Building a Nation

New World Diasporas

UNIVERSITY PRESS OF FLORIDA

Florida A&M University, Tallahassee
Florida Atlantic University, Boca Raton
Florida Gulf Coast University, Ft. Myers
Florida International University, Miami
Florida State University, Tallahassee
New College of Florida, Sarasota
University of Central Florida, Orlando
University of Florida, Gainesville
University of North Florida, Jacksonville
University of South Florida, Tampa
University of West Florida, Pensacola

Building a Nation

Caribbean Federation in the Black Diaspora

ERIC D. DUKE

Kevin A. Yelvington, Series Editor

University Press of Florida

Gainesville · Tallahassee · Tampa · Boca Raton

Pensacola · Orlando · Miami · Jacksonville · Ft. Myers · Sarasota

This book may be available in an electronic edition.

First cloth printing, 2016
First paperback printing, 2018

23 22 21 20 19 18   6 5 4 3 2 1

Library of Congress Cataloging-in-Publication Data
Duke, Eric D., author.
Building a nation : Caribbean federation in the black diaspora / Eric D. Duke.
pages cm — (New world diasporas)
Includes bibliographical references and index.
ISBN 978-0-8130-6023-1 (cloth)
ISBN 978-0-8130-6496-3 (pbk.)
1. Blacks—Caribbean Area—History. 2. Blacks—Latin America—History. 3. African
diaspora. I. Title. II. Series: New World diasporas series.
F2191.B55D84 2016
304.8096—dc23
2015030169

The University Press of Florida is the scholarly publishing agency for the State University
System of Florida, comprising Florida A&M University, Florida Atlantic University,
Florida Gulf Coast University, Florida International University, Florida State University,
New College of Florida, University of Central Florida, University of Florida, University
of North Florida, University of South Florida, and University of West Florida.

University Press of Florida
15 Northwest 15th Street
Gainesville, FL 32611-2079
http://upress.ufl.edu

For my daughter, Mya Gabrielle Duke, and my son, Xavier Zion Duke—
this is your history. May you come to appreciate and understand it,
no matter where life takes you!

Contents

Tables

Acknowledgments

The completion of a book inevitably involves the accumulation of debts of gratitude both personal and professional. While it is impossible to thank all who have supported me during my previous studies and this endeavor, many people deserve recognition.

My interest in history evolved considerably during my childhood in Mobile, Alabama. What began simply as a general subject discussed by my family, especially my father, became for me a passion for Black History as a tool for social change and a means to challenge others seemingly intent on continuing the status quo. Those years included both meaningful discussions and "cuss and fuss" sessions with just about anyone who was willing. Along the way, some friendships were maintained, new ones made, and others lost. I want to thank all—friends and foes—who shaped these formative years, but especially those friends who stood by me through tumultuous times, and at times believed in me more than I did: Shadia Tilahun, Jessica Pierce, Dante Baker, Alex Padgett, Brian Kittrell, Sylvester Kidd, Nick Miller, and Adair Padgett.

By the time I entered Florida State University, I had known for some time that I wanted to study Black History, and one day become a professor. Undergraduate studies in history and Black Studies were more than just a major for me. Beyond the classroom, Eric Heard, Michell Clark, and Shenitta Clark also became part of my extended family and offered significant support in these and subsequent years. When I entered the MA program in history at FSU, I began to understand the difference between an interest in history and a career as a historian. The handful of graduate students working on African American history within the department—Dawn Herd-Clark, John Wess Grant, Walter Pierce, Pamela Robbins, and Barbara "Annie" Fuller—made these years enjoyable and became my first cohort of colleagues. Also at this time my focus expanded beyond African

American history to include Caribbean and black diaspora histories—all of which form the basis of this book. Professors who deserve special recognition are Joe M. Richardson, Darrell E. Levi, Maxine Jones, and especially C. Peter Ripley.

Doctoral studies at Michigan State University brought the most enjoyable and engaging times of my college years, largely due to my participation in the Comparative Black History program founded under the visionary leadership of Darlene Clark Hine. The dynamic CBH group of students and professors created a unique environment where the various national and international histories of black peoples took center stage in the department, quite unlike the peripheral standing I had witnessed in my other programs. I would like to salute all of the students in our "CBH family"—my contemporaries and alumni of the program—with whom I shared countless classes, discussions, and debates. Professors involved with our CBH program who deserve recognition include Leslie Page Moch, Daina Ramey Berry, and David Robinson. Peter Beattie's "writing boot camps" and our many conversations were particularly helpful during my early years at MSU. Laurent Dubois's steady support of my studies, his research in the Caribbean and black diaspora, and his professional example proved especially important to my development as a historian. Darlene Clark Hine has my eternal gratitude for her commitment and multifaceted contributions—teaching, mentoring, research, and program building—in African American and black diaspora history. Without her, few of us could have done what we did, and there could not have been a CBH family!

Several others influenced the writing of the book. Rebecca Scott and David Barry Gaspar offered important insights and questions during the early stages. Winston James, whose scholarship offered a model of what I hoped to do in linking the history of the British Caribbean and Black America, gave significant feedback during informal and formal discussions at various times over the years. I am grateful for Jason Parker's encouragement and insistence that the history of Caribbean federation deserved multiple studies. Joyce Moore Turner, who has not only written on aspects of this history but experienced it firsthand as the daughter of Richard B. Moore, kindly offered opinions on some portions. To participants at the numerous conferences where parts of this work were presented, and to the three anonymous reviewers for the University Press of Florida, my thanks as well. I am grateful to my former colleagues at the University of South Florida for encouragement in recent years: Kevin Yelvington, Barbara Cruz, Cheryl Rodriguez, Daphne Thomas, Edward Kissi, Deborah Plant, and the late

Trevor Purcell. FUFO, FUH, and FUASPO! And I look forward to working with my new colleagues at Clark Atlanta University.

I would like to recognize the many librarians and archivists at institutions visited during my research, whose helpfulness extended at times to debates over what sources offered insights into the history of Caribbean federation, which proved interesting and useful as I pushed my project (and some of them) beyond the bounds of the West Indies Federation as *the* history of Caribbean federation. Thank you to the various staffs in Jamaica (University of the West Indies—Mona special collections, National Library, and National Archives and Records Department); in Trinidad (University of the West Indies—St. Augustine special collections); in Barbados (W.I. Federal Archives Centre); in Great Britain (National Archives, Institute of Commonwealth Studies, Rhodes House at Oxford University, People's History Museum, Black Cultural Archives, and British Library); and in the United States (Schomburg Center for Research in Black Culture, Library of Congress, Moorland-Spingarn Research Center, National Archives, University of Florida libraries, and University of Massachusetts libraries). I also wish to thank the interlibrary loan staff at Michigan State University and the University of South Florida (especially Sandra Law) who tracked down numerous small publications that proved important to this study. Several of these research trips could not have been completed without short-term grants from Michigan State University, the University of South Florida, the American Historical Association, and the National History Center. The National History Center's Decolonization Seminar was an especially fruitful opportunity to interact with colleagues and complete crucial research in Washington, DC.

Several from my CBH family became much more than professional colleagues and remain important members of my extended family: Sowande Mustakeem (with whom I shared many conversations, especially during the book's earliest stages), John Wess Grant (with me at both FSU and MSU), and Pero Dagbovie (whose passion for history in and out of academia has been influential). Also, a special thanks to "Tasty," whose sometimes ridiculous self-centeredness provided laughs and motivation too!

Significant portions of the research, writing, and especially revisions of this book took place under trying circumstances. Three from my CBH family deserve special recognition for helping see me through. To Kenneth Marshall, who has become my brother—thank you for your support and assuaging sarcasm. To Meredith Roman, who has long been my sister—thank you for always taking the time, no matter how busy you were, to offer your relentless encouragement. I look forward to more time with you, Ken, and my godsons Julius and Vaughn. To Kennetta Hammond Perry (A.W.)—thank you for the numerous conversations and boundless support as we both worked through the research and writing of our books. I owe you all so much! I also wish to thank the University Press of Florida staff, especially my editor Sian Hunter and series editor Kevin Yelvington, for wise guidance and patience through unforeseen delays.

Finally, I wish to thank my family. My parents, Billie and Alice, and sisters, Angela and Katrina, have always expressed encouragement and pride in my work and goals. To my in-laws, Merlin, Moyne, Chelsea, Floyd, and Lando Perkins, thank you for your general support and our many conversations on Jamaica and the larger Caribbean, Black America, race, migration, and related topics over the years. A special thanks to Aunt Val and cousins Joan, Paul, and David, whose hospitality afforded me extended months of research in London, a "Jamaican sanctuary," and interesting discussions on Jamaica, Black Britain, Black America, and more.

I reserve my greatest gratitude for my wife, Jody, and our children, Mya and Xavier. You all deserve special recognition for putting up with me! To Mya and Xavier—thank you for understanding when Daddy was too busy working or when my mind was elsewhere when it should have focused more on enjoying my time with you. To Jody—no words can express the love and gratitude I have for you. You have been with me since the early days of graduate school at FSU. I am certain I would not have accomplished what I have without you. I thank you the most for being always by my side.

Note on Terminology

Numerous terms in my study have fluid meanings and may be defined differently by others. I should therefore note my specific use of certain terms.

While my definition of "black diaspora politics" shares some similarities with definitions of Pan-Africanism, I find the latter term more monolithic and constrictive than "black diaspora politics," an umbrella term encompassing the wide-ranging activities and goals of various race-based or race-focused organizations and activists across the political spectrum, from conservative to radical, and including both nationalist and internationalist endeavors. Moreover, the intentional use of "black diaspora" rather than "African Diaspora" helps to highlight and center the various dispersed black communities outside continental Africa, such as those in the Caribbean, Black America, and Black Britain.

Several forms of "nationalism" are also represented within this study, including local nationalisms centered on and within individual colonies and regional nationalism focused on the British West Indies. Although both local and regional nationalisms could be considered forms of West Indian nationalism, this study generally reserves that term for those whose interests and focus encompass the entire region rather than individual colonies. It also employs the term "islandism" and "islandist" for colony-specific nationalisms, and "regionalism" and "regionalist" for more regional (West Indian) nationalism.[1] Despite these distinctions, these nationalisms were not mutually exclusive for many.

Although "black nationalism" and "black internationalism" are often defined by distinct perspectives—with the former focused on, among other things, the creation of "black nations" and the latter viewing the struggles of black peoples as part of the struggle by various nonwhite colonial peoples (as well as the white working class) against the capitalist system upon which imperialism and colonialism were constructed—many activists and organizations operated at times as both black nationalist and international-ist movements. As Lara Putnam argues, "Many black nationalists were also black internationalists, and some black internationalists were also black nationalists. The two approaches could well be mutually reinforcing, but they did not everywhere and always coincide."[2]

Likewise, while "black diaspora activism" is a form of transnationalism, this study tries to distinguish between "West Indian transnationalism," as an expression of West Indian nationalism beyond the borders of the region but focused primarily on that region, and "black diaspora activism," which focused on the broader black diaspora (including the West Indies) as well as the African continent. Therefore, much as activists and organizations could operate as both black nationalists and internationalists, many but by no means all of the activists and organizations reviewed operated as both expatriate, transnational West Indian and black diaspora activists and organizations.

Given the extensive discussion of race and region within this study, it is necessary to clarify my usage of associated terms. In many West Indian set-tings, "black" refers to persons of (supposedly) "unmixed" African descent, and "coloured" (with the British spelling) to persons of African descent with a "mixed" heritage. These traditional divisions in the Caribbean are noted at times, but since many of the activists and organizations reviewed sought to unite all peoples "of African descent" as "black peoples," this study employs these latter two terms as inclusive of both groups. Moreover, the term "Afro-Caribbean" also includes both black and coloured West In-dians. This study does not use "colored" or "coloured" as a broad label in-cluding everyone except white people (unless in a direct quote). Instead it uses "nonwhites" because some black diaspora activists employed a more limited use of "coloured" or "colored" people as synonymous with "black" people. Therefore, it should not be assumed that "coloured" always referred to all nonwhites, even if there was much cooperation between black and other nonwhite peoples at times. Although there are distinctions between "multiracial(ism)" and "transracial(ism)," given that both terms advocate cooperation between races—either by bringing different racial groups to-gether or by claims of racelessness in which racial groups are not recog-nized—these two terms are often used synonymously in this study as an alternative to different racial nationalisms.

As for geographic locations, "West Indies" is used primarily as a term for the Anglophone Caribbean, rather than the entire region, and is often used interchangeably with "British Caribbean" and "British West Indies." Finally, while some activists and organizations referred to African Americans as "Black Americans," this study uses the term "Black America" to refer to the overall black population of the United States, which is not limited to African Americans.

Abbreviations

AACA	American Association for Caribbean Advancement
AACC	Anglo-American Caribbean Commission
AAWIA	American Association for West Indian Advancement
ABB	African Blood Brotherhood
ACWIF	American Committee for West Indian Federation
AFWIF	American Friends of the West Indies Federation
ANLC	American Negro Labor Congress
APU	African Progress Union
AWIA	American West Indian Association
AWIACA	American West Indian Association on Caribbean Affairs
BLP	Barbados Labour Party
BPL	Barbados Progressive League
BWIR	British West Indies Regiments
BWIS	British West Indian Society
CAA	Council on African Affairs
CARIFTA	Caribbean Free Trade Association
CARICOM	Caribbean Community
CLA	Caribbean League of America
CLC	Caribbean Labour Congress
CU	Caribbean Union
CUC	Closer Union Commission
CWIF	Committee on West Indian Freedom
DLP	Democratic Labour Party
FDLP	Federal Democratic Labour Party
IAFE	International African Friends of Ethiopia
IASB	International African Service Bureau
ITUCNW	International Trade Union Committee of Negro Workers
JLP	Jamaica Labour Pary

JPL	Jamaica Progressive League
LCP	League of Coloured Peoples
NAACP	National Association for the Advancement of Colored People
NNC	National Negro Congress
NWA	Negro Welfare Association
PAF	Pan-African Federation
PNM	People's National Movement
PNP	People's National Party
SCAC	Standing Closer Association Committee
SPAO	Society of Peoples of African Origin
TWA	Trinidad Workingmen's Association
UAPAD	United Aid for Peoples of African Descent
UCAC	United Caribbean American Council
UCWI	University College of the West Indies
UN	United Nations
UNCIO	United Nations Conference on International Organization
UNIA	Universal Negro Improvement Association
WICA	West India Committee of America
WICC	West Indies Conference Committee
WIDC	West Indian Defense Committee
WIF	West Indies Federation
WIFA	West Indian Federation of America
WIFLP	West Indies Federal Labour Party
WINC	West Indies National Council
WINEC	West Indies National Emergency Committee
WISU	West Indian Students' Union

Introduction

On 18 October 1959 the prime minister of the West Indies Federation (WIF), Grantley Adams, spoke before a large audience in New York City that had gathered under the auspices of the Caribbean League of America (CLA) to hear news regarding the federal union of British Caribbean colonies which had been launched in 1958 after several decades of pursuit by an array of interested parties within and beyond the region. While the Federation elicited many celebrations among West Indians and others upon its inauguration, its first year had been characterized by significant internal tensions and divisions. Over the course of his lengthy speech, Adams provided an overview of various economic, social, and political matters. He confirmed multiple lingering and formidable questions such as taxation, a customs union, freedom of movement, and the rights of individual units within the union. Despite these issues, Adams assured the crowd that the Federation was in no danger of dissolution and "that all such problems would be resolved and the future unity of the embryo nation assured."[1]

The public meeting with Adams had been arranged to provide US-based supporters of the Federation a firsthand account of the new West Indian nation. The visit of the prime minister was certainly a focal point, but the meeting also provided an opportunity to acknowledge the past, present, and future importance of these supporters to the cause of federation. Following Adams's address, a message was read from Norman Washington Manley, the premier of Jamaica and a key figure within the historical efforts to build the Federation, which acknowledged the great importance of "the development of the West Indies" to the "coloured people of America," particularly but by no means solely those of West Indian origin. Manley also noted the positive contributions that these communities could continue to make to the development and prestige of the West Indian nation. Hope Stevens, an executive member of the CLA and a longtime West Indian activist in New York, spoke next and echoed the sentiments of Manley. He recognized other expatriate West Indian activists in the audience, including Richard B. Moore, W. A. Domingo, Reginald Pierrepointe, and Daisy Brooks-Johnson, who along with many others had "dedicated themselves to the cause of West Indian nationhood" throughout their decades of activism in the United States.[2]

Although many appreciated the update provided by Adams, some remarks drew the ire of the aforementioned West Indian activists. On the matter of the Federation's still unrealized pursuit of independence and commonwealth status, Adams claimed the Federation's current status was "the fault of the people of the West Indies" rather than the British Colonial Office. Equally troubling to some were Adams's stereotypical remarks, such as "the Barbadians are the most intelligent and industrious in the West Indies" and "the average Trinidadian would rather sing a Calypso than do any hard work," as well as exaggerated estimations of Jamaican illiteracy.[3]

After his speech Adams responded to written questions from the audience. Richard B. Moore, a Barbadian, a self-proclaimed "Caribbean-American," and one of the most prominent activists within New York's multinational black community, posed two questions to Adams. Moore asked why West Indian political leaders had not secured independence, commonwealth status, and "all the other essentials of genuine nationhood." Also, given Adams's crude stereotypes of the different islanders within the Federation, Moore asked Adams, "How can you as Prime Minister, foster the development of Federal National Consciousness when you make such insular and provincial comparisons?" In his response, Adams largely ignored the first question and claimed his characterizations of the various islanders of the Federation were humorous and harmless. When questioned by W. A. Domingo, another longtime and prominent activist in the area, regarding the accuracy of his claim that 50 percent of Jamaicans were illiterate, Adams retorted that those were the figures provided to him and that many people were likely reluctant to admit their illiteracy.[4]

While Adams's responses largely dismissed the concerns of these "Away-men," as Moore referred to himself and other West Indians in New York, their questions represented decades of concern and activism on behalf of West Indian liberation and self-determination—a cause they pursued and, at times, led from abroad as vigorously as any within the West Indian colonies. For Moore and other longtime supporters of a Caribbean federation, a unifying, regional West Indian consciousness beyond familiar island-based insularities was crucial and far from a joking matter. Adams's failure to address why West Indian leaders in the region had not done more toward securing complete self-government and independence for the Federation, which many supporters had assumed should have been attained upon its initial creation in 1958, also proved disconcerting. These issues compounded, and in some opinions confirmed, the inability of Adams to lead and achieve an independent, united West Indies Federation. In an interview shortly after this meeting, Moore went so far as to as ponder "Would it not be helpful to this desired end of free nationhood, if the British Government would immediately accord Commonwealth Status to the West Indies Federation, appoint Sir Grantley Adams as Governor General, and permit the Caribbean people to elect a Prime Minister more satisfactory to the people?"[5]

In the following weeks, an editorial appeared in the *Barbados Recorder* related to the exchange between Adams and Moore at the New York meeting. It criticized Moore for his questioning of Adams and defended Adams's controversial remarks as both true and evidence of a "healthy spirit of rival inter-island pride" that did not "influence the achievement of an independent and unified nation." The author wondered if Moore (and seemingly other West Indian expatriates) lacked a clear understanding of the Caribbean, given their long stay outside the region. For this reason, the editorial suggested "West Indians in America" restrict their interest in the Caribbean "to sending quantities of food and clothing or other material and civic assistance" and "concentrate on this charitable side a little more and on the political front a little less."[6]

Moore penned a contentious response, claiming that the editorial misrepresented his exchange with Adams. More important, Moore lambasted the editor for attempting to "deprive natives of the Caribbean now domiciled in New York even of the right to ask questions" and for attempting to "prohibit us from sharing knowledge, giving advice and counsel, warning against dangers, or pointing out ways and means for basic improvement and necessary advancement." Moore continued, "You seem not to understand that our fraternal interest in the welfare of our sisters and brothers in the Caribbean embraces not only the material and financial but also the cultural, social, and political phases of their welfare."[7]

Moore's defense of the right of expatriate West Indians to involve themselves in West Indian affairs from abroad, as well as his remarks on the need for the affirmation of a united West Indianness beyond insular island identifications, highlights many important issues embedded in the wide-ranging efforts to create a united West Indian nation—most commonly proposed via a Caribbean federation—during the twentieth century. Far from being outsiders, unfamiliar with and disconnected from the politics of their homelands, US-based West Indians along with some African Americans with whom they lived and interacted in the multinational black communities of the United States, particularly Harlem and the surrounding New York City areas, proved an invaluable source of support for West Indian nation building from the early-mid twentieth century.[8] Of course, this support was often rooted in and connected to far more than narrow island-based nationalisms (islandisms) or broader regional nationalism (regionalism). Many within these multinational black communities, from which a significant number of prominent black diaspora activists emerged in the early and mid-twentieth century, viewed West Indian nation building as but one portion of the larger freedom struggles of African and African-descended peoples across the globe.

Given the long tradition of migration from the Anglophone Caribbean and the significant number of people involved, Afro-Caribbean migrants from these islands have been described as "the most peripatetic of all African peoples."[9] In the late nineteenth and early twentieth centuries, thousands of these migrants converged with local and other international black populations in metropolitan areas such as Harlem and London, as well as various peripheral locations of the Caribbean and circum-Caribbean. Although assimilation was rarely sought or realized within such settings, various populations of African descent were melded into collective, but by no means homogenous, racialized black diaspora communities. For many Afro-Caribbeans, migration involved the production and promotion of multiple overlapping identifications by themselves and others: insular (colony specific), regional (West Indian), and racial (black or African-descent).[10] While not discounting the strong racial consciousness and diaspora activism of many within the islands, it was often beyond the bounds of the British West Indies that migrants came to view both their insular and regional identifications as part of a larger international "black citizenry" composed of various other peoples of African descent. At the same time, the conditions and respective struggles of the West Indian colonies themselves became part of a racialized global struggle encompassing both African and black diasporic struggles. The interests in and ramifications of West Indian nation building, therefore, stretched far beyond the seascape of the Anglophone Caribbean and across the broader black diaspora.

The diasporic dimensions of the campaigns for a Caribbean federation—a means to achieve West Indian liberation and self-determination as well as racial uplift and unity—demonstrate what Frank Guridy calls the "process of diasporization . . . the complex social, political, and cultural interactions between people of African descent across national, cultural, and linguistic boundaries that are based on a perceived commonality."[11] Diasporization, which in many cases equated to racialization, did not preclude intraracial rivalries between black populations, or result in the loss of insular or regional identifications among Afro-Caribbeans and others. It did, however, demonstrate how assumed commonalities—perceptions of a shared racial heritage, history, and status—led to concern for and cooperation with "other" peoples of African descent across such divisions.

Given these circumstances—the diasporization and racialization of West Indians and West Indian struggles in the late nineteenth and early-mid twentieth centuries, as well the fact that "West Indian" identification and "West Indianness" were largely forged and often more prominent and practical within these other black diaspora locations than within the British Caribbean colonies—diaspora support for and conceptualizations of West Indian nation building beyond the Caribbean must be considered. Moreover, if Afro-Caribbean émigrés from the British Caribbean were among the leading figures within the wide-ranging black diaspora politics of the early-mid twentieth century, and at the same time key supporters of a Caribbean federation (as Moore and various others were), it is precarious to dissociate their activism on behalf of the latter from the former. Nevertheless, this disassociation is prominent. Indeed, although much has been written on the significance of Afro-Caribbean activists in the numerous movements associated with black diaspora politics in the twentieth century, including their important roles as both leaders and rank-and-file members in a variety of black nationalist and internationalist movements, from Pan-African to Black Marxist organizations, few of these works examine their activism in support of their West Indian homelands. Equally scant attention has been given to how the various West Indian colonies themselves were envisioned by Afro-Caribbean and other black diaspora activists within the multidimensional black diaspora politics of these years.

Building a Nation addresses these and associated issues through an examination of the relationships between West Indian freedom struggles and nation-building endeavors and black diaspora politics from the late nineteenth century through the onset of independence in the Anglophone Caribbean in the early 1960s. More particularly, it examines and employs the broader diasporic history of Caribbean federation as a case study through which to explore a range of related questions. What was the place of West Indian self-government and nation building within black diaspora politics? What was the relationship between West Indian nationalism and black diaspora activism in and out of the Caribbean? What were the particular connections between African and African American freedom struggles and the pursuit of Caribbean federation? In what ways did ideas of "race" inform conceptualizations of West Indian nation building, as well as the very West Indianness that this nation was to be built upon or was to create? How did West Indian and black diaspora activists employ race as a tool to garner support for the building of a West Indian nation? While the answers to these questions may be found in the twentieth-century history of the British Caribbean and other locales of the black diaspora, the atmosphere in which they were operated was rooted in the pre-twentieth-century history of the region.

Race and the Future of the British Caribbean

Anadelia Romo concludes in her recent study of Bahia (Brazil) that "demography is not destiny."[12] While it is true that the existence of an overwhelmingly African-descended population does not dictate an area's future, one cannot overlook or dismiss the place of race in shaping the past, present, and future of a region. Within the long colonial history of the British Caribbean, for example, the region's demography and connected, ubiquitous questions and concerns involving race indelibly marked the region's past while also shaping many visions of its future. Given the centrality of race within justifications for British colonialism, both colonizer and colonized, rulers and reformers, those in power and those who sought to become empowered, were forced to address inextricable questions related to the connections between race and the future of the British Caribbean.

British colonization of the West Indies was but one part of the broader European expansion into the Caribbean. Beginning in the 1620s and 1630s, the British, French, and Dutch Empires broke the monopoly of the Spanish Empire in the Caribbean and established their own colonies alongside the older Spanish communities created in the sixteenth century. Over the course of the next three centuries, these Caribbean colonies increased in both number and importance as the West Indies became a source of great wealth and power for European empires. The plantation system, based on forced labor extracted from millions of enslaved Africans, developed and expanded exponentially and created significant black majorities in most Caribbean colonies.

The British Empire ultimately became one of the major colonial powers in the Caribbean, with a range of island and mainland colonies established over approximately two hundred years. The majority of the British colonies of the early seventeenth century were located in the Lesser Antilles of the eastern Caribbean, including St. Kitts, Barbados, Nevis, Antigua, and Montserrat. The British expanded their Caribbean holdings in this century with further settlements in Anguilla, the Cayman Islands, the Virgin Islands, and the Turks and Caicos. The most significant addition was Jamaica, a former Spanish colony conquered in 1655. From the 1760s to the 1790s, other eastern Caribbean islands, including Dominica, Grenada, St. Vincent, and St. Lucia, changed hands several times between the British and French Empires. By the early nineteenth century, Great Britain controlled all of these islands, as well as Trinidad, Tobago, and mainland areas that were to become British Guiana and British Honduras.

Although slave labor produced an array of crops in the British West Indies for the wider Atlantic economy, including coffee, cacao, and various tropical fruits and spices, the "sugar revolutions" that engulfed the Caribbean beginning in the mid-late seventeenth century and continuing into the nineteenth century most strikingly shaped many aspects of these colonial Caribbean societies. As Franklin Knight argues, "Imposed on the initial settler societies, the sugarcane agro-industrial complex changed fundamentally the basic economy, the demographic structure, the internal politics—as well as the relationship of the region to the wider world."[13] Sugar, with its high demand for labor and potential for great riches, provided the primary impetus for the influx of enslaved Africans, who became the vast majority in most British Caribbean colonies, and transformed the region into a key site within what Charles Wagley famously termed Plantation-America.[14]

The institution of the plantation system produced a hierarchy of race, color, and class that remained a prominent characteristic of the region well into the twentieth century. At the top of these colonial societies was a small white population consisting of planters (both local and large numbers of absentees), merchants, small landholders, colonial officials, and in some islands (notably Barbados) small numbers of poor white laborers. Free people of African descent, both black and mixed-race "coloureds," often occupied an expanding middle ground. Finally, enslaved Africans formed the extensive bottom of the social pyramid. Despite the existence of rivalries and divisions within each of these sections of plantation society, its hierarchical nature created a degree of racial and class solidarity within the broader social categories. For instance, among many white colonial communities the demographic imbalance forged a sense of solidarity resting largely upon broader fears of, and feelings of superiority to, the Afro-Caribbean populations, including the majority enslaved and smaller "free" communities. As Robin Blackburn argues, "Fear and privilege, both constituted with reference to black slaves, possessed the ability spontaneously to 'interpellate' white people, making them see themselves . . . as members of a ruling race—and thus to furnish them with core elements of their social identity."[15] Similarly, despite divisions among the enslaved populations, there were interethnic plots and rebellions, including cooperation between African-born and Creole slaves, based upon a solidarity fashioned by their common enslavement.[16] These racialized social divisions created an ongoing cycle of fear, control, and resistance within the colonial British West Indies for much of slavery's existence.

From the early decades of the nineteenth century, when the bulk of the West Indian colonies remained slave societies, through the transition of abolition, and into the post-emancipation and Crown Colony eras, political and ideological debates over the capacity of the Afro-Caribbean majorities to participate as equals within colonial society or to achieve self-government significantly shaped British policies in the Caribbean. Even as other "nonwhite" peoples, including Chinese and Indian laborers, settled in the post-emancipation West Indian colonies via a system of indentured servitude designed to offset the loss of enslaved African labor, the demography of the region as a whole, as well as gradations within white supremacist attitudes toward different nonwhite groups, meant the suitability and capabilities of the African-descended populations remained one of the most pressing and prominent issues in most of the British Caribbean. At the very heart of this matter was the trepidation, and in some cases outright fears, of many Europeans regarding possible black majority rule in the region.

From the 1770s through the 1830s, the abolitionist movement became a powerful force in the British Empire and a potent threat to the British West Indian slave societies. White planters in these colonies faced both continued slave resistance and a lengthy ideological debate with the antislavery movement.[17] The abolition of the British slave trade in 1807, as well as subsequent efforts to "improve" slave conditions, failed to produce a dramatic amelioration or a cessation of slave rebellions.[18] Despite the staunchness of the planters, continued slave resistance and an increasingly potent abolitionist movement were major factors, though not the only ones, in the gradual death of plantation slavery in the early nineteenth-century British West Indies.[19]

Whatever the ultimate reason, as David Brion Davis recalls, "Britain moved quickly from being the world's leading purchaser and transporter of African slaves" to outlawing the slave trade in 1807, and ultimately slavery itself in the 1830s.[20] In August 1833 a compromise was reached between the antislavery movement and West Indian planters with the Slavery Abolition Act in the British Parliament. This act, which became law on 1 August 1834, emancipated approximately 750,000–800,000 enslaved people, although a mandatory apprentice system delayed final emancipation until 1838. In return, former owners were paid £20 million sterling.[21] The abolitionist movement seemingly won a major victory through this peaceful concession. Nonetheless, the transition to a "free society" included many unresolved matters. One of the most pressing was the possibility of black majority rule, which appeared inevitable should the franchise be extended to the black male populations of the colonies. What was to be the place of the Afro-Caribbean population, especially the formerly enslaved? How, if at all, could they be integrated into their societies as citizens?[22]

The interjection and eventual rejection of British liberalism in the former British West Indian slave societies took center stage in the post-emancipation era, as the empire reorganized local colonial governments to address the realities of vast black majorities in most colonies. In 1837 colonial secretary Lord Glenelg wrote that "the apprenticeship of the emancipated slaves is to be immediately succeeded by personal freedom, in that full and unlimited sense of the term in which it is used in reference to the other subjects of the British Crown."[23] Glenelg also called for the various governors of the West Indies to remove all remnants of racial discrimination to ensure the former slaves' economic, social, and political freedom. Despite the optimistic tone of Glenelg's decree, many in the Colonial Office knew that such a proposal would encounter serious opposition from the white populations in the West Indies who had exercised significant power within their colonies in prior decades and centuries.

From the seventeenth to the mid-nineteenth century, the overwhelming majority of local assemblies in the British West Indies operated under the Old Representative System.[24] Given the "fantastically limited franchise . . . they represented, at best, only the planter, merchant, and legal classes." They were the domain of the local planters or, in the case of colonies with a great number of absentee planters, their agents and associates.

These oligarchical assemblies saw themselves as the legitimate colonial power against imposed governors and nominated executive councils.[25]

In the post-emancipation era, the small white elite remained determined to maintain dominance of West Indian societies, and most were leery of Glenelg's vision. The franchise remained severely restricted, but given the numerical superiority of the recently freed Afro-Caribbean population, the possibility of black participation in colonial and local affairs made many planters worry that the African-descended majorities would soon overwhelm them.[26] Acutely aware of these attitudes, some government officials in the metropole openly questioned whether it would be possible for free societies to be created in the British Caribbean colonies if local power remained in the hands of former masters determined to retain the colonial hierarchy. However, local whites in the British Indies were not the only ones concerned by the prospect of black majority rule.

By midcentury even the Colonial Office, which was often at odds with local planters, retreated from the liberal experiment of Glenelg and sought ways to "blunt the impact of black political participation."[27] Some colonial officials believed that the only possible solution to the problem of local government in the British West Indies, with its social divisions between an undemocratic white oligarchy on one hand and a black majority whose political capacity was questioned on the other, was the abolition of the Old Representative System where it existed and the installation of more direct rule from the Crown. Such governance had been debated in previous years within some circles, but the proposals were generally shelved, as the assemblies were not expected to relinquish willingly their powers and the metropole was not ready to force such concessions. This changed in 1865, however, when a major rebellion at Morant Bay in Jamaica sparked a remarkable voluntary dismantling of the local assemblies and opened the door to widespread changes in colonial governments throughout most of the British West Indies.

The Morant Bay Rebellion was a watershed moment in British Caribbean history. Like many other West Indian colonies, Jamaica saw much discontent in the decades following the formal end of slavery. Low wages, high taxes, land alienation, poor living conditions, and the continued domination of the island's economic, social, and political institutions by the small white oligarchy created significant resentment within the black peasant class. While there were sporadic protests and even small episodes of violence before the 1860s, the crescendo came in October 1865 in Morant Bay, the principal city of St. Thomas in the East parish.[28]

On 11 October 1865, after a turbulent weekend of small-scale confrontations between peasants and authorities over an assault case and a trespassing case, Paul Bogle, a Baptist preacher and small landowner, led hundreds of protestors into Morant Bay. Clashing with the local militia, the protestors took control of the city, with casualties of approximately twenty-five dead, including seven of their own members, and thirty-one wounded. Over the next few days, many others joined the rebellion, ransacking area plantations and killing two planters.[29]

In response, Governor Edward John Eyre dispatched British troops and Maroons against the rebels and declared martial law in the parish. These forces swiftly and brutally suppressed the rebellion—shooting, hanging, and flogging captured and suspected rebels. Hundreds were arrested, court-martialed, and eventually executed, including Paul Bogle. Moreover, in a controversial step, Governor Eyre ordered the arrest of George William Gordon, a local "coloured" Jamaican Assembly member who was known as a critic of the current colonial government and a religious leader associated with Bogle's church. Gordon was arrested in Kingston, which was outside the martial law area, taken into St. Thomas in the East parish, and summarily tried and executed.[30] Estimates for the tally of the Morant Bay repression include 1,000 houses burned, approximately 600 men and women flogged, between 439 and 608 rebels killed, and numerous others sentenced to death through the courts after martial law ended. The rebels, in contrast, killed none of Governor Eyre's troops.[31]

Eyre's authoritarian and violent repression of the rebels, and especially the questionable trial and execution of Gordon, were much debated in the metropole; however, the immediate fallout within Jamaica and the other West Indian colonies proved more far-reaching. While scholars have noted both race and class issues in the Morant Bay Rebellion, for many of the island's whites who still controlled the local assembly, as well as some officials in England, this was the beginning of a larger race war that many had long feared.[32] Coupled with the general fear of the black majorities eventually gaining power within colonial assemblies, this led the Jamaican Assembly to abdicate voluntarily all of its powers for a more direct rule from the Crown.

The events of Morant Bay led to the wider adoption of Crown Colony rule in the second half of the nineteenth century and to the end of local representative government in every British Caribbean colony except Barbados, British Guiana, and the Bahamas.[33] Supporters of Crown Colony government cited several reasons for these constitutional changes in the British

West Indies. Many noted colonial inefficiencies, both fiscal and political. To some officials of the Colonial Office, "the white oligarchies" who controlled the local assemblies "proved to be incapable not only of good government but even of stable and orderly government."[34] Nevertheless, one should not underestimate the role that questions of race played in the installation of Crown rule. As Morley Ayearst notes, the Old Representative System "was based upon the assumption that the colonies were and would remain areas of European settlement . . . [with] a fairly homogeneous society. [However,] this had long ceased to be the case in the West Indies."[35] Many questioned, therefore, the extent to which this system could survive in a region populated by a black majority, especially with much of that majority recently removed from slavery and living alongside their former "masters."

The idea of black majority rule had worried not only local whites but the metropolitan government ever since the slavery period. There was striking continuity between the old fears of slave rebellions and the paranoid assumptions of what would happen if free black populations gained "control" of the region in the post-emancipation era. The fear of black majority rule was not simply fanciful, however, as the successful Haitian Revolution of the late eighteenth century demonstrated. More than just a confirmation of the ability of enslaved peoples to throw off their chains permanently, the transformation of the Saint-Domingue slave society into the independent Haitian republic in 1804 created a genuine example of black self-rule that reverberated throughout the hemisphere.[36] Unfortunately, racist and stereotypical accounts of both the revolution and the ensuing Haitian state stiffened many Europeans' opposition to black self-rule, especially in the broader Caribbean.

Notions of African inferiority and European superiority supposedly gained credibility and legitimacy with the development of assorted scientific racisms in the mid-nineteenth century. Scientific studies spouted new biological understandings of race that justified racial hierarchies of "superior" and "inferior" peoples, with Europeans at the top and peoples of African descent invariably at the bottom. Racial determinism became popular in intellectual and governmental circles, consistently influencing and justifying policies of European imperialism.[37] What became known as the "white man's burden," the duty to lead, nurture, and civilize inferior races while withholding self-determination until such peoples were "fit to rule," became a cornerstone of British imperialism with its imperial trusteeships, guardianships, and patronizing notions of tutelage.[38] There is little doubt that these ideas influenced the decision to institute obstructionist

Crown Colony rule in the face of ever-increasing Afro-Caribbean demands for self-determination.

As Neil MacMaster argues, "By the late 1860s the predominant thinking among colonial officials and policy-makers in London was that black populations in the Caribbean, Africa and elsewhere—unlike the colonies of white settlement like Canada and Australia, which could be prepared for self-government—would have to remain under the 'benevolent guardianship' of their white masters."[39] Crown Colony government provided the means to institutionalize these ideas in the British West Indies. As James Patterson Smith notes, "Racial thinking dictated this authoritarian solution to West Indian problems. Broadening the franchise would have required considerably more thought, energy, attention, and willingness to [take] risks. The racial reasoning that supported authoritarianism provided an escape from this burden."[40]

The Colonial Office presented Crown Colony rule as an "efficient and impartial" system of "benevolent paternalism."[41] On one hand, they claimed, it would serve to check local oligarchies' abuses and misuses of power. "The Crown was the guardian and representative of the masses, the protector of popular interests against the oppression of the landowners."[42] As such, not all whites in the British West Indies welcomed Crown intervention in local affairs. Some saw this as a challenge to their rights of representation as Englishmen, and to their economic well-being. Nevertheless, many within the planter and merchant oligarchy saw Crown Colony government as the best means to prevent black majority rule.[43] As Thomas Holt notes in the case of Jamaica, Crown Colony government was "justified as saving Jamaica from the perils of a black-dominated democracy."[44] Moreover, the idea that the Crown system would defend the masses at the cost of alienating or dominating the white elite proved a fallacy. Local whites, especially prominent planters and merchants, maintained great influence within the new colonial systems. In her study of colonial Trinidad, Bridget Brereton explains:

> It was the great myth of Crown Colony government that Governors and officials were impartial administrators and, at the same time, the special protectors of the poor. The Crown was the representative of the unrepresented masses; hence the need to keep power and responsibility in the hands of the Governor. But the written constitution of a Crown Colony was one thing, reality another. . . . It was too much to expect that British officials would have operated as truly impartial

arbiters between the contending socio-economic groups. For these English gentlemen by and large shared the planters' general political and social views.[45]

Therefore, well into the twentieth century, Crown Colony government proved to be more of a check to Afro-Caribbean participation in West Indian politics than an impartial arbiter of good government.

The racialized justifications of the Crown Colony system were part of a broader ideological debate over the future of the British West Indies. The uncertainty of the post-emancipation era, continued unrest and resistance among the working classes, economic insecurity, the rise of new scientific racisms, and a general decrease in the importance of the Caribbean colonies within the British Empire combined to paint a dim future for the British Caribbean. Though a range of reasons existed for the depressed state of the British West Indies, not least Britain's removal of preferential treatment for West Indian sugar imports and the subsequent overall negative impact of free trade upon the region, numerous British intellectuals and government officials bound the fate of the region to questions about the intellectual and cultural "fitness" of the Afro-Caribbean majority. While some colonies received significant numbers of Chinese and Indian indentured servants in the mid-late nineteenth century, the latter becoming a prominent population in Trinidad and British Guiana, their addition did not alter the racialized views of the region.[46] Many Europeans also considered these new arrivals inferior, though less so than those of African descent, who still overwhelmingly outnumbered all other groups in the West Indies as a whole. The ideological debates over the future of the region thus remained primarily focused on the capabilities, or lack thereof, of the Afro-Caribbean majorities.

Thomas Carlyle, the famous Victorian intellectual, penned one of the most prominent condemnations of the British West Indies in his polemical 1849 essay "Occasional Discourse on the Negro Question," which was expanded and reprinted in 1853 as the more crudely titled "Occasional Discourse on the Nigger Question."[47] In this text Carlyle presented a caricatured image of black West Indians as "Quashee." A happy disposition, funny speech, rhythm, an ability to dance and sing, and an appetite for "pumpkins" (various tropical fruits) marked this figure. More important, Quashee was a consumer rather than a producer.[48] Carlyle repeatedly imputed laziness to the black population, and declared emancipation a mistake because slavery created order and extracted labor from a population that would otherwise not work. According to Catherine Hall, "Carlyle argued that white people were born to be lords and black people to be mastered."[49]

Throughout his essay Carlyle claimed the region would fall into decay and ruin without the leadership of the white population, who he maintained developed and, therefore, rightfully owned the region. "But under the soil of Jamaica, before it could even produce spices or any pumpkin, the bones of many thousand British men had to be laid."[50] Carlyle also offered a willfully distorted image of Haiti as a warning on the future of the British West Indies without white presence and guidance. "Look across to Haiti, and trace a far sterner prophecy! Let him, by his ugliness, idleness, rebellion, banish all White men from the West Indies, and make it all one Haiti, —with little or no sugar growing, black Peter exterminating black Paul, and where a garden of the Hesperides might be, nothing but a tropical dog-kennel and pestiferous jungle."[51] Such claims justified continued British control of the British West Indies and fueled racialized conceptualizations of a doomed region.

In response to Carlyle's essay, John Stuart Mill penned his own essay on the British West Indies and its black majority, "The Negro Question" (1850). While Mill did not take an anti-imperialist stand, he defended emancipation and the ability of the black population to be equals, noting how slavery, not nature, hindered the development of the enslaved. In response to Carlyle's contention that the West Indian colonies owed their development to the British, Mill responded:

According to [Carlyle], the whole West Indies belong to the whites: the negroes have no claim there, to either land or food, but by their sufferance. "It was not Black Quashee, or those he represents, that made those West India islands what they are." [But] I submit, that those who furnished the thews and sinews really had something to do with the matter. "Under the soil of Jamaica the bones of many thousand British men" . . . How many hundred thousand African men laid their bones there, after having had their lives pressed out by slow or fierce torture? They could have better done without Colonel Fortescue, than Colonel Fortescue could have done without them.[52]

As for Carlyle's use of Haiti as a warning to the British West Indies, Mill argued, "We are told to look at Haiti: what does [Carlyle] know of

Haiti? . . . Are we to listen to arguments grounded on hearsays like these? In what is black Haiti worse than white Mexico? If the truth were known, how much worse is it than white Spain?"[53]

With such challenges, Mill eloquently dismissed many of Carlyle's blatantly racist assumptions, though he too maintained a belief in the ultimate benefits of British colonialism. Nevertheless, Carlyle's view that the British West Indies faced a bleak future because of its black majority remained prevalent within the British Empire. In the coming years, such ideas continued to be espoused by various British authors and intellectuals, such as Anthony Trollope, Charles Kingsley, and James A. Froude, who weighed in on the future of the British West Indies in the mid-nineteenth century to the dismay of Afro-Caribbean intellectuals and activists.[54]

The aftermath of the Morant Bay Rebellion provided another opportunity for metropolitan debate over the West Indies. In response to Governor Eyre's repressive tactics, the Crown recalled him to England in 1866. The "Jamaica Committee," which included John Stuart Mill, Charles Darwin, and Herbert Spencer, pushed for prosecution of Eyre on murder charges, while the "Eyre Defence Committee," which included Thomas Carlyle, Charles Dickens, Alfred Lord Tennyson, and Charles Kingsley, defended Eyre as "a savior of besieged Anglo-Saxons in Jamaica."[55] The Eyre case continued until the end of 1860s, with the former governor prosecuted but never convicted, and remembered fondly by many whites in the Caribbean and Great Britain.

Although the Carlyle-Mill clash and the Eyre controversy provoked major debate in the metropole, in the British West Indies themselves the publication of Froude's *The English in the West Indies* (1888) was equally, if not more, provocative. Froude, the Regius Professor of Modern History at Oxford University and a close friend and protégé of Thomas Carlyle, briefly traveled to the British Caribbean in 1887. Upon his return he wrote in this inflammatory volume that the West Indian colonies, once the pride of the British Empire, were slipping out of English hands and becoming a ruined society. He argued that the prospects of any country relied on the "character" of its population, and that in the British West Indies the vast majority of the population were of an inferior race that could not rise to the level of the white race without the guidance of white men.[56]

Froude supported the extension of self-government in the British Empire; however, he believed this should be done cautiously. "The danger now is that it will be tried in haste in countries either as yet unripe for it or from the nature of things unfit for it."[57] Echoing the sentiments of Carlyle and others, he claimed that turning the West Indian colonies over to the black majorities would create another Haiti, which he portrayed as a barbarous land.[58] He claimed that despite the presence of British culture in the islands for many years, the "old African superstitions lie undisturbed at the bottom of [the black populations'] souls. Give them independence, and in a few generations they will peel off such civilisation as they have learnt as easily and as willingly as their coats and trousers."[59] Therefore Froude declared the British obligated to maintain their presence and control over the region.

Froude's volume is a prime example of the intellectual support that existed for British colonialism, and the role race played within such imperial justifications. Eric Williams, famed West Indian historian and politician, claimed, "No British writer, with the possible exception of Carlyle, has so savagely denigrated the West Indian Negro as Froude did in his analysis of Negro character."[60] Not unexpectedly, it drew the ire of many. Reacting much as they had to similar vilifications by other British intellectuals and authors in recent years, Afro-Caribbeans and their allies mounted a defense of both the West Indies and its African-descended populations with editorials in colonial periodicals such as *New Era* in Trinidad as well as more lengthy responses to Froude.[61]

C. S. Salmon, a former British colonial official with experience in the Caribbean and Africa, offered one of the most pointed rebuttals to Froude within a broader call for reform and self-government in the British Caribbean.[62] Writing during the golden jubilee of the final abolition of slavery, Salmon in *The Caribbean Confederation* (1888) defended the capabilities of the Afro-Caribbean populations and called for their equal inclusion within West Indian societies. Salmon maintained that these "Black British men" were among the most loyal in the empire. He opposed the ongoing extension of Crown control over the region. Instead he asserted that Afro-Caribbeans were both capable and ready for self-government. To deny this, Salmon argued, was to risk alienating the region's loyalty.[63] "If the British people and their Government fail to place their black fellow subjects in the West Indies on an equal footing within the Empire with the white races, they will be using their position to perpetuate a wrong, or rather to prolong it, for in all human probability to perpetuate it they will not be able. They will be prolonging a social and political blunder."[64]

Salmon challenged several aspects of Froude's book. He claimed Froude's depiction of the region demonstrated "how ready some are to re-forge [the black populations'] chains."[65] He noted that Froude's visit to the West Indies included stops at only four of fifteen colonies, and a few hours at two others. During that time, Froude primarily associated with government officials. Given such a short visit, as well as the lack of contact with the population he so thoroughly condemned, Salmon declared that Froude's assumptions about the black population and West Indian conditions were not only false but the "result of prejudices formed in England long ago." Salmon also dismissed Froude's use of Haiti as a "warning" to the British West Indies as nothing more than racist stereotypes.[66]

Overall, Salmon's defense of Afro-Caribbeans, as well as his call for an inclusive and expanded local self-government in the British West Indies—by a former colonial official, no less—proved a powerful rejoinder. However, while Salmon's reply is noteworthy, another publication in the same year proved even more significant within the West Indies.

In 1888 J. J. Thomas published *Froudacity: West Indian Fables Explained*, a book many consider one of the earliest West Indian nationalist texts. In this work the black Trinidadian schoolteacher Thomas confronted the white Oxford professor Froude.[67] Although Thomas was no British professor, he had received some acclaim within the West Indies and England for his 1869 book *The Theory and Practice of Creole Grammar*. Nevertheless, it was his reply to Froude that sealed his fame within West Indian circles.

Thomas's treatise challenged both the paternalism and the racialism of Froude's account. Upon receiving a copy of *The English in the West Indies* in February 1888 while on vacation in Grenada, Thomas wrote a series of articles in the *St. George's Chronicle* and *Grenada Gazette* which were republished as *Froudacity* shortly thereafter.[68] Thomas began his reply with a reference to Froude's book as "the dark outlines of a scheme to thwart political aspiration in the Antilles." He, like Salmon, whom he thanked for his rebuttal of Froude, noted various mistakes in Froude's account and argued that the residents of the British West Indies were capable of managing their own affairs. Thomas rejected Froude's claims of black inability, as well as the idea that allowing all citizens to participate would inevitably lead to a vengeful black rule of the region. In Thomas's view, "No one can deserve to govern simply because he is white, and no one is bound to be subject because he is black."[69]

One of the most significant aspects of Thomas's reply was that it came from the very population Froude criticized. Given the ways in which race was used to "doom" the future of the West Indies, Thomas was implicitly charged with defending both the region and his race. As Faith Smith notes, Thomas challenged Froude's and other metropolitan assumptions by "offering the accomplishments of black people throughout the African diaspora as proof of the imagination and creativity that would rehabilitate African people, and stressing the ability of British Caribbean residents generally to chart their own destinies."[70]

Faith Smith argues that to "know" Thomas, one must consider the multiple contexts in which he lived: "black nationalist, Caribbean resident, defender of francophone Creole traditions in a British-ruled territory, British subject proud of his mastery of British canonical texts, middle-class elite with working-class roots." It is also important to understand the multiple reasons Thomas took the stand he did. His defense of the British West Indies was not merely a stand for democracy and equality within the British Empire. It also connected to broader ideas of racial self-determination and racial uplift embedded in both his regional and his pan-African interests and activities. Thomas's West Indian nationalism and British cultural attributes coexisted and included a prominent racial consciousness, which would become a familiar characteristic of many West Indian nationalists in the twentieth century. He, like many West Indian and black diaspora intellectuals after him, "challenged some of the racial and cultural assumptions . . . even as he shared some of these assumptions."[71]

Outside of these discussions within the empire, the future of the British Caribbean and its connection to other areas of the black diaspora, particularly Africa and Black America, were also discussed prominently in the nineteenth century. Many noteworthy figures within the struggle against slavery in North America, such as Prince Hall, Denmark Vesey, and John Brown Russwurm, had Caribbean roots. Slave rebellions in the Caribbean, particularly the successful Haitian Revolution, also proved influential and inspiring to African American abolitionist movements. In Robert Alexander Young's *Ethiopian Manifesto* (1829), the black messiah for enslaved people in the United States was prophesied to come from the British West Indian island of Grenada. Moreover, from the mid-late nineteenth century, several black nationalists in the United States, including Martin R. Delany, Edward Wilmot Blyden, Henry Highland Garnet, James T. Holly, and Alexander Crummel, also connected the plight of African Americans, Afro-Caribbeans, and Africans in the nineteenth century.[72] The various islands of the Caribbean region were proposed as sites for possible emigration from the United States or other black nation-building endeavors.[73]

Ideas of the Caribbean as the location of new black nations were not restricted to black activists. In the early nineteenth century, famed German explorer and naturalist Alexander von Humboldt believed the region could become an "African Confederation of the free states of the West Indies."

Similarly, Thomas Jefferson noted the West Indies could be an "ideal place for a black kingdom" for repatriated slaves.[74]

As the nineteenth century ended, there was little consensus on the future of the British Caribbean. Was the region a ruined, lost land? Was it simply in decline, or doomed? Did it require white guidance? Could it be developed as a site of transracial unity within the bounds of the British Empire? Could it become an example of the power and abilities of people of African descent? What role did black diaspora politics play in the British West Indies, and how was the region conceptualized and connected with other areas of the black diaspora? Such questions and the disparate answers to them would be debated within and beyond the empire for much of the twentieth century. It was in this context that twentieth-century debates over self-government, self-determination, and the creation of a West Indian nation via federation would take on varied and potent political meanings in and out of the British Empire and Caribbean.

Reexamining Caribbean Federation

Various conceptualizations of Caribbean federation between some or all of the British West Indian colonies existed in the late nineteenth and twentieth centuries. British colonial officials proposed and debated federation as a solution to the economic and political problems they claimed plagued the region. As those ideas took shape, many West Indian reformers and activists co-opted the idea of a regional union as a means to achieve self-government and self-determination. Although federation was not the only idea of West Indian nation building or the only way West Indians pursued such goals, it would become one of the most prominent political visions for the region during these years. Still, even West Indian supporters of federation had diverse goals and motivations. For some, it was a path to local economic, social, and political advancement. Others, however, embraced federation as the ultimate goal, through which the entire region would advance as a united West Indian nation. Likewise, while many black diaspora activists and their organizations favored Caribbean federation as a means to liberate and empower people of African descent—reflecting the persuasive power of race in shaping support for the idea—there were both similarities and differences among these supporters too.

Despite the historical significance of Caribbean federation, its importance is often underestimated and at times overlooked. Much of this can be attributed to the existing presentation of the topic. Within both British and

Caribbean historiography, studies of Caribbean federation remain largely dated and limited. Most of them focus primarily on the rise and fall of the short-lived West Indies Federation (1958–62), with significant discussion of the reasons for its failure. However, this experiment's creation was the culmination of decades of debate, and it remains only one portion of the longer history of the idea of a Caribbean federation. Unfortunately, the failure of that endeavor has led many to view the history of federation as ultimately a study in failure. Much of this can be attributed to the boom of federation studies in the 1950s and 1960s prior to, during, and following the rise and demise of that particular federal experiment. Such studies largely examined the post–World War II planning and launch of the West Indies Federation as a regional decolonization and nation-building effort within the British Empire. Even works that do include and examine the longer history of federation do so overwhelmingly within the bounds of empire, while the broader importance of federation outside the Caribbean is generally disregarded.[75]

Building a Nation explores the broader, diasporic history of Caribbean federation as a window through which to examine the place of the British Caribbean within the multidimensional black diaspora politics of the early-mid twentieth century. Moving beyond a focus on the formal West Indies Federation and its failure, it expands on traditional studies of federation by exploring the longer history of the idea of federation and its relevance to the history of black diaspora. This includes visions of and support for federation and West Indian nation building circulating in and between the Caribbean, Black America, and Black Britain. It argues that efforts to create a federation in the British Caribbean were much more than merely an imperial or regional nation-building project. Federation was also a black diasporic nation-building endeavor intricately connected to notions of racial unity, racial uplift, and black self-determination. By placing the pursuit of West Indian self-government and nation building in the transnational and diasporic framework from which much debate and support emanated, this study addresses the overlapping and interconnected histories of the black diaspora, and moves the British Caribbean from the periphery of black diaspora studies.

Given the presence of Afro-Caribbean populations in so many locales within the black diaspora—North, South, and Central America, Europe, Africa, and the broader Caribbean itself—there are numerous areas where one could explore the idea of Caribbean federation and its connections to black diaspora politics in the twentieth century. Many people undoubtedly recognize the historical and contemporary existence of a "Caribbean diaspora" in many of these areas. While not discounting *that* diaspora, this study contextualizes these locations and the West Indies themselves primarily as parts of the broader "black diaspora"—as did many of the activists and organizations examined in this study.[76]

Building a Nation does not attempt to cover all of these areas and instead centers on the United States (particularly Harlem and the greater New York City area), Great Britain (particularly London), and the British West Indies themselves. My focus on these areas does not discount the relevance and importance of the other locations. As recent scholarship by historians such as Lara Putnam, Glenn A. Chambers, and Frank Guridy has shown, West Indians in the circum-Caribbean of Central and South America, as well as other Caribbean islands such as Cuba, constructed regional and racial identifications and took part in the burgeoning black diaspora politics of the twentieth century.[77] Nevertheless, these areas are not the focus here.

Several factors influenced the decision to focus on the United States, Great Britain, and the British Caribbean. While various locations in Black America are included in this study, a preponderance of my subjects and sources center on Harlem and the greater New York City area. Considering the designation of this area as the "Capital of the Caribbean" in the early-mid twentieth century and its long-recognized status as a center of black diaspora activism, this is likely unsurprising. Despite the significant number of studies produced on such topics in this area, as well as the need to "escape from New York" in order to situate the history of black activism in the wider diasporic, global context in which they operated, there remains much history to be uncovered here.[78] Similarly in Great Britain, although some areas of the circum-Caribbean had larger West Indian migrant communities than London, particularly in the years prior to World War II, its status as the center of the British Empire and a crossroads of anticolonial activism among black and other colonial peoples in the twentieth century makes it an important location in which to examine the topics within this study. Finally, perspectives from the British Caribbean are included, given the region's history of black diaspora activism as well as its being the focal point of efforts to create a Caribbean federation in the twentieth century.

Rather than a counternarrative that attempts to correct or contradict previous studies, this book is a parallel narrative to much of the existing historiography of Caribbean federation. It seeks to expand the subject to include and examine often overlooked perspectives, particularly visions of and support for Caribbean federation among the aforementioned black diaspora activists and organizations.

It is grounded in archival research in the United States, Great Britain, Jamaica, Trinidad, and Barbados. Although official collections on federation were consulted, one of my primary goals was to move beyond government and diplomatic records to investigate sources related to West Indian, African American, and black diaspora activists and organizations. These include personal and organizational records, government surveillance reports, periodicals, pamphlets, and other contemporary materials and writings. Black newspapers, particularly within the United States, also provide significant insight on the diasporic history of Caribbean federation. Indeed, the black press proved to be a valuable source on the agendas and activities of individuals and organizations, including the various local, ad-hoc, and temporary organizations at the center of much expatriate West Indian and black diaspora activism in the early-mid twentieth century that do not have their own archives. In many cases, black press accounts are the only records of these activities, while at other times they provide verification or alterative perspectives. These periodicals, many with wide circulation, provide both public and popular accounts of events and perspectives otherwise unnoticed. Finally, while my study does not aim to merely provide a narrative account of these histories, it does make a concerted effort to include the rhetoric employed in diaspora and expatriate support for federation, and to establish more than simply the existence of these organizations through passing mention.

While this book aims to expand the history of Caribbean federation, as with any historical study, there remain limitations. The focus on West Indian and black diaspora activists and organizations, as well as the sources employed, undoubtedly results in a study of primarily black middle-class perspectives. Granted that most of the individuals discussed were male and "educated"—some even considered among the elite of their communities— many of these activists and intellectuals were non-state actors who have been overlooked or excluded in prior studies of federation. Although their perspectives may not represent views of Caribbean federation from "the bottom," they do provide insight "from below" in contrast to studies of federation that prioritize discussions among government officials.

In addressing the diasporic dimensions and history of Caribbean federation, *Building a Nation* connects with and contributes to existing historiographies. In recent years, various studies have appeared on the history of expatriate Caribbean communities in the United States and United Kingdom.[79] Many of these have established the presence and, in some cases, the political activities of West Indians in these areas. However, while the participation of West Indians within black diaspora politics is well known, few studies address their anticolonial and nation-building efforts on behalf of their own homelands, including support for Caribbean federation and its connections to other black diaspora and African struggles. There has also been a significant increase in historical studies focused on African American participation in, and connections to, international black freedom struggles. Such studies have examined a wide range of issues from the place of racial politics in US foreign affairs (notably the Cold War) to African American international activism across the globe.[80] Unfortunately, despite the long presence of Anglophone Caribbean populations within the United States and their close work with African Americans within domestic and international black freedom struggles, few of these studies have sufficiently examined anticolonial activities and nation-building efforts centered on the British Caribbean colonies. When Caribbean federation is mentioned, it is rarely examined or analyzed but is instead noted only in passing.

There are, however, two recent exceptions to this treatment of Caribbean federation. Jason Parker's *Brother's Keeper: The United States, Race, and Empire in the British Caribbean, 1937–1962* is the more significant. Parker's work examines the pursuit of the West Indies Federation within the diplomatic negotiations of American, British, and West Indian governments during World War II and the Cold War. Though Parker does offer some significant reflection on racial politics and diaspora activism in World War II–era Harlem, his study prioritizes official diplomatic relations and opinions, and it overlooks discussions of Caribbean federation in earlier decades of the twentieth century. Gerald Horne's *Cold War in a Hot Zone* also discusses the pursuit of a West Indies Federation. Similar in focus to many of his other publications, this study primarily considers the role of labor and leftist politics in the cause of West Indian independence in the mid-twentieth century. The disparate ideas of federation, diasporic support for it, and its place within black diaspora politics, however, are not examined. Moreover, like Parker, Horne begins his study in the 1930s and largely omits the long history of federation in preceding decades. It is my hope that *Building a Nation* addresses some of the topics not covered in these studies and advances the history of Caribbean federation as they have done.

Chapter 1 establishes the disparate support for and conceptualizations of a united West Indian nation from the late nineteenth century through the 1920s. While some federal experiments were proposed prior to the twentieth century, it was during the years surrounding World War I that federation became increasingly debated by an array of politicians, activists, and organizations within and beyond the Caribbean. Multiple proposals were put forth by the "colonial power brokers" of the region—a group that included colonial officials in the colonies and the metropole as well as the white elites of the colonies, whom the Crown viewed as the only "responsible" portion of the colonial population. These proposals sought to create a "united status quo" aimed only at administrative efficiency and economic opportunity. Support for federation, however, was not limited to these proposals. The idea of federation also came to be embraced by an array of local and regional reform associations that sought changes to the existing economic, social, and political systems. Though some within these groups agreed that federation was an important step in the region's political evolution toward self-government *within* the British Empire, others embraced federation as a means to achieve unity for additional reasons. Given that race was routinely used to dismiss and limit black political participation in the region, many Afro-Caribbean reformers, and their respective organizations, avidly pursued racial uplift, unity, and empowerment in conjunction with their reform efforts. For many such activists, these ideologies supported and bolstered the cause of federation as a black diaspora project. Likewise, in diaspora centers such as Harlem and to a lesser extent London, Afro-Caribbean migrants were regionalized as West Indians, while both West Indians and West Indian issues were overtly racialized as part of a global black identity and freedom struggle. For many West Indian expatriates and other black diaspora activists, federation became a means to unite and empower the region for the good of West Indians, particularly the black majorities of the islands. Federation, therefore, was a common answer to disparate and competing goals, and existed simultaneously as a tool of colonial control and a means to varying ideas of liberation and empowerment.

Chapter 2 examines the history of Caribbean federation through the 1930s and World War II. Dire economic conditions, social upheaval (particularly various labor rebellions), and the rise of numerous political movements marked much of this era within the British Caribbean colonies, while anticolonial and Pan-African activism continued to flourish in the region and other sections of the black diaspora. During these years, federation remained a central goal for both the Crown and most local political parties and labor unions in the West Indian colonies. Alongside the rise of organizations within the region, expatriate West Indian and diaspora-focused organizations were increasingly created and active in diaspora centers, especially Harlem, whose honorary designation as the "Capital of the Caribbean" became solidified in this era. Much more than simply auxiliary units of material support, many of these organizations and activists outside the region participated in, led, and in some cases even helped found progressive political movements within the Caribbean. In addition to the wide range of Caribbean-focused associations active in the broader diaspora, various race-based organizations operating on both side of the Atlantic—including the conservative League of Coloured Peoples, the moderate NAACP, and the more radical International African Service Bureau—also championed Caribbean federation within a prioritized, racialized anticolonialism that connected the freedom struggles of the Caribbean, Black America, and Africa. Therefore, multifaceted visions of West Indian nation building via a Caribbean federation continued to exist and flourish in both British imperial and black diaspora politics throughout the tumultuous years of the 1930s and early 1940s.

Chapter 3 investigates the transition of Caribbean federation from a long-standing dream to an impending reality in the closing years of World War II and the immediate postwar era, with a particular focus on the continued cross-pollination between black diaspora and intra-regional West Indian politics. Within British imperial politics, the Crown increasingly proposed the creation of federations throughout the crumbling empire—in the West Indies, Africa, and Asia—as a means to control decolonization. In 1945, Secretary of State for the Colonies Oliver Stanley directed the legislatures of the West Indian colonies to officially debate the issue of political federation, which began a decadelong series of meetings between West Indian political leaders and colonial officials. Though West Indian and black diaspora organizations outside the Caribbean were largely excluded from the official planning of federation, they continued to offer crucial moral and material support. These relationships demonstrate the racial dimensions of West Indian nation building with connections to broader black diaspora struggles of the postwar era.

Chapter 4 explores the final steps in the creation of a Caribbean federation in the 1950s leading to the launch of the West Indies Federation in 1958. Expatriate West Indian and black diaspora activists were by now largely confined to auxiliary roles, but they maintained a watchful eye on the ongoing federal negotiations. Within the official meetings between the Crown and colonies, federation was promoted as a regional project within the British Empire. Nevertheless, to some it remained part of the broader struggles of the black diaspora and a racialized endeavor focused on black self-determination. As the formal federation took shape, many within the region struggled to build a collective sense of West Indianness, which proved far more concrete outside the West Indies. Given the significant ties between race, West Indianness, and West Indian nation building in previous decades, this chapter also examines the ongoing debates on the place of race within the emerging nation, and juxtaposes parallel visions of the federation. On one hand, supporters of federation, especially within the region, trumpeted the creation of a multiracial (or transracial) nation. At the same time, others, particularly beyond the Caribbean, heralded federation as the launching of a "black nation" intimately connected to the African American and African freedom struggles of the era. In both cases, federation was a symbolic venture—a lesson for the world to admire, whether it was the creation of a nation beyond race or another example of black self-rule.

Finally, the epilogue addresses the short existence of the West Indies Federation. This study has intentionally attempted to avoid reproducing a familiar history of federation as primarily the planning and construction of the official West Indies Federation (1958–62), which is but one portion of a much larger history of the idea of federation, and sought to deprioritize the formal federation and its failure. Nonetheless, since many view its creation as the culmination of the previous decades' efforts, the epilogue includes discussions of the inherent problems of the new nation, the divisive nature of internal relations between member units, its untimely collapse only four years after its creation, and the reactions to its demise. This includes not only the views of West Indian officials within the Federation but expatriate and diasporic voices from beyond the Caribbean. It also ponders the legacy of the idea of federation within the postcolonial Anglophone Caribbean and black diaspora, as well as insights garnered from a diasporic history of Caribbean federation.

By examining the idea of Caribbean federation within the various contexts in which it existed, beyond the limited scope of the West Indies Federation and inclusive of the long history of support from the black diaspora, one can more fully appreciate the multiple, often overlooked dimensions of West Indian nation building in the twentieth century. Though the goal of liberating and unifying the West Indies was not as pronounced as the struggles of the African continent within black diaspora politics in the twentieth century, that goal was not forsaken or forgotten by the activists from its shores, or by their African American and African counterparts. Indeed, this history of federation presents another important example of Caribbean connections to the black diaspora, and establishes the ways in which the Caribbean itself became, at least to some, a site for transnational and diasporic black nation-building efforts beyond Africa.

1

A Common Answer to Disparate Questions

Envisioning Caribbean Federation
in the Late Nineteenth and Early Twentieth Centuries

The twentieth century began with much uncertainty in the British Caribbean. To some within the empire, much of the region had become a "synonym of ruin."[1] In the words of Joseph Chamberlain, the area was the "Empire's darkest slum."[2] Economically, many of the colonies remained mired in depression, several because of the continuous boom-and-bust cycle of the still-dominant sugar industry. Politically, the installation of the Crown Colony system in all but a few colonies, a move that was supposed to bring good government, social order, and prosperity, more often only added another layer of bureaucracy and economic inefficiency. The region also remained deeply divided along racial and class lines, with the bulk of the Afro-Caribbean population suffering at the bottom of the economic ladder with little say in the functioning of the colonial governments.

Despite differences of opinions on the specific "ills" affecting the British Caribbean, a common remedy emerged within many conceptualizations of the West Indian future in the twentieth century—federation. As Hume Wrong notes in his *Government of the West Indies* (1923),

> When one contemplates the wide circle of British possessions around the Caribbean Sea . . . one is left with the impression that here is to be found a waste of effort, an untidiness that calls for rearrangement, diffusion and variety where concentration and symmetry should prevail. In other parts of the British Commonwealth the tendency has been for distinct units which are geographically related gradually to coalesce for some or for all political purposes. Why should the West Indies remain almost as scattered and distinct politically as they were a hundred years ago?[3]

Ideas of a regional union between different countries and colonies of the Caribbean were not confined to the British West Indies. In the nineteenth century, one can find proposals for an Antillean Confederation between Cuba, Puerto Rico, and the Dominican Republic, as well as plans involving Haiti and other islands of the region. Nevertheless, it was within the British Caribbean that the idea persisted and endured the longest.[4]

Although proposals for federation and other variations of regional unification in the British West Indies existed before, the idea reemerged in the late nineteenth and early twentieth centuries among an array of politicians, activists, and organizations within and beyond the British Caribbean. Given the disparate and often opposing groups that proposed and supported federation, there were inherently different motivations and expectations of what a federation would, could, and should do. Indeed, one finds a wide range of ideas related to political and economic reform in the region within the various proposals for federation between some or all of the British West Indian colonies. All told, the idea of federation purported to be the answer to contrasting and competing goals, existing simultaneously as a tool of colonial control and also a means to achieve varying degrees of liberation and empowerment within or outside the British Empire.

This chapter explores support and conceptualizations of a united British West Indies (alternatively proposed as a federation, confederation, or closer union) from the late nineteenth century through the 1920s among the "colonial power brokers" of the region, West Indian activists within the Caribbean, and various other activists beyond the Caribbean. It provides an overview of proposals for federation from the Crown and white oligarchies of the West Indies in order to establish what many prior studies have assumed to be *the* history of the subject in this era. However, the greater part of the chapter examines the co-opting of the idea of federation by West Indian activists in the Caribbean (especially Afro-Caribbeans within the emerging West Indian nationalist movements) and a range of black activists in the broader black diaspora. It is interested particularly in the ways in which concepts of "race" shaped perceptions and pursuit of Caribbean federation during these years.

The colonial power brokers of the region—a group that included colonial officials in the colonies and metropole as well as the white elites of the colonies whom the Crown viewed as the only responsible portion of the colonial population—put forth multiple proposals in the early twentieth century. Despite historical tensions among this group, and differences within their proposals, overall they sought primarily to create a "united status quo" aimed at administrative efficiency and greater economic productivity and opportunity. Support for federation, however, was not limited to these proposals.

Various local and regional reform associations, most middle-class led and many of which came to be predominantly composed of the vast Afro-Caribbean majority in most of the West Indian colonies, also embraced the idea of federation in the early twentieth century. These included colony-specific organizations focused on local struggles, as well as the burgeoning regional West Indian nationalist and labor movements. In both local and regional organizations, one could find those who supported federation as *an* important step in the pursuit of self-government, which often included demands for an expanded franchise, increased representation, responsible government, and eventually dominion status *within* the British Empire for the individual West Indian colonies. At the same time, one could also find in both local and regional organizations those who had many of the same aims, but who viewed the creation of a united West Indian nation (via federation)—in or out of the empire—as *the* ultimate goal in their pursuit of self-government and self-determination. For the latter group, the advancement of the region as a whole outweighed the insular concerns of individual colonies. These distinctions, however, often proved fluid, given the overlapping membership and sentiments between many local and regional organizations.

In either case, whether viewed primarily as a means to achieve local or regional reforms, the pursuit of a Caribbean federation by West Indians within these movements often included additional motivations. Given the centrality of racial justifications of British colonialism, the programs of many such groups incorporated overt calls for racial equality not only in the West Indies but worldwide. Many Afro-Caribbean reformers and their organizations within the British West Indies ardently pursued racial uplift, unity, and empowerment and embedded these ideas within their demands for self-determination. These pursuits aligned with and bolstered their support of a Caribbean federation, which in turn became more than a regional, West Indian project. It also became a racialized project with diasporic implications.

Beyond the Caribbean, in diaspora centers such as Harlem and London, where Afro-Caribbean migrants more concretely identified as West Indians than they did *within* the colonies in the early twentieth century, West Indians and West Indian issues, including social and political reform and empowerment, were overtly racialized. With much the same racially conscious support displayed by some West Indians within the region, and often with direct communication and connections to them, many Afro-Caribbean, African American, and other black activists in these diaspora centers viewed federation as a means to unite and empower the region for the good of West Indians, particularly the black majority who many assumed were *the* West Indians. They too presumed the creation of a Caribbean federation would be beneficial to far more than just West Indians.

Colonial Power Brokers and Proposals for Caribbean Federation

Twentieth-century visions of a united British Caribbean were rooted in a series of proposals, investigations, and experiments for regional cooperation that circulated the region between the seventeenth and nineteenth centuries. These efforts most often originated in the metropole and represented imperial efforts to institute efficient government via the streamlining of colonial administration in the region. Such proposals often irritated the local planter-merchant oligarchies, who wished to maintain control of their particular colonies and economic interests through their powerful representative assemblies. Moreover, many of the West Indian colonies competed against each other economically, which created island-based rivalries that tended to undermine regional reform projects. For many within the dominant white oligarchies of the Caribbean, especially those in more prosperous colonies, the prospect of formal association with rival or poorer West Indian colonies was unappealing. Nevertheless, in rare cases, these groups did accept projects for regional cooperation if they deemed it to be in their best interests.

In many ways, projects for Caribbean federation represented a return to the mechanisms of governance that previously prevailed in the region. The original "Caribbee" colonies were governed together under a proprietorship granted to the Earl of Carlisle between the 1620s and 1670s.[5] In the following decades, however, governance was repeatedly disaggregated and reaggregated as the colonies became more prosperous and demanded more control over their own affairs. Perhaps the earliest attempt at uniting different colonies took place in the late seventeenth century with the creation of the Leeward Island Association.[6] Various other Leeward and Windward Island groupings were attempted on and off in the eighteenth century; however, rivalries between the colonies and the desire for local representation within the Old Representative System generally limited or prevented the successful establishment of long-term and stable intra-regional associations.[7]

New attempts to unite the British Caribbean colonies appeared in the nineteenth century. Although planters and merchants often thought of themselves as sharing a common (white) West Indian identification and cooperated in associations and occasional meetings designed to protect and promote their interests, such as the Society of West India Planters and Merchants, the West India Committee, and Colonial Congress of 1831, this tendency did not make them more welcoming to proposals for regional unification in the Caribbean itself.[8] Other than the reorganization in 1831 of Berbice, Demerara, and Essequibo into the single colony of British Guiana, the local white oligarchies generally remained opposed to political unions of the West Indian colonies.[9]

During the reorganization of colonial rule in the post-emancipation era, the Colonial Office proposed and instituted various new colonial unions in the British Caribbean. The success of the Canadian confederation of 1867 rejuvenated the Colonial Office's hopes of successful amalgamations in the West Indies, which they increasingly proposed in the 1870s and beyond.[10] There was even some debate of a more far-reaching imperial federation of the British Empire.[11] With such ideas gaining popularity in circles of colonial governance, an 1871 parliamentary act created the Leeward Islands Colony. This federation, however, remained rather weak, with most legislative and financial power reserved for the individual island legislatures.[12]

In the mid-1870s the Colonial Office proposed a merger between Barbados and the Windward Islands of Grenada, St. Vincent, St. Lucia, and Tobago. There was some support among the working classes of these colonies for such a grouping, but the middle and upper classes of Barbados strongly resisted the suggestion, which they saw as a threat to their economic well-being and a potential hindrance to the continued development of the colony. An island-wide riot occurred in 1876, driven in part by resistance to the planned merger. As a result, the reigning governor of Barbados was transferred to Hong Kong and the federal initiative dropped.[13]

Despite these events, Barbados and the Windward Islands retained a joint governorship until 1885, when Barbados was disassociated completely from all other colonies. Grenada, St. Lucia, St. Vincent, and Tobago were grouped into a Windward Island association in 1885 with a common governor, though they maintained their individual legislatures. Tobago was removed from this association in 1889 and joined with Trinidad to form a single colony.[14]

Crown efforts at colonial reorganization continued in the 1890s. In 1893–94 a royal commission, organized to investigate conditions in Dominica, issued a report that argued that there would be important benefits gained from a federation of the entire British West Indies under the administration of one governor-general. However, the report also noted that the time for such a move was not yet ripe, and the Crown initiated no formal plans.[15] A few years later, an 1897 royal commission rejected suggestions for a federation under a single governor-general and a combined West Indies civil service.[16] In 1898 the British House of Commons issued another call for a "single government for all the islands," but that too proved unsuccessful.[17] As the century closed, what remained of projects for federation was only a series of loose associations between some, but not all, of the British Caribbean colonies.

With few exceptions, such proposals for varying levels of cooperation and association between the colonies were limited to visions of administrative efficiency and increased commercial prowess. They originated primarily in the metropole, which sought, generally unsuccessfully, to impose them on the colonies. Some within the planter-merchant oligarchies had, at times, relaxed their opposition to such schemes when they believed regional cooperation, in one form or another, could aid them financially during times of economic depression. Generally, then, debates about closer union, confederation, or federation were almost exclusively about how these plans would affect colonial administration or the local white oligarchies.

A notable exception was Charles Spencer Salmon's 1888 proposal for a Caribbean Confederation in the British West Indies. Salmon called for full and equal integration of the Afro-Caribbean populations and a federation of *all* British West Indian colonies.[18] He ridiculed the duplicative and inefficient nature of the current West Indian colonial governments.

> For the fifteen colonies there are now eight governors, all receiving their orders from Downing Street direct, each with his staff, and nine lieutenant-governors, administrators, or presidents, four of whom receive orders from the Governor of the Windward Islands, and five from the Governor of the Leeward Islands. This makes seventeen governors and administrators for the fifteen colonies, because the Windward and Leeward Islands have every one not only their separate administrators, but a governor for each of the two groups.[19]

Salmon lambasted such colonial bureaucracy for needlessly wasting resources, "as if each of these colonies were large, distant, rich, and powerful communities, that had nothing in common, and that could never be amalgamated."[20] These complaints aligned with other calls for some form of political union between the West Indian colonies. However, given Salmon's demand for racial equality alongside political reforms, the implications of his plan for a broader social and political transformation of the West Indies were quite different from other plans by colonial officials and the planter-merchant oligarchies.[21]

Although nothing came of Salmon's idea for confederation, it was important as a precursor to the alternative visions of a united West Indies that would gain importance in the twentieth century. It also shows that while many ideas for regional unification appeared similar on the surface, the content and possible implications of these proposals could differ significantly in what they sought to achieve and whom they hoped to aid. This became increasingly evident in the twentieth century when new bases of support coopted the idea of a Caribbean federation.

Plans for different levels of regional cooperation and union continued to appear among colonial power brokers in the early decades of the twentieth century. Unlike previous centuries, in this era the proposals for uniting the West Indies emanated from both the metropole and the colonies. The Colonial Office remained one of the staunchest supporters of the idea based on continued calls for administrative efficiency. These initiatives were bolstered by periodic plans associated with the planter-merchant oligarchies, which, despite their general long-standing opposition to federation, began to view some level of cooperation as a means to combat their weakened economic status. Many of these proposals, like those from the Colonial Office, supported the consolidation of smaller colonies as not only efficient but essential to the prestige and development of the region.

Federation remained connected with notions of progress, order, and modernity popular within colonial administrative discourse. Some proposals included visions of a future marked by the widespread return of representative government and eventually responsible self-government, possibly with dominion status in the British Empire. Like the nineteenth-century proposals, however, few if any plans emanating from the colonial power brokers of the region directly sought to challenge social hierarchies, or to increase the political participation and economic status of the Afro-Caribbean majority.

Interest in regional cooperation among the colonial power brokers reappeared early in the first decade of the twentieth century. In 1902 Norman Lamont, a member of Parliament (MP) who also owned a large estate in

Trinidad, called for the British West Indies to "be united into one great Colony with a Cromer or a Curzon at the head of it, advised by a council of the best men we can send out." This, he believed, would allow for greater trade through reciprocity treaties with Canada and the United States.[22] Over the next few years, Lamont continued his support for a federation with a "strong central administration, under a benevolent despot," and dismissed suggestions of trading the West Indies to the United States for the Philippines, which he assumed would not benefit the Crown or be welcomed by the United States. Instead he maintained that colonial unification in the West Indies was essential to the future of the region.[23] Lamont's early calls for a strong federal center displayed little concern for the jealously guarded local interests and institutions of the planter-merchant oligarchies. However, by 1912 his idea for federation—likely influenced by other proposals from the period that asserted the need for more local autonomy—included safeguards for local institutions and "the greatest possible autonomy retained by the constituent units."[24]

G. B. Mason, a founding member of the West Indian Club, a social organization connected with the West India Committee, also supported some form of regional unification in the British Caribbean. In 1903 he proposed a "common West Indian legal, medical, and civil service." By 1908 Mason proposed a more extensive association between the colonies through the creation of "the Antilles"—a union of the Windward Islands, Leeward Islands, and Barbados under a single governor—above which would be a Confederate Council consisting of four governors from the Antilles, Trinidad, British Guiana, and Jamaica.[25]

In 1907–8 other proposals for colonial consolidation came from Joseph Rippon of the Direct West India Cable Company, a man noted by one of his contemporaries as "a gentlemen most zealous in the cause of West Indian federation and of the advancement of the West Indies."[26] Rippon believed the West Indian colonies still held significant value for the empire, and that some form of "effective union" between them would provide a united voice, better representation, and increased prestige. Among other benefits, such an arrangement would create a united West Indian trade capable of commanding "permanent attention from other parts of the Empire, like Canada, as well as from foreign countries." In conjunction with these ideas, Rippon devised a draft "United West Indies Consolidation Act" in which he suggested the formation of a general council composed of representatives of the various executive and legislative bodies of the entire British West Indies.[27]

R. H. McCarthy suggested a confederation of Barbados and the Windward and Leeward Islands in 1908.[28] In response to criticism that the islands were too remote and lacked effective communication between them, McCarthy countered that both Australia and Canada, two existing federation models within the empire with extremely large landmasses and numerous remote areas, had been able to unite successfully. Moreover, McCarthy argued, the Caribbean Sea was in some ways easier to cross than extensive unsettled lands. "Were the Atlantic land instead of water," he wrote, "probably the West Indies would still await their discoverer."[29] To claims that there was little advantage in confederation, McCarthy responded that there was power in numbers, that strength through unification had helped push the success of confederation in Canada and Australia and would lead to the success of such projects in South Africa in the near future. As suggested by others, a Caribbean confederation would increase the power and raise the international status of the West Indies too.

In 1910 D. S. DeFreitas, a representative of the Agricultural and Commercial Society of Grenada, presented his ideas for regional consolidation to the Royal Commission on Trade Relations between Canada and the West Indies. He proposed the creation of a "central authority," with representatives from the British West Indian islands and British Guiana, which would deal with a series of "common subjects and questions." Like many other proposals of this era, his idea of what constituted "common interests" was largely economic: commerce, trade, and communications. DeFreitas also echoed others who argued that such an institution would increase the region's power to influence imperial policies, claiming that "any policy or decision stamped with the concurrence of Demerara and of the British West Indies will carry weight and call for clear recognition."[30] The initial step he proposed would, he hoped, in time lead to the "formation of a real union."[31]

In a series of articles published between 1908 and 1911, the West India Committee responded to these and similar calls for West Indian unification.[32] The committee generally supported Mason's early idea of uniting the medical, postal, and civil services of the West Indies. McCarthy's broader proposals, however, were dismissed. The committee believed that it would be too difficult to merge the colonies that he suggested, since they did not all share the same constitutional structure.[33] Rippon's plan proved more appealing to the West India Committee because it coincided with their desire for a "federated commercial and industrial West Indian Parliament" which would look after the economic interests of the region. Though the Committee rejected the idea of political federation between West Indian colonies at this time, they did see the creation of a commercial federation as a positive first step toward that goal.[34]

The most significant proposal for federation in the prewar era came from C. Gideon Murray, the administrator of St. Vincent (and later of St. Lucia), who designed two detailed schemes in 1911 and 1912. When Murray presented his *Scheme for the Federation of Certain of the West Indian Colonies* to the West India Committee in London on 22 November 1911, Sir Owen Philipps, presiding at the meeting, attempted to set a positive tone. "These are days of great federations, not only of labour and capital, but also of states." In response to those who opposed federations of labor and capital because of possible abuses, Philipps declared that he saw "the federation of small states into dominions [as] perfectly natural development[s] in the progress of the nation, where it is practicable. It is, in my opinion, perfectly futile and worse than useless to fight against what is one of the laws of the development of our civilisation." Noting the successful creation of Canada (1867), Australia (1901), and the Union of South Africa (1910), Philipps said that the West Indies must now decide if they would "sink local differences and combine together to form a West Indian Dominion, and thus fall into line with the other British Dominions beyond the seas." To do so would allow them to take their proper place within the empire.[35] This introduction mirrored various recent calls for some form of a regional union, but also more explicitly connected federation with ideas of national progress and modernity, presaging the future development of proposals for federation.

Murray noted at the beginning of his talk that he understood discussions of federation "tread upon very delicate and debatable ground," yet the issue was of "vital importance."[36] Despite the vastness of the British West Indian seascape, with some colonies separated by a thousand miles of ocean, and the distinctive local histories of many islands with closely guarded local interests and different levels of development, Murray believed that federation was both workable and needed. "The various colonies," he wrote, "are waking up to the fact that unity means strength, progress and prosperity, while disunion spells weakness and even poverty."[37]

Dismissing the idea of immediately uniting all the colonies into a single federation as impractical, Murray suggested a federation of the southeastern portion of the West Indian colonies.[38] As for the other colonies, particularly Jamaica, they could join later should they choose to do so.[39] Murray argued that a federation of the southeastern West Indies was necessitated by "weighty subjects of common interest calling for solution" including commerce, trade, and communication.[40] Murray's "Federated Colonies" were to have a federal council primarily elected by and from the members of the various colonial legislatures under a high commissioner. The council would have limited legislative powers over agreed-upon common interests.[41] The proposal called for some rearranging of governorships and political associations between the islands, particularly within the Windward and Leeward Islands. Murray did not wish to alter significantly the local constitutions and colonial governments of the individual colonies, believing that "purely local affairs and taxation" should remain controlled by local governments, with "the delegation to a central body of all affairs of common interest."[42]

At the conclusion of Murray's talk, he took questions and comments from the audience. Joseph Rippon welcomed the discussion, though he had minor qualms about Murray's terminology, and made sure to reiterate his own contributions on the subject.[43] Others, however, were more critical of Murray's proposals. A Mr. Rutherford noted he was glad that Murray's plan included no constitutional alterations, but he questioned the advantage of a high commissioner and wondered if there was a large enough leisure class to fill the positions on a federal council. Regarding federation in general he seemingly disagreed, arguing, "When things are well, leave well alone."[44] Murray responded that there was actually some debate on whether things were "well" in the West Indies. As for the leisure class, he claimed that the "planters and others" had the time to participate in a federal council, and clarified that he was not calling for wider political participation in the government.[45]

In 1912 Murray republished his ideas in a new book, *A United West Indies.* The text included few significant changes to Murray's proposal from the previous year, though he offered additional information to bolster his plans along with a draft constitution for a United West Indies. Murray reiterated that the future of the West Indies rested upon the creation of a regional union, an idea he again clearly connected to notions of progress and modernity.

> For what is to be the destiny of our British West Indian Colonies? Are they to remain single, isolated, disintegrated units, each striving to work out its own salvation in the haphazard way that has hitherto been the case; coming together through delegates when some cause demands concerted action and then only at the last moment and in a spirit of reluctance and hesitation, like so many strangers entering

into negotiations, suspicious of each other's business intention and motives? Or are they to face modern conditions in a modern way and to form such a combination amongst themselves for political and commercial purposes as will give them that status in the Empire and the world that their growing importance warrants.[46]

The following year, an article in the *Times* expressed mixed feelings on federation. It said that a union of only a portion of the colonies would make matters even worse for those left out, because they would face an additional powerful competitor, one from within the same empire. The author rejected any federation that would require an assembly with powers to make joint laws or control the finances of all members, but did support some level of cooperation on matters of agriculture, education, and the civil service, as well as some arrangement that would allow the West Indian colonies to speak with a single voice in the international arena.[47] This was consistent with many previous federation proposals that spoke in terms of regional "common interests" but demanded "local autonomy." The author also commented directly on the need to avoid alteration of the islands' constitutional structures, lest the region become dominated by the black majority.

> Few persons acquainted with the West Indies would contemplate with equanimity any concession which would have the effect of giving to the coloured voter, who would, unless the franchise were very strictly limited, be in an enormous majority, a position of predominance. It is unnecessary to enlarge on this aspect of the case for federation. The experience of Haiti and San Domingo is too recent and too adjacent to escape attention.[48]

Though rarely articulating such concerns so openly, previous proposals had also avoided calling for greater participation, arguing that any new organizations or government bodies would draw from the current legislative councils, which were overwhelmingly white.

In the post–World War I era, debates over federation continued with proposals from the local oligarchies alongside official investigations from the Colonial Office. Some of the most prominent support for regional cooperation came from the Associated Chambers of Commerce in the West Indies, an organization established in 1917 and led by Edward R. Davson, an Englishman whose family held business interests in British Guiana.[49] This group proposed periodic meetings where "the commercial men of the different Colonies will take counsel together over such questions as tariffs, customs, trade statistics, and the many other subjects which chambers of commerce discuss." It also hoped to represent the region as a whole at the triennial Congress of the Chambers of Commerce of the Empire.[50] In the early 1920s, Davson and the Associated Chambers of Commerce formally approached the Colonial Office with projects to create a more permanent conference system under a joint central committee or council that would meet periodically to address issues of common interest, but little came of their proposals in these years.[51]

Surprisingly, until this period the vast majority of these early twentieth-century proposals for regional unification emanated from individuals or commercial organizations, rather than government agencies. Though several of the individuals actually held government positions, their proposals were not formal inquiries or initiatives from the Colonial Office, but rather their own presentations. However, in the early 1920s, the Colonial Office formally reexamined the issue of federation and other constitutional matters of the West Indies. At the behest of MPs Gideon Murray and Samuel Hoare, and with the approval of Winston Churchill, then serving as secretary of state for the colonies, a formal visit to the British West Indies was organized.[52]

In December 1921, Under-Secretary of State for the Colonies E.F.L. Wood began a three-month tour of the British West Indies.[53] In each colony visited, Wood, along with MP William Ormsby-Gore and R. A. Wiseman of the Colonial Office, investigated a range of constitutional questions, as well as economic, health, and medical issues. The committee's ensuing official report, commonly known as the Wood Report, also addressed the possibilities of a federation in the West Indies. The Wood Report largely agreed with previous schemes that emphasized the need for regional unification to provide a more powerful voice within the empire.[54] However, in line with Colonial Office policy, it maintained that there needed to be support for such an initiative from the colonies themselves. Any advances on the question of federation could "only be as the result of a deliberate demand of local opinion, springing from the realisation of the advantages of co-operation under modern world conditions"—something the Wood Commission claimed they had not seen during their brief visit.[55]

The Wood Report concluded it was "both inopportune and impracticable to attempt amalgamation of existing units of government into anything approaching a general federal system."[56] It cited familiar reasons of geography, constitutional differences between the colonies, and fierce local sentiments as the primary obstacles.[57] The Wood Commission also dismissed suggestions for the wider introduction of representative government, given the sharp social divisions and the considerable numbers of "backward and politically undeveloped" people in the region.[58] "West Indian political unity" was ultimately declared "likely to be a plant of slow and tender growth."[59]

In the wake of the Wood Report, the constitutional structures of the various West Indian colonies remained largely unchanged.[60] Notwithstanding the introduction of some political reforms, including the addition of small numbers of elected "unofficial members" to legislative councils in Trinidad and Tobago, Grenada, St. Vincent, St. Lucia, and Dominica, Crown Colony rule was still the dominant system for the vast majority of the British West Indian colonies.[61]

Despite the Wood Report's comments on federation, proposals and meetings regarding regional cooperation continued in the latter half of the 1920s along similar lines to those of the previous years. In 1926 a West Indian Conference was organized in London to "consider and report upon the desirability of setting up a Standing Conference to deal in a consultative and an advisory capacity with matters of concern to all of the colonies."[62] The delegates drafted a constitution for the Standing Conference as a "purely advisory board, with no executive powers, meeting at regular intervals and performing for its constituents functions analogous to those which the Imperial Conference performs for the Empire as a whole."[63] For the most part, this plan emulated the previous plans of Edward Davson and the Associated Chambers of Commerce to hold periodic meetings to discuss matters of common interest in the West Indies. Its successful creation led to a West Indies Conference in Barbados in 1929, which Davson chaired. As expected, economic issues predominated, with political reform not part of the agenda.[64]

In thirty years of debate, the vast majority of plans for federation (or other forms of closer association) from colonial power brokers focused on administrative efficiency and increased commercial prowess, with little consideration for changes to the status quo. Colonial officials sought to sustain rather than undermine the colonial system in the Caribbean, which remained firmly tied to white supremacist notions of the white man's burden that claimed to have the best interests of the "uncivilized races" at heart, and characterized by policies of trusteeship and tutelage for the nonwhite colonies. The white oligarchies shared many of these sentiments, and their reliance on the maintenance of a subjugated labor force in the British Caribbean further ensured there was little interest in empowering the West Indian masses economically or politically.

There may have been some who believed that the "advantages" garnered from federation would eventually trickle down and positively affect the majority of the West Indian population. However, the overwhelming lack of interest in, and in some cases outright opposition to, political reform or significant alteration of the West Indies economic system shows that these federal schemes were rarely conceived as a way of expanding political and economic opportunities for the nonwhite populations of the British Caribbean, particularly Afro-Caribbeans. In fact, the vast Afro-Caribbean majority within most colonies, and their perceived inferiority even in comparison with other "inferior races" in the region, remained one of the most troubling aspects of the West Indian future among many whites in the West Indies and the broader empire. Nevertheless, regardless of the restricted goals of federation among the colonial power brokers, their appeals for it in this era created a foundation and atmosphere in which others pursued the same political goal for different ends.

"West Indian" Support for Caribbean Federation— Within the West Indies

Although many within the Colonial Office and planter-merchant oligarchies deemed themselves the only responsible voices from which to elicit opinions on the West Indies, numerous West Indian activists and organizations emerged in the late nineteenth and early twentieth centuries determined to have their voices heard and their demands considered. The various reforms proposed by West Indians in this era included an expanded franchise, greater participation by West Indians in more representative forms of local government, and in some cases self-government (dominion status). In conjunction with these goals, federation also became a goal of several local reform associations, and a crucial cornerstone within the regional West Indian nationalist movement such as the British Guiana and West Indies Labour Congress.[65] While common "power in numbers" and "unity as strength" rationales for federation served different purposes for West Indians than for colonial powers, the former's support for federation, like the latter's, was not one-dimensional or static even as there were similar overarching goals.

Rather than a means to establish a united status quo, federation became one of the key ways through which West Indians hoped to challenge and change the current conditions in the British Caribbean. Those primarily concerned with political advancement and empowerment for individual colonies often supported federation as an avenue to achieve their goals, assuming that some degree of political reform would have to take place in order to unite the various colonies—an idea shared by some opponents of federation among the colonial power brokers. On the other hand, those who pursued similar reforms for the region as a whole often viewed federation as the ultimate goal rather than simply a step in the advancement of individual colonies, although the latter would inevitably occur too. Whereas some activists prioritized their local colonies, and others the region as a whole, there was not an inherent conflict between the two. Indeed, it was rather common to find West Indian activists participating in both local and regional reform movements, successfully juggling the islandism and regionalism of the era, though this would not always be the case.

Whether driven by islandist or regionalist sentiments, the pursuit of federation by West Indians remained more than simply a matter of colonial peoples attempting to attain a greater say in and control of their homelands. Writing in 1923, Hume Wrong declared, "The two great political problems of the West Indies are federation and the form of representative government." The issue that connects them, and "lies behind all discussion of the political future of the West Indies, is the fitness of the negro to play his part in a self-governing community."[66] Unlike in the former and current "white colonies" of the British Empire with more sizeable or predominantly white populations, but as in many "nonwhite colonies," the debates and various efforts undertaken in regard to the future of the West Indian colonies inevitably, given the demography of the British Caribbean (see tables 1.1 and 1.2), had to address the issue of race.

The embedded racism of British colonialism was obvious to most West Indians in the early twentieth century. While not formal segregation of the kind found in the US South, there was an obvious racial caste system throughout the region. Crown Colony rule and an ambiguous path toward self-government in the West Indies contrasted starkly with the representative systems and clearer path toward self-government for the so-called white dominions of the empire. While white colonies such as Australia, New Zealand, Newfoundland, and South Africa sped to dominion status with internal self-government, the West Indian colonies remained stifled under an imperialist doctrine that promised "self-government when fit for it."[67] Despite significant numbers of Afro-Caribbeans in various civil ser-

Table 1.1. British Caribbean population by race (early twentieth century)

Colony	Year	White	Mixed	Black	East Indians	Chinese	Caribs	Aborigines	Others and Unknown
Bahamas	1943	7,923	3,214	57,346	—	178	—	—	185
Barbados	1921	10,429	34,216	111,667	—	—	—	—	-
	1946	9,839	33,828	148,923	136	—	—	—	74
British Guiana	1921	3,291	39,762	117,169	124,938	2,722	—	18,850	659
	1946	2,480	46,228	143,385	163,434	3,567	—	16,322	285
British Honduras	1946	2,329	18,360	22,693	1,366	50	4,112	10,030	280
Jamaica	1921	14,476	157,223	660,420	18,610	3,696	—	—	3,693
	1943	13,809	216,348	965,960	26,507	12,394	—	—	2,045
Turks and Caicos	1921	210	1,503	3,900	—	—	—	—	7
	1943	115	1,935	4,081	—	—	—	—	—
Cayman Islands	1921	1,994	2,431	828	—	—	—	—	—
	1943	2,086	3,518	1,051	—	—	—	—	15
Leeward Islands	1921	2,281	13,864	69,038	—	—	—	—	—
	1946	1,726	12,156	94,388	99	4	—	—	464
Grenada	1921	905	11,673	51,032	2,692	—	—	—	—
	1946	635	14,769	53,265	3,478	16	113	—	111
St. Lucia	1921	—	—	49,316	2,189	—	—	—	—
	1946	343	26,326	40,616	2,635	—	13	—	180
St. Vincent	1931	2,173	11,292	33,257	653	—	—	—	586
	1946	1,906	12,631	45,042	1,817	—	242	—	9
Dominica	1921	556	11,563	24,940	—	—	141	—	—
	1946	142	35,524	11,862	4	1	40	—	51
Trinidad and Tobago	1931	—	—	268,584	138,960	5,239	—	—	—
	1946	15,283	78,775	261,485	195,747	5,641	26	—	1,013

Source: Data taken from Kuczynski, *Demographic Survey,* 3:28–29.

Note: Figures for the Leeward Islands include Antigua, British Virgin Islands, Montserrat, St. Kitts and Nevis. Dominica is listed separately, having transferred from the Leeward to the Windward Islands in 1940.

Table 1.2. British Caribbean population: percentage by race (early twentieth century)

Colony	Year	White %	Mixed %	Black %	Asiatic %	Aborigines %
Bahamas	1943	11.5	4.7	83.0	0.3	—
Barbados	1921	6.7	21.9	71.4	—	—
	1946	5.1	17.6	77.2	0.1	—
British Guiana	1921	1.1	13.0	38.2	41.6	6.1
	1946	0.7	12.3	38.1	43.5	4.4
British Honduras	1946	3.9	31.1	38.4	2.6	17.0
Jamaica	1921	1.7	18.4	77.3	2.6	—
	1943	1.1	17.5	78.1	3.1	—
Turks and Caicos	1921	3.7	26.8	69.5	—	—
	1943	1.9	31.4	66.5	—	—
Cayman Islands	1921	37.9	46.3	15.8	—	—
	1943	31.3	52.7	15.7	—	—
Leeward Islands	1921	2.7	16.3	81.0	—	—
	1946	1.6	11.2	86.7	0.2	—
Grenada	1921	1.4	17.6	76.9	4.1	—
	1946	0.9	20.4	73.7	4.9	0.2
St. Lucia	1921	95.7			4.3	—
	1946	0.5	37.6	58.1	3.8	—
St. Vincent	1931	4.6	23.8	70.2	1.4	—
	1946	3.1	20.5	73.1	3.0	0.4
Dominica	1921	1.5	30.9	67.3	—	0.4
	1946	0.3	74.6	24.9	—	0.1
Trinidad and Tobago	1931	65.1			34.9	—
	1946	2.7	14.1	46.9	36.1	—

Source: Data taken from Kuczynski, *Demographic Survey*, 3:28–29.
Note: The figures for the Leeward Islands include Antigua, British Virgin Islands, Montserrat, St. Kitts and Nevis. Dominica is listed separately, having transferred from the Leeward to the Windward Islands in 1940.

vice positions across the colonies, political power and formal participation in government remained largely restricted under white colonial rule based upon racist assumptions of the "ability of the Anglo-Saxon to govern" the region until the colonies could "stand by themselves."[68] The importation of whites from England and other British colonies to rule over the local West Indian populations, and the overwhelmingly white and restricted nature of colonial legislative councils, was especially frustrating to the aspiring Afro-Caribbean middle classes, both black and coloured.[69]

Despite the predominance of the Afro-Caribbean population within the West Indian colonies and, as some would come to argue, their hegemonic position within the various reform movements of the region and association by many as *the* West Indians, the place of race within the pursuit of federation was not monolithic or static among the different reform movements of the region.[70] In both local and regional organizations, some West Indian activists, including Afro-Caribbeans, deemphasized race through the presentation of their efforts as transracial or multiracial movements of "British citizens" seeking the same colonial advancement they observed in other areas of the empire. At the same time, some noted their purported rights as British citizens but also espoused their support for reforms and federation in overtly racialized terms with obvious connections to other black struggles.[71] Much like the tug-of-war between islandism and regionalism, at times activists adopted both characterizations of their struggles as they emphasized and deemphasized race within their support and visions of federation. Both approaches challenged imperial notions of inferior peoples, and yet questions remained. Given the ways in which race was used to justify British colonialism, should race be downplayed and moved beyond? Alternatively, was race itself a useful tool with which to organize opposition against a racist system?

The development of West Indian reform movements in the early twentieth century, including the rise of more regionally focused West Indian nationalism and the pursuit of racial unity between the black majorities, built upon prior patterns of Afro-Caribbean activism in the region.[72] Jamaica was home to many important examples. One of the most significant precedents was the work of Dr. J. Robert Love, a Bahamian immigrant who came to Jamaica in the 1890s after living in the US South and Haiti.[73] Until his death in 1914, Love worked for both better economic conditions and greater political participation in Jamaica's government for the black and coloured populations. He gave public lectures on Toussaint L'Ouverture and Haiti, among other topics, and established the *Jamaica Advocate*, which became a significant forum for the black middle class of Jamaica. In its pages, Love and his constituents pushed for economic, social, and political equality and reform in the island.[74] In 1898 Love established the People's Convention as an organization to address a range of issues, especially the plight of black people in Jamaica.[75] Such efforts actually led to the election of a few black men to Jamaica's Legislative Council; however, their numbers remained very small.[76] Like other black and coloured activists of this era, and undoubtedly influenced by his own migration experiences, Love connected the local Jamaican struggle with the global struggle of black peoples for racial uplift and racial unity, even helping to establish a Jamaican branch of Sylvester Williams's Pan-African Association.[77]

Another important example in Jamaica is the work of the National Club and S.A.G. "Sandy" Cox. Cox, a fair-skinned coloured or "brown" man, and H.A.L. Simpson, a "Jamaican white," founded the National Club in 1909.[78] The National Club focused primarily on constitutional reform, including the extension of representative government in Jamaica. Despite the middle-class orientation of most of its members, the group instituted some of the earliest calls for labor organization and improved working conditions.[79] Cox also published a biweekly newspaper, *Our Own*, which echoed much of the National Club's platform. Like Love, Cox connected the plight of Jamaica's Afro-Caribbean population, including coloured and black people, to the struggle of peoples of African descent in the black diaspora. Writing in 1911, Cox declared, "The coloured and black people in Jamaica can only hope to better their condition by uniting with the coloured and black people of the United States of America and with those of other West Indian islands, and indeed with all Negroes in all parts of the world."[80]

Trinidad was also a center of significant and vibrant political activism during the late nineteenth and early twentieth centuries. Although other West Indian colonies shared a history of colonial rule under multiple European powers (Spanish, French, and British), Trinidad was distinguished by the significant diversity of its population. This included, as did British Guiana's, a substantial Indian populace that arrived in the colony via the indentured servitude system that replaced enslaved African labor earlier in the nineteenth century. Aspiring middle-class Afro-Trinidadians ("Creoles") therefore faced not only the racism of white colonial rule but, in the view of some (by no means all) black activists, an additional challenge for potential power from the Indian community. At times, Afro-Trinidadian reformers collaborated with white liberals in the colony for alterations to the Crown Colony system, including increased representative government. As for their relationship with the Indian middle classes, who were increasingly active in political reform efforts in the early twentieth century, while there were periodic cooperative efforts between the Afro- and Indo-Trinidadian communities, there remained far more mutual suspicion than collaboration in this era.[81]

Like their middle-class Afro-Caribbean counterparts in other West Indian colonies, Afro-Trinidadian activists of the late nineteenth and early twentieth centuries often displayed a strong racial consciousness as they simultaneously pursued reform efforts in Trinidad and connected them to broader regional and diaspora struggles of peoples of African descent. Their various reform-minded organizations were supported by a strong print culture that carried their platforms to readers in the colonies and beyond, particularly in the late nineteenth century.

As Selwyn Cudjoe argues, "The rise of a vigorous press . . . among the black and coloured inhabitants opened an avenue whereby adult Africans and coloreds could comment about the goings-on in their society. These newspapers also offered their readers a larger diet of foreign news, which allowed them to keep in touch with international events."[82] Many of these black newspapers carried articles and editorials that articulated the racial consciousness and pride of the Afro-Trinidadian middle class, as well as coverage of and responses to the racism black people faced.[83] For example, the *New Era* (1869–90) under Samuel Carter and Joseph Lewis aimed to "vindicate and defend the African race against its enemies home and abroad." Upon leaving the *New Era* in 1874, Carter operated the *San Fernando Gazette* (1874–95), in which one could find calls for constitutional reform and for the termination of state-supported Indian immigration, along with a wide array of other columns in defense of Afro-Trinidadians.[84] William Herbert, considered "a great coloured patriot" by his peers, owned multiple newspapers in the late nineteenth century (the *Trinidad Press*, *Trinidad Colonist*, and *Telegraph*) that displayed similar commitments to race pride and consciousness.[85] Beyond these newspapers, activists such as Norman Alleyne worked to raise the racial consciousness of Afro-Trinidadians and push for intra-racial unity in Trinidad, the West Indies, and the black diaspora, including support for fellow Trinidadian Sylvester Williams's Pan-African Association.[86]

These are but a few examples of the British Caribbean's activists and organizations that, though often island-based, connected their local activism to the broader West Indies, other locations of the black diaspora, and Africa. Given the ways in which racism, colonialism, and imperialism affected the lives of African-descended people worldwide, they viewed their local struggles as "but a local phase of a world problem."[87] Likewise, many of their programs in the twentieth century, including the pursuit of federation, were but local and regional phases of worldwide efforts by peoples of African descent for self-determination.

In her study of decolonization in the British Caribbean, Elizabeth Wallace notes that by the late 1930s and early 1940s, "pressures for federation were no longer based mainly on the white planters' interest in economy or on Britain's administrative convenience, but on black and brown West Indians' desire for more control over their own affairs."[88] Wallace's assertion, however, could have been applied to previous decades as well.

One of the earliest examples of support for federation from the coloured and black communities of the British Caribbean is the work of William Galwey Donovan in Grenada. Donovan was the editor of the *Federalist and Grenada People* newspaper from the 1880s through the pre–World War I era. Edward Cox describes Donovan as a "race man" and "champion of the black man" who "clearly linked his demand for local empowerment to black racial solidarity."[89] Beyond his local campaign for the empowerment of Afro-Grenadians, and in line with contemporaries such as his fellow newspaper editors Robert Love and S.A.G. Cox, Donovan connected the struggle for political power in Grenada and other areas of the West Indies with the global struggles of black peoples.[90]

Described by some as the "First of the Federalists," Donovan proved a staunch supporter of local, regional, and racial empowerment—ideas that he combined and pursued through his early and consistent advocacy of federation. Donovan believed that federation, "by uniting West Indians, and uniting [his] race in the West Indies," would form a crucial foundation for Afro-Caribbean advancement. "For Donovan, political advancement and federation were useful vehicles through which blacks could truly become masters of their home."[91] While Donovan did not go so far as to suggest a break from the British Empire, he did envision a West Indian nation with local self-government where the majority population of African descent would have equal opportunity and full political participation. Given his involvement and avid support for pan-African activities in the early twentieth century, including his coverage of and support for the 1900 Pan-African Conference and subsequent efforts to establish Pan-African Association branches in the Caribbean, it seems clear that he connected his idea of a federated West Indies to the wider struggle for self-determination.[92] In such circumstances, federation was both a regional movement within the British Empire and part of an international project of racial uplift within the black diaspora.

Similar support for federation can be found in *Confederation of the British West Indies versus Annexation to the United States of America: A Political Discourse on the West Indies*, published by Jamaican doctor and dentist Louis S. Meikle in 1912. No doubt influenced by his education and employment in the United States, Meikle denounced the possible annexation of the British West Indies by the United States or Canada, which had been debated periodically since the late nineteenth century.[93] Despite the fact that the British Empire placed the West Indies on a different path from the white dominions, Meikle, like many of his contemporaries, believed it to be better than the other imperial powers of the era. Nonetheless, he opposed Crown Colony rule in the West Indies as "autocratic in principle, and a gigantic farce," a "government of subjugation, under which the people are semi-slaves," and called instead for a West Indian confederation with self-government within the British Empire.[94]

Meikle sought confederation as a means to "preserve the West Indies for the West Indians."[95] On the surface, this goal was not connected overtly to issues of race or the struggles of black peoples for self-determination. His stand against US annexation of the West Indies and his support for federation, however, portrayed a striking racial consciousness that clearly illuminated the racial dimensions of his call for a united region. Meikle rejected any association with the United States because of its overt racism toward people of African descent, an issue he warned went far beyond the racism of British colonialism. "With the Americans you must be White! White!! White!!! You must be white to be truthful and honest. You must be white to hold any position of trust outside of the political realm . . . and so it is wherever the Stars and Stripes float as the controlling power."[96] Moreover, annexation would sidetrack the goal of a self-governing West Indian confederation, which he maintained was a means to empower and develop the region for the good of West Indians—a people he defined as "negro."[97]

Meikle's appeal for a "federation, with responsible government" was "made with the negro in the foreground."[98] He argued this was not a selfish act or done with malice toward the white population, but because people of African descent formed the vast majority of the West Indian population and therefore deserved primary consideration in the discussion of a possible federation.[99] Meikle believed a federation would create a homeland and a land of opportunity for people of African descent. Although he never suggested the expulsion of the white population from the West Indian colonies, Meikle noted, "These islands [were] not the home of the white man," and the "white population could migrate, if conditions did not suit them in the change of authority."[100] This "change of authority" would no doubt involve the empowerment of the Afro-Caribbean majority in place of white oligarchical rule.

Meikle's visions went well beyond the proposals of federation made by the Colonial Office and the local oligarchies during that era. While agreeing that regional unification would create greater economic opportunities, he was staunch in his demand for federation with self-government, "a government by the people for the people," not simply commercial ties under the current colonial regimes. A federation without self-government,

Meikle believed, would only keep power in the hands of the "*Official Masters*, namely 'The West Indian Committee,' who, acting in conjunction with the 'Colonial Office' dominate the West Indies."[101] Like Donovan's, Meikle's vision of a united West Indies encompassed ideas of racial uplift and unity, with connections to similar racial struggles beyond the West Indies.

Calls for some form of regional unity also emerged from the World War I experiences of the British West Indies Regiments.[102] The BWIR became one of the most prominent groups associated with the affirmation of a regional West Indian identification in the early twentieth century.[103] Created in response to demands by local West Indians eager to demonstrate their loyalty to the Crown, the Regiments offered an opportunity for West Indians to prove themselves as equals within the British Empire.[104]

After much debate within the empire over the recruitment and participation of black men in the war effort, the BWIR were created. Some argued that their formation demonstrated the loyalty and capabilities of the black population in the British Empire. A 1915 article in the *Dominica Guardian* proclaimed, "It is the proud boast of all coloured West Indians that they have now been called upon to fight alongside Englishmen, Canadians, Australians, South Africans, New Zealanders, East Indians and others of the British Empire."[105] In the following year another article called the BWIR a "concrete symbol of inter-racial unity . . . a splendid brotherhood in the service of the Empire of men who have overcome the slavery of racial distinctions," and claimed that their actions would help "pave the way for that inevitable Federation . . . The Dominion of the West Indies."[106] Referring to one military rally, a British newspaper noted, "A sturdy party of the British West Indian Contingent was there to remind us once again that loyalty under the English flag is no matter of race."[107]

The BWIR's experience abroad, away from their individual colonies and beyond the insularity that at times stymied regional cooperation, undoubtedly fostered a regional West Indian identification among the troops. However, despite descriptions of these regiments as symbols of the unity and transracial character of the British Empire, their actual wartime experiences did little to prove the irrelevance of race within the empire. The BWIR, like many other nonwhite colonial regiments, faced widespread discrimination during the war at the hands of their supposed imperial brethren. These soldiers often operated under trying, unequal conditions, barred from official commissions, used primarily as laborers instead of "fighting men," subjected to racist slurs and hostility from white soldiers, paid on an unequal scale, and generally relegated to a segregated life.[108] On numerous occasions the BWIR witnessed the racism of their white allies. Once, as the BWIR marched into camp in Alexandria, Egypt, singing "Rule Britannia," they were confronted by white British troops who asked, "Who gave you niggers authority to sing that?"[109] On another occasion when a protest of their ill-treatment reached Brigadier-General Carey Bernard, a South African camp commandant, Bernard replied that "the men were only niggers . . . [and] they were better fed and treated than any nigger had a right to expect."[110] Overall, one West Indian soldier remembered, "The men were treated 'neither as Christians nor British Citizens, but as West Indian Niggers.'"[111] For many soldiers of the BWIR, such experiences helped to entrench racial consciousness in their emerging regional West Indianness and connected them to the global struggles of black peoples, including other black troops who suffered similar mistreatment.

The frustrations of the BWIR exploded into rebellion at Taranto, Italy, in December 1918. Though the rebellion itself was important, the aftermath proved equally significant. Shortly after the rebellion, between fifty and sixty sergeants of the BWIR organized an intra-regional group called the Caribbean League. Topics at the initial meeting included "black rights, self-determination, and closer union in the West Indies."[112] At a later meeting the correlation between these issues was stated more bluntly when one sergeant said that the "black man should have freedom to govern himself," and take it by force if necessary. In reporting these activities, a British official noted that the League's discussion "drifted from the West Indies and became one of grievances of the black man against the white."[113] The official seemingly did not see the connection, but in the minds of many members of this Caribbean League, discussions of the West Indies and the problems of the black man were intimately related. As such, their desire for self-determination and closer union in the West Indies incorporated racial, regional, and international ideas of unity and power in numbers.

In the immediate postwar era, there was much concern within the Colonial Office and colonial West Indian governments about the demobilization of black troops and the effect that these returnees, fresh from their mistreatment abroad, would have in an already tense situation. The war had led to food and supply shortages in the Caribbean, and inflation with no corresponding increase in wages. Upset by poor wages and working conditions, workers held strikes in several colonies between 1916 and 1919.[114] Marcus Garvey's Universal Negro Improvement Association had also become increasingly popular, and viewed by some colonial officials as inciting "racial hatred" in the region.[115] Some colonial officials in the West Indies even proposed a ban on Garvey's *Negro World*, given what they believed to be its inflammatory content, such as a February 1919 article that not only attacked colonialism but also claimed that the colonies were "the property of the Blacks" who should gain control of them "even if all the world is to waste itself in blood."[116]

Though the government's postwar fears proved exaggerated, strikes and riots in 1919 did occur. In July during a riot involving ex-servicemen in Belize, British Honduras, one police officer reported hearing people say that "'the white man had no right' in Belize as this is 'our country' and 'we want to get the white man out.'"[117] In Trinidad, ex-soldiers participated in a longshoremen's strike, which spread throughout the island, causing chaos over several weeks.[118] These episodes displayed the overlapping and inter-connected racial and class consciousness growing in the British West Indies in the postwar era; however, they were not the only forms of protest.

There were also numerous "peaceful" protests against Crown Colony rule in the post–World War I West Indies. A 1919 petition from St. Kitts and Nevis noted that local West Indians were "quite fit and capable to have a voice in the management of their own public affairs," and that they de-served the "full citizenship" enjoyed by other colonists who were no more loyal than West Indians.[119] Such demands became common within the nu-merous political reform organizations founded throughout the British Ca-ribbean in the late 1910s and 1920s.[120] Many of their leaders and members incorporated the race and class consciousness of the era into their respec-tive reform efforts. While most of the organizations focused on constitu-tional reform, particularly representative government, several included a demand for federation. As Allister Hinds has argued, support for federa-tion marked the conjunction of political aspirations and a heightened racial consciousness among the "black and colored intelligentsia" within these island societies.[121]

Out of these reform movements emerged two of the most famous West Indian nationalists, renowned for their extensive and prolonged support of, and leadership within, the push for federation in the early twentieth century: T. A. Marryshow and A. A. Cipriani. As friends and allies, Cipriani and Marryshow worked for better social, economic, and political condi-tions in their own islands and advocated the establishment of a federation as an essential step in the overall advancement of the region as a whole.[122]

As a result, both men came to be called the Father of Federation, though that title is most often associated with Marryshow.

Despite their parallel action, the careers of the two men also symbolize different aspects of West Indian nationalism and the accompanying federation movement. Cooperation between Marryshow (a black Grenadian) and Cipriani (a white Trinidadian of Corsican descent) suggested and symbolized a multiracial vision of West Indian nationalism and unity. Both, at times, together and individually, represented what Deborah Thomas has referred to as "creole multiracial nationalism."[123] Such nationalism focused on, among other things, island or regional development, with little overt attention to matters of race. In fact, this strand of nationalism implicitly put forth transracial and multiracial images of reform efforts in specific islands and the entire region that suggested the West Indies were "beyond" conventional racial ideologies and politics. Nevertheless, this did not deter some West Indian nationalists from maintaining a racially conscious component to their activism—a racialized nationalism alongside their appeals to creole multiracial nationalism. West Indian nation building, including federation, therefore could and did exist as both a transracial and racial venture.

Arthur Andrew Cipriani rose to fame in Trinidad and the West Indies as a military officer, labor leader, local politician, and staunch supporter of West Indian federation. Cipriani, born in 1875, divided much of his early life between his cocoa estates and horse racing interests.[124] This changed, however, with the outbreak of World War I. Cipriani first came to prominence with his support for the creation of the British West Indies Regiments, and his service as an officer with one of those regiments.[125] Captain Cipriani earned his reputation as a friend and defender of West Indians through his representation of several BWIR soldiers facing unjust court-martial. His experiences with the regiments, which included his frustration at the lack of fighting opportunities for West Indians until late in the war, furthered his conclusion that West Indian peoples were more than ready to have political representation. The only thing lacking, he came to believe, was opportunity offered by the Crown.[126]

Upon his return to Trinidad, Cipriani continued his advocacy of West Indian advancement and became more actively involved in colonial reform. One of his most prominent positions was the presidency of a resurgent Trinidad Workingmen's Association (TWA) in the postwar era. With Cipriani at the helm, the TWA experienced unprecedented expansion, adding thousands of members and numerous branches. As C.L.R. James notes,

Cipriani had "faith in the local black men," and in return they shared "an unshakeable affection for and confidence in the man who stood by them so firmly."[127]

In spite of contemporary claims that "if he raise[d] his finger he [could] cause a riot," Cipriani, who was a socialist, was much more a reformer than a radical or revolutionary leader.[128] In the 1920s Cipriani formally entered Trinidadian politics, serving as an elected member of the colony's legislative council (after the limited constitutional reforms put in place by the Wood Commission) as well as city councillor and mayor of Port-of-Spain. Beyond Trinidad, Cipriani was also involved in the regional West Indian nationalist movement of the 1920s, particularly through the prominent role he played within the intra-regional British Guiana and West Indies Labour Congress. In these roles he advocated numerous reform measures: poor relief, worker safety, health, housing, education, a minimum wage, eight-hour workday, old-age pensions, and competitive exams for entry into the civil service. In addition, Cipriani became one of the most vocal supporters of expanded franchise, representative government, and especially a Caribbean federation with self-government and dominion status within the British Empire.[129] The West Indian population, he believed, was ready for such reforms:

> It is all very well and good to talk of us as "subject races." I laugh that to scorn. We are free people of the British Empire. We are entitled to the same privileges and the same form of Government and administration as our bigger sisters, the Dominions, and we have got to use everything in our power, strain every nerve, make every effort—I go further and say to make every sacrifice to bring self-government and Dominion status to these beautiful colonies.[130]

In many ways the career of Captain Cipriani characterized, and seemingly verified, the vision of West Indian nationalism as a transracial project. His rejection of the moneyed white classes in favor of the TWA's primarily black, and to a much lesser extent Indian, members endeared him to many as a great West Indian patriot and a friend of the "barefooted masses." Cipriani also downplayed the significance of race and claimed his program and that of the wider regional movement was not based on color or class.[131] Accordingly, he became a popular and powerful symbol of creole multiracial nationalism. However, while it is true that Cipriani's strand of West Indian nationalism was transracial to a large degree, his leadership and ideals did not eliminate the prominent racialized motivations for reform among members of organizations like the TWA, or within the larger push for representative government and federation among many of his supporters and contemporaries.[132] West Indian nationalism in this era remained simultaneously a racial and a transracial endeavor, often with proponents emphasizing or deemphasizing race to suit the time and place.

T. A. Marryshow provides one of the best examples of how West Indian nationalists ably juggled racial and transracial visions of federation. Given his long-standing and consistent support for federation, he was recognized eventually as the "greatest and most accomplished protagonist of Federation" and the "first citizen of the united West Indies."[133] Born Theophilos Maricheau in 1887 to a small black planter, but raised by his housekeeper godmother after his mother's death, Marryshow rose to prominence in the early twentieth century as a journalist, political activist, local colonial politician, and labor leader.[134] Through his positions as co-owner and editor of the Grenada-based *West Indian* newspaper, a leading member of the Representative Government Association (RGA) in Grenada, president of the Grenada Workingman's Association, an elected member of Grenada's legislative council, and an important figure (along with Cipriani) in the British Guiana and West Indies Labour Congress, Marryshow worked for racial and class equality, labor rights and organization, an expanded franchise, the return of representative government to the British Caribbean, and a Caribbean federation with self-government. While the cooperative work of Cipriani and Marryshow on many of these issues displayed the transracial nature of West Indian nationalism, much of Marryshow's activism—his journalism, race consciousness, and involvement in black diaspora politics—added a familiar racial element to his West Indian agenda and shaped his ideas of a federation within the British Caribbean.[135]

The *West Indian* became an important outlet for Marryshow and other West Indian nationalists in the early twentieth century. No doubt influenced by his time as a delivery boy and protégé of William Donovan, Marryshow created a newspaper whose title asserted a regional identification and agenda, and which provided coverage of and commentary on local, regional, and black diaspora events.[136] In this manner Marryshow carried on Donovan's legacy in Grenada, the West Indies, and the broader black diaspora. Though Marryshow was not the sole contributor to the *West Indian*, as editor he was largely in charge of selecting its contents, and even those articles and editorials not penned by Marryshow in many ways represented his ideals.

A particularly common topic of discussion in the *West Indian* was the idea of a federation. From the first issue on 1 January 1915, Marryshow noted the newspaper's support for an "administrative and fiscal union" of the West Indian colonies. A few days later the paper advertised an essay competition on "West Indian Federation."[137] In February an editorial called for the subordination of the various insular island identities in favor of a regional West Indian identification that would seemingly pave the way for the creation of a federation.

> There should be neither Grenadians, nor Barbadians, nor Trinidadians, nor any such "ians" among us, but West Indians and, fundamentally, none other. . . . only in this way can a West Indian Dominion come into being which will cause us to be a respectable force in the affairs of the world. We should all leave the "outgrown shell" of insular limitations and aspire to the more "stately mansions"—the mansions of nationality.[138]

Articles and editorials related to federation continued to appear with some regularity in the *West Indian* during World War I and the immediate postwar era. These included calls for "a nearer West Indies, a united West Indies," and for federation as a means to give the region a greater voice in the empire.[139] Discussions of the possible annexation of the West Indies by Canada or the United States were dismissed on multiple occasions, in many cases in favor of a West Indian union of their own.[140] Upon hearing rumors that the empire was considering creating a new Pacific dominion of British islands and recently captured German islands, one article asked why a new dominion among the British Caribbean islands was not being considered.[141]

As talk of federation increased in the postwar era, Marryshow welcomed discussion by the Colonial Office and the local oligarchy, but like many other West Indians, he demanded federation with self-government—a step few if any in the Colonial Office and local Crown governments considered feasible.

> We are ardent Federalists but primarily we are staunch believers in the rights of the intelligent and law-abiding governed to have a voice in their government. We desire to see a West Indian Commonwealth, but not a huge West Indian Crown Colony, which will the more easily be boxed at the whim of each successive Governor-General! We want the Ship of Federation, but the people should have the power and right of anchorage, the power to set sail, no matter who the pilot

may be. . . . We tell our people that a Foul Federation is gaining attraction in these days, and ask them not to touch it. It is dead and rotten. It has no life of Representation; no soul of Liberty. There is a true Federation which will be presented if we are wise to reject this dead one. When that time comes, West Indians will have something worthy of attention.[142]

Marryshow's demands for a self-governing federation mirrored those of other West Indian nationalists like Donovan, Meikle, and Cipriani who viewed federation as an avenue for change rather than a structure to bolster the status quo. Likewise, in a February 1920 editorial, Marryshow reminded the Associated Chambers of Commerce to "discuss men and not only material materials," and called for the implementation of representative government—a call he believed was "a reasonable demand . . . a British demand."[143] These appeals presented federation as a key step in the development of the region, a "summit," which could only be attained through representative government.[144]

Few of these calls for federation in the *West Indian* overtly mentioned race. Within the broader context of the newspaper, however, such discussions were connected to Marryshow's racial consciousness, and his support for racial unity and black self-determination. As Marryshow noted in a letter to W.E.B. DuBois in later years, the *West Indian* was "pro-Negro from apogee to perigee."[145]

Alongside support for federation, Marryshow's *West Indian* included numerous antiracist editorials, coverage of and support for black diaspora groups and activities, and demands for representative government. In August 1917 the *West Indian* reprinted a *New York News* article on the transfer of the Danish Virgin Islands to the United States in which C. H. Emanuel noted: "We, as natives of this island, want it to be distinctly understood by those already here, as well as by every other Caucasian newcomer who may have occasion to pitch his tent among us, that this island is ours by divine right. . . . the purchase of our liberties was not included" with the acquisition of the islands.[146] Emanuel's comments and the *West Indian's* republication of them highlight the heightened racial consciousness in many parts of the Caribbean and black diaspora in the era.

Marryshow and the *West Indian* also reported on the struggle to organize the BWIR, and their wartime experiences, as well as the activities and treatment of African American soldiers.[147] Additional coverage of black diaspora activism included defenses of Garvey's *Negro World* in the face of postwar sedition charges, reports on the UNIA's activities, and the program of the African Progress Union in London. In 1920 Marryshow published an original poem in praise of the famous African American leader Frederick Douglass.[148] By December 1922 Marryshow even drew the attention of the NAACP, which lauded his work for self-government in the region and called the *West Indian* a "paper which ought to make Negro American editors sit up and take notice."[149] Taken as a whole, such writings speak to the race consciousness and racial activism of Marryshow in this era.

If these issues appear disconnected from Marryshow's support for federation, which would be hard to assume, one of his most famous writings draws his views on race and nation building together more obviously. In 1917 Marryshow penned a series of editorials in the *West Indian* titled "Cycles of Civilisation" in reply to a May 1917 speech by General Jan Christian Smuts of South Africa in which the Boer general addressed the problem of creating a "White South Africa" and "outlined a programme for the suppression of Africans in the interest of white members of the Empire." Though Marryshow lamented that "In the West Indies, when public men speak on race questions they are condemned by some who think they have no right to discuss such questions," these articles, shortly thereafter published in book form as *Cycles of Civilisation*, spoke directly to the issue of race.[150]

One of the major components of *Cycles* was Marryshow's staunch defense of a glorious African past. In his speech, Smuts had asserted that despite the foothold that civilization once held in some regions of ancient Africa, the continent was marked at that time by widespread barbarism and the need for European colonization. Marryshow replied that Africa was not a foothold but a stronghold of civilization, which "held sovereign sway when the inhabitants of England were in the sheerest infancy of human development—when they were unmitigated savages, who fed on the barks and roots of trees, and were scantily clothed with the skins of animals."[151] Marryshow spent a number of pages detailing the place of Africa and black peoples in the Bible, including a discussion of Egypt as a former black nation, and of Jesus as looking quite different from contemporary European notions of him as a white man.[152] In response to praise of Cecil Rhodes for building a "civilised Rhodesia out of a mere forest which was inhabited by black men," Marryshow noted that the ruins of that region, which included "wonderful fragments of art and glimpses of the high standard of scientific thought to which Africans attained when white men were savages," showed a past perhaps much greater than anything the present Rhodesian colony could hope to be.[153] With such rebuttals, Marryshow directly challenged white supremacist notions that claimed Europe as the cradle of civilization, and provided inspiration to black peoples in Africa and the black diaspora, especially those suffering under European colonialism.

Marryshow's key argument, however, was that history showed a cyclical pattern in which nations (and races) rose and fell. He argued that recent and current European dominance was simply "their time" and but a small fraction of world history. Marryshow challenged the idea that European civilization was the zenith in human development, or in any way a permanent fixture. He believed this era was temporary, and forecasted that its demise was near. In Marryshow's estimation, France, Italy, and Portugal were already in decline, and modern Europe as a whole was "not in a very hopeful position."[154] "Who knows whether London will not become the capital of a decayed Libya, and Paris of Persia, and Berlin of a Babylon." In the future, he noted, a "superior Chilian [sic], Brazilian, Negro, or aboriginal Indian" may gather "fungi in the damp devastation of the Reichstag, or beetles where once stood the lofty Campanile of some famous Italian Cathedral."[155] As for the British Empire, Marryshow believed that the recent patriotic enthusiasm for the Crown during the war years would likely subside, and the empire might well come to an end because of racial issues.

> United in spirit in war and disunited in peace, may be the verdict of tomorrow. . . . There are strong indications that certain parts of the Empire will not be able to endure, for long, certain monstrous inequalities of the British order, and on racial grounds is this wonderful Empire of ours likely to break up. . . . The rocks ahead on which the waves of the British Empire might spend themselves are the Rocks of Race.[156]

In conjunction with the eventual demise of European nations, Marryshow predicted the rise of new nonwhite nations, particularly within Asia and the Americas. Africa, he said, would have its time again soon too.[157] While *Cycles* was in many ways an anticolonial treatise that appealed to various nonwhite readers, Marryshow focused primarily on the past, present, and future of people of African descent, especially those of English-speaking Africa, the West Indies, and North America. Marryshow asked rhetorically, "Is there to be no place under the sun . . . where Negroes are to experience free human development?"[158] He answered emphatically, "He, who is 'too wise to err and too good to be unkind' did not send the Negro in His world to be sport and toy of nations. As Negroes, and in the highest spiritual instinct, we look up to . . . the long-expected dawning of a truer world."[159] Marryshow declared, "The great Negro Race has had its turn, and its turn is coming again."[160]

More than just a reference to the possible redemption of the African continent, this "turn" also alluded to the rise of a West Indian nation. Marryshow declared, "Taken as a unit, the West Indies, in all departments of thought and activity, are a coloured man's West Indies." He asserted, "The indication of the times point to a great prosperity that shall dawn for the West Indies and a high type of civilisation that shall come a-wooing in these parts. And we feel that we are being sufficiently grounded to stand on our rock, keeping the West Indies of the future true to our particular identity."[161] The next great rise of people of African descent, therefore, might not occur in Africa, but possibly in the diaspora, specifically in the West Indies. The only obstacle was "that so many [West Indians] are blind to the value of unity of purpose and direction, and prefer loose and easy compromises which do not make for race identity and dignity."[162] Marryshow's strong support in these passages for the development of a united West Indies via federation shows that it was not simply Caribbean nation building but a black diaspora nation-building project as well—connected to ideas of racial uplift, racial unity, and self-determination for people of African descent internationally.

The publication of *Cycles*, combined with his political activities within the West Indies, provided Marryshow much political currency within the broader black diaspora. While in Barbados in 1919, Marryshow met with a Mr. Anthony Crawford who brought "the best wishes of a large majority of coloured people in New York to the Editor of the *West Indian*." Crawford noted that both the *West Indian* and *Cycles of Civilisation*, which sold thousands of copies in the United States, circulated from hand to hand among many people in New York, securing Marryshow a presence on a wider international stage. Apparently an offer was made for Marryshow to move to New York and join the burgeoning black diaspora movements in that area, but Marryshow declined to make such a permanent move, preferring to stay and fight in the West Indies despite efforts by colonial officials to curtail black periodicals and pamphlets in the postwar era.[163] He did, however, visit the United States briefly, became a "corresponding member of the Negro Society for Historical Research," and spoke at the Second Pan-African Congress in London in 1921.[164]

Throughout the 1920s Marryshow continued to be an active force in both West Indian and diaspora politics in his roles as editor, politician, labor organizer, West Indian nationalist leader, and pan-African activist. During the latter half of the decade, he periodically exchanged letters with W.E.B. DuBois. Some of these concerned the ultimately failed plans to host a Pan-African Congress in the West Indies in 1925, and the successful Fourth Pan-African Congress in New York in 1927.[165] In 1926 Marryshow and his constituents sent a contribution of $55 to help fund the defense of Ossian Sweet, an African American who, along with other family members, was on trial for assault and murder following their use of armed self-defense against a white mob that attacked the Sweet family home in a previously all-white neighborhood of Detroit, Michigan. DuBois thanked him for the contribution and referred to this support as an example of the "binding together of men of black blood in all the Americas and in Africa for the honor and defense of Negro manhood."[166]

Marryshow's connections to black diaspora politics and his obvious racial consciousness should not diminish or be disassociated from his work for local (Grenadian) and regional (West Indian) reform efforts. Like many other West Indian activists, Marryshow's racial consciousness and activism merged with and added an extra dimension to these activities.[167] Marryshow provides a significant example of how West Indian nationalism, including the often-accompanying support for federation, cannot easily be characterized as either transracial or racial—nor can it be confined to the bounds of intra-regional debates within the empire, ignoring the crucial connections between Caribbean federation and broader black diaspora politics.

Debates over the possibilities and purposes of Caribbean federation continued throughout the early twentieth-century British West Indies. At the same time, it is important to recognize that support for and conceptualizations of such a West Indian nation were not confined to the Caribbean. Federation also emerged as a subject of debate and concern among black activists and groups outside the Caribbean. These contributions bolstered and expanded visions of a united West Indies as an important project within black diaspora politics.

Beyond the West Indies

The early twentieth century has long been recognized as a significant era for the development and proliferation of race-conscious movements in the black diaspora. Activists in various black nationalist and black internationalist organizations pursued a range of goals connected to overarching programs of racial uplift and the liberation of black populations across the globe. Similar to the efforts of some West Indian nationalists within the Caribbean, who, as argued in the previous section, were deeply involved in black diaspora politics and in some cases active in common movements, many black activists outside the West Indies sought intra-racial cooperation and unity between peoples of African descent as one of the most crucial means through which to attain their respective objectives. As had occurred in previous years, there were concerted efforts by black diaspora activists and organizations in various locales to increase awareness of the common, though not necessarily identical, freedom struggles of peoples of African descent worldwide.

The unequal status shared by many, if not most, black populations in the early twentieth century undoubtedly helped forge and further conscious efforts by black peoples to unite beyond their own ethnic and national differences. While one should not dismiss the ways in which black peoples came to recognize the benefits of racial cooperation and unity on their own, the realities of white supremacist rule across much of the globe in this era also provided an unfortunate example. White countries and empires were by no means monolithic or always cooperative. They engaged in a variety of conflicts with each other in the late nineteenth and early twentieth centuries, often over larger shares of the nonwhite world that had been or was soon to be overwhelmingly under white colonial control. Yet despite their divisions and animosities, most shared assumptions of themselves as the "superior race," and in venues such as the Berlin Conference (1884–85) and the Paris Peace Conference (1919) they established or maintained white supremacist control over much of the nonwhite world. Many black diaspora activists argued for a similar setting aside of intra-racial differences and a commitment to unite as people of African descent.[168]

One of the most significant means through which black people came to realize the global dimensions of black oppression was by travel or migration beyond their respective homelands and subsequent encounters with others of African descent. This was particularly true for West Indians, whose long history of migration continued in the late nineteenth and early twentieth centuries.[169] As Winston James argues, "No other national grouping of Africans in the Americas—not that in the USA, not that in the Spanish Caribbean, not that in Brazil, and not even that in the French territories—has produced such a large and widely scattered diaspora as the British Caribbean, especially over so many centuries."[170] Migration within the wider Caribbean remained common in the early twentieth century. The

Table 1.3. Black immigrants to the United States from the Caribbean and Central America (1900–1925)

Year	Caribbean		Central America	
	Number of Immigrants	% of All Black Immigration to United States	Number of Immigrants	% of All Black Immigration to United States
1900	703	98.5	N/A	N/A
1901	520	87.5	N/A	N/A
1902	805	96.8	N/A	N/A
1903	1,134	52.2	1	—
1904	1,762	73.8	3	—
1905	3,034	84.3	37	1.0
1906	3,018	79.7	91	2.4
1907	4,561	87.2	99	1.9
1908	3,563	77.0	116	2.5
1909	3,340	77.5	107	2.5
1910	3,769	75.9	120	2.4
1911	4,973	74.0	154	2.3
1912	4,885	72.3	245	3.6
1913	4,891	73.7	277	4.2
1914	5,724	67.8	348	4.1
1915	4,104	72.5	252	4.5
1916	3,257	70.6	160	3.5
1917	5,769	72.0	662	8.3
1918	3,993	70.0	906	15.9
1919	4,027	69.2	799	13.7
1920	6,059	74.1	417	5.1
1921	7,046	71.4	543	5.5
1922	4,424	84.3	188	3.6
1923	6,580	86.6	254	3.3
1924	10,630	86.8	511	4.2
1925	308	38.9	174	22.0

Source: Statistics from W. James, *Banner of Ethiopia*, 356–57.

Note: While "Caribbean" here includes the entire region, the majority of these immigrants were from the British Caribbean. Likewise, the Central American data include a great many British West Indians moving from stays in Central American nations like Panama and Costa Rica. Between 1900 and 1930, US destinations for such immigrants included New York (about half), New England, and Florida. See W. James, *Banner of Ethiopia*, 9–49; Holder, "West Indian Immigration to New York." The significant decline in Caribbean migration in 1925 reflects new US immigration restrictions.

United States also became an important destination in these years, while West Indian migration to Great Britain occurred on a much smaller scale. Moreover, the history and importance of West Indian migration to various South and Central American nations of the circum-Caribbean in these years cannot be overlooked.[171] In each of these areas, one can find noteworthy examples of the forging of racial and diasporic consciousness within the black diaspora.

West Indian immigration to the United States, especially to Harlem and surrounding New York City areas, came to play a particularly important role in the proliferation of black diaspora activism in the early twentieth century. Although the West Indian colonies were by no means free from racial strife, Afro-Caribbean immigrants to the United States encountered an overt and virulent racism that differed from the prejudices of their homelands. While these immigrants arrived as Jamaicans, Barbadians, Trinidadians, Guyanese, or members of other island communities, and often viewing themselves through the lens of common West Indian class and color distinctions, they were quickly confronted with an American racism that largely collapsed such divisions into an overarching and damning blackness. The "majority consciousness" with which many arrived was displaced as they were transformed into members of a race-conscious "minority."[172] The migration process also helped construct an additional regional West Indian identification alongside insular identifications, as well as the subsequent association by many that both categories were but subsections of a global black community in Africa and the diaspora.

The affirmation of one identification did not necessarily entail the loss of others. Instead, many immigrants from the West Indies and other regions of the Caribbean willingly adopted multiple, situational identifications.[173] As Louis J. Parascandola argues in the case of Harlem, "They exhibited a fluidity of identity, describing themselves as Black, as West Indian or Caribbean, as British, as Jamaican (or whatever their homeland was), and, when it suited their purpose, American, feeling no need to choose between multiple identities."[174]

Writing in 1925, W. A. Domingo, a popular and influential West Indian (Jamaican) activist of the era, noted of the various international black populations converging in Harlem,

> Here they have their first contact with each other, with large numbers of American Negroes, and with the American brand of race prejudice. Divided by tradition, culture, historical background and group per-

spective, these diverse peoples are gradually hammered into a loose unit by the impersonal force of congested residential segregation. Unlike others of the foreign-born, black immigrants find it impossible to segregate themselves into colonies . . . they are inevitably swallowed up in black Harlem.[175]

Within the seventy to eighty blocks of an increasingly black Harlem, the men and women of the British West Indies established themselves as members and leaders in the economic, social, and political life of their new communities through a myriad of activities that encompassed all of their allegiances rather than one in particular. Numerous West Indians established and participated in various insular community organizations and societies based upon their land of origin: the Jamaican Benevolent Association, Montserrat Progressive Society, St. Lucia United Association, St. Vincent Benevolent Association, Trinidad Benevolent Association, and many others. Additionally, various regional organizations connected British Caribbean migrants together as "West Indians": the American West Indian Ladies Aid Society, American West Indian Association, Caribbean Union, West Indian Protective Society, West India Committee of America, and more. At still another level, West Indian men and women often associated with African Americans and other black peoples in churches, local politics, and race-based fraternal and social organizations, as well as black nationalist and internationalist movements.[176]

Despite the participation of some West Indians and African Americans in common organizations, an all-encompassing racial unity beyond tensions of nationality was not easily or always produced. As Irma Watkins-Owens notes in her study of Caribbean immigrants in Harlem during this era, "Churches and fraternal lodges, through their leaders especially, bonded the newer Caribbean community to larger African American Harlem, although this connection was not always smooth."[177] At times there was cooperation between African Americans and West Indians, but stereotypes, condescending attitudes, and jealousies were also common. The "national" differences between the two groups often became inflated as both sides jockeyed for economic, social, and political power. Simple disagreements between individuals could take on more meaning should the opponents be from different communities *within* Harlem's international black communities.[178]

Given these circumstances, many who sought racial unity between black communities understood such sentiments had to be forged. The writings, speeches, and programs of black diaspora activists and organizations centered in Harlem toward the end of World War I and in the postwar era provide numerous examples. Hubert Harrison, a Danish Caribbean immigrant noted by some of his contemporaries as "the foremost Afro-American intellect of his time," was one of the chief proponents of a Race First philosophy. Writing in 1917, Harrison boldly stated,

> Any man today who aspires to lead the Negro race must set squarely before his face the idea of "Race First." Just as the white men of these and other lands are white before they are Christians, Anglo-Saxons or Republicans; so the Negroes of this and other lands are intent upon being Negroes before they are Christians, Englishmen, or Republicans.[179]

In the fall of 1918 the launch of the *Crusader* by Cyril V. Briggs, the "angry blonde Negro" from Nevis who had recently been ousted as editor of the *New York Amsterdam News*, offered another forum for coverage of black freedom struggles across the globe and discussions of the need for intraracial cooperation and unity.[180] Appeals for the latter appeared in some of the first issues of the *Crusader*, even before it became officially connected to the African Blood Brotherhood (ABB) which Briggs helped found the following year. In September 1918, Briggs published a short article titled "Race Catechism." Among the questions and answers posed, it asked, "What are one's duties to the Race?" and answered, "To love one's Race above one's self and to further the common interests of all above the private interests of one."[181] While the catechism did not specifically name African Americans and West Indians, there is little doubt that they were two of its main targets as the largest black populations in Harlem.

In the September 1918 edition of the *Crusader*, Briggs reprinted an article from the *New York Amsterdam News* headlined "Sowing Dissension" that noted, "There have been several attempts made of late to sow the seeds of dissension between the American Negro and his West Indian brother." Clearly defining West Indians as black people, the writer argued, "The American Negro and the West Indian Negro are one in blood, one in achievement, and one in the aspiration for equal rights and opportunities. They are both the seed of Africa." The article asked readers to follow the example of Jewish people who refused to weaken or divide their widely scattered race.

Let us, recognizing that in unity there is strength, focus our eyes upon, and move forward the consummation of a united Race that shall recognize neither geographical lines nor European superimposed governments; smoking out in the process all the conscious or unconscious traitors to the Race who would create a rift between any of its members.[182]

Similar calls for racial unity, particularly between African Americans and West Indians in the 1920s, demonstrated the continued importance of the issue to many as well as its elusiveness. Speaking to a Harlem audience composed of both groups at a February 1923 forum, "The Problem of the Relationship between the American and West Indian Negroes," Chandler Owen, a black socialist leader and coeditor of the *Messenger*, called for African Americans and West Indians "to unite and fight for the betterment of conditions affecting them as a race." Unfortunately, those remarks came after what some considered multiple negative comments about West Indians over the course of his speech. W. A. Domingo, who worked with Owen at the *Messenger*, responded a few weeks later at a similar forum. He rebutted Owen's recent comments on the possible restriction of West Indian immigration to the United States and the un-assimilability of West Indians and African Americans. "It is a dangerous thing for an oppressed people to advise cutting off their own numbers," Domingo argued, and, "One can understand the Anglo-Saxon saying he cannot get along with the Negro but to say or infer that two groups of Negroes cannot assimilate is the height of ridiculous."[183] Later in the decade, the *West Indian American* also called for racial unity between African Americans and West Indians. "The colored man, wherever he may be found, cannot afford to draw fine distinctions . . . or indulge in inter-racial strife. 'One for all and all for one,' must be the motto if he hopes to come out from under."[184]

Although many activists and organizations targeted intra-racial unity within the Harlem community in the post–World War I era, they also spoke to West Indians who remained in the colonies as part of their efforts to forge racial unity in the cause of black liberation across the globe. An October 1918 *Crusader* article titled "The Black Man's Burden" admonished West Indians in the West Indies for maintaining insular identities, given their common oppression, which seemingly called for and connected the need for an increased regional and racial awareness among them. The following year, a brief article noted: "The white man can afford divisions and diversions. The Negro cannot. It's Negro first, last and all the time or perish for us." Similarly, a 1920 letter from Trinidad to the editor of the *Crusader* derided West Indians for their allegiance to Great Britain and their claim of a British identity at the expense of race patriotism, believing that white Britons viewed West Indians by their race and not as fellow Britons.[185]

Alongside the calls for black peoples to adopt a Race First ideology, many periodicals in Harlem also carried news and informational pieces on the British West Indies. These served not only to keep West Indians in Harlem aware of their homelands and to educate African Americans on their "brothers abroad" but also to help forge the international black consciousness that many diaspora movements believed was necessary to counter the current global oppression of black peoples. Mainstream African American newspapers like the *New York Amsterdam News*, organizational periodicals such as the UNIA's *Negro World* and the ABB's *Crusader*, and socialist magazines like the *Messenger* contributed news and notes on the British West Indies, as well as other key sites of struggle for peoples of African descent.[186]

Throughout the early twentieth century, black diaspora organizations called for an end to the Crown Colony system in the British Caribbean and the installation of majority rule. The notion of "strength in unity" underlay most of these movements, and they did not wish to see the creation of small, struggling self-governing nations. Instead, parallel with projects for uniting portions or all of Africa under majority rule, there was a call for the British West Indies to unite in a strong and sizeable black nation that would bring both respect and power to peoples of African descent throughout the world. A united, federated West Indies was often seen as one of the most logical and powerful embodiments of racial unity and black nation building in the West.

Marcus Garvey and the Universal Negro Improvement Association (UNIA) galvanized millions in the late 1910s and 1920s.[187] Garvey, like many black diaspora activists of the era, focused primarily on the African continent—in his case, the desire for a united Africa and the Back to Africa movement for which he is likely most remembered. Many studies and scholars of Garvey and the UNIA, and of Caribbean federation, have overlooked, diminished, and in some cases dismissed outright any interest by Garvey in Caribbean federation.[188] If one focuses on Garvey's work only during his Harlem heyday, this appears justified. For instance, in the early

1920s Garvey himself stated, "The future of the Negro . . . outside of Africa, spells ruin and disaster."[189] However, racial unity and black nation building in the West was also very important in his movement—including the creation of a Caribbean federation.

As Robert A. Hill argues, before Garvey's vision of an "African Empire," he imagined a federated West Indies as the basis of a "Black West Indian Empire."[190] One of the earliest illustrations of Garvey's views on federation appears in a 1913 article in the London-based *African Times and Orient Review*.

> There have been several movements to federate the British West Indian Islands, but owing to parochial feelings nothing definite has been achieved. Ere long this change is sure to come about because the people of these islands are all one. They live under the same conditions, are of the same race and mind, and have the same feelings and sentiments regarding the things of the world.
>
> As one who knows the people well, I make no apology for prophesying that there will soon be a turning point in the history of the West Indies; and that the people who inhabit that portion of the Western Hemisphere will be the instruments of uniting a scattered race who, before the close of many centuries, will found an Empire on which the sun shall shine as ceaselessly as it shines on the Empire of the North today. This may be regarded as a dream, but I would point my critical friends to history and its lessons. Would Caesar have believed that the country he was invading in 55 B. C. would be the seat of the greatest Empire in the World?[191]

Following his return to Jamaica in 1914, an article appeared in the *Gleaner* that summarized a recent letter from Garvey to the newspaper. Garvey noted his support of Louis Meikle's call for a West Indian federation, which Meikle had reiterated in his own letter to the newspaper the previous week. Garvey expressed his admiration for Meikle, a "true West Indian patriot," and urged "all critics of sense and reason to lend their support to . . . bring about the realization of a united West Indies."[192]

Within the overall program of Garvey and the UNIA, African redemption did receive greater focus during their most prominent years in Harlem during the late 1910s and early 1920s. In the UNIA's "Declaration of Rights of the Negro Peoples of the World," the West Indies receive only a brief mention. Nevertheless, it is likely that he did not dismiss the idea of federation in the West Indies altogether, but instead continued to view it as a step in the broader unification and empowerment of black peoples throughout the world.

Upon his return to Jamaica in the late 1920s, West Indian federation reappeared as a more explicit goal within Garvey's political program. As Tony Martin notes in his study of Garvey's activities in this era, particularly his People's Political Party in Jamaica, Garvey demanded majority rule for the Caribbean, dominion status (self-government) for Jamaica, and the establishment of a Caribbean federation which he hoped would come to include even non-English-speaking islands. Writing in the *Blackman* in May 1929, Garvey said, "Federation of the West Indies with Dominion Status is the consummation of Negro aspiration in this Archipelago."[193] Without a doubt, Garvey's support for federation represented a black nation-building project in the Western Hemisphere.

The African Blood Brotherhood (ABB) was another black diaspora organization with Caribbean ties and interests in the early twentieth century. During its brief existence (1919–24) the ABB, founded in postwar Harlem by Cyril Briggs, Richard Moore, W. A. Domingo, and Grace Campbell, shuffled between black nationalism and black internationalism based on revolutionary socialism. In spite of some key ideological differences and disagreements with other black diaspora movements, particularly Garvey's UNIA, the ABB did share a fundamental belief in the need for racial unity and uplift for black people throughout the diaspora and on the African continent. Alongside goals of racial equality, race pride and harmony, and political and economic liberation for black peoples, the ABB sought

> to organize the national strength of the entire Negro group in America for the purpose of extending moral and financial aid and, where necessary, leadership to our blood-brothers on the continent of Africa and in Haiti and the West Indies in their struggle against white capitalist exploitation.[194]

Like the UNIA and other movements of this era, the ABB supported self-determination and nation-building efforts in both Africa and the diaspora. In fact, one of their stated goals, pushed in editorials and articles in their *Crusader*, was to "awaken the American Negro to the splendid strategic position of the Race in the South American and the West Indian Republics."[195] In conjunction with the "rising tide of colour" against the "alien overlords" across the globe, the ABB and its supporters called for the development of the West Indies for West Indians, and black nation-building initiatives in the West.[196] This would seemingly include the idea of a West Indian federation.

> Let us unite from the ends of the earth on the common purpose of liberation and redemption of our motherhood and the rejuvenation of the great states that in ages past held Africa securely for her children. . . . Let us even include in our aims the lands of the New World for which our blood was shed and where still we are numerically predominant. Let us aim for a greater rule that will include Haiti and the rest of the West Indies and the vast republic of Brazil in South America with the ancient homeland.[197]

While actual discussions of federation appear to be rare in the ABB program, one news note in the October 1919 edition of the *Crusader* claimed, "Falling in line with the world-wide sweep of the Negro movement for national existence and freedom from the white heel, residents of Dominica, B.W.I., have started a movement for an independent federation of the West Indies on the principle of national freedom."[198] Though it is debatable whether these undefined residents of Dominica considered their actions to be connected with black diaspora politics, it did not matter to the ABB.[199] They, like most involved in black diaspora politics, viewed such efforts as part of the struggle for racial uplift and self-determination. Caribbean federation, therefore, was once again overtly racialized as a means to unite black peoples through the linking of regional and racial concerns.

Early twentieth-century London offered fewer race-based and diaspora-focused organizations than Harlem—a fact that spoke more to the small numbers of "permanent" black residents and communities in London (and England as a whole) than to a strikingly different atmosphere. Still, London remained one of the most important "crossroads at which black people came to a greater sense of group consciousness."[200] Here, as in Harlem, both working-class and middle-class Afro-Caribbean migrants encountered racism, interacted with other international black populations, and joined various organizations that sought to unite and fight for a range of racialized goals in and out of the empire.

Notwithstanding the smaller black population of England, which included a small number of permanent residents along with temporary sojourners such as colonial students and seamen, similar examples of black diaspora activism existed. Periodicals like Duse Mohamed Ali's *African Times and Orient Review* ("devoted to the interests of the coloured races of the world") offered a familiar venue through which black and other nonwhite anticolonial activists presented their respective platforms, and coverage of the plight of the "dark races" in the empire. While broader anticolonial organizations supporting the struggles of all colonial peoples existed, organizations such as the African Progress Union (APU) and the Society of Peoples of African Origin (SPAO) focused more specifically on racial uplift and empowerment among peoples of African descent, including cooperation between West Indians and Africans.[201]

The APU and SPAO worked together in the immediate postwar years under the leadership of John Eldred Taylor, a Sierra Leonean businessman, and F.E.M. Hercules, a Venezuelan-born Trinidadian. Similar to both Caribbean and Harlem-based periodicals, their *African Telegraph*, owned by Taylor and edited by Hercules, offered readers in England important coverage of black struggles in Britain, the West Indies, and the broader black diaspora. This included the plight of black soldiers in World War I, the various race riots in Britain in the postwar years (similar to ones that wreaked havoc in the British West Indies and United States), and the everyday indignities black people faced in all of these locales. As for their specific interest and activism in the West Indies, Hercules, described in one colonial report as an agitator "believed to be working with a view to the ultimate independence of negro countries," and the SPAO published a report on economic and social conditions in Jamaica that called for, among other things, a "federation of the British West Indies."[202] Given the scope of their activism, it is quite reasonable to assume they were interested in federation primarily as a means for the Afro-Caribbean population to unite and gain self-determination within the region. As such, it was connected to the broader freedom struggles of black peoples in Africa and the diaspora.

The minutes of the Pan-African Conferences and Congresses of the early twentieth century also show the racialization of West Indians and the West Indies, and their place within black diaspora politics. The role of West Indians in the formal Pan-African Conferences and Congresses in these years is well chronicled. From the Pan-African Conference in London (1900), organized by Trinidadian barrister Sylvester Williams, through the Fourth Pan-African Congress in New York (1927), numerous West Indian delegates joined with African American activists and smaller numbers of Africans.[203] At most of these meetings, the future of the British West Indies was connected with Africa, Black America, and other Caribbean areas as sites of struggle for peoples of African descent, with the redemption of the African continent taking precedence. Many of the declarations from these meetings sought reforms to the colonial system including greater degrees of self-determination for black people in these areas, such as representative and responsible self-government in the colonies. According to W.E.B. DuBois, the 1900 Pan-African Conference called for the British Empire to provide "responsible government to the black colonies of Africa and the West Indies" which would ostensibly create majority rule in these areas.[204] Similar calls were made about the West Indies in the first three Pan-African Congresses in 1919, 1921, and 1923. After failed attempts to organize the Fourth Pan-African Congress in the Caribbean in 1925, the meeting finally took place in New York in 1927 with the usual calls made for "self-government" for the colonies. As for the West Indies specifically, the constituents at the New York meeting resolved to "urge the peoples of the West Indies to begin an earnest movement for the federation of these islands."[205] No explanation is given for why federation was needed in the British Caribbean, but once again, given the context, it is reasonable to assume these delegates viewed federation as the best means to empower and unite the West Indies, which they viewed as a black region.

Calls for federation litter the writings of other black activists in the early twentieth century. For instance, Hubert Harrison included discussion of a West Indian federation alongside discussion of the broader Caribbean in one of his "West Indian New Notes" columns in the *Negro World* in March 1922.[206] W.E.B. DuBois, who had previously referred to the West Indies as a "new Ethiopia of the Isles," supported the cause of West Indian federation in his 1925 article "The Negro Mind Reaches Out." Noting Europeans' fear of black self-rule, DuBois asked, "Why is there not a great British West Indian Federation, stretching from Bermuda to [British] Honduras and Guiana, and ranking with the free dominions? The answer was clear and concise—Color."[207]

Caribbean federation also became a goal in the late 1920s among many Black Marxists who would continue their support over several decades. Richard B. Moore, a founding member of the ABB and an important supporter of federation well into the 1960s, represented the American Negro Labor Congress (ANLC) at the International Congress Against Colonial Oppression and Imperialism and for National Independence held in Brussels in 1927. The various resolutions "for the benefit of the oppressed Negro peoples in the world" included a demand for an end to imperialist occupation of nations such as Haiti, Cuba, and the Dominican Republic and self-government for Caribbean colonies, including a "Confederation of the British West Indies."[208] In 1928 George Padmore, one of the most prominent black communists in this era, penned an article for the ANLC's *Negro*

Champion that noted the growing movement for federation in the West Indies and called for the colonial masses of the region to support such an initiative "in their own interest" rather than the reasons colonial governments and middle classes pushed it. Padmore urged West Indians in the United States, whose "group life in America [had] tended to unite them and establish a common fellowship," to support the cause of federation, and closed by stating that the *Negro Champion* "stands ready to give its full support to a militant movement among the islanders for the federation and the freedom of the West Indies."[209] Similarly, a 1929 article in the *Liberator* (the successor of the *Negro Champion*) presented Caribbean federation as a means to fight British colonialism and end the Crown Colony system in the West Indies. Once more there was a call for workers to resist colonial and middle-class ideas of federation and instead "seize the movement and turn it to their own advantage in a relentless struggle against both native and foreign exploiters ... for a Free Independent West Indies!"[210] Although race is not overtly mentioned in these articles, given Black Marxists' refusal to set aside race as prescribed in orthodox communism, their race and class consciousness, and their condemnation of the conjoined forces of racism and capitalism under which black and other colonial peoples struggled, was surely a consideration in these articles, particularly in the case of Moore and Padmore.[211]

Support for federation in the late 1920s can also be found among the various moderate West Indian organizations based in Harlem that commonly occupied a middle ground between the more radical Garvey and Black Marxist movements. Among the broad array of colony-specific and regionally focused organizations that flourished in this era, one of the most noteworthy of the latter appeared in November 1927 when a group of "West Indian Negroes living in Harlem, prominent in business and the professions," launched the West India Committee of America (WICA). The WICA, which included representatives from several benevolent societies in the area, presented their platform at a public meeting in late January 1928. Described as "more comprehensive than that of the many benevolent societies," the platform sought to influence the development of community life in Harlem and to improve "the conditions for the West Indian, both here [United States] and in his native home." Economically, the new organization hoped "to stimulate the development of West Indian business enterprises" and to provide West Indians with "dignified and lucrative employment."

On their own, these goals portray the WICA primarily as a transnational

West Indian organization intended to act on behalf of the West Indian communities in Harlem as well as their colonial homelands. However, in step with many other race-conscious groups of the era, there was also a specific intent to bolster racial unity between West Indians and African Americans for the good of the race as a whole. The WICA endeavored to "co-operate in any endeavor to promote the economic welfare of the race," not simply West Indians. In addition to its economic goals, the WICA aimed "to promote friendly relations between American and West Indian Negroes" and promoted naturalization "to the end that [West Indians] may be better able to enjoy the advantages to be derived from American citizenship"—objectives with ramifications for the overarching black communities' political advancement, rather than only West Indians'.[212] In doing so, the WICA became more than simply a transnational West Indian organization. It also came to operate as a black diaspora organization that recognized and dedicated itself to ideas of racial unity and uplift for peoples of African descent, including Caribbean federation.

One of the most prominent members of the WICA was A. M. Wendell Malliet, who served as its secretary. By the time the WICA launched, Malliet, a Jamaican immigrant who arrived in the United States in 1918, had established himself as a reporter for several black newspapers in the United States. Among his most noteworthy contributions was a four-part series in the *Pittsburgh Courier* during the summer of 1927 titled "Why I Cannot Become Americanized." In these articles Malliet recalled a familiar West Indian immigrant tale of his arrival in the United States, encounters with the American brand of racism, intra-racial problems between African Americans and West Indians and the need to unite, as well as his determination to better black life in America and his West Indian homelands.[213] Malliet does not appear to have been involved in the more radical black diaspora organizations of Harlem, though he maintained relationships with several who were, including W. A. Domingo and Richard B. Moore of the ABB. Instead, like the WICA in which he participated, Malliet represented a more moderate strain of black diaspora activism. Over the next several decades, he became an influential and well-respected activist through his interest and involvement on behalf of the West Indies, Black America (which included the West Indian expatriate communities), Africa, and the broader black diaspora.

Although the WICA platform does not specifically mention Caribbean federation, one can draw some conclusions through Malliet's activism. His publication *The Destiny of the West Indies* (1928) provides one of the most explicit examples of the pursuit of a Caribbean federation as a racialized, diasporic project with benefits for West Indians at home and abroad, as well as African Americans. In this text Malliet claimed that the British Caribbean offered the most opportunities for people of African descent in the New World, as there was "room in those colonies for the coloured man to grow to full stature."[214] However, for the region to reach its full potential, he called for the end of Crown Colony rule and the establishment of a West Indian federation. Knowing that such a demand required the colonial governments to abandon their belief that the black populations of the West Indies were not yet "fit" for self-government, Malliet spent the bulk of his booklet arguing that the West Indians were more than ready for such a responsibility. He pointed to the numerous positions already capably held by Afro-Caribbeans in the West Indies, and claimed that those who ignored such examples and held fast to the idea that the region required a trusteeship were hampered by the "pernicious influence of the Anglo-Saxon race philosophy."[215] Like many other activists of the era, in and out of the Caribbean, he noted the advancement of the white dominions of the empire and called for the same opportunities for the British Caribbean so that they could take their place as a united, "self-governing nation within the British Commonwealth of Nations."[216]

Despite Malliet's desire to assure his readers that a united West Indies would not be "governed on the principle of race," his appeal certainly portrayed a prominent racial consciousness like many of his contemporaries.[217] He envisioned a federated British Caribbean as a key step in the transformation of white-ruled colonies into a strong black homeland in the West where peoples of African descent could reach their full potential. These ideas aligned closely with various other diaspora visions of the West Indies and federation popular in the early twentieth century and coming decades.

In comparing visions of federation from outside the Caribbean to those of the colonial power brokers and West Indian nationalists in the region, one finds both similarities and differences. The vast majority, if not all, of the government officials' and oligarchies' ideas of a united West Indies sought to maintain and bolster the status quo of the British West Indies. Like many Afro-Caribbean conceptualizations from within the Caribbean, support for federation among expatriate West Indians and other black peoples outside of the region directly challenged the status quo. They viewed federation as a means to develop the region—a region thoroughly racialized as part of the broader black diaspora—for the good of the local West Indian populations, but with benefits for other peoples of African descent too. At the same time, although black support for West Indian self-government and federation shared many overarching similarities, whether in or out of the Caribbean, it was by no means monolithic. For instance, one can find both transracial and racial appeals within the activism of many West Indian nationalists in the Caribbean, including those deeply involved in black diaspora politics such as Marryshow. However, the bulk of support for federation by expatriate West Indian and other black diaspora activists outside of the region more directly, consistently, and freely appealed to the racial consciousness of their target audiences as a means to rally support for federation as a liberating, empowering, black nation-building project. Nevertheless, even as ideas of racial unity and uplift served to bring black radical and moderate activists together in their support of federation, there remained differences, including the anticapitalist critiques embedded in the support of many Black Marxists that contrasted with the more pro-black-capitalist appeals of the WICA and Malliet.

Overall, all of these perspectives are important within the history of Caribbean federation. The connections, overlaps, and divergences between the multiple conceptualizations speak to the complicated history of efforts to build such a West Indian nation, which expanded in the following decades. As West Indian nationalists within the Caribbean were increasingly empowered in the region in the 1930s and 1940s, their diaspora counterparts outside the West Indies also continued to be a major source of support in the pursuit of Caribbean federation.

2

Moving Toward the Crossroads of Our Destiny

Black Diaspora Politics and the Pursuit of West Indian Nationhood,
1930–1945

The 1930s and early 1940s proved to be an era of much chaos and significant change across the globe. Worldwide economic depression, military invasions, rebellions, war, and increasingly powerful anticolonial movements substantially challenged and altered the imperialist stranglehold over many sections of the colonial world. If the First World War and its aftermath inspired important ideological attacks on European colonialism, the turmoil of the interwar years and Second World War furthered significantly many of these anticolonial challenges. By the time World War II ended in 1945, much of the colonial world stood on the verge of a new era as old empires lay weakened and new nations appeared poised to emerge from the ashes of war.

The British Empire, in particular, faced significant challenges in the 1930s and early 1940s. Internally, the 1926 Balfour Act and the 1931 Statute of Westminster solidified a different status within the empire for the so-called "white dominions" than for the nonwhite colonies of Africa, Asia, and the Caribbean.[1] These actions further undermined already precarious notions of equal standing within the empire as white dominions—Canada, Australia, New Zealand, South Africa, and the Irish Free State—became self-governing equals voluntarily aligned with the former mother country, while the nonwhite colonies remained exploited and unequal under familiar racist ideologies of trusteeship and tutelage. As a result, the demand for reforms and the anticolonial activities within and between many of these colonies expanded, with intensified calls for self-determination and self-government. For the West Indian colonies, the claim of being one of the oldest parts of the empire increasingly became a "scarlet letter" rather than a badge of honor. Externally, the empire faced the rise of fascism in the 1930s, and the outbreak of World War II exacerbated many of the tensions within their colonies. Though the haughty boast that "the sun never set on the British Empire" survived into the postwar era, ominous storm clouds forewarned of the "setting sun" to come in many parts of the British colonial world.

In the 1930s the West Indies, with the exception of Barbados and the Bahamas, remained under the antiquated Crown Colony system with severely restricted economic, social, and political opportunities. Even in the two colonies where Crown Colony government was not formally established, the dominance of the white oligarchies and colonial system remained the norm, with obvious race and class discrimination against the bulk of the population throughout the region. Though some reforms in the 1920s added minuscule elected representation in many Caribbean colonies, the vast majority of West Indians remained largely disfranchised and outside the decision-making processes in their homelands. West Indian activists, especially from the Afro-Caribbean majorities in most colonies, continued to push for political reforms that they believed would increase their participation and lead eventually to responsible self-government. Unfortunately, colonial officials remained ambivalent and reluctant to initiate substantial reforms, which could undermine the power of the governors and nominated legislative council members.

Political matters were far from the only problems. Economically, the British Caribbean continued to flounder. The depression that gripped much of the globe in the 1930s was especially severe in the region. The struggling export economies worsened as the foreign markets that typically purchased West Indian goods suffered through their own economic woes. Many in the middle and working classes found their traditional migration outlets closed, leaving them stuck in their respective colonies with limited opportunities. Moreover, thousands of West Indian migrants were forcibly repatriated, including significant numbers of Afro-Caribbeans expelled from circum-Caribbean countries of Central and South America where these migrants had long worked and established their own communities, due to the rise of anti-black immigration legislation.[2] Socially, although lacking the formal Jim Crow policies found in the United States, the colonies remained staunchly divided along race and class lines.

Overall—notwithstanding some level of reforms in the British Caribbean—the undemocratic nature of colonial rule, the economic stagnation, lacking and lost job opportunities, poor wages, shameful working and living conditions, poverty, and general dissatisfaction with the constrained economic, social, and political opportunities of the colonies produced a volatile atmosphere. Against this backdrop, labor unrest and activism, heightened racial consciousness, and continued demands for political reform, from within the West Indies and the broader black diaspora, combined to challenge the status quo of the British Caribbean in the 1930s and early 1940s.

Throughout these tumultuous years, the creation of a federation between most or all of the West Indian colonies continued to be viewed by many as a solution to the region's political and economic woes and a key to the West Indies' future. Supporters within the Colonial Office and white oligarchies maintained their views of federation as the means to institute "better" colonial government, administrative efficiency, and greater economic strength. As in previous decades, the Crown sent multiple investigative commissions to the region in the 1930s, including the Closer Union Commission, which was created to explore the possibilities of federation, and the Moyne Commission, whose investigations into a series of labor rebellions later in the decade also came to explore the issue indirectly. Nevertheless, the vast majority of the colonial and oligarchical support for a Caribbean federation still did not seek to empower the West Indies for the West Indian populations.

For many reformers and activists in the British Caribbean colonies, whether focused on colony-specific reforms or the region as a whole, federation continued to promise facilitation of a range of political, economic, and social reforms for the good of the West Indian population themselves. Although substantial reform movements existed prior to the 1930s, their numbers and activism now increased exponentially. A notable development was the founding of formal, overwhelmingly middle class–led political parties in several West Indian colonies in the late 1930s.[3]

Alongside increased West Indian activism within the colonies during the 1930s and early 1940s, West Indian and other black activists based outside the Caribbean further solidified themselves as important forces in the cause of West Indian self-government and liberation. During these years, there was significant and increased cooperation and cross-pollination between local and regional reform movements in the Caribbean and transnational West Indian and black diaspora organizations based in the United States and Great Britain (particularly Harlem and London). More than simply auxiliary sources of material and moral support, many participated in, and in some cases led and helped create, political movements within the Caribbean. Some even believed themselves mandated to speak for the region, whether in collaboration with or independently of their counterparts in the West Indies. As in previous decades, West Indian struggles for self-government and self-determination, including the pursuit of federation, proved to be a focal point within black diaspora politics and the international struggles of black peoples against anachronistic and exploitative white supremacist ideologies.

This chapter examines the continued pursuit of self-government and a West Indian nation, particularly via federation, in the British Caribbean from the 1930s through the Second World War. Imperial and intra-regional conversations are included, but the primary focus is the scale and scope of black diaspora activism in support of these endeavors, particularly among the various transnational West Indian and black diaspora activists and organizations in the United States and Great Britain. Given this focus, the chapter also interrogates the ways in which ideas of race shaped perceptions of and support for West Indian self-government and nation building in this era. These struggles in the West Indies were obviously part of the broader anticolonial struggles of various nonwhite colonial peoples. At the same time, they were conceptualized, contextualized, and prioritized by many black activists explicitly as part of a racialized fight for self-determination and connected to parallel and overlapping struggles in Africa and Black America. Indeed, from the earliest years of the 1930s, through the turmoil of the Italian invasion of Ethiopia and West Indian labor rebellions in the mid-late 1930s, and into the war years of the 1940s, the status and future of the British Caribbean remained important within black diaspora politics.

Early 1930s

The 1930s began much as the previous decade had ended. Most agreed the economic, social, and political conditions of the West Indian colonies required reform. There remained much debate, however, over the specific issues that required reform and the extent of any initiatives to address them. Within these discussions, the new decade opened with continued inquiries into the possibilities of federation. The West Indian Sugar Commission of 1929–30, organized to investigate the dire economic situation, made the familiar recommendation of unifying some colonial governments to reduce costs and achieve better efficiency. In 1930 some members of the legislative council in Antigua petitioned for a federation of the Leewards, Windwards, and Trinidad, while officials in Dominica requested a federation of the Windwards and Leewards as a step toward a union of all British Caribbean colonies.[4] Federation continued to receive support from some West Indian reformers at both local and regional levels. West Indian nationalists like Cipriani and Marryshow sustained their campaign in the colonies for federation with self-government, directing West Indians to "agitate, educate, and confederate," while new local organizations, such as the St. Kitts Worker's League, founded in 1932, incorporated the goal of federation into their programs.[5]

Some of the most important discussions of federation within imperial and intra-regional deliberations of this era occurred in 1932–33. In 1931 a dispatch from the secretary of state for the colonies to the governors of the Windward Islands, Leeward Islands, and Trinidad noted "the time is ripe for an enquiry to be held into the possibilities of closer union and co-operation between Trinidad, the Windward and the Leeward Islands, or some of them." Lord Passfield's direction ultimately led to the creation of the Closer Union Commission (CUC) in November 1932.[6] Before that official commission launched, however, West Indians organized their own conference.

The Dominica Taxpayers' Reform Association hosted the West Indian Conference, commonly referred to as the Roseau Conference, in their capital from 28 October to 2 November 1932. The conference brought together a diverse collection of interested parties from eastern Caribbean colonies, including some current and formerly elected members of the various legislative councils, newspaper editors, representatives of labor organizations, and West Indian nationalists. A large number of the attendees were Afro-Caribbeans, though a few white representatives from the planter and merchant class were present. The composition of the delegates made the conference unusual for the era, especially in comparison with the official conferences held in previous decades at which the local West Indian representation was minute or nonexistent. The charge of this meeting was to discuss a series of common problems facing the West Indian colonies, particularly the need for political reform. The most pressing topics were the need for an end to antiquated Crown Colony rule, and the installation of a federation of the eastern Caribbean islands with self-government and dominion status (open to additional units joining later). For some activists in attendance, particularly among the West Indian nationalists focused on regional reform and unity, these issues obviously coincided.[7]

Roseau delegates discussed at length the idea of federation as the means to improve the current inefficient government and to increase the economic prowess of the area—for the good of all West Indians and not just the ruling oligarchies or Crown. The vast majority of the participants rejected federation of the colonies under the current Crown Colony system, which they assumed would not provide increased participation by West Indians themselves via a wider franchise and greater representation. Instead they called for a self-governing federation.

In the official report of the conference, the delegates offered an extensive blueprint for federation in the eastern Caribbean, including the numbers, procedures, and powers of the federal government. They resolved it "desirable in the general interests of the Colonies of Trinidad, Barbados, Grenada, St. Vincent, St. Lucia, and the Leeward Islands that a Federation of such Colonies should be effected." The conference also cabled the secretary of state a resolution requesting that the soon-to-arrive CUC's "terms of reference" expand to include investigation of self-government for the region and proposed federation.[8] Overall, in the words of its chairman Cecil E. A. Rawle, the conference marked "the end of a Chapter in West Indian history, and the beginning of a new era, for in taking the initiative and sustaining to a successful end the effort necessary to devise a programme of political reform and the outline of a democratic constitution for a United West Indies, the people of these islands proclaim that they have definitely freed themselves from the Crown Colony mentality, and from the prejudice of insular myths."[9]

Given the hopes that the conference would lay the "foundation stones of West Indian Nationality," represent "West Indian Solidarity," and provide a base for a new "West Indian Nationhood," the conference took it upon itself to offer a definition of who was a West Indian.[10] Unsurprisingly, the issue of race proved one of the most intriguing aspects of that question. Captain G. F. Ashpitel, a planter and former nominated member to the Dominica Legislative Council, helped initiate this discussion. As recounted in both the official report and newspaper coverage, "Mr. Ashpitel, speaking on behalf of the English communities having interests in the West Indies indicated that doubts should be removed as to their position under the proposed federation."[11] It is safe to assume that Ashpitel was alluding to the common notion that Afro-Caribbeans, who were the vast majority of the West Indian population, would dominate a self-governing federation, and the implicit fears of many whites in the colonies of black majority rule. C. L. Elder from Barbados responded that "Federation was for all classes of the West Indies," and Cipriani replied, "Confederation had nothing to do with class, colour, or creed." In the end, the "term West Indian was defined . . . as including all persons born, domiciled, or having a permanent stake in the West Indies.[12] Thus both federation and West Indianness emerged from the Roseau Conference as largely a transracial regional project within the bounds of the British Empire.

Shortly after the close of the Roseau Conference, the CUC arrived in November 1932 "to examine on the spot the possibilities of closer union between Trinidad and the Windward Islands and Leeward Islands, or some of them." Over the course of approximately three months, the commission visited Antigua, St. Kitts and Nevis, Montserrat, Dominica, St. Lucia, St. Vincent, Grenada, and Trinidad and Tobago.[13] Though they allowed some testimony concerning self-government, as the Roseau Conference requested, the bulk of their focus remained the viability of a federation in the eastern Caribbean as a means to achieve economic and administrative efficiency. This mission was similar to many of the previous official investigations of the region, in which federation was contemplated by the empire as a system for better colonial control rather than to empower or improve the West Indies for West Indians. Ultimately the commission reported that they heard some support for federation, but the deep-seated insularity of most of the islands and their reluctance to agree to any unions that might restrict their local autonomy prevented the institution of an eastern Caribbean federation. While the commission did suggest uniting the Windwards and Leewards into one colony with one governor over the separate colonial administrations, several of the colonial governments in these islands rejected this limited proposal as well.[14]

Despite the fact that ideas of federation emerged from the Roseau Conference, and many of the testimonies to the CUC, as a project for political advancement for the region as a whole and not for any particular race or class, there was some trepidation within the Colonial Office about local West Indian support for federation from among the Afro-Caribbean majorities. In January 1933 a memo by S.E.V. Luke of the Colonial Office described the Roseau Conference delegates as representing a "negro separatist movement strongly tinged with a political socialism," ignoring the presence of the whites at the conference. The desire for dominion status, Luke believed, would place the West Indies in the hands of a "negro population" who viewed Crown Colony government as not only "irresponsible" and "unrepresentative" but also white supremacist.[15] Though it is true that many West Indians did wish to achieve self-determination and overturn the obvious racism of the colonial systems, the notion of a "separatist movement" was largely paranoid folly, as the Roseau Conference's request for federation with dominion status clearly showed a desire to maintain ties with the Commonwealth, though with an elevated standing more equal to other nations.

While the Roseau Conference avoided direct talk of black self-determination by arguing for self-government with a wider franchise, many delegates certainly knew that the federation proposed would indelibly empower black majorities in ways that official appeals for federation eschewed, and that this concerned many whites within the region and empire. Randall H. Lockhart's lengthy memorandum to the CUC expresses many of these sentiments. Lockhart, a former elected member of the Dominica Legislative Council, secretary of the Dominica Taxpayers' Reform Association, and Roseau Conference delegate, addressed a range of issues, including the possibilities of federation and self-government, and the stifling race and class structures of the West Indies. Some of his most eloquent remarks referred to the flawed Crown Colony system in the Caribbean and British notions of "trusteeship for natives."

Such systems and ideologies could never accomplish their purported goal of making the local populations fit for government, Lockhart wrote, because many in the white population would resist it. "A class of officials anxious to uphold the prestige of their race and to continue its privileged position as a ruling people are not likely to be over-anxious to train a subject people to oust them from that position, nor will they readily acknowledge that the time has come for their own gradual eviction."[16] Lockhart claimed that those who did not believe in "the complete educability of the Negro" dismissed much of the political activity West Indians undertook, which demonstrated their eagerness and readiness for self-government, as communist plots, or rejected them for their supposed lack of character.[17] If only white people populated the West Indies, he argued, they would have free democratic institutions, and the question should not be whether West Indians were fit for self-government, but whether they had the right to it.[18] Lockhart believed they did and noted the great strides West Indians had made in such a short time since the horrors of slavery. To refuse their demands for self-determination was not only detrimental to black people but also an indictment of English notions of liberty which they held so dear.[19]

Lockhart's memo impressed some colonial officials, but it produced no tangible results in the struggle for self-government and federation in the West Indies. His many valid points, made by others in preceding years and echoed in years following, fell upon deaf ears among white colonial officials who may have appreciated his "extremely interesting and well-written account of the situation" but did little to advocate the demise of British colonialism—as Lockhart himself had predicted.[20] At the very least, Lockhart's memo emphasized how race remained intricately tied to debates over self-determination and self-government for the black majorities of the colonies. For some, however, rather than a burden to be overcome, race proved a popular and efficient tool through which to rally support for the cause of West Indian liberation and nation building.

The plight of the British Caribbean and West Indians remained an important topic within the social and political atmosphere of Harlem. As they did in previous decades, African American, transnational West Indian, and black diaspora organizations in Harlem provided regular coverage of and support for the various reform and nation-building activities of the West Indies. These groups hosted activists from the colonies when they came to New York, while activists in the two regions maintained regular contact. As historian Jason Parker has established, Harlem, with a population at least one-quarter of West Indian origin in the early twentieth century, came to be the figurative "capital of the Caribbean" and the "Harlem Nexus" (as Parker dubbed the communication between the two regions) proved a powerful transnational connection.[21]

W.E.B. DuBois, who remained one of the most prominent and influential African American activists associated with black diaspora politics, continued to receive regular correspondence from the Caribbean in this era, and reported on British Caribbean activities alongside other international news in the pages of the NAACP's *Crisis*.[22] Around the time of the Roseau Conference and CUC, for instance, the *Crisis* reported and offered support for another Marryshow-led delegation to London in pursuit of political reform and federation in the West Indies, and described the Roseau Conference as "one of the most important meetings ever held in the West Indies."[23] DuBois himself received copies of the Roseau Conference report from the Dominica Taxpayers' Reform Association, who asked him to compare their political aspirations and demands with those of the CUC.[24]

Black Marxist organizations remained active in the early 1930s, with a considerable presence in and connections to Harlem, home to multiple movements and leading figures (many of whom were West Indian).[25] In these years, support for West Indian liberation and self-determination continued to be linked to the broader struggle against capitalism and imperialism, with the creation of a federation considered particularly important for the relief and empowerment of the toiling black masses of the British Caribbean. Otto Huiswoud's 1930 article "World Aspects of the Negro Question" described the pursuit of a "Federated West Indies" as a fight for "native rule" and "political and economic control" of the colonies.[26] Writing in January 1931, George Padmore noted the shared plight of the "Negro masses in the West Indies [who were] just as viciously exploited as the natives of Africa or the black toilers in the United States," and extended the support of the International Trade Union Committee of Negro Workers (ITUCNW) for the "economic and political demands of the toiling population of the West Indies in their fight against the imperialists and the native capitalist exploiters."[27]

In the months prior to the launch of the CUC, the *Negro Worker* published a letter from Trinidad concerning the ongoing "agitation for freedom and Federation." The author condemned the British Labor Party for failing to extend self-government in the islands as promised, and for its decision to send yet another commission to investigate the topic. As indicated in the closing of the letter, the West Indies needed self-determination and freedom from colonialism, not another fact-finding commission and the possibility of colonial reform. "Down with British Imperialism! Long Live the Free Federated West Indies! Long Live the 'NEGRO WORKER'!"[28]

Although there was unquestionable interest among some African Americans and African American organizations, as well as Black Marxist circles, expatriate West Indians organizations remained among the most important forces advocating the cause of West Indian nationhood from abroad in the early 1930s. Various activists and a multitude of transnational (island and regionally focused) benevolent societies and social-political organizations flourished, with some becoming deeply involved in black diaspora politics too.[29]

Charles A. Petioni was one of the most significant Afro-Caribbean activists in Harlem, yet he receives little more than passing mention in most studies of Harlem-based West Indian and black diaspora activism in this era.[30] Petioni was born in Trinidad in 1883. After attending the Government Training College for Teachers and the Royal Victoria Institute, he worked as a reporter for the *Morning Mirror* and *Daily Evening Argus* before being fired for his anticolonial activities. Told that he would not find work in Trinidad again, Petioni arrived with his wife in New York City in 1917. After working briefly in the area shipyards, as an elevator operator, and as a porter, Petioni did premed studies at City College. Upon completion of his medical degree at Howard University in 1925, Petioni moved back to Harlem, where he established himself as a prominent physician as well as an activist for the black communities—both West Indians and African Americans.[31]

Like several of his contemporaries, Petioni participated simultaneously over the course of his career in a variety of organizations, whose platforms ranged from local Harlem community issues, to insular concern for fellow Trinidadian immigrants, to broader West Indian causes in Harlem and the Caribbean and to the general uplift of all people of African descent. In his role as a physician, Petioni was a leading figure within the National Medical Association (an association of black physicians), the North Harlem Medical Association, and the Howard Medical Society.[32] He also helped create the Trinidad Benevolent Society in New York and served as its first president, as well as vice president of the West Indies Societies Protective League and chairman of the West India Committee of America.[33]

In 1930 Petioni and colleagues established the Caribbean Union (CU). Under Petioni's leadership, the CU proved to be one of the more active West Indian organizations in Harlem in the 1930s and the early years of the Second World War.[34] Though a specific platform is difficult to establish, the group sought "to encourage naturalization of the foreign born and to bring about better understanding between the natives and foreign born" as a means to empower the West Indian community in Harlem and build racial unity between peoples of African descent in the area.[35] In July 1932 the CU joined with the Brotherhood of Sleeping Car Porters, the Unemployed Citizens League of Harlem, and other groups to demand proportionate employment for "Race Citizens" within the New York subway system.[36] Speaking at a CU meeting the following year, Petioni urged both naturalized West Indians and African Americans to vote in upcoming elections to increase their influence in local politics. While tensions between some West Indians and African Americans surfaced periodically, Petioni and the CU continued working "sedulously though quietly" for West Indian and African American unity for the good of the race.[37]

Despite subsequent claims by the FBI that the Caribbean Union "confined its interests to purely local politics," Petioni and the CU actively supported West Indian progress in the Caribbean, including federation.[38] In the mid-1930s Petioni wrote multiple articles in the pages of the *New York Amsterdam News*. Two of these articles clearly illuminate the ways in which Petioni conceptualized the future of the British Caribbean and its connection to racial uplift ideologies. While not explicitly dismissing (or acknowledging) the presence of other races in the region, he depicted the Caribbean as a black homeland and land of opportunity for Afro-Caribbeans and African Americans.

In September 1935 Petioni's "Better Times in the West Indies" detailed expatriate West Indian support for and interest in Caribbean reform and nation-building efforts. In addition to the importance of these developments for West Indians outside the region, he presented their significance for African Americans "who should take interest in the conditions of the islands because they are a potential source of emigration, of social improvement as well as commercial, political and racial advancement." Petioni, who had returned recently from a visit to the Lesser Antilles, reflected upon the economic and social history of the islands, noted the growing power of Afro-Caribbeans in almost all sectors of colonial life in the region, and called for continued reform efforts and political activism. He also lauded the considerable positive impact, in his opinion, of West Indian and African American influence from the United States. In so doing he presented a rather positive view of the region and the opportunities for both Afro-Caribbean and African American populations. As for the latter, Petioni noted, "the American capitalist of color" would "be welcomed with open arms by his fellows in the islands." In closing, Petioni said that approximately twenty years earlier former president Theodore Roosevelt had woefully pondered "Why these beautiful islands had been virtually abandoned by the teeming white population which formerly inhabited them." Petioni claimed, "Were [Roosevelt] alive today to see the tremendous changes in the social, political and economic fields made by the colored West Indian, owing in considerable measure to the influence of the colored American . . . he would conclude that the knell of white domination, not only in the West Indies but in the world, is being mournfully tolled."[39]

A week later Petioni's "Black Man's Paradise" appeared. After establishing the reality of social divisions in the region between mulattoes and blacks—an issue less prominent in the United States than in many West Indian colonies—Petioni argued that the black majorities were "awakening" and coming into greater power in the West Indies. He referred to the rise of black professionals and officials, and a growing sense of "colored solidarity" across color and class distinctions between peoples of African descent, particularly among "returned natives from the United States." Looking to the "eventual removal of the petty lines and jealousies and foolish class distinctions," Petioni claimed that the dream of a "West Indies for the West Indians" was close at hand with a "federation of the West Indies" as the personification of this quest. More than just an important step for West Indians, Petioni believed federation held promise for black peoples elsewhere, especially African Americans. He argued, "The American Negro can play no unimportant part" and "will be given a better and heartier welcome than he could ever receive elsewhere." The African American "will be invited to stay to spread his psychology and his education; and to invest his money for the advantage of himself and the islanders. He will be made to realise the essential brotherhood of the so-called West Indian and American."[40]

Petioni's articles presented familiar visions of Afro-Caribbean liberation and the achievement of a black homeland through the creation of a Caribbean federation as beneficial to West Indians and to other diasporic black communities as well. Some of his appeals also mirrored nineteenth-century calls by black nationalists for the emigration of African Americans to Africa or other parts of the black diaspora where they could achieve the still-sought-after right to self-determination and self-rule.

The West Indian Federation of America (WIFA) shared many traits with the Caribbean Union, as well as previous groups such as the West India Committee of America. Created in March 1933 following a conference between more than a dozen West Indian benevolent societies, the WIFA launched their program in the summer of 1933 with a focus on local (New York), West Indian, and black diaspora interests. As announced by their secretary A. M. Wendell Malliet and again by the NAACP's *Crisis* shortly thereafter,

> the West Indian Federation of America was organized having as its immediate objectives: to advocate the early federation of, and self-government for, the British West Indies, British Guiana, British Honduras, Bermuda, and the Bahama Islands within the British Commonwealth of Nations; to stimulate among British West Indians in America a keen interest in West Indian affairs, particularly in the development of the political, economic, educational, and social conditions in the Homeland and to foster among West Indians and Afro-Americans the development of such industrial and commercial enterprises as may be considered necessary for the economic welfare of the group.[41]

Over the next few years the WIFA, sometimes in conjunction with the CU and other allied groups, pressed their agenda in various public meetings in Harlem and surrounding New York City areas. Some of the most noteworthy took place in August in each year of their existence to mark the anniversary of emancipation in the British Caribbean.[42] In these celebratory gatherings, the progress of West Indians (and black peoples in general) was heralded, as was the need for West Indian and African American unity and support for black political advancement. At an August 1933 meeting marking the ninety-ninth anniversary of emancipation in the British West Indies, Justice James S. Watson of the Municipal Court asserted, "West Indian and American Negroes should join hands in the spirit of brotherhood and work for the common racial welfare, without prejudice or national bias."[43] The WIFA's commitment "to co-operate with all movements and projects designated to promote racial well-being" was even more pronounced at the centenary celebration of West Indian emancipation in 1934.[44] This meeting included speakers from the WIFA and CU as well as other West Indian and African American guests. A local minister "brought greetings on behalf of the American Race people and praised West Indians in America for the contribution which they have made towards the culture and progress of the Race in this country."[45] As the *New York Amsterdam News* report of the event proclaimed, "The heritage of America's black citizens of the future will be richer for the gifts of the Antilles."[46] While this meeting included significant praise for the general progress of the race and stressed racial unity, it also addressed political reform and advancement in the Caribbean, including federation.

The possibilities of and the need for a Caribbean federation received much attention in the year leading up to the centenary celebration. In November 1933 Malliet penned a lengthy article calling for the development of a "spirit of nationalism, a sense of oneness." Echoing sentiments from his *Destiny of the West Indies*, Malliet presented federation as the political solution through which the West Indies could progress and achieve dominion status within the British Commonwealth of Nations. Like Petioni, Malliet made an explicit appeal for African American support for a Caribbean federation. "The West Indies offer the finest opportunity for the black man in the new world," including a site for African American economic investment.[47] In June 1934 the WIFA called a meeting to discuss the report of the Closer Union Commission, which had investigated the possibility of a federation in the West Indian colonies.[48] At the actual centenary celebration in August, several speakers broached the topic of West Indian nationhood and federation, among them Petioni, representing the Caribbean Union, with "The Blight of Crown Colony Government" and Helena M. Benta with "The Role of Women in the Development of West Indian Nationhood." Joseph C. Morris, a Guianese immigrant and president of the WIFA, addressed the issue of federation more directly. He noted "the trend of the times . . . towards larger political units" and affirmed the group's support "for the federation of the nine crown colonies in the Caribbean into one self-governing dominion." Morris asserted, "It is time to let Great Britain know that the West Indies are no longer willing to remain the Cinderella of the British Empire." Malliet repeated his support for federation and proposed the creation of a new organization with branches and representatives in each Crown Colony. "To this end a number of West Indian leaders are in the near future to be invited to this country for a West Indian national congress."[49]

The programs of moderate transnational West Indian organizations like the Caribbean Union and the West Indian Federation of America demonstrate the involvement of expatriate West Indians in the black diaspora politics of the early 1930s outside of the radical political organizations with which many West Indians were associated. Moderate and radical groups remained connected by ideas of racial uplift and liberation within the inclusive black diaspora politics of the era, often with common objectives. Nevertheless, common support for such things as West Indian self-government and federation did not homogenize their agendas. Many Black Marxists continued to emphasize the need for economic reforms, especially for the good of the West Indian working classes, and criticized capitalism as a major component of black exploitation in the West Indies and elsewhere. Conversely, both the CU and WIFA supported and appealed to forms of cooperative capitalism among black populations in the cause of racial uplift in a manner much more similar to the National Negro Business League (founded in 1900 by Booker T. Washington) and Marcus Garvey's Negro Factories Corporation (incorporated in 1920) than their Black Marxist counterparts.

It is also important to recognize the place of these moderate West Indian transnational organizations alongside various other groups within black diaspora politics in these years. This includes the ways in which race shaped visions of the West Indian future, and how activists employed it to seek support of Caribbean federation through appeals to the increasing racial consciousness of black peoples in the diaspora in the 1930s. West Indian residents in Harlem and surrounding areas undoubtedly dominated their memberships. However, to describe them simply as "West Indian" overlooks the ways in which they also operated as black diaspora organizations concerned with more than simply their homelands. Their calls for racial unity between African Americans and West Indians, and the clear associa-

tion of West Indian political development and federation with racial uplift and self-determination were only portions of the larger black diaspora
politics of the early-mid 1930s. Nevertheless, they were just that—a key
component within the larger racial politics of the day.

Written about and discussed within racialized spaces and discourses,
with both explicit and implicit appeals to race, support for West Indian
nationhood and federation proved to be much more than simply a political
movement within the British Empire. In the coming years, the connections
between West Indian, African American, and African struggles, and the
reform and freedom movements associated with them, became even more
pronounced.

Mid-Late 1930s

In the mid-late 1930s, the Italian invasion of Ethiopia and the various labor
rebellions that swept the British Caribbean garnered the attention of West
Indian and black diaspora communities and activists. While the war *in*
Ethiopia may have been thousands of miles from the shores of the West
Indies, or the streets of Harlem and London, the war *over* this invasion took
place in these areas as well.[50] Likewise, the labor rebellions by the working
masses of the various colonies increased not only imperial and regional
interest and action in the British Caribbean but interest and action within
other sections of the black diaspora. These overlapping events spawned
waves of activism, in and out of the West Indies, which further shaped and
sharpened racialized conceptualizations of the West Indies and the possibilities of a West Indian nation.

For people of African descent, Ethiopia long existed as a symbol of Africa's glorious past, and one of the few symbols of "black" independence during the height of European colonialism.[51] The Italian invasion of this sovereign nation, therefore, sent shock waves throughout the black diaspora. It
forged and stimulated both increased race consciousness and anticolonial
activities among people of African descent across the globe, which in turn
spurred more than a defense of Ethiopia.[52] Not simply an imperialist invasion of one of only three "black nations" at this time, many black people
viewed this "as a setback to their own struggle for self-determination."[53]
Still, some believed that something positive might come from the invasion.
Amy Jacques Garvey, for instance, described Mussolini as "a weapon being
used by the Almighty God to bring Negroes to a realization of their true
position in the world" and "the Italian invasion of Ethiopia as a blessing to

the coloured peoples since it would . . . draw closer together the Coloured Races."[54]

As news of the Ethiopian conflict spread, a range of reactions emerged from across the British Caribbean. These included general resolutions of protest, requests to enlist as soldiers in the Ethiopian military, and demands to the Crown for Great Britain to sanction Italy and support Ethiopia within the League of Nations. At a Friends of Ethiopia meeting in St. Lucia in 1935, attendees "resolved that we, the friends of African freedom, resident in St. Lucia, British West Indies, view with grave concern the present impasse between Italy and Ethiopia, and we feel it is our bounden duty as lovers of peace to express our deep sympathy towards Ethiopia in her present struggles." If Italy was allowed to conquer Ethiopia, they suggested, it would "shatter the hopes of His Britannic Majesty's coloured subjects for the future peaceful and harmonious intercourse between the various Races of Mankind."[55] From British Guiana a group who described themselves as "loyal subjects of Georgetown, British Guiana, and representatives of various Organisations and Societies of all parts of British Guiana, under the auspices of the Universal Negro Improvement Association" petitioned the Crown for permission to "organise groups of African descent as Contingents, who would voluntarily go to East Africa to assist the said Ethiopian Government to protect and maintain her Liberty and Independency to which Your Majesty's Government had pledged itself."[56] In August 1935 the Afro-West Indian League in Trinidad asked "His Majesty's Government to do all in its power in order to ensure that the independence and sovereignty of the ancient Empire remain inviolate and respected" and expressed "regrets that His Majesty's Government has placed an embargo on the shipment of arms to Ethiopia."[57] In Barbados, supporters of Ethiopia held prayer meetings and raised money for the Ethiopian Red Cross.[58] From Dominica, J. R. Ralph Casimir wrote directly to the Ethiopian minister in London to assure him that "Negroes (Africans and people of African descent) throughout the World are prepared to help Ethiopia in her hour of distress."[59]

There was also an outpouring of support for Ethiopia in Jamaica, where the Rastafarian movement originated earlier in the decade, and where Garveyism remained a potent ideology. The resolution of a public meeting in early October 1935 among "loyal coloured Jamaicans" in Kingston claimed it was "part of [their] racial duty to express unanimous resentment against any effort to infringe upon the sovereignty of Ethiopia."[60] Around the same time, the UNIA branch of Spanish Town asked to "be given a chance to go and fight for the purpose of preserving the glory of the one and only Negro

Empire." They urged that their request "be speedily granted so as to save what we regard as a symbol of our own civilization."[61] In the same month, the UNIA of Kingston petitioned King George V along similar lines for the right to fight for Ethiopia. While they offered assurances that they would not be "less loyal to Your Majesty's Crown and Person and to the British Empire," they argued it would be a "sad condition" if they were "unable to rush to the assistance of others of their Race."[62]

For many West Indians, their defense of Ethiopia provided an opportunity and catalyst for action within the Caribbean, for their own self-determination, and not simply a rhetorical imagining of diasporic bonds. Colonial officials on the ground in the Caribbean closely monitored these activities. In a letter to the Colonial Office, the Jamaican governor noted, "There is undoubtedly strong feeling in this Colony in support of the Abyssinians against Italy. There is also a risk of this feeling being inflamed on racial grounds and being used as a pretext for demonstrations which have nothing to do with the War."[63] In the fall of 1935 a colonial official described a meeting about "the Ethiopian business" where "the crowd refused to sing the National Anthem," and hinted at the possible growth of anti-British sentiment as well.[64] Another report claimed "this wretched Italy Abyssinia business has done an enormous amount to cause bitter feeling amongst the West Indians of African descent in these islands," and reported that a crowd gathered near the cable station in Grenada cheered, "We win, we win," after a false report of an Abyssinian victory and the death of an Italian garrison.[65] Two telegrams from the governor of British Guiana noted that the "African community is powerfully affected by Italian Abyssinian conflict which presents itself to them as [a] colour question." He even suggested that a warship be kept in the area in case more widespread trouble ensued.[66] The governor of the Windward Islands, who believed that the Italian-Ethiopian conflict "intensified" racial feelings in both St. Lucia and St. Vincent, put forth a similar suggestion.[67]

Following a public meeting in St. Kitts that included a speech by Marryshow ("the champion of black people of the British West Indies"), the acting governor of the Leeward Islands echoed concerns about possible racial strife in the colonies. While Marryshow's speech contained "nothing of such a nature as to require serious notice . . . it has not served to do anything other than to create animosity amongst ignorant and excitable people and to elevate in their minds the idea that Mr. Marryshow and those of his persuasion are destined to rescue the coloured races from the harshness of British rule, and to provide them with a desirable alternative."[68] As

J. L. Maffey summarized in his letter to the Lords Commissioners of the Admiralty, "the Italo-Abyssinian conflict has aroused feelings of indignation amongst the negro population of those dependencies, which, it seems certain, have already been exploited in certain colonies in such a way as to provoke active disorder and to stimulate anti-white feeling."[69]

Outcry and protest over the Italian invasion of Ethiopia was also widespread among the expatriate West Indian and African American communities of Black America. In the United States, black newspapers offered extensive news and opinions on the conflict.[70] In May 1935 the *Crisis* carried a long article by George Padmore titled "Ethiopia and World Politics." Padmore placed the invasion within the context of ongoing conflicts in Europe between older imperialist powers and fascist regimes that sought to expand their territories. Noting the racism inherent in both ideologies, including a shared belief that black peoples were not fit for self-rule, Padmore urged "every black man and woman to render the maximum moral and material support to the Ethiopian peoples in their single-handed struggle against Italian fascism, and a not too friendly world."[71]

This support was evident in the numerous public meetings held under the auspices of various societies. New groups such as the Provisional Committee for the Defense of Ethiopia, the Friends of Ethiopia, and United Aid for Ethiopia, as well as several existing ones, answered the call for Ethiopia.[72] The West Indian Federation of America, for example, expressed their dismay at the British embargo of arms to Ethiopia and called "upon England to take definite action to frustrate Mussolini in the attempt to subjugate Ethiopia."[73] Though composed primarily of West Indians, they made a concerted effort to work with African Americans for the cause of racial uplift. The defense of Ethiopia provided a concrete opportunity. In late July 1935 a WIFA meeting of "1500 West Indians and Americans unanimously pledged loyalty to Ethiopia in her defensive measures against Mussolini's aggression" and "expressed the grave concern of the 15,000,000 Negroes in the Americas in the Italo-Ethiopian crisis."[74] The following year, a meeting cohosted by the Caribbean Union and United Aid for Ethiopia protested "the attitude of Great Britain, particularly, and France, in deciding to lift sanctions against Italy and concede the annexation of Ethiopia." Their resolution stated, "West Indians and Americans of African descent demand British Government maintain sanctions against Italy, and keep pledged word to maintain Ethiopian independence."[75]

Across the Atlantic, the Ethiopian conflict helped politicize some black organizations and fueled the creation of others in Great Britain. Although its black population remained small in comparison to Harlem, London during the 1930s increasingly came to play a crucial role in the development and expansion of black diaspora politics. Here, as in the United States, one could find an assortment of race-conscious activists and organizations, from moderate reformers to radical internationalists. Within these black communities there were undoubtedly intra-racial tensions between Africans and West Indians, similar to those between African Americans and West Indians in the United States. Nevertheless, as in Harlem, many were still able to cooperate often in the common struggle for black liberation in Africa and the black diaspora, without the homogenization of their tactics and more specific goals.[76]

The League of Coloured Peoples (LCP) was one London-based organization that took up the cause of Ethiopia. Founded in 1931 by Harold Moody, a Jamaican physician, the LCP began as a conservative Christian-oriented group that worked for interracial cooperation and against the "colour bar" in England.[77] Although it was firmly pro-British and quite moderate, ideologies of racial uplift and black self-determination shaped much of the LCP's actions in the 1930s. There was some debate on whom the LCP meant by "coloured peoples," given that some members of the LCP applied this inclusively to all nonwhites, while Moody and others largely restricted their definition to peoples of African descent.[78] Although the LCP welcomed the participation of all races, and was undoubtedly interested in the welfare of all colonial peoples, the organization overwhelmingly focused on and prioritized peoples of African descent and the issues affecting them.[79] With such a focus, it is unsurprising that the LCP took up the cause of Ethiopia following the Italian invasion. In the midst of the conflict, the LCP moved beyond its limited program within England to rally support for Ethiopia, including protests to the Crown and the raising of funds for refugees.[80] This expanded role within black diaspora politics set the stage for the LCP's increased activism over the next decade alongside other black diaspora-focused groups.

Various other black organizations in England also supported Ethiopia. The West African Students' Union (WASU), which included African and Afro-Caribbean students, protested the invasion of Ethiopia and condemned England's inaction.[81] More important, in 1935 Amy Ashwood Garvey and C.L.R. James created the International African Friends of Ethiopia (IAFE), which brought together a collection of West Indian and African activists including such Pan-Africanists as George Padmore, T. A. Marryshow, and Jomo Kenyatta. Though the IAFE would exist for only a few years before giving way to a more virile reincarnation, it proved an important group in rallying support for Ethiopia, especially in London. The IAFE worked "to assist by all means in [its] power, in the maintenance of the territorial integrity and the political independence of Abyssinia."[82]

The Italian invasion of Ethiopia galvanized black diasporic action in the mid-1930s. In many ways it increased black activism on both sides of the Atlantic and strengthened the bonds between the British Caribbean, Black America, and Africa. For black populations in the British Empire, the invasion of Ethiopia did more than raise racial consciousness. In the case of Afro-Caribbeans, the inaction of the Crown in defense of Ethiopia further fractured their tenuous bonds to the empire. The notion of colonials as equal British citizens had already been rendered precarious by the previously discussed conditions within the West Indian colonies, as well as the disinterest and failure of the empire to protect its "black citizens" against discrimination in other locales in which they resided (such as antiblack immigration legislation in the circum-Caribbean).[83] Thus, although the invasion of Ethiopia may have taken place on the African continent, its ramifications were far more widespread.

Beginning in British Honduras in 1934 and continuing almost annually through 1939, a series of West Indian labor rebellions (see table 2.1) rocked the British Caribbean. In several colonies these uprisings and strikes spurred the creation of formal, largely middle-class-led political parties with ties to the laboring masses. These events marked a more pronounced entry of the region's working class into the ongoing reform efforts in the West Indies. The political fallout of this era stimulated and bolstered demands for reforms in the region (including self-government and federation), shook the empire's general disregard for the Caribbean colonies, and fueled increased diasporic interest in the area, bringing about what Cary Fraser has called "the twilight of colonial rule" in the West Indies.[84]

The causes of these rebellions included a range of frustrations with existing economic, social, and political conditions. The poor economic state of the colonies, including limited job opportunities, dismal wages, and a high cost of living, combined with poor housing, education, and health services, added to the misery the working class had lived under since emancipation. In addition, the continued exclusion of most West Indians from the various colonial governments of the region, and the obvious racial and class discriminations embodied in these institutions, created an explosive situation.[85]

Table 2.1. Labor rebellions in the British Caribbean (1934–1939)

Year	Colonies
1934	British Honduras
1935	British Guiana, Jamaica, St. Kitts, St. Lucia, St. Vincent, Trinidad
1936	St. Kitts, Trinidad, Barbados, Jamaica, British Guiana
1937	Bahamas, Barbados, Jamaica, Trinidad
1938	British Guiana, Jamaica
1939	British Guiana

Source: Bolland, On the March, passim.

The assortment of activists and organizations that emerged from the labor rebellions displays the continued multiple dimensions in which West Indian reforms were demanded and different nationalisms constructed: islandist, regionalist, and diasporic. Much as in the reform efforts of prior years, some activists focused on their respective colonies and others on the region as a whole. The labor rebellions also produced strong antiracist condemnations of colonialism through both racialized and transracial appeals and visions of the West Indies. In colonies with substantial Afro-Caribbean majorities, working-class rebellions demonstrated the merging of race consciousness and class consciousness among some workers. In colonies with substantial Indo-Caribbean working-class populations, such as Trinidad and British Guiana, labor activism often stressed, albeit with limited success, the shared plight of black and Indian workers in an effort to move beyond divisions of race and ethnicity in the name of working-class solidarity.[86]

The West Indian labor rebellions received significant attention from black activists outside the Caribbean. Similar in surge and range to the protests produced in the wake of Italy's invasion of Ethiopia, which came to deal with far more than simply the struggles of Ethiopia, the reactions of transnational West Indian and black diaspora organizations in Harlem and London to the labor rebellions were swift. While these groups and the black press in the United States reported on the strikes and lent their support to the workers of the region, they also took the opportunity to address what they saw as the bigger issues to which these uprising were connected. Given the racialization of the West Indies, many activists in these organizations described the revolt of West Indian workers primarily as yet another black struggle against colonialism.

The class dimensions of these rebellions and their connections to an inclusive anticolonial struggle were by no means ignored, especially among organization with more internationalist leanings. Black communists were especially interested in the wave of labor protests across the region. In conjunction with the ITUCNW's aim "to defend the independence of Abyssinia, Liberia, Haiti and to fight for the full independence of the Negro toilers in Africa and the West Indies and their right of self-determination in the Black Belt of USA," the *Negro Worker* offered coverage and support for West Indian workers.[87] The front covers of the *Negro Worker* in early 1937 included the image of a muscular black man breaking his chains over a globe with maps of the United States, the West Indies, South America, and Africa. This image portrayed views on the West Indian rebellions as part of a black diaspora struggle quite well.[88] In March 1937, Charles Alexander published an article titled "1937—A New Year of Struggle for West Indian Masses." Alexander offered readers brief summaries of the 1936 strikes in St. Kitts, Trinidad, Barbados, Jamaica, and British Guiana. He also noted support of the Scottsboro Boys within the protests in British Guiana, and praised the widespread support of Ethiopia in almost all of the West Indian colonies. From these actions, he said, "we draw the only logical conclusion: the Negro masses of the West Indies are moving into action." Although the 1936 protests were primarily "economic in character," he concluded that the New Year would see a broadened focus "to include political demands" for the region.[89]

In Harlem, black newspapers such as the *New York Amsterdam News* carried reports of the West Indian labor uprisings and associated violence against West Indian workers, as both old and new organizations supported West Indian labor in conjunction with their broad support of reform and against racial discrimination in the British Caribbean colonies. In an August 1937 meeting marking the 103rd anniversary of emancipation in the West Indies, previously established and new organizations met to outline "an ambitious and far-reaching program of political, economic and social reform in the West Indies." Attendees took up a range of topics—support for the Scottsboro Boys, Ethiopia, and African colonies, protests against Crown Colony government in the Caribbean, and discrimination against black passengers on steamships between the United States and the West Indies—and created resolutions against recent shootings of Trinidadian laborers and in support of labor in the Caribbean.[90]

It was during these years that another important organization appeared within the multinational black community in Harlem—the Jamaica Progressive League (JPL).[91] The JPL was formed in New York City in 1936 by W. A. Domingo, Ethelred Brown, and W. Adolphe Roberts with a specific agenda focused on self-government and dominion status for Jamaica. As declared in *Self-Government for Jamaica*, a booklet based upon speeches by JPL president W. Adolphe Roberts to the British-Jamaicans Benevolent Association in 1936, "Firmly believing that any people that has seen its generations come and go on the same soil for centuries is, in fact, a nation, the Jamaica Progressive League pledges itself to work for the attainment of self-government for Jamaica, so that the country may take its rightful place as a member of the British Commonwealth of Nations." The JPL advocated "universal suffrage in Jamaica and the removal of property qualifications for candidates for public office," as well as "the right of labor unions to function legally." Its immediate concerns were to:

(1) Study economic and social problems of the Island and press for necessary reforms

(2) Foster inter-Caribbean trade and commerce, and all other relations which tend to bring about a closer union of the British West Indian countries

(3) Encourage study of the history, geography and literature of Jamaica, and give aid to all forms of artistic expression by the people

(4) Stimulate among Jamaicans and the United States and other foreign countries a keen interest in home affairs

(5) Adopt any other measure, or take any other action, consistent with the principles and objects stated above[92]

While the JPL was founded in New York, its broad objectives were written so as to be applicable to other expatriate Jamaican communities and to Jamaicans in the colony. The founders planned initially to form additional branches in other US cities, in London, and especially in Jamaica itself. They succeeded in the latter when a Kingston branch opened in 1937 under Walter G. MacFarlane. In coming years the JPL would play a significant role within the politically charged atmosphere of Harlem and in Jamaica, where it became closely associated with Norman Manley's People's National Party (PNP)—a political party formed in Jamaica in 1938—and the push for Jamaican self-government. The vanguard role of the JPL in helping to forge and push the case for self-government in Jamaica both from within the colony and from abroad, including an influential role in helping to establish the PNP itself, offers another example of the importance of transnational and diasporic communities in West Indian freedom struggles.[93]

That said, the JPL proved somewhat of an anomaly within the bustling political scene of mid-1930s Harlem. Islandist organizations based upon specific West Indian colonies had long existed, including the wide range of benevolent societies that focused on their respective communities in Harlem and in the West Indies. And since the late 1920s, many new groups with more regional (West Indian) or diaspora identifications and agendas had been formed, such as the West Indian Federation of America and the Caribbean Union—both of which received support as well as leadership and members from the various islandist benevolent societies. The JPL, however, proved different. Whereas organizations such as the WIFA and CU confirmed regional West Indian identifications and represented the connections between transnational West Indian organizations and black diaspora politics, the JPL, as a transnational Jamaican organization, demonstrates that the regionalism that took root among many West Indian expatriates in these years did not negate all expatriates' islandist perspectives and allegiances.[94] Moreover, such islandism could be and was connected to black diaspora politics in this era too.

Given its specific islandist agenda, ascertaining the JPL's relationships with transnational West Indian and black diaspora organizations in the United States can be perplexing at times. Nevertheless, for many years of its existence, especially from the mid-1930s to the immediate post–World War II era, the islandism of the JPL and the regionalism of other organizations coexisted without too many difficulties. Much of this can be attributed to inherent similarities in many of their demands, as well as overlapping memberships. Some of the leading JPL figures were also leading figures in transnational West Indian and black diaspora organizations.[95] Indeed, despite their stated focus on Jamaica, some members of the JPL did support West Indian regionalism, even over their own coexisting islandism. Like other West Indians, several JPL members capably juggled their islandism and regionalism, emphasizing one or the other at various times.

While the JPL claimed that race would have no place within the movement, as in many other organizations, its members often showed striking racial consciousness. Indeed, while the JPL did not make any direct reference to race within its objectives, as some other groups did, many JPL members connected their objectives in Jamaica to larger regional and diasporic struggles of black peoples. In a 1937 letter to the *Negro Worker*, Domingo claimed that the significance of the JPL was that it demonstrated "some West Indians have realized that their primary fight is right where they are—in the West Indies—and not in Africa. . . . If Jamaica with over a half of the total Negro population of the Caribbean area of the British Empire makes a dent, then others will be inspired to make similar or greater demands."[96] This was strikingly similar to commentary among transnational West Indian and black diaspora groups on a possible Caribbean federation as well as more general demands for self-government. The JPL's goal of self-government may have focused on Jamaica specifically, but the argument that Jamaicans deserved it and were prepared for it did not differ from similar appeals by other groups in support of self-government for the broader West Indies.[97]

Although the JPL shared a common pursuit of self-government with many transnational West Indian and black diaspora groups, its indifference (and at times opposition) to federation did distinguish it from some of these other groups. Because one of the JPL's immediate concerns was to "foster inter-Caribbean trade and commerce, and all other relations which tend to bring about a closer union of the British West Indian countries," and because of the pro-federation stance of some members, many contemporaries (as well as later studies of the group) assumed that the JPL supported a political federation that would include Jamaica—an assumption that, as Birte Timm has noted, was not warranted. In fact, the JPL held no official position on federation in its early years other than periodic remarks by JPL members that before any such configuration could even be contemplated, self-government must be achieved, which was not strikingly different from the position of other groups.[98]

It is important not to read the staunch anti-federation stance of some JPL members in later years, which was often in reaction to specific suggestions or plans for a Caribbean federation, back into these prior years. Moreover, JPL members were divided among themselves over federation. For instance, given his participation in some organizations that did advocate a self-governing federation with dominion status, W. A. Domingo has often been assumed to have supported federation before supposedly betraying the idea in later decades. Yet Domingo was rarely, if ever, as outspoken in favor of federation as some of his associates, especially if Jamaica was to be included. When he did address the subject, he often said that any federation scheme that included Jamaica should be interrogated to insure it truly helped and did not burden Jamaica. At the same time, other JPL members like Ethelred Brown proved to be among the more vocal supporters of federation.[99]

Although the islandism of some Jamaicans within and outside the JPL, as well as the debates over Jamaica's involvement with federation, would prove prophetic in subsequent decades, in the mid-1930s this should not be exaggerated, as the above-noted similarities and cross-pollination between the JPL and other groups of this era matched, if not outweighed, their differences. The JPL, therefore, become another component in the broader struggle for West Indian self-determination and its connections to broader black diaspora struggles.

In the fall of 1937 Reginald Pierrepointe, a Barbadian immigrant who worked as a reporter for the *New York Amsterdam News*, created the West Indian Defense Committee (WIDC) with the help of other Afro-Caribbean activists in Harlem. Outraged by the repressive violence against the striking workers, Pierrepointe and the WIDC sent protests to the Crown and sought to raise relief funds for their defense and general welfare.[100] In October the WIDC organized a mass meeting in Harlem to protest "against the wanton slaughter of West Indians in Trinidad-Barbados-Jamaica-St. Kitts and the Bahamas," and offered support for Grantley Adams of Barbados, who was in London pleading the case of Barbadian workers still held in jail.[101] A few months later the WIDC hosted a meeting of five hundred people "to raise funds and map plans for the aid of the victims of the recent labor strife in the islands of Trinidad and Barbados."[102]

Though the WIDC was based in Harlem, its reach extended into the West Indies themselves. In 1938 Hope Stevens, a local Harlem lawyer and WIDC member, was planning a trip to the West Indies to visit family in Nevis. Before his departure Pierrepointe, Richard B. Moore, and others in the WIDC requested that Stevens use this trip to inquire into the ongoing labor disturbances in Barbados and Trinidad. Upon arriving in Barbados, Stevens met with W. A. Crawford, editor of the *Barbados Observer*, and other Barbadian activists. From this meeting sprang the Barbados Labour Party (BLP), renamed the Barbados Progressive League (BPL) before reverting to BLP in subsequent years. The creation of the BLP/BPL further established the ways in which West Indian transnational and black diaspora groups outside the Caribbean helped lead West Indian political development in the colonies on some occasions.[103] Of course, it would be unwise to assume such a group could not have been organized in the West Indies without aid and support from abroad. It would be equally imprudent, however, to diminish the role of activists from the broader diaspora.

Analogous attention to the West Indian rebellions occurred in London. In 1937–38 the *Keys*, one of the League of Coloured Peoples' periodicals, carried various articles that not only informed readers on the labor strife but offered analysis of the problems of the Caribbean and demands for reforms.[104] In December 1937 Grantley Adams spoke before a special meeting of the LCP regarding labor unrest. In town to petition the Colonial Office on behalf of Barbadian workers, Adams offered attendees firsthand reflections on the riots and the causes of them, which he laid at the feet of the "unsympathetic and selfish attitude of the minority of wealthy landowners, merchants and industrialists."[105] By the summer of 1938 the LCP submitted a resolution to the secretary of state for the colonies in support of Jamaican workers involved in strikes there. Moody and the LCP expressed their horror at the killings and general violence "which arose from the effort of the Jamaica workers to improve their intolerable conditions." It also called for an official inquiry into the political and economic structures of the islands and demanded universal free education and the establishment of a University of the West Indies. To ensure that these measures were not "thwarted by local vested interests," the LCP called upon the "the British Government to grant to the people of Jamaica and of all the British West Indies, the same constitutional rights and the same civil liberties as are enjoyed by the people of Britain, including universal adult suffrage, [and] the removal of the property qualification for members of the Legislature." It also requested "a Federation of the West Indies, with complete self-government."[106] Overall, the LCP connected the plight of West Indian workers and the need for reform in the West Indies to the organization's broader diasporic concerns for peoples of African descent.

In the spring of 1937 a new London-based black diaspora organization appeared—the International African Service Bureau (IASB).[107] The IASB grew out of the International African Friends of Ethiopia (IAFE) and included many from that organization, including George Padmore (chair), Amy Ashwood Garvey (vice chair), Jomo Kenyatta (vice chair), and C.L.R. James. One of the primary functions of the IASB was to "enlighten public opinion in Great Britain, especially the working and middle classes, as to the true conditions in the various colonies, protectorates and mandated territories in Africa, the West Indies and other colonial areas."[108] Through their *African Sentinel*, "a journal devoted to the interest of Africans and peoples of African descent, all over the world," followed by the *International African Opinion*, which carried the IASB's motto "Educate-Co-Operate-Emancipate: Neutral in nothing affecting the African Peoples," the IASB came to play a major role in radical anticolonial activities for the next several years.

While cooperative with all who supported their agenda, the IASB's dedication to internationalism, anticolonialism, and antiracism did not belie an explicit prioritization of the black diaspora within the broader struggle against imperialism and fascism. The IASB supported "the demands of Africans and other colonial peoples for democratic rights, civil liberties and self-determination," but described itself specifically as "an organisation representing the progressive and enlightened public opinion among Peoples of African descent."[109] In the first edition of the *African Sentinel*, the IASB stated their goal "to create a connecting link between Africans at home (in Africa) and the Africans abroad (in the West Indies, United States of America and other Western countries) by the transmission of messages and informations, news and views, from one to another, in the most accurate and concise forms." They claimed a willingness to share this information with all "who may be interested in the cause of the progressive advancement of the Africans and peoples of African descent, or who may be disposed to enlighten the public through our medium on matters of social, economic, political, educational and other importance, as well as on questions of international and inter-racial significance, regardless of colour or creed." Nonetheless, they affirmed a "desire to make it clear also, that why we shall, at all times, be willing to co-operate with one and all in the above lines, we cannot afford to overlook the fundamental cause for which we are out, and which is to advocate and defend, as far as it may be possible, the cause of the oppressed sections of humanity, and particularly of the great majority of Africans and peoples of African descent who are scattered all over the face of the globe."[110] In fact, while the organization accepted as *associate* members "Europeans and members of other races, who sympathize with the aims and objects of the Bureau and desire to demonstrate in a practical way their interest in Africans and peoples of African descent," it reserved active membership for Africans and people of African descent.[111]

Some of the earliest activities of the IASB focused on the West Indian labor rebellions. Numerous articles and editorials, alongside various public demonstrations in London, offered extensive coverage of the strikes and support for the workers in the late 1930s.[112] In 1938 the IASB published "An Open Letter to the Workers of the West Indies and British Guiana" thanking the West Indian workers for their actions which "served to dramatise before the world and to bring home to the British people the fact that all is not well in [their] island homes" and forced the empire to note publicly the dreadful social and economic conditions of the West Indies. Pledging support for all the workers in the West Indies, irrespective of race, as part of their push for working-class solidarity, the IASB letter urged the workers to maintain their struggles for justice and equality via trade unionism and continued political action, lest the British Government forget them. Such actions, the IASB believed, would form "a solid and firm basis for the building of a West Indian Liberation Movement striving for self-determination and political federation."[113] While the organization demonstrated support for class solidarity and interracial cooperation, given its overall focus and the ways in which the West Indies were invariably perceived as part of the black diaspora, one cannot dismiss the racial dimensions of the IASB's interest in and support for the Caribbean colonies.

As intra-regional and black diaspora activists offered their assessments of the continuing labor unrest, the British launched their own investigations in the late 1930s. Following the pattern of previous decades, various commissions and reports examined the disturbances.[114] The West India Royal Commission of 1938–1939 (better known as the Moyne Commission) undertook the most substantial investigation. Organized in August 1938, the Moyne Commission investigated "the social and economic conditions in Barbados, British Guiana, British Honduras, Jamaica, the Leeward Islands, Trinidad and Tobago, and the Windward Islands" and was charged to make recommendations on these issues.[115]

Designed to take a broad survey of opinions on conditions in the region, the Moyne Commission went far beyond previous commissions. Some within the Colonial Office hoped the Moyne Commission would reaffirm British control in the region and reinvigorate West Indian faith in the empire. As Cary Fraser has argued, "The establishment of the West Indian Royal Commission was perceived as providing breathing room for the development of new policy" and a chance to reinvigorate the empire's "*mission civilisatrice*."[116] Ultimately, however, "What distinguish[ed] the Moyne Commission from its predecessors was the recognition by the Colonial Office, for the first time, that the unrest in the West Indies was neither the work of agitators, nor blind protest, but the expression of a more fundamental malaise in the region as a whole."[117]

During its investigation, the Moyne Commission received some 789 memoranda in the West Indies and London.[118] These testimonies offered a wide range of opinions on the reasons for the unrest in the Caribbean and on possible cures for the region's problems. While most submissions supported some level of reform, the extent of these reforms was dictated by the political attitudes of the witnesses. Some people and organizations, which remained staunchly pro-British, recognized the economic aspects of the unrest but called for little more than moderate reforms of current fiscal policies in the region.[119] Others argued the West Indies' backward and immoral nonwhite majorities constituted the biggest deficiency of the region, and called for a rededication of Britain's presence and policy to aid in the continuing civilizing mission of British imperialism.[120] These testimonies mirrored those of many previous commissions. However, unlike the previous investigations, the Moyne Commission also received a significant amount of testimony from the very populations damned by others. Indo-Caribbean populations, which were especially significant in Trinidad and British Guiana, submitted various memoranda on their particular status within the colonies.[121] Specific Afro-Caribbean concerns were also addressed in various testimonies, such as one from the Negro Progress Convention of British Guiana, which petitioned the commission for support of agricultural and industrial education in the colony similar to the Tuskegee model in the United States.[122]

Aside from the economic and social concerns within many testimonies to the Moyne Commission, several organizations used the opportunity to press for political reform in the West Indies, including representative government, self-government, and even federation. In January 1939, elected members of the legislative council in Trinidad and Tobago demanded an increase in the number of elected council members, the right of women to run for council seats, and an expanded franchise.[123] West Indian labor unions also submitted numerous testimonies. The *West Indian Pilot*, the "Official Organ of the Trade Union Movement" in Trinidad and Tobago, critiqued the educational and health systems on the islands, called for an end to discrimination in employment, and demanded the right of assembly, freedom of speech, and peaceful picket.[124] Progress toward federation proved an important goal among several labor unions and their supporters, including the Trinidad Labour Party, the Committee for Industrial Organisation, and the British Guiana and West Indies Labour Congress. The Committee for Industrial Organisation urged Parliament to "take early and active steps to grant to British Guiana and the West Indies SELF-GOVERNMENT and FEDERATION," which they claimed the vast majority of the West Indian population believed was required to improve conditions in these "neglected . . . outposts of the British Empire." The British Guiana and West Indies Labour Congress had supported federation since the 1920s, and at their recent conference in 1938, Marryshow famously said the region could "federate or disintegrate." In their memo to the Moyne Commission, the organization asked for a federal constitution for the region "if they are to have efficient and progressive Government."[125] In such cases, federation appears defined largely as an intra-regional project of colonial advancement within the empire.

As can be expected, transnational West Indian and black diaspora organizations based outside the West Indies also took the opportunity to submit memoranda and testify before the Moyne Commission. Many activists within these groups doubted the effectiveness of another British commission in addressing the woes of the West Indies, especially one that was all-white.[126] Following the announcement of the Moyne Commission, the IASB immediately criticized its composition. "Besides an overweight of Conservatives, the membership of the commission includes no African or person of African descent," and therefore, the IASB argued, "the Royal Commission to the West Indies can inspire no initial confidence in the success of its efforts."[127] The IASB also wondered what another commission could possibly accomplish. "The Royal Commission is a bluff. The Government knows the condition of the people. Commissions, Royal or otherwise, have reported it over and over again. Why is nothing done? Because the white officials are the friends of the white capitalists; by means of dividends and large salaries, golf, tennis and whisky, bravely, bearing the white man's burden."[128] A few months later the IASB warned the workers of Barbados to "not be misled by belief in the efficacy of the Royal Commission. There have been many Commissions and too little action. This is just a method of killing time, in the hope that the temper of the masses may die down and the long-awaited reforms be staved off."[129]

From Harlem, W. A. Domingo offered similar criticism and doubt regarding the Moyne Commission.

After all, the men and women on the Commission are just human and subject to all frailties of humanity. They were born in England and were doubtless taught many things about the glorious mission of their countrymen to civilize the world. They have been perhaps subtly convinced of the essential superiority of their own racial stock. It is difficult to conceive that they have not been at some time thrilled by the eloquent imperialistic poems of the late Rudyard Kipling. They have heard and perhaps accepted the doctrine of the "white man's burden." It is most likely that they have read or heard about Haiti and concluded in a hazy fashion, like most white people, that self-government by people of African descent is bound to be a ghastly failure.[130]

Despite such initial concerns, several West Indian and black diaspora activists and organizations *outside* the Caribbean submitted testimonies to the Moyne Commission, among them the League of Coloured Peoples, International African Service Bureau, Negro Welfare Association (NWA), Jamaica Progressive League, and United Aid for Peoples of African Descent (UAPAD). Just as important as their actual testimony was the mandate that many of these organizations claimed to hold to speak *for* the West Indies.[131] Given the overarching focus of most of these groups on the larger black diaspora, their testimonies further demonstrate how many saw the West Indies as an integral part of the black diaspora, and the racial dimensions of West Indian political development.

Acting upon their professed mandate to speak on behalf of the West Indies, and interestingly referring to themselves as "West Indian organizations in London," the IASB, LCP, and NWA submitted a lengthy memorandum to the Moyne Commission in September 1938.[132] Within its discussion of poverty, poor housing, health, education, illiteracy, and overcrowded conditions, the memo provided both racial and class analyses of the West Indian situation. Noting the continued domination of these colonies by the small white population, which it estimated as only 3.5 percent of the total, the memo called for the extension of civil liberties and the institution of democratic government. It demanded representative government, universal adult suffrage, the removal of property qualifications for legislators, the abolition of the Crown Colony system, and the creation of a federation. "The establishment of democratic government fully representative of the people of these territories is an essential prerequisite to the abolition of the inhumane conditions now prevailing, and a first step on the road towards that goal, which is *Federation and Dominion status*." At the conclusion of their memorandum, the groups issued a stern warning to the Colonial Office—one that hinted at a growing racial consciousness among Afro-Caribbeans, whose numbers they estimated as 82 percent of the West Indies' population.

> In 1833 there was reason to apprehend a universal Negro rebellion for freedom, and emancipation was granted from above to prevent the cataclysm of emancipation from below, as had occurred in San Domingo. Similarly today, when the rape of Ethiopia has given a great stimulus to growing Negro consciousness, it is not a question of rebellions if, but rebellions unless, democratic government is granted. In the words of the report of Hon. E.F.L. Wood (Lord Halifax), "it would

be wise to avoid the mistake of endeavoring to withhold a concession ultimately inevitable until it has been robbed by delay of most of its usefulness and all of its grace."[133]

Harold Moody, president of the LCP, and Peter Blackman, president of the NWA, presented further oral testimony before the Moyne Commission on 29 September 1939 in conjunction with this joint memorandum. Their presentation continued their general critique of the Crown Colony system and the need to build a stronger "West Indianness" in the region. Blackman said that a federation would go far in building such a regional conscious-ness, though his call here for federation appeared more gradual than the immediate creation demanded by many others in this era.[134]

This joint memorandum and the accompanying oral testimony provide a prime example of the ways in which groups operating upon different po-litical philosophies, with dissimilar approaches and objectives, were able to cooperate in pursuit of a common goal through the frame of black diaspora politics. In this case, a self-governing federation in the British West Indies was just such a goal. Considering the respective platforms of these organi-zations, we can assume there remained some differences in the visions of Caribbean federation between Padmore and the IASB, Moody and the LCP, and Blackman and the NWA. The LCP's more moderate and pro-British attitude primarily viewed federation as a means through which the region could gain its equal place as a dominion within the British Commonwealth. On the other hand, the IASB's more radical political program, with a focus on both the race and class dimensions of colonial oppression, envisioned federation as a more transformative project for the good of the working-class masses and with less concern for continued connections to the empire. Given the communist orientation of the NWA, their views of federation likely mirrored those of the IASB.[135] Despite these differences, and likely some tensions between the IASB and the NWA owing to Padmore's depar-ture (or expulsion) from the Comintern and subsequent personal attacks on him by former colleagues in the Communist Party, these organizations were able to move beyond their own specific political philosophies (at least temporarily) to find a common ground for cooperation based upon their dedication to the achievement of black self-determination.

The Jamaica Progressive League also submitted a memorandum to the Moyne Commission in the fall of 1938.[136] Even before this formal submis-sion, some JPL members had participated as delegates within the Jamaica Deputation Committee, which testified before the Moyne Commission earlier in the year.[137] As for the JPL's own memo, much of it consisted of copies of three JPL booklets: *A Social and Economic Programme for Jamaica* (1938), *Why We Demand Self-Government* (1938), and *Self-Government for Jamaica* (1936). These publications were already well circulated among Jamaican, West Indian, and black diaspora activists, but their submission to the Moyne Commission sought to place the JPL's demand for Jamaican self-government and dominion status directly before the British government.[138]

In February 1939 the New York–based United Aid for Peoples of African Descent submitted a memorandum to the Moyne Commission through the Colonial Co-Operative Society in British Guiana. Active since at least 1937, the UAPAD, like many parallel organizations, represented both African Americans and West Indians and cooperated with a variety of black organizations in the New York area. Although the group had focused primarily on providing aid to Ethiopia in previous years, by the end of the 1930s their objectives turned to, among others things, colonization and development in British Guiana. In their memorandum to the Moyne Commission, the UAPAD issued a particularly race-conscious call for the development of British Guiana for Afro-Caribbeans. Without any mention of the significant Indo-Caribbean population already residing in the colony, the UAPAD claimed, "The Colony of British Guiana constitutes the rightful heritage of the people of African descent in the British Caribbean area; and this heritage ought not to be surrendered to another race." Although the issue of federation was not mentioned specifically in their memorandum, the presentation of British Guiana as a potential site for West Indian migration and a black homeland undoubtedly connects with the long-standing support of federation with distinctive undertones of racial uplift by some UAPAD leaders, including A. M. Wendell Malliet, their executive vice president.[139]

As the Moyne Commission completed its far-reaching investigation of the West Indies, many in and out of the West Indies anxiously awaited the completion of the report. Although there remained substantial doubt about what would come of the investigations, rumors swirled of possible far-reaching economic, social, and political reforms. At the close of 1938, an article in the *Pittsburgh Courier* claimed that the Moyne Commission appeared ready to propose the creation of a self-governing West Indies federation with dominion status similar to Canada's. It doubted, however, that self-government would solve all the ills of the region "because the great estates will still be in the hands of the few white folk who spend their time and money abroad."[140] In the summer of 1939, Malliet noted in the *New York Amsterdam News*, "Standing at the crossroads of destiny, 3,000,000 Negroes in the British West Indies look to the report and recommendations of the West Indies Royal Commission to open the way for a New Deal under the Union Jack."[141]

Unfortunately, the outbreak of World War II, which had been mounting and eventually erupted as the Moyne Commission was completing its mission, delayed the complete release of the commission's report. Fearful that it could be used as negative propaganda during the war, the British government would not release the full report until 1945. Instead, an abbreviated "recommendations" report was published in 1940. On the issue of constitutional reform, the commission took a middle ground between the demands for "immediate and complete self-government" and the calls for an extension of autocratic rule favored by some officials, with recommendations to make the various legislative councils "as truly representative as possible" through universal adult suffrage, though the committee differed on whether this should be immediate or gradual. On the matter of closer union or federation, the commission found that instituting such a structure would not alone solve the "pressing needs of the West Indies." However, it was "the end to which policy should be directed." For now, they suggested "combining the Leeward and Windward Islands in one federation on the lines of that existing in the former group."[142]

These suggestions were far from what many had envisioned. Upon their release, the LCP submitted a "Memorandum on the Recommendations of the West India Royal Commission" to the Colonial Office detailing its analysis of the commission's recommendations. Overall, there was frustration that the Moyne recommendations had not done enough. Moody and the LCP maintained that the recommendations were at their "weakest on economic and political questions."[143] In regard to federation, the LCP was pleased to see that the Moyne Commission recognized the need for federation in the region, but was troubled that the commission only advocated a small-scale federal experiment combining the Leeward and Windward colonies at this time. The LCP rebuffed the suggestion that a limited administrative federation in the eastern Caribbean could offer definitive conclusions on larger political federation, and counter-suggested a larger political (rather than solely administrative) federation in the eastern Caribbean to include British Guiana, Trinidad, Barbados, and the Windward and Leeward Islands.[144] "Rightly or wrongly," the LCP concluded, "West Indians are 'fed up' with protestations that Britain holds democracy for them as their ultimate achievement; they will judge the Colonial Office by what it offers now, and not what it promises for the future."[145]

For now, many of the reforms were inevitably put on hold due to World War II. Just as the chaotic atmosphere of the 1930s labor rebellions had created an opportunity for increased activism in the West Indies and the black diaspora, so would the Second World War.

World War II

During World War II, the British Empire struggled for its very existence on multiple fronts. On one hand, the British faced the obvious military threat of Nazi Germany and its Axis allies in Europe, as well as in various colonial areas of Asia and Africa. Compounding the ways in which these military struggles pushed the empire to the brink of destruction at times, particularly in the early years of the war, the empire also faced challenges from both its allies and its own colonial populations. The United States, which had already established significant spheres of influence within the Hispanophone and Francophone Caribbean, was encroaching on the British West Indies during the war years. And various vigorous anticolonial movements that confronted the empire used the chaos of the war years to push their demands further.

The war certainly stalled many of the official inquiries and discussions on reform in the West Indian colonies, but in most cases it did not abate the continued demands. Labor unrest and the associated expansion of West Indian nationalisms (islandist and regionalist), both of which drew support from various anticolonial groups in the broader black diaspora, continued the push for self-government and, on the part of many, federation throughout much of the war. While the Crown did institute some reforms within the Caribbean in the midst of war, including the Colonial Development and Welfare Act and the liberalization of some colonial constitutions, such actions did not subdue the increasing calls for self-government and self-determination in these colonies.

Within the anticolonial struggles of the late 1930s and early 1940s, many black diaspora organizations, particularly those associated with black internationalism, supported and collaborated with various other colonial peoples in their fight against imperialism and colonialism. In recent years, scholars such as Gerald Horne and Nico Slate have examined connections between African American and Indian freedom struggles in the twentieth century. Robin D. G. Kelley, Minkah Makalani, and Marc Gallicchio, among others, have also noted connections between black anticolonial activism and Asian nations such as China and Japan.[146] These activities speak to the dedicated internationalism of many black diaspora activists. However, it is not unreasonable to assume some of these anticolonial collaborations were also based on the adage "My enemy's enemy is my friend." For instance, many black diaspora activists certainly supported the right of India to self-government, while also recognizing that its liberation would be a significant blow to the British Empire. Support of an inclusive anticolonial activism for all colonial peoples did not belie the coexistence of a prioritized, racialized anticolonialism focused on the struggles of Africans on the continent and African-descended populations in the black diaspora—not least the British West Indies, whose struggle for liberation continued to be perceived by many as having significant connections to African, African American, and other black freedom struggles, given the racial heritage of the Afro-Caribbean majority.

The IASB's *The West Indies To-day* provides an example of such anticolonial activism. Published in the late 1930s as labor unrest continued in the West Indian colonies and Europe moved closer to war, this booklet offered readers a fairly de-racialized overview of the historical background and current social, economic, and political conditions in the region, but its call for the building of a "New Jerusalem" presented a particularly race-conscious vision of West Indian liberation and nation building. "How long it will be before black humanity comes into its own on the shores of the Caribbean no one can tell, but the prospect is a challenge which West Indians, at home and abroad, will not leave unanswered."[147]

In 1939 IASB executive secretary T. R. Makonnen's "Plea for Negro Self-Government" more explicitly demonstrated this sense of a racialized anticolonialism within the broader anticolonial struggle. While his focus on black self-government aligned with the agenda of the IASB, his article addressed more than self-determination. It questioned the very idea of cooperation among colonial peoples, given the antiblack sentiments among other nonwhite populations in some colonies.

All sections of humanity, including the exploited of other lands, try to subject the Negro. Many people deserted and despised like the African in their own historical homeland—Jews, Indians, Assyrians, Chinese, Arabs, etc.—as soon as they come into contact with the Negro, whether in his homeland Africa or in the West Indies, at once become one with a dominating class in interest and outlook, endeavoring in common to exploit him. For some reason or other they cease to regard him as one among them, ruthlessly exploited and dominated by an alien oppressor. Their class interest and class psychology becomes at once a basis for unity. They discover that their interest, instead of being one with the Negro in their home of adoption, is tied up organically with a deeper historical past founded upon language, cultural similarity, and sentimental attachments.

In spite of this inescapable fact which stands as a monument in Africa and the West Indies, the Negro is being advised by those among his own people, who are attempting to lead him, that his interest and future are much more secured by an alignment with the supposedly oppressed racial groups who are also his own economic oppressors. While desiring at times to accept this as a tactical programme for a basis of unity among the oppressed, I cannot allow myself to be misled, and at the same time mislead the masses of our people into believing that this policy will result in their benefit.[148]

While recognizing the important diaspora connections between black colonial struggles, Makonnen also recommended that peoples of African descent outside Africa focus primarily on the struggles within their own homelands first, which would aid the cause of Africans on the continent as well.

If the African peoples of the West are to advance, they must intensify their growing desire for complete national independence. They must aim in political philosophy and corresponding action at the establishment of a complete economic, social and political control of their own destinies. By all means let them enshrine Africa in their hearts, but let them also be conscious of their duty to the country in which they live and from which they draw their sustenance. Let them combat imperialism on their own doorstep, for only by so doing can they precipitate the emancipation of all the African races and by attacking on many fronts, at last deliver the continent of Africa from bondage.[149]

As an expatriate West Indian himself (from British Guiana), it is likely that Makonnen's plea intended to speak directly, though not solely, to the Afro-Caribbean majorities in the British West Indies. While some of his colleagues in the IASB were not as candid on the issue of antiblack racism among other colonial peoples at this time, much of Makonnen's plea, especially the call for black populations in areas outside Africa to not forsaken the black freedom struggles in their own lands, aligned with the IASB's agenda. From this perspective, West Indians (and their allies) needed to commence their own version of Black America's "Double V" (or "Triple V") campaign for victories abroad and at home, including the fight against fascism, against colonialism, and for self-government.[150]

In the early years of World War II, black diaspora activists and organizations debated the reasons for the war, questioned whether either side should be supported, and shared a determination to not allow the war to sidetrack their programs and the progress made in recent years. From London, the IASB issued multiple manifestos in opposition to the war. Appealing to all colonial peoples, as well as white workers, the IASB argued that the war was not about saving "poor little Poland" or Czechoslovakia, but an imperialist war to prevent Germany from expanding its own empire at the expense of colonial powers such as Britain and France. Much like the First World War, this Second World War was not about saving or extending democracy, especially given the fact that Britain and France denied it to "hundreds of millions of coloured peoples in Africa, India, the West Indies, Indo-China, Morocco, Tunis, Algeria and the other territories too numerous to mention." In specific sections dedicated to black populations, the IASB asked:

> What do black folks know about democracy? There is as much democracy for the natives in Africa . . . as for Negroes in Mississippi. The Africans have as much freedom and liberty in their own countries as the Jews enjoy in Hitler's Germany. . . . And what do the Negroes get out of the last war which should make them enthusiastic about the present? Nothing. Today they enjoy less democracy in their own countries than they did in 1914. As for self-determination? Abyssinia, the last of free Africa, is sufficient answer.[151]

As for the West Indies specifically, the IASB declared, "after a hundred years of so-called emancipation, [they] are still denied the most elementary right of human beings. When you ask for bread they give you hot lead!"[152]

Despite concerted efforts by British officials to sway the influential expatriate West Indian communities in the United States to maintain their alleged loyalty to the empire in the early years of the war, transnational West Indian and black diaspora activists did not unequivocally do so.[153] Shortly after the beginning of World War II, an article by Reginald Pierrepointe in the *New York Amsterdam News* presented several concerns about the war. Following a brief summary of West Indian working-class opposition to conscription in service of the empire, as reported by the *Barbados Observer*, and for many of the same reasons as the IASB's stance against the war, Pierrepointe worried that the war would impede the momentum for reform in the West Indies by giving the merchants and planters "a new lease on existing conditions and a new grip on affairs." He also lamented how war regulations would inevitably be enacted that could be used against activists in the region. Pierrepointe closed with a "hope for war's speedy conclusion, or the opportunity an Empire crack-up might give them to strike for confederation and perhaps nationhood under the protection of the Monroe Doctrine."[154]

Various groups weighed carefully the costs and rewards of the war in relation to their respective agendas. During the fall of 1939 a series of proclamations and public meetings in Harlem and the wider New York City area addressed the war's connections to both the wider black diaspora and the West Indies specifically. In September the Jamaica Progressive League hosted a public meeting concerning the war. The JPL's resolution pledged support for the empire but also took the occasion to reemphasize that all nations, regardless of size, race, or status, deserved self-government. Moreover, they argued, their support of the empire in the current war did not mean the JPL would "abate its campaign or abdicate its right to struggle for self-government in Jamaica in order that the people of the island may enjoy some of the political blessings for which they are willing to make the supreme sacrifice on behalf of others."[155]

The following month the Caribbean Union hosted a forum, "The European War in Relation to the West Indian People," which featured familiar West Indian and black diaspora activists such as A. M. Wendell Malliet, W. A. Domingo, Richard B. Moore, Charles A. Petioni, and Hope Stevens. As in most such meetings, there was not a unanimous "West Indian" opinion. Malliet argued in favor of assistance to the Allies with subsequent conferences on the status of colonies, while Moore countered with what would become his familiar stance against support for the British. Overall, the "majority of the speakers were for the non-participation of the islanders in the war on the ground that it is a white man's war or an imperialistic war." The meeting's resolution denounced the war as another imperialist venture and argued that "colored peoples of the world" should not support Britain and France as long as those empires denied self-rule to African and West Indian colonies.[156]

At a CU meeting in mid-November, the debate over support of the war continued. In the course of this meeting W. A. Domingo argued, "British Negroes should fight for Britain if she is in danger of defeat, not because we love her but because . . . we hate Fascism more than we do British Imperialism." He claimed that while he disliked "both intensely as the stranglers of the legitimate aspirations of our people in Africa and elsewhere to control their own affairs in their own interests," at this time fascism was the greater threat to the cause of black liberation, which he consistently prioritized within his anticolonial activism.[157]

In the months between December 1939 and June 1940, Domingo and Richard B. Moore took part in a series of debates in Harlem and surrounding communities on whether or not "British Colonial Negroes" should support the empire. Domingo recalled that most of these meetings were characterized by his own continuous support for the British in the face of the greater evil of fascism, while Moore repeatedly argued against supporting the British, given their own record of horrendous treatment of black colonials throughout the empire.[158]

As expatriate West Indian and other black diaspora activists debated the war and its possible negative effect upon the momentum for reform, the pursuit of self-government, and for many federation, remained a crucial concern. In July 1940 the *Crisis* reprinted an article from the *Chicago Defender* as its "editorial of the month." Within a discussion of loyalty to the Crown, the author presented the creation of a federation as a means to meet demands for West Indian self-determination while also rallying support for the Crown beyond the current dubious debates. "We believe that if West Indians were told they were at liberty to create a federation of the West Indian peoples, a government of their own, for themselves and their posterity, such a flood of loyalty and love for the 'mother' country would go forth that the ranks of the liberation army would be filled overnight."[159] Though such a move would likely have raised support for the Crown, the future status of the British West Indian colonies, including their very existence as a part of the empire, remained a matter of much debate in the early years of the war.

The speed and ease of Nazi victories in Europe during the first year of World War II led to much speculation. As many pondered the possible fall of Great Britain and the collapse of her empire, England increasingly sought greater support from the United States. In the midst of the discussions between the British and Americans, US annexation of the British West Indies, which had been debated periodically since the early twentieth century, reemerged. Among the reasons given for the possible transfer was as (partial) payment of British war debt, or as a security measure to keep the islands from falling into the hands of the Axis should Britain fall.[160] The latter was particular important, considering that the fall of France in the summer of 1940 technically placed French Caribbean colonies under Axis rule.

As US and British officials discussed the possible transfer of the West Indian colonies to the United States, so did the multinational black communities of Harlem. Many of these conversations focused on the impact annexation would have on black people and their respective freedom struggles in the United States and the West Indies. Both pro- and anti-annexation groups, each with some African American and West Indian adherents, routinely employed racial appeals to garner support for their respective stances.

In May 1939 the *New York Amsterdam News* ran an editorial in support of US annexation of the colonies "not only for military and naval protection but also for the social, political, economic and cultural advancement of the millions of people who inhabit them." Though they recognized that many West Indians worried how the overwhelmingly black region would be treated under American rule, they believed such a move provided a clearer path to self-government than continued British rule.[161] Charles Petioni rejected such pro-annexation arguments, which did not consider "the opinions of three million inhabitants of the West Indies, simply because it suits two white nations."[162] Another rebuttal a few weeks later argued for West Indians to continue their push for federation and an eventual place within the British Commonwealth of Nations. Not surprisingly, the racial dimensions of West Indian nation building were emphasized. "West Indian blacks are not only thinking of 'full stomachs.' They want honor, prestige and equality with whites. We also hope that our American brothers will benefit greatly when we gain our hopes in the West Indies. American blacks should, therefore, use what influence and other help they can render to bring about federation of all the British West Indians and mainland colonies."[163]

Debates over the annexation of the British West Indies continued the following year. At a meeting in early January 1940, the Council of Pan-American Democracy, Caribbean Union, Jamaica Progressive League, and several Latin American organizations in the United States employed both racial and pan-American appeals in their protest against "the proposed transfer and sale of the Negro and other peoples inhabiting the European possessions of the Western Hemisphere" without regard to the wishes of the inhabitants themselves.[164] In April another community forum discussed the possible annexation of the West Indies, its effect on West Indians (in and out of the Caribbean), and how it could possibly "influence the American Negro problem."[165]

In May 1940 approximately eight hundred people attended the symposium "The Political Future of the West Indies." Ashley L. Totten, international secretary of the Brotherhood of Sleeping Car Porters and president of the Virgin Islands Civic Association, argued in favor of annexation, stating that it was "ridiculous to hold up the British flag with one hand" and "eat Uncle Sam's food with the other." Much the way activists appealed to notions of racial unity and uplift to garner support for West Indian self-government and federation, Totten used these tactics to rally support for annexation, which he believed would benefit the black populations of both the West Indies and the United States. "The cultural and economic benefits that would come from unity of the American and West Indian Negro in the Western World, would bring us far closer to the solution of the race problem than anything else." Other speakers at the symposium, ones who had long maintained the need for cooperation between West Indians and African Americans, and who routinely used racial appeals to solicit support for West Indian self-government and federation, did not support annexation. Hope Stevens, general secretary of the Caribbean Union, contested Totten's position. He argued the West Indies deserved self-government under a federation, rather than annexation by the United States. Charles Petioni continued his opposition to annexation and stressed "his utter contempt for all who looked upon the West Indies and its people as cattle for sale or barter, and wondered why nobody mentioned a plebiscite or referendum when talking about transfer of the islands to the United States."[166]

In June a letter from Philip Francis, a Jamaican resident of Harlem, addressed the subject further. Despite a recent *New York Times* poll that claimed 81 percent of those surveyed favored US annexation of the West Indies, Francis said the fate of three million West Indians was being settled with little input from West Indians themselves. Like many others who opposed annexation, he argued for greater autonomy and self-government, viewing annexation as a setback for the region. He asked, if American colonists had deserved independence from Britain, why did not West Indians? "Is it because they are a people of African descent?" Francis closed by appealing to the racial consciousness of readers. "It should be remembered that the future of the Negro peoples of the world depends to a very large extent upon their untrammeled freedom to work out their own ways of life as independent peoples. The race will be forever a slave race unless it becomes its own master in it its own land."[167]

The following month, a letter from H. T. Penny appeared to accept annexation as inevitable, and called for the affected populations to make the most of it. "Any practical person should in these times come to grips with realities." Unlike some others, Penny did not assume annexation would prevent a Caribbean federation, and viewed it as a prerequisite to self-government, as opposed to the creation of a self-governing federation many supporters pursued. Therefore, "West Indians who look squarely at the situation should work for the progress of their homelands if and when they are taken over by America. The United American Negro groups with the help of other peoples can secure great advantages for both the American and the West Indian Negro."[168]

Although formal annexation of the British Caribbean colonies remained possible, given the fall of the Netherlands and France to Nazi Germany in the spring and summer of 1940 and the precarious position of Great Britain, the creation of a (temporary) protectorate or trusteeship over British, French, and Dutch Caribbean colonies under United States control emerged as a more likely possibility. Supporters of the idea believed it would keep these colonies from Axis control and provide the security with which many in the US government were most concerned. While the measure could be justified under the Monroe Doctrine, the United States did not wish to act unilaterally and possibly alienate other American republics in the hemisphere. Instead, these and connected matters would be discussed at a Pan-American Conference scheduled for late July 1940 in Havana.[169]

W. A. Domingo, who had doubted the United States would annex the British West Indies because many white Americans would not welcome the formal acquisition of the colonies, given the region's overwhelmingly black population, believed a trusteeship over the colonies to be a more likely scenario.[170] Though Domingo, like many of his counterparts, had long maintained a far-reaching anticolonial agenda, particularly focused on Africa and the black diaspora, in this moment he asserted the immediate focus should be on the West Indies. "My greatest concern now is the future of the colored race. Africa is gone. There is nothing we can do about it. . . . Jamaica and the other Caribbean areas are in the balance." Therefore, despite ridiculing the idea of the region being placed under American and Latin American caretakers, given his belief that West Indian "civilization and culture is equal if not superior to those of most Latin-American coun-tries, and large sections of the United States," he understood this was now a possibility that had to addressed.[171]

As with the recent proposals of US annexation, it appeared the future of the West Indies would be decided without considering West Indian opin-ions. Once again, transnational West Indian and black diaspora activists outside the Caribbean took it upon themselves to speak for their region from abroad. While the various delegates from across the Americas pre-pared to discuss plans for the British and other Caribbean colonies at the Havana Conference, without any direct representation of those islands, West Indians in the United States scrambled to ensure the islands would not be voiceless at this meeting.

In June 1940 a group of West Indian residents of Harlem, most of whom had long been active within black diaspora politics, organized the West In-dies National Emergency Committee (WINEC). With limited time before the Havana Conference, the WINEC took it upon themselves to represent the region.[172] Though small in numbers, this pan-Caribbean group, which included W. A. Domingo (Jamaican) as president, Richard B. Moore (Bar-badian), Charles A. Petioni (Trinidadian), and Ivy Bailey-Essien as vice presidents, Herman P. Osborne (Trinidadian) as secretary, and Arthur E. King (Guianese) as treasurer, came to play a symbolic if not significant role in debates over a possible inter-American trusteeship over the Caribbean colonies.[173]

The WINEC's primary objective was to "lobby for self-determination and self-government of the Caribbean people" at the Havana Conference, especially through appeals to Latin American nations that they assumed might not be receptive to an extension of US hegemony in the hemisphere. Over the next month, Domingo and Moore drafted the WINEC's "Dec-laration of Rights of the Caribbean Peoples to Self-Determination and Self-Government," which declared the organization's official position on the question of a protectorate over European colonies in the Caribbean, es-pecially as it pertained to the British West Indies.[174] On 15 July the WINEC presented its platform to a mass meeting of "more than 2000 West Indians and their friends" in Harlem. Given the reported unanimous approval of its declaration by the cheering audience, the WINEC decided to send a delegate to the Havana Conference "in an effort to protect the rights of the Negro populations of the West Indies, Guianas, and [British] Honduras."[175] Some within the Harlem community doubted the WINEC would gain a favorable result at the conference. Nevertheless, the group's efforts were applauded by some for their "race-consciousness" and the "racial feeling" that prompted their actions.[176]

Hope Stevens, the chosen delegate, arrived at the Havana Conference in late July armed with the WINEC's declaration. With no official standing at the conference, Stevens would not be allowed to formally present the declaration, but it had already been circulated to President Roosevelt, Secretary of State Cordell Hull, foreign ministers' offices, and various press agencies, as well as translated into Spanish and Portuguese. Now he distributed copies to various conference delegates.

The declaration repeatedly stressed the WINEC's firm and irrevocable opposition to "any sale, transfer, mandate, trusteeship, or change of sovereignty" of Caribbean colonies, and voiced displeasure that these matters were being considered without consent of the Caribbean peoples. It began with reference to the inalienable rights of "life, liberty, and the pursuit of happiness." Despite the striking racial consciousness of WINEC members, the declaration presented a rather de-racialized and Pan-American appeal for the right to self-determination and self-government in the Caribbean. "Every nation in the New World developed from the status of a colony or colonies to its present position," which the WINEC believed "should justly render every Pan-American nation sympathetic to the aspirations of the West Indian and Caribbean peoples." The declaration also included two appendices, one of which offered "evidence of the widespread and urgent character of the demands of the Caribbean peoples for self-government and self-determination." That appendix summarized the progress within the British Caribbean toward self-government and included excerpts of various memoranda on the subject to the Moyne Commission from Caribbean organizations within the colonies and the United States. It closed with a final plea for "all the Pan-American Republics to assist them to realize their manifest and inevitable destiny as self-governing and self-determined members of the Pan-American family of nations."[177]

The impact of the WINEC on the Havana Conference and the resulting Havana Act is debatable. On one hand, the WINEC delegation hoped for the support of Latin American delegates who did not want to see an extension of the United States' power in the Caribbean. They received such support from the Argentine delegate Leopoldo Melo, who "championed the rights of the Caribbean peoples to self-government," as well as Cuban leader Fulgencio Batista, who supported Caribbean independence over a mandate or trusteeship in the case of a British defeat in World War II.[178] By the close, however, all twenty-one nations represented at the Pan-American Conference agreed to support the Havana Act and its idea for a Pan-American trusteeship over the region. This undoubtedly disappointed many who had hoped to see a stronger consensus for self-government and against any form of possible occupation. Some, like Metz Lochard, foreign editor of the *Chicago Defender*, claimed the Havana Act provoked "the gravest apprehension among the peoples in the Caribbean," and described it as "one of the most brazen pieces of contemplated international banditry engineered by the United States in recent years."[179]

The Havana Act did authorize a collective Pan-American trusteeship over Caribbean colonies should Great Britain also fall to the Nazis. However, it included a clause that "any act of occupation of those regions would be transitory and provisional, whilst the populace are consulted, in order to enable them freely to form their own Government." This led some to rate the effectiveness of the WINEC in Havana much more positively. In Domingo's view, though some people might underestimate this clause, it marked an important acknowledgment of the right of Caribbean peoples to self-determination and provided a "firm political foundation" for them.[180]

Regardless of the mixed outcomes and interpretations of the Havana Act, the WINEC, renamed the West Indies National Council (WINC) shortly after the Havana Conference, proclaimed the results a major victory and trumpeted its own role over the next several years. Many of the celebratory remarks regarding these actions alluded to the ways in which West Indian nation building remained to many a racialized project with ramifications for and connections to black peoples throughout the diaspora. Multiple newspaper articles referred to the efforts of the WINEC/WINC at the Havana Conference as representing "the demands of the Negro people of the West Indies" despite no explicit mention of race in the WINEC declaration presented in Havana.[181] Similarly, at a roundtable discussion at the University of Chicago, one speaker praised the "powerful influence" of the WINEC in Havana and described it as "West Indian Negroes fighting for the democratic rights of the people."[182] In an August 1940 letter to a colleague in Jamaica, Domingo reflected on the WINEC's/WINC's efforts in Havana and the Havana Act, which he referred to as "the Magna Carta of our future should England be beaten." "At one stroke, and without shedding a drop of blood, the peoples of the West Indies have been guaranteed more rights than they now enjoy . . . [and] won a victory of great value to the Negro race, if properly understood."[183]

Over the next few months, W. A. Domingo claimed growing recognition from "prominent Negroes [who] are beginning to realize the value of the work we did in Havana" that included commendations from Howard Law School dean and NAACP lawyer Charles Hamilton Houston, Howard history professor Charles Wesley, and Max Yergan of the Council on African Affairs.[184] Though Domingo was disappointed that more African Americans did not seem to realize the importance of the WINC's recent activism, possibly because of their focus on their own national problems, he hoped African Americans would come to recognize "the deeper implications of the war and what an improved political status for West Indian Negroes will mean to American Negroes." In a November 1940 letter to the NAACP, Domingo declared that the actions of the WINEC/WINC and the ensuing Havana Act represented "a substantial political gain for the colored race in the Western World." He argued, "I think it is safe to say that this is the first time in the history of the Western World, since the Haitian Revolution, that a group of Negroes, without the backing of a State, succeeded in influencing an international gathering along the lines they desired. This fact and its logical consequence, the possibility of creating new black nations in the Caribbean, should be of the highest significance to American Negroes." If the Germans should win, he said, there was a good chance that the United States itself would become fascist. In that case, "American Negroes will be grateful for the existence of Haiti and perhaps an autonomous West Indies and British Guiana capable of offering them asylum."[185] The reference to an "autonomous West Indies and British Guiana" is vague, but given the fact that the WINC leadership included many longtime and staunch supporters of a Caribbean federation, it likely referred to the WINC's support for "the independence of the West Indian islands and the formation of these islands into a federation of states."[186] Overall, Domingo's pronouncements on the WINC's activities related to the Havana Conference and Act obviously played to notions of diasporic connections between black peoples, and of the potential black homeland(s) in which West Indians and other black populations in the diaspora could prosper.

Much as the possibilities of annexation or the establishment of a trusteeship appeared to threaten these ideas, so did renewed discussions of resettling European refugees in the British Caribbean. As early as 1934, West Indians had noted their disapproval of a League of Nations proposal to resettle 20,000–30,000 Assyrians from Iraq in British Guiana.[187] In 1938, Charles Petioni and A. M. Wendell Malliet cabled the prime minister to register West Indian opposition to the resettlement of German and Austrian (presumably Jewish) refugees. Though they empathized with people suffering under the racist policies of the Nazi regime, they maintained such an addition to the British Caribbean colonies would exacerbate already intolerable economic, social, and political conditions.[188] The UAPAD's 1939 memo to the Moyne Commission, which explicitly established claims over British Guiana as "the rightful heritage of the people of African descent in the British Caribbean area," shared many of the same sentiments. Though they deplored the persecution of Jewish populations in Central Europe, they opposed "any attempt to settle an alien European group within the Colony of British Guiana." One of the most criticized aspects of such a plan was the likelihood of settling refugees in separate sections of the colony, away from the native population. The UAPAD argued that such a resettlement of "subsidized whites" in a segregated area, similar to European settlements in Kenya, would result in the "oppression and exploitation of the Colonial peoples."[189]

Although W. A. Domingo asserted that the struggle for self-government in Jamaica was "not and cannot be waged along racial lines," he was well aware it would give people of African descent in the island "considerable power" with reverberations for black people in other British colonies and the United States.[190] These concerns lay at the heart of his opposition to the settlement of European refugees in Jamaica. Writing in November 1940, he argued that an influx of Europeans to Jamaica, without consulting Jamaicans, would "aggravate the local economic, social and racial" conditions of the colony.[191] "The arrival of the Refugees in the island is a matter of prime social significance" but many "stupid natives don't seem to be able to grasp that fact. They are so pitifully British that they subordinate their own racial interests to those of the Empire—an Empire that is ruled and controlled directly by white people. Whereas there were only about 15,000 whites in the islands today we have or will soon have 25,000."[192] Domingo assumed the arrival of these European refugees could sidetrack progress toward self-determination and self-government. His comments may have addressed conditions in Jamaica, but his overall sentiments spoke to other British Caribbean colonies too.

In the coming years, Harlem-based activism on behalf of the West Indies remained in the vanguard. While various political parties emerged and increased their presence and prowess within the islands, and groups such as the IASB and LCP continued their activism from London, the wartime turmoil and realties of censorship within the empire made US-based activism particularly important in the early year of World War II, especially as US presence in the region increased. As George Padmore claimed in a letter to the *New York Amsterdam News* in August 1940, "Because of the not inconsiderable influence they do and can exert, West Indians in the United States must raise the call for action now. Their brothers in their native lands from their very circumstances rely upon them at this time to push the struggle . . . seeking to exercise imperialistic pressure in the West Indies." He and other West Indians in London suggested the creation of a "constituent assembly" in the United States to consider a program including political independence in the West Indies under a federation to include both British and French colonies, an offer of military bases in the Caribbean colonies in exchange for US military protection of the islands and a nonaggression pact and economic agreements with the United States. Padmore believed this program "would find considerable support among the Negroes of the United States, [with] whom the people of the West Indies are already closely linked culturally, historically, and geographically" and draw these populations even closer together.[193]

While the United States' presence in the British Caribbean had been expanding since the late 1930s, its influence increased significantly in the fall of 1940 with the Bases-for-Destroyers Deal. With this agreement, the United States provided fifty destroyers to the British navy in exchange for a series of ninety-nine-year leases of naval and air bases in various mainland and island British Caribbean colonies, as well as Bermuda and Newfoundland. According to Jason Parker, this deal "signaled British endorsement of the Havana Declaration, essentially inviting the United States to enforce it."[194] This action increased the already growing US hegemony in the region and ensured that any discussion of the West Indian future would now be a three-way conversation between the West Indies, the United Kingdom, and the United States.[195]

West Indians and their allies reacted swiftly to news of the Bases-for-Destroyers Deal. Once again, they were upset that West Indians were not consulted in such a deal, which opened the door for greater US presence in many colonies. Many noted their displeasure at how their lands were given to the United States by the empire, whereas predominantly white colonies like Newfoundland and Bermuda, which were also part of the deal, had been consulted. In a letter to the People's National Party's annual conference in Jamaica, the WINEC/WINC protested "this plain discrimination in favor of Newfoundland."[196] A *New York Amsterdam News* article shortly after the deal said, "West Indian leaders expressed the view that the British wished to save the white populations of Newfoundland and Bermuda the humiliation of having any part of their territories bartered or sold. But the colonies with predominant Negro populations were bartered without consultation or consent." Beyond condemnation of how the deal came to be, was criticism of the deal itself. Speaking on behalf of the Caribbean Union, Charles Petioni maintained the Bases-for-Destroyers Deal was a "subterfuge to defeat the resolutions of the Pan-American Conference held at Havana recently and to frustrate the legitimate political aspirations of the people of the West Indies, who may not hope to attain self-government for 99 years." Despite such protests, there were differing opinions on the possible economic aspects of the deal for the West Indies. Some, including Petioni, contended that the bases could prove to be an economic advantage for the people of the colonies, while others claimed the best jobs would be reserved for imported white workers.[197]

Whether they were pro- or anti-deal, most West Indian and African American observers shared concerns over the possible, and in many minds likely, introduction of US-style Jim Crow discrimination in and around the bases, as well as Americans' disregard of local West Indian laws, customs, and rights.[198] In the fall of 1940, the PNP in association with the WINEC/WINC noted such concerns to the colonial secretary of Jamaica and proposed guidelines for the bases and American workers.[199] In December 1940 the WINC wrote President Roosevelt to ask that Americans in the West Indies not enact Jim Crow policies, and that American soldiers and workers on the bases not exercise what they believed were racist American social customs in the colonies, as they had in the Panama Canal Zone in previous decades.[200] In January and February 1941 the WINC made similar pleas to the secretary of state for the colonies, and requested that the British government protect the local West Indian populations "from all forms of racial discrimination and segregation on the leased areas." In their opinion, "By completely excluding the West Indian peoples from direct participation in the negotiations of the leases . . . the British Government [had] inescapably assumed the heaviest moral responsibility" for protecting West Indians in areas where the bases were being constructed.[201] Writing from Grenada, T. A. Marryshow requested that both local and imperial governments ensure that "the deal will be of social and economic advantage to the people of the West Indies, and that all of their rights and privileges . . . be fortified and safeguarded."[202]

The Bases-for-Destroyers Deal presented additional opportunities for collaboration and cross-fertilization between African American, West Indian, and black diaspora organizations. The NAACP, one of the most prominent African American organizations, had been expanding its in-

ternational and diasporic interests beyond its primarily national platform
in recent years. NAACP interest in the British Caribbean dated at least to
March 1939. In that year Walter White and Norman Manley shared correspondence concerning the platforms of the NAACP and PNP, with the
latter noting his desire to become a subscriber to the NAACP's *Crisis*.[203]
A few months later the NAACP declared its solidarity with the Caribbean
Union against new proposals for immigration restrictions, which both
groups believed aimed to restrict black immigration. White noted the need
to safeguard the "rights of all persons who are classified as belonging to the
colored race" who faced white supremacist theories "aimed with increased
severity at Negroes in all parts of the world."[204] By the fall of 1940, Walter
White acted as fact-finder for Charles Taussig, who, as a member of President Roosevelt's "Brain Trust," was planning a tour of the Caribbean.[205]
When Taussig undertook this tour, he carried with him a letter from White,
which Jason Parker has argued opened many doors for the American during his journey and spoke to the respect for the NAACP within the region.[206] Given these activities, it was predictable that the WINC and others
would seek the aid of the NAACP in their investigation of possible discrimination within the new American bases.

With the formal introduction of the United States into the British Ca-
ribbean, the already recognized power of black protest from the United
States remained crucial. Domingo claimed, "It is my long-held belief that
American Negroes by intelligence, [and] unselfish action can do more to
influence the foreign policies of this country than they can to influence
its domestic policies." Although Domingo had been frustrated that Walter
White had not replied to correspondence trumpeting the "success" of the
WINEC/WINC at the Havana Conference or mentioned the organization's
activities in the *Crisis*, he continued to push the NAACP to recognize the
WINC's efforts in pursuit of Caribbean self-government, and to demonstrate the NAACP's recently proclaimed activism in support of West Indian
rights in the colonies.[207] In the coming months, the NAACP did just that.

In communications with the WINC and various US government agencies, the NAACP demonstrated a commitment to deter the spread of Jim
Crow to the Caribbean and to investigate others forms of racial discrimination. One of the more prominent issues was a rumor that the British had
asked the Americans not to allow African Americans to work on the new
bases. That rumor proved false, though there were some who still believed
it to be unofficial policy at least.[208] Despite clear tensions at times between
the NAACP and the WINC, these and connected activities did establish

a precedent for postwar activism and cooperation in which the NAACP would join, albeit briefly, the long-established tradition of connecting West Indian and African American struggles.

Through the rest of the war years, the pursuit of self-government and self-determination in the British Caribbean remained highly important to West Indian and black diaspora activists. Within the Caribbean, "national parties" that had begun to form within some colonies in the late 1930s (and continued to expand over the next two decades), as well as various labor organizations, carried these struggles forward.[209] The impact of their activities was bolstered by the institution of key reforms by the empire, including the Colonial Development and Welfare Act (1940) and the liberalization of some colonial Caribbean constitutions, especially in Jamaica and Trinidad. The Atlantic Charter (1941), which asserted the right of all people to self-determination, further strengthened the resolve of many in and out of the colonies to press for significant reform. Nevertheless, there remained skepticism about and criticism of these reforms as inadequate to address the dire conditions of the region. Some argued the constitutional reforms did not do enough to curtail the authority of Crown Colony governors, who would still wield unmatched power even over an expanded electorate. Likewise, there was considerable debate over whether the Atlantic Charter applied to nonwhite regions. While Churchill claimed it did not, the United States actually argued it did.[210] Despite these issues, West Indian nationalists continued to assert themselves with growing stature in the colonies.

Likewise, the West Indian struggle, as part of a black diasporic struggle, continued in Harlem. In June 1941, W. A. Domingo returned to Jamaica to help the PNP in their renewed campaign for self-government and in support of the new constitution. Upon his arrival, colonial authorities under orders of the Jamaican governor detained Domingo as a threat to public safety, and interned him for the next few years along with other political activists in the island. These actions would elicit much outcry and support for Domingo from within the Caribbean and the United States.[211] Even with one of their key leaders imprisoned, Harlem-based activists continued to help shape the pursuit of Caribbean self-government in the face of joint US-British policies. Their resolve to be heard and have their say in the West Indian future persevered after the United States entered the war following the bombing of Pearl Harbor in December 1941.

In March 1942 the British and Americans created the Anglo-American Caribbean Commission (AACC) to address social and economic problems in the Caribbean, which would become one of the most important and influential manifestations of US-British cooperation in the wider Caribbean in the 1940s.[212] Following the launch of the AACC, both West Indians and African Americans sought to ensure a black presence on the commission. Eventually William Hastie, an African American with some Caribbean experience as a judge in the Virgin Islands, was appointed to the Caribbean Advisory Committee for the US section of the AACC. While this satisfied the goal of at least a black presence on the commission, some West Indians expressed disappointment that an American of West Indian descent was not chosen.[213]

Throughout this era, as in previous ones, neither African Americans nor West Indians were monolithic in their thinking. In many cases there was significant cooperation and disagreement between these groups, as well as within the groups themselves. Rarely did national lines alone dictate outlooks. For instance, despite the fact the WINC had intentionally included members of various political ideologies throughout its short existence, the concerns of some over a growing "communist" influence in the group led in 1942 to the creation of the more conservative American West Indian Association on Caribbean Affairs (AWIACA).[214]

The AWIACA fits the model of a race-conscious transnational West Indian and black diaspora organization. As stated in its charter, "The American West Indian Association [holds] itself free at any time to adopt any measure, or to take any action consistent with the aims or conducive to the attainment of its immediate and general objectives . . . and also generally to lend its support, in its discretion, to any movement calculated to enhance the interests of peoples of African descent."[215] This policy demonstrates that while black activists may have differed in their political philosophies enough to spur the creation of an alternative organization in the case of the AWIACA, there remained a commitment to work for the general cause of racial uplift, which included the West Indian struggle for self-government.

Notwithstanding the differences of opinion between groups such as the WINC and AWIACA, as demonstrated in newspaper columns and political rallies in this era, seemingly rival organizations shared a resentment of white interference. As Malliet said, "White people continue to treat the Negroes like children by making decisions for them about their homeland and not allowing them to have anything to do in these matters."[216] On the purported communist influence in the WINC, AWIACA president Joseph C. Morris argued, "It was not the business of the Government to decide with whom [we] should associate," and "the white man was only trying to bring disunity among the Negroes by setting one against the other . . . trying to muzzle the Negroes."[217] In fact, despite their differences, the WINC and AWIACA would eventually, albeit uneasily, work together to suggest candidates for appointment to the AACC. One can conclude, therefore, that while there were certainly limitations to racial unity in the anticolonial activities of West Indian and African American activists in this era, race remained an influential tool through which many groups cooperated.

As the war turned in favor of the Allies, postwar planning for the Caribbean increased. The AACC acted as the primary agency through which the United States and the British Empire tried to assert their agendas in the region. While there was certainly cooperation between the two, there were also significant differences of opinion at times. Many of these issues were discussed, with varying degrees of success, at the 1944 West Indian Conference held in Barbados.[218] Outside of these official meetings, West Indian and African American activists also took it upon themselves to discuss the postwar Caribbean, as in the formal conference "The Economic Future of the Caribbean," held at Howard University in 1943. This meeting addressed a variety of topics on the entire Caribbean—both independent nations and colonies—and included several papers on the British Caribbean, among them discussions of federation by W. Adolphe Roberts of the Jamaica Progressive League and African American historian Rayford W. Logan.[219]

Throughout the years of World War II, there remained a variety of opinions on the specific form of self-government desirable in the West Indies. Some prioritized and pursued self-government for their individual colonies, while others maintained the need for a federation. Within official colonial circles, federation remained a tool to improve the region, though questions over the sort and extent of reform continued. In the early years of the war, some assumed the British might institute a "Federation of the West Indian, North American, South and Central American colonies of Britain under the direction of the Duke of Windsor, as governor-general." In 1941 a program of "economic federation" between the British Caribbean colonies and other Caribbean countries was proposed to President Roosevelt. By 1943 General Smuts suggested uniting the Caribbean colonies into a "West Indian Federation under a joint Anglo-American Commission in which Canada will participate."[220] At the same time, within the Caribbean, several political parties, labor unions, and other organizations continued to pursue a self-governing federation as a means to create a larger, more powerful nation than could be achieved through individual self-government.[221] Many expatriate West Indian, African American, and other black diaspora activists supported a Caribbean federation for the same reason. Moreover, like some Afro-Caribbeans within the region, they explicitly racialized West Indian nation building as part of the broader struggle for self-determination and the liberation of black peoples. In fact, the *Chicago Defender* reported that in a January 1945 poll conducted in Chicago and New York, 95 percent of respondents believed it was time to establish a federation.[222] In a few short months, they would be proven correct.

For much of the twentieth century, through the end of World War II in 1945, the empire offered only limited official support for a British Caribbean federation, claiming it did not want to force it upon the region. However, with the end of the war there was a shift in Crown policy toward the idea of a West Indian federation. On 14 March 1945, Secretary of State for the Colonies Oliver Stanley issued the "Stanley Dispatch," which directed the legislatures of the West Indian colonies to officially debate the issue of political federation as a goal that would "quicken the progress" toward self-government within the British Commonwealth of Nations. Though Stanley said that no colony would be forced to participate in such a scheme, the Crown had taken a significant step to suggest and support federation.[223] The long-imagined goal of federation now appeared poised to become a reality. However, the question remained—whose vision of federation would reign?

3

From Long-Standing Dream to Impending Reality

Caribbean Federation and the Mobilization of Black Diaspora Politics,
1945–1950

The Stanley Dispatch of 1945 launched a new wave of official and unofficial discussions on the issue of Caribbean federation in the post–World War II era. In this dispatch Oliver Stanley, the secretary of state for the colonies, asserted the Crown's professed policy "to quicken the progress of all Colonial peoples towards the ultimate goal of self-government" and addressed how this should take place within the British West Indies. "The aim of British policy should be the development of federation in the Caribbean at such a time as the balance of opinion in the various Colonies is in favour of a change, and when the development of communications makes it administratively practicable. The ultimate aim of any federation which may be established would be full internal self-government within the British Commonwealth." Like many others, Stanley believed that "under modern conditions" it would be difficult for "small units, whatever their outward political form may be, to maintain full and complete independence." Therefore, as suggested by the Moyne Commission, a Caribbean federation should be the end to which policy was directed.[1] As summarized in a 1945 *Times* article, "Federation [was] presented as the final objective of West Indian constitutional progress for the conclusive reason that federation alone can create a political unit sufficiently large and diverse to be capable of full self-government in the modern world."[2]

In the British Caribbean, Stanley's instructions to the various colonial legislatures to formally consider federation coincided with a general liberalization of colonial policies, and postwar efforts by the Crown to dictate the terms and speed of decolonization. In Jamaica, where "national parties" such as the People's National Party and the Jamaica Labour Party developed in the late 1930s and early 1940s, a new constitution based on universal adult suffrage was instituted in 1944. Universal suffrage was instituted in Trinidad and Tobago in 1945, but the development of cohesive national parties did not occur until later in the 1950s. In Barbados the income qualification was lowered in the early 1940s, followed by an expansion of the franchise a few years later, and finally universal suffrage in 1951. Constitutional reform in the Windward and Leeward colonies took longer, but the push for self-government increased alongside the development of national parties in these colonies as well. In spite of these reforms, in the immediate postwar years the dominant power remained the governor in all British Caribbean colonies, including Barbados and the Bahamas, which were not Crown Colonies.[3] Even so, many West Indians and their allies were optimistic that the dawn of a new day was at hand. While the Stanley Dispatch surely helped set the West Indian colonies on the road to federation, the journey remained long and at times uncertain.

The Crown's support for federation in the West Indies was not unique in the post–World War II era. It was but one example of the expanding support by the Crown for the creation of federations among Britain's colonies, which were debated, attempted, and in some cases implemented (with varying success) in East Africa, Central Africa, Nigeria, Malaysia, and the West Indies from the end of World War II through the 1960s. These efforts reflect a discernible shift in colonial policy from prewar efforts to preserve empire to postwar efforts to accelerate but control decolonization. Federations were not the only means through which this could occur. Nonetheless, many colonial officials, like some supporters of federation within the colonies themselves, believed small countries faced much greater obstacles for successful and lasting self-government and independence than did larger countries with the resources to face the challenges of nationhood.[4]

The political and economic interests of the United States in the West Indies, which had expanded significantly during World War II, also played an influential role in West Indian decolonization. In the immediate prewar years and over the course of the war, the United States had generally supported decolonization and self-determination for the colonies in line with the Atlantic Charter, which at times proved a source of contention with Britain. In the postwar era, however, US commitment to decolonization and the rights of colonial peoples to choose their own form of government became strained by the realities of Cold War politics, which shifted US interests and policy from ending imperialism in the Western Hemisphere to the creation of anticommunist bulwarks. In the case of the West Indies, many US officials believed a well-planned federation of the colonies could provide such a safeguard.[5]

British and American interests in decolonization were only part of the larger process of postwar planning and reconstruction. Nevertheless, they exemplified some of the key deliberations in the aftermath of World War II including the future of imperialism and colonialism, as well as the significant influence of the Cold War within international politics. The victorious nations of the recent war certainly shaped many of the conversations related to the rebuilding and restructuring of the world in this era. However, the governments of old imperial powers (Great Britain and France) and new superpowers (United States and Soviet Union) were not the only parties concerned and involved in postwar planning. In regard to the colonial world, the various nationalist and anticolonial movements active within or on behalf of the colonies were also determined to have their voices heard, especially when it came to their own futures.

As for the West Indian future in this era, in conjunction with the solidification of Crown support and the increased power and presence of the various national parties of the colonies within *official* discussions on the subject, the pursuit of a Caribbean federation was increasingly characterized by many as an intra-regional nation-building project. Nevertheless, the interactions of these groups remain only part of the larger history of federation in this era too. Although most of the transnational West Indian and black diaspora organizations outside the colonies would find their roles diminished by 1950, they remained significant and influential sources of moral and material support in the cause of Caribbean federation in the immediate postwar years. While not dismissing the intra-regional dimensions of federation, a significant number of these activists and organizations continued to trumpet the racial dimensions of federation and Caribbean nation building, as did some local West Indian political leaders who strategically played to black diaspora politics for continued support.

This chapter investigates the transition of Caribbean federation from a long-standing dream to an impending reality in the closing years of World War II and the immediate postwar era, with a particular focus on the continued ties and collaborations between West Indian political movements in the Caribbean and transnational West Indian and black diaspora organizations abroad. It examines the support of federation within the preparations for and during the founding meeting of the United Nations, as well as the Fifth Pan-African Congress in 1945. Following these events, it explores the debates over the possibility of Caribbean federation from the Stanley

Dispatch in 1945, through two seminal conferences in 1947, and up to the release of the Rance Report in 1950, which marked the beginning of formal negotiations over the scope and structure of federation.

Postwar Planning for the British West Indies and Black Diaspora Politics

During the closing years of the war, the allied nations and interested parties, including colonial peoples themselves, held a variety of meetings to discuss war efforts and, in many cases, postwar policies in Europe and throughout the colonial world. These included conferences between government representatives of the Big Three—the United States, Great Britain, and the Soviet Union—in Tehran (1943), Yalta (1945), and Potsdam (1945). The Dumbarton Oaks Conference (1944), which would create the framework for the United Nations, also included the Republic of China. Alongside the formal planning by these national and imperial governments, various anticolonial activists and organizations continued to push their respective agendas, with an eye toward the postwar world. Their demands ranged from varying levels of reform to the eradication of the colonial systems that dominated the lives of many throughout Africa, Asia, and the Caribbean. As in previous decades, the future of the British West Indies remained an integral part of these general, and at times more specifically black diaspora, anticolonial activities.

While the Yalta and Potsdam Conferences of 1945 are remembered particularly for the shaping of postwar policies, the creation of the United Nations has gained greater recognition as one of the most significant moments for the investigation of colonial and other subject peoples' perspectives. The United Nations Conference on International Organization (UNCIO), held 25 April–26 June 1945, proved especially important. More than simply the organization of an international body, the UNCIO provided an opportunity for nations and various interest groups to put their respective platforms in front of an international audience. In the months leading to the UNCIO, various black diaspora activists and other anticolonial advocates, mobilized in preparation for the conference, which some would attend as formal delegates, observers, and uninvited guests.[6]

The reformist and anticolonial activities of black diaspora political movements were familiar to both the United States and Britain. As the war came to a close, followed by the start of the Cold War, there was growing scrutiny of the connections between and collaborative efforts of African

American, West Indian, and African activists. In the United States, the government monitored "radical" black organizations such as the National Negro Congress (NNC), the Council on African Affairs (CAA), and the West Indies National Council (WINC) with purported communist agendas, or at the very least the presence of communist sympathizers within them.[7] In the case of the WINC, the FBI continued the surveillance that had begun shortly after the original creation of the preceding WINEC. In 1944 the FBI authorized wiretaps on Hope Stevens and Charles Petioni of the WINC, which they feared was a communist organization that aimed to extend its program to the Caribbean colonies.[8] In 1945 they recommended the continuation of this surveillance for "the excellent coverage that it provides on general Communist activities, particularly among the Negroes in Harlem, and also Communist activities relative to political problems affecting the West Indies where they advocate liberation from the colonial rule of Great Britain and a federation of the various islands."[9]

Within the empire concern over connections between what were deemed "Subversive Negroes and Subversive Organizations" intensified.[10] In early 1944, Foreign Office officials became increasingly concerned with the black press in the United States and its coverage of and interest in British colonial issues.[11] Later in the year, John Harrington, an administrative officer in the Colonial Office, highlighted the shared uneasiness of the British and US governments over connections between Afro-Caribbeans and African Americans.

> The position as I see it is that we must be prepared to meet a certain amount of disaffection in our West Indian Colonies after the war when the removal of the Defence Regulations and other wartime restrictions will give our local agitators a freer hand than they have had for the last five years. . . . As you know, even before the war there was a certain link-up between the more subversive elements, at any rate in Jamaica, and similarly minded organisations in New York. It seems possible that America's negro problem may become acute after the war. If it does, it is certain to have troublesome repercussions in the West Indies.[12]

Though not particularly concerned with the domestic struggles of African Americans, Harrington said the Colonial Office would appreciate any additional information on associations "between subversive negroes or negro organisations in the USA and organizations or parties in the West Indies." They also requested any information on "how the negro problem

is developing in America [which] may help [them] to forecast possible reactions in the West Indies."[13] Around the same time, internal Colonial Office memos show exchanges of information with the FBI, and the desire
for further information on the development of black political movements
"whether subversive or merely political within the British Empire and in
connected movements outside the British Empire." Additional information was solicited from MI6, while MI5 created a special department on
"Negro political movements."[14] Such apprehensions over the connections
between various black diaspora organizations and black populations in the
United States and West Indies, as well as with other colonial peoples, reflected the two governments' awareness of these historical and continued
collaborations.

From London, groups like the League of Coloured Peoples continued
to press for change in the closing and postwar years. In July 1944 the LCP
pressed the Crown to support a "Charter for Coloured Peoples." This included demands for equal economic, educational, legal, and political rights
for all men and women, irrespective of color. It called for colonial powers to
establish comprehensive plans for the development and eventual self-government of dependent territories. Foreshadowing the creation of the UN,
the charter called for imperial powers "to account for their administration
of dependent territories to an international body with powers of investigation, and, in particular, to make regular reports on the steps taken towards
self-government."[15]

Despite the failure of the LCP to garner support from colonial powers
for this charter, several of its demands were included the following year
in the "Manifesto on Africa in the Post-War World." This manifesto, created by colonial delegates at the World Labor Conference held in Britain in
early 1945, was to be presented to the UNCIO in April 1945. Its cosponsors
were a variety of black organizations in Britain, including the West African
Students' Union, International African Service Bureau, Negro Association,
Negro Welfare Centre, Coloured Men's Institute, and representatives from
trade unions in the Gold Coast, Nigeria, Gambia, and British Guiana.[16]
Compared to the LCP's "Charter for Coloured Peoples," it had a more explicit focus on Africa and peoples of African descent in the postwar era.

Similar efforts took place in the United States among various black
diaspora organizations. The Council on African Affairs hosted multiple
meetings in April 1944 with a focus on Africa, including "Towards Democracy for Africa" on 8 March and "What About Africa?—Africa and
the World-Wide War" on 8 April. On 14 April the CAA hosted a larger

meeting, "Africa—New Perspectives," which included representatives from various Indian organizations in the United States, as well as the WINC representing West Indian interests. At this meeting Paul Robeson argued that the Atlantic Charter's support for self-government should apply to all colonies, and pushed for concrete plans for its implementation. The following year, in April 1945, the CAA published "The San Francisco Conference and the Colonial Issue," which called for the UNCIO to discuss colonial questions more widely, and for the establishment of an International Colonial Commission to monitor the advancement of colonial peoples toward self-government.[17]

The CAA's focus on postwar planning for colonized peoples represented the broader scope of anticolonial activities, which included nonblack populations that suffered similarly under colonialism in their respective territories. Nevertheless, like many other black diaspora organizations in the mid-twentieth century, such cooperation did not negate the racial consciousness and prioritized anticolonialism of the CAA. As James Meriwether argues, "Yet even as CAA leaders placed the anticolonial struggle in the context of a broad history and the worldwide political economy, at the same time, they specifically promoted strong connections with Africa and concern for its problems. The CAA and its more prominent proponents, particularly Robeson, illustrate that radical internationalism could be blended with a black nationalism, with its emphasis on racial consciousness and unity."[18]

The NAACP continued anticolonial activities in this era too. Following the 1944 Dumbarton Oaks Conference, the organization protested that meeting's lack of attention to the plight of colonial peoples and the colonial question. The following year, in March 1945, the NAACP adopted a resolution regarding colonial issues and the upcoming UNCIO, which it sent to the US secretary of state, calling for "a declaration of racial equality" between the "great groups of mankind in international law, and urged that a provision be made against economic and governmental exploitation of colonies." It asked if the future status of the colonies would be discussed at the UNCIO, and if colonial and subject peoples, including African Americans, would be allowed to speak for themselves regarding "their aspirations and progress." On the latter issue, the resolution emphasized the NAACP's diasporic scope and connections with colonial black populations. It demanded representation of "American Negroes at the San Francisco meeting in order that they may advocate and advise measures for their own social progress and also be given an opportunity to speak for other peoples of African descent whom they in a very real sense represent." Finally, it urged the adoption of four principles regarding the ownership and control of colonies and dependencies: (1) the ruling country should immediately give the people of such areas a voice in their own government, (2) by a given date these populations should be given the opportunity to choose whether to become integrated into the ruling country with full citizenship rights or allowed to become independent and autonomous nations, (3) the natural resources of the colonies should be owned and used for the benefit of the people in these areas, and (4) an international Mandates Commission should be created under UN control.[19]

Shortly after the NAACP's resolution, W.E.B. DuBois hosted a Colonial Conference on 6 April 1945 at the Harlem Branch of the New York Public Library. A concerted effort was made to bring together a wide range of colonial peoples, rather than limiting the conference to Africa and the West Indies. Attendees represented Puerto Rico, India, Burma, East and West Africa, and the Netherlands East Indies, alongside more familiar African Americans and West Indians, including A. M. Wendell Malliet and Ethelred Brown (Jamaica Progressive League), Charles Petioni, Richard Moore, and Herman Osborne (West Indies National Council), W. A. Hunton (Council on African Affairs), and Rayford Logan (Howard University).[20] Among the proposals put forth by conference delegates, Kwame Nkrumah sought complete independence for dependent territories at the end of the war. As for the West Indies, given the recent constitutional reforms in Jamaica, Malliet and Brown seemed to favor a gradual approach to responsible self-government in that colony, while Moore urged colonial peoples to make demands at the UNCIO for the "forthright recognition of the inalienable right of self-government for the Caribbean, the right of voluntary federation, and guarantees for the abolition of all discriminatory practices everywhere."[21]

By the end of the meeting, the Colonial Conference adopted a resolution with four key demands: (1) an end to colonialism, which caused poverty, illiteracy, and disease in the colonies and wider world and threatened world peace; (2) the creation of an international body to oversee the transition of peoples from colonial status to whatever form of autonomy they desired; (3) representation of colonial peoples within this body; and (4) the use of this body to improve the economic and social conditions of the colonial peoples. The WINC objected to some aspects of this resolution, which they believed could impede the progress of the West Indies and other colonies toward self-government, but they did agree with other recommendations regarding the West Indies, including significant limitations to colonial West

Indian governors' often unmatched power, land redistribution, increased wages for workers, and an end to poverty in the region.[22]

WINC plans for the UNCIO were also shaped and shared at other meetings in early 1945. Inspired by and looking to duplicate their "success" at the 1940 Havana Conference, the WINC's Conference Committee, led by Richard B. Moore and Barbara Watson, held a special meeting on 30 March. "Declaring the great moment has at last arrived for the achievement of voluntary federation and complete self-government and that the stage is now set for the consummation of West Indian liberation," the WINC announced it would press for a hearing at the UNCIO.[23] The seven-point program it intended to present included demands for

(1) the right of Caribbean peoples to representation at the United Nations Conference by delegates of their own choosing;
(2) recognition of the inalienable right of the Caribbean peoples to self-government and self-determination;
(3) recognition of the age-long objective of the West Indian peoples for voluntary federation;
(4) equal representation for Caribbean peoples in the regional organizations of the Americas, including the making of policy;
(5) abolition of all discriminatory laws and the assurance of life and liberty for Caribbean, African, and all other people without regard to race, creed or color;
(6) equality of rights for all people without regard to race, creed, or color, and full democratic rights, including universal suffrage; and
(7) inclusion of Caribbean peoples in the plans for postwar rehabilitation.[24]

In the following weeks, WINC members presented the program at DuBois's Colonial Conference in early April and various public meetings later in the month. On 16 April the WINC presented its nominations for delegates to the UNCIO and its seven-point program to the local West Indian and African American community for ratification. The program was approved by the meeting, and the five nominated delegates confirmed: Richard B. Moore, Charles Petioni, Hope Stevens, Mabel Staupers, and Godfrey Nurse.[25]

Despite its collaborative efforts with many other black anticolonial organizations in this era, the WINC opposed the creation of an international trusteeship over colonies under a mandates commission, which the CAA, NAACP, and other activists supported, and remained committed to independence, self-government, and federation in the West Indies.[26] Herman Osborne, secretary of the WINC, emphasized the group's opposition to the trusteeships and mandates at one of these pre-UN meetings. Speaking "for men of African descent who are at the same time colonials," Osborne began his speech by noting that the single aim of the WINC was "to liquidate the scourge of imperialism." After yet another recollection of WINC success at the Havana Conference, Osborne declared,

> The colonial peoples hate the very sound of the word "trusteeship." We resent it no less than the way all men of African descent resent and hate the word "nigger." For us "trusteeship" represents the fountainhead of that system of psychological warfare that has been waged and skillfully conducted against the colonial peoples—especially those of African descent—for over three hundred years.[27]

Osborne also dismissed the goal of "dominion status" within the British Commonwealth. He proclaimed,

> Men of African descent are no longer to be assailed in their racial integrity with impunity. Yesterday, we were considered patient "jackasses." Do you remember? Today, we might be considered as jackasses alright but with the power to kick out all the front teeth of these dingoes. . . . we fight together side by side with them in this fight today, tomorrow, one minute after the Victory our paths can quickly diverge. This much is clear. We say categorically: We are not interested either in the continuity or in the salvation of Empire.[28]

Instead he called for federation as "essential to the economic development and cultural growth of the West Indian people . . . Nationhood is our goal and we make apologies to no one for holding to this goal." Osborne closed his speech with a call for racial unity between peoples of African descent and support of each other's freedom struggles.

> Let us continue to work for a free Africa. . . . If Africa is not free we cannot be free. Let us work conscientiously for the unity we need. Let [us] close ranks, American and West Indian and African peoples. Let us achieve a new type of unity that will break the hearts of our enemies. Tomorrow, we too will insist upon the right to reap with others the fruits of the Victory over world fascism.[29]

As Marika Sherwood notes in her study of African American and Caribbean participation at the UNCIO, "Though the war was not yet over, for two months from April 25, the attention of the 'free' world was on the meeting . . . in San Francisco. Besides 282 official delegates of the 51 countries represented, every person and organization which sought to have its wrongs redressed sent lobbyists to the city."[30] Over the course of this meeting, anticolonial activists and reformers from across the globe sought to place their proposals before the new international body. Despite several prior indications that colonial issues would not receive the amount of discussion desired by many, there remained optimism over the conference. For instance, Mary McLeod Bethune, who attended as a consultant to the US delegation, declared, "The Negro in America has an unprecedented opportunity" in San Francisco. "Through this conference, the Negro becomes closely allied with all the darker races of the world, but more importantly he becomes integrated into the structure of the peace and freedom of all people, everywhere."[31] Her words undoubtedly expressed the hopes of the various black people, as well as other colonial people, who attended.

Although many activists came to San Francisco to press their respective programs, very few attended as official delegates or consultants.[32] Nevertheless, their presence was felt through their lobbying efforts, which included routine meetings and proposals, and the general distribution of their propaganda among each other and to official delegates. Here various organizations—the WINC, JPL, Universal Negro Improvement Association, federated bodies consisting of multiple groups, such as the Federation Organization of Colored Peoples of the World and the Provisional World Council of Dominated Nations—presented their case for the postwar Caribbean, alongside other colonial territories.[33]

The WINC made the most prominent appeal focused on the West Indies. Richard B. Moore and Charles Petioni, the two WINC delegates who attend the UNCIO as observers, shared the Council's "Appeal to the United Nations Conference on International Organization on Behalf of the Caribbean Peoples" with any who would hear it. The WINC claimed the appeal was made "on behalf of the peoples of the British, French, and Dutch West Indies, the Guianas and British Honduras." After noting general support and hope for the creation of the United Nations, it recapped the vital support Caribbean peoples provided in the war, argued that the abolition of imperialism was essential to world peace, called for economic rehabilitation, demanded self-determination, and said that the trusteeship idea was discredited. It also presented the seven-point program adopted in New York, including the cause of federation within the British Caribbean.[34]

Upon Petioni's return in mid-May, he told the *New York Amsterdam*

News that the "West Indian observers were very active in propagandizing members of delegations against trusteeship for colonies and in favor of federation and self-government for the West Indies."[35] Following Petioni's departure from San Francisco, Moore continued to press the WINC's agenda before various delegates and organizations. He was even able to persuade General Carlos P. Romulo of the Philippines "to take a stand to include independence as the goal of all colonial peoples."[36] Notwithstanding the extensive efforts of the WINC and other interested parties, the future of colonial peoples in the West Indies, much like others across the globe, emerged from the UNCIO with few guarantees. Nevertheless, such activism gave the various anticolonial movements, including those focused on the Caribbean, important momentum in the coming years.

Although much of the postwar activism in 1945 focused on the UNCIO, it was not the year's only major international gathering of colonial peoples. In London, where black activists had continued their anticolonial activities during the closing years of the war, and even sent resolutions to the UNCIO via the "Manifesto on Africa in the Post-War World," black diaspora organizations planned a Pan-African Congress, the first since 1927, for October 1945 in Manchester.

The Fifth Pan-African Congress, also known as the Manchester Conference, was largely organized through the efforts of George Padmore and the recently created Pan-African Federation (PAF). This new organization superseded the IASB, which dissolved in 1944. Organized as a "federation of organisations of African Peoples and Peoples of African descent throughout the world," the PAF adhered to four basic objectives: (1) to demand self-determination and independence of African peoples and other subject races; (2) to secure equality of civil rights for African peoples and the abolition of all forms of racial discrimination; (3) to promote the well-being and unity of African peoples and peoples of African descent throughout the world; and (4) to strive for cooperation between African peoples and other peoples who share their aspirations. As with its predecessor, membership was reserved for persons of African descent, with associate memberships open to all others who supported their objectives.[37] Like several other black diaspora organizations, it placed an explicit focus on black peoples but also supported other colonial peoples in the fight against colonialism.

The Manchester Conference proved to be one of the most important Pan-African meetings for its numbers and the increased participation of Africans, rather than primarily African Americans and West Indians as at previous meetings. To be sure, numerous West Indian delegations from the colonies attended, and many of them included the cause of Caribbean federation in their resolutions before the congress. E.D.L. Yearwood of the Barbados Progressive League and Workers' Union noted the League was a "keen supporter of the federation of the West Indies" as the only means to solve the economic and social problems of the region.[38] D. M. Harper of the British Guiana Trades Union Council demanded self-government and a West Indies Federation.[39] Representatives of the St. Kitts Workers' League and the Executive Committee of the St. Kitts-Nevis Trades and Labour Union called for a greater unity that would only be achieved through federation, noting, "The time for West Indian Federation is overripe."[40] A supplementary resolution submitted by the UNIA of Jamaica voiced support of a Caribbean federation, which the UNIA claimed both the Colonial Office and West Indians desired.[41] As a group, the "accredited and recognised representatives of the people of the British West Indies and British Guiana in attendance at this Fifth Pan-African Congress" demanded federation "on a voluntary and equal basis founded upon complete Self-Government."[42] While delegates at the Manchester Conference supported and extended well-wishes to colonial peoples who were not of African descent, presentations and discussions of Caribbean federation within this Pan-African Congress undoubtedly characterized it as principally a black nation-building project—one part of the broader freedom struggles of black peoples in Africa and the diaspora.

In the context of these various 1944–45 meetings focused on postwar planning, the pursuit of Caribbean self-determination and self-government, via federation, was a common goal. On one hand, these efforts were just one example of the overarching demands by various colonial areas seeking significant reforms in their postwar status. That is to say, their struggle was part of a general anticolonial struggle between colony and imperial power. At the same time, West Indian struggles remained tied to the more explicitly racialized anticolonial activism of black diaspora politics. The pursuit of Caribbean liberation and the creation of a united, self-governing federation remained an intra-regional and diaspora project, as well as a transracial and racialized one, as the official planning of the federation took shape.

The Stanley Dispatch and the Possibilities of Federation

The Stanley Dispatch announced the Crown's support for a federation among the postwar West Indian colonies with instructions that it be "announced [with] full opportunity given for public discussion" and for the colonial legislatures to debate the matter at their earliest opportunity. Rather than providing a definitive path to a federation or a clear outline of its possible structure, the dispatch spoke more to possible steps the colonies could undertake toward that goal. Given the continued belief among many officials that "movements towards such political unity must come from within and not from outside the area," it is not surprising the dispatch offered no specifics other than Stanley's own statement that some might conclude that two separate federations were preferable to a single federal unit of all colonies—one among eastern Caribbean colonies and another between the western Caribbean colonies. Stanley also indicated that although federation was by no means a guarantee within the West Indies, the ongoing reforms in the region that served the "more immediate purpose of developing self-governing institutions in the individual British Caribbean Colonies should keep in view the larger project of their political federation," as should other "political developments in each colony." Overall, he declared, "British policy should aim at the fostering of a sense of West Indian unity and of the removal of the present obstacles in the way of federation."[43] While Stanley's Dispatch failed, by design, to act as a sort of rallying cry for federation, it did establish the atmosphere in which federation would be debated at this time within the colonies.

The Stanley Dispatch is of considerable importance, given its representation of the shift in Crown policy on the matter of federation. Although many colonial officials had voiced their support of a Caribbean federation at various times during the early twentieth century, the Crown never took a decisive stance. On many occasions the Crown dismissed the readiness of the region for federation, argued federation was not yet workable for a variety of reasons, or claimed an unwillingness to force such a structure on the region without popular support among the "responsible" populations in the West Indian colonies. Many of these assumptions were based upon the reports of official commissions that had investigated the possibilities of federation at various times largely through the limited scope of the small white minorities' opinions on the subject. Regardless of the significant support for federation among some portions of the "native" West Indian populations, particularly the various middle-class reform movements and some regional labor organizations during the early twentieth century, the Colonial Office essentially ignored this segment of the West Indian population on the issue, other than the recording of their opinions by the 1930s Moyne Commission, which received memoranda and testimony from the broadest range of West Indian societies up to this time. Just as a blind eye was turned toward the native West Indians for many years, opinions on federation among many transnational West Indian and black diaspora organizations based outside the Caribbean were never sought, though some also submitted memoranda and testimony to the Moyne Commission. The issuance of the Stanley Dispatch in 1945, however, changed the course of these restrictive discussions to some extent, even as it helped set a course for the initiation of others.

The Crown's shift to support and urge federation, arriving shortly after or in conjunction with the institution of political reforms and the rise of more formal political parties in many colonies, ushered in a new era in the history of Caribbean federation. Now the voices of the "native" West Indians, particularly the Afro-Caribbean middle class, would be heard within the discussions of Caribbean federation more than at any previous time. While the Stanley Dispatch created an atmosphere for more open discussion of federation within the West Indies, it also led indirectly to the development of a more restrictive atmosphere in some regards in the ensuing years. The dispatch set the stage for a series of official meetings between representatives of the Crown and the colonies from the late 1940s to the late 1950s. In these official discussions, federation became increasingly, and more restrictively, viewed as an intra-regional venture to be negotiated between West Indian political leaders in the colonies and the Crown.

The limited capacity in which federation came to be negotiated within the colonies had two significant flaws. First, given the middle-class status of most Caribbean political leaders, particularly those involved in these final steps toward federation, consideration of the West Indian working masses' opinions remained dubious. Indeed, in many ways the debates over federation continued to be a top-down discussion, even as new members were added to the "top."[44] Next, and more central to this study, limited visions of federation as primarily, and in some opinions exclusively, an intra-regional endeavor also affected the long-standing and significant support of federation within black diaspora politics. Given the enhanced regional characterizations of federation, as well as the persistent trepidation of the British about racial activism among their colonial populations, it is not surprising that the racial and diasporic dimensions of West Indian nation building, which had long existed alongside along these other visions of federation, were increasingly downplayed or dismissed as the views of "outsiders."

Immediately after the Stanley Dispatch, discussions of federation ensued among the colonial legislatures and some political movements within the colonies. Over the next two years, the various British Caribbean colonial legislatures debated the possibilities. Ultimately, all but the Bahamas agreed that federation warranted further discussion. This decision was crucial, particularly given the specific instructions of the Stanley Dispatch. However, it quite symbolic that as these legislatures debated the matter, the first meeting to discuss and confirm the Stanley Dispatch took place outside official governmental bodies.

The founding conference of the Caribbean Labour Congress (CLC) took place in Barbados in September 1945. Building upon the legacies of prior regional labor movements, most notably the British Guiana and West Indies Labour Congress, the CLC was established upon a regionalist spirit that many assumed was necessary for a federation to ever come into existence. The conference began with a moment of silence for Arthur Cipriani, who had died in April, before tackling the tasks of establishing the new organization's statements and resolutions. These included such matters as economic development, education, and social and industrial legislation.

One of the most important matters to be resolved was the CLC's stance on federation. Prior regional labor organizations had long supported the goal of federation with self-government. The BGWILC had supported federation since the 1920s and more recently at its 1938 conference and in its memorandum to the Moyne Commission in 1939. At its 1945 conference, the CLC continued its predecessor's tradition and offered support to the recent Stanley Dispatch. It called for a regional conference where delegates chosen by elected officials of the region would draft proposals for federation acceptable to their constituencies, and devise plans to remove any obstacles to its creation. Among the most important components of the CLC's official position on federation were demands for "a federal constitution with responsible government" and "wholly elected legislatures based on universal adult suffrage with policy making Executive Councils responsible to the legislatures."[45] The CLC's demand for a federation with self-government was far from unique. Still, appearing as it did so soon after the Stanley Dispatch, it marked an important moment within intra-regional politics as the idea of federation transitioned from aspiration to imminent possibility.

While there was significant support for federation immediately after the Stanley Dispatch, it was not without its critics. As John Mordecai notes in his study of federation, the timing of the Stanley Dispatch proved ironic. In previous years, activists driven by islandist sentiments supported federation because they believed that the British would never grant self-government to individual colonies, but only to the region as a whole within a federation. However, given the constitutional reforms in several West Indian colonies in the mid-1940s, which gave more power to elected members within the various West Indian colonial governments, some realized they could now achieve self-government without federation, and indeed "federation began to be seen as an obstacle. . . . The desire for self-government now began to work against federation, instead of in its favour."[46] Although there were certainly some who would disagree, particularly regionalists who prioritized regional cooperation above concerns for individual islands, this does not negate the validity of Mordecai's argument.

One of the chief obstacles to federation within the colonies, therefore, remained the continued and refocused islandism among some West Indians. The islandist tendencies of many Jamaicans provide explicit examples. While some Jamaicans, including Norman Manley and the PNP, had long supported federation, activists in the eastern Caribbean colonies had been more prominent supporters. In those colonies, several intercolonial associations had existed, and federation appealed to many because of the colonies' small size. By contrast, Jamaica was quite distant from many other West Indian colonies and, in many minds, sizeable enough to seek self-government on its own. Others simply thought there were too many inherent shortcomings in federation, especially in one that would include Jamaica.

Some of the most critical assessments of federation came from W. A. Domingo of the JPL. In January 1945, a few months before the release of the Stanley Dispatch, Domingo, who was still in Jamaica following his recent internment, published an article in *Public Opinion* against the idea. As Birte Timm argues, while he had more quietly opposed Caribbean federation in previous years, especially schemes that included Jamaica, he now "felt it was about time to publicly express his concerns." Domingo listed numerous reasons that Jamaica should oppose federation, including the significant distance between some of the colonies, lack of contact and communication between many of them, no economic benefit, the different stages of political development among the colonies, and the general lack of a united West Indianness.[47]

Given the atmosphere of federation discussions and its increased characterization as primarily an intra-regional project in the years following the Stanley Dispatch, it may be tempting to undervalue the role of expatriate West Indian, African American, and other black diaspora activists' support *outside* the West Indian colonies, or to dismiss their perspectives as out of step with those within the British Caribbean. To do so, however, would be to ignore the fact that, despite the more limited vision of federation by many political leaders within the region during the final years leading to its creation, Caribbean federation remained intricately tied to black diaspora politics and freedom struggles.

The lack of "official recognition" by some within the Caribbean does not mean these activists and organizations should be discounted. Before the formal federal negotiations took shape around 1950 with the release of the Rance Report, black diaspora support for Caribbean federation remained crucial, particularly given the continued collaborative efforts between many West Indian political leaders and movements from the region and activists and organizations within the multinational black communities of the United States and Great Britain, where many continued to racialize West Indian affairs and merge them into the larger frame of the black diaspora in familiar ways.[48] Indeed, racial appeals for federation and conceptualizations of it as a black nation-building project remained a potent tool through which to rally support. In fact, several West Indian politicians and activists from the region, including some who deemphasized or evaded discussing race and the diasporic scope of federation while in the Caribbean, emphasized and played to black diaspora perceptions of federation when visiting these locales throughout the 1940s and into the 1950s.

Organizing and Mobilizing for Caribbean Federation

Although the postwar era saw a more concerted focus on domestic civil rights by African Americans, there remained within Black America, which had long included more than just African Americans, an interest in the international struggles of black peoples in Africa and the black diaspora. In Harlem, which remained the center of black diaspora activism in the United States, and other (primarily urban) locales, articles and editorials in black newspapers, as well as the programs, speeches, and meetings of various African American, transnational West Indian, and black diaspora organizations, provided extensive coverage of the anticolonial and antiracist struggles of black peoples across the globe, much as in previous decades. Although African struggles may have continued to be the focal point for many, black diaspora freedom struggles such as the continued pursuit of self-government and federation in the British West Indies also received significant coverage and support.

Between the preoccupation of many diaspora activists with the UNCIO and the delayed release of the Stanley Dispatch to the public, some of their first reactions to the Dispatch did not appear until the summer of 1945. In late June, Malliet congratulated Secretary of State for the Colonies Oliver Stanley on his recent interest in the colonies he oversaw, noting his recent travels to West Africa and to Jamaica. Malliet also shared with his readers the details of the Stanley Dispatch, and emphasized the long-held goal of federation as "the only road toward unity and progress" for the West Indian colonies. The article was not overly celebratory, however, as Malliet noted the uncertainty over the place of British Guiana and Jamaica in any future federation, which would prove prophetic in the coming years.[49]

The following month, another Malliet article on the Stanley Dispatch and federation gave the perspectives of many leading West Indians in the New York area. Reginald Pierrepointe, editor of the West Indies News Service and longtime activist in various black diaspora political movements, offered this cautious reaction: "The dispatch of Colonel Stanley . . . came as welcome, but not surprising news. Immersed as I have been for many years in agitating for federation and independence for the West Indies, I feel a sense of satisfaction at this belated but progressive step." Yet Pierrepointe noted his initial skepticism of a "federation imposed from the outside" and wondered, "Federation under whose auspices?" Citing the failures of the post-emancipation eras in the United States and the West Indies, he argued there was still much to be done to secure the federation, lest the British government lose interest and disregard its current goal. He urged, "Don't for one moment cease the necessary agitation that in my opinion wrung this gesture from the masters." Joseph C. Morris, former president of the West Indian Federation of America (WIFA), offered a more optimistic tone. In his view, the benefits of a federation were "too obvious to need emphasis." Charles Petioni, president of the WINC, claimed the Stanley Dispatch was "not very reassuring" given that a simple order from the secretary of state for the colonies could do more than the debates that would shortly ensue. "However," Petioni said, "as an advocate of federation for the past 40 years, I welcome this step as being in the right direction."[50] Overall, these perspectives demonstrate an overriding sense that much work remained to be done, and that the road to federation was hopeful but uncertain.

Diaspora centers such as Harlem (and its surrounding communities) remained a crucial site in rallying support for Caribbean federation. British and colonial officials, West Indian politicians, and other activists routinely visited the area to keep the expatriate West Indian and broader black community abreast of the situation in the colonies, but more importantly, at least for some West Indian politicians and activists, to solicit their support for West Indian self-government and federation. In October 1945, during his visit to New York City, the Trinidad colonial governor Bede Clifford, who favored federation "because it has the blessing and sanction of the British Government," took time to meet with West Indian activists, including Petioni, Malliet, Herman Osborne, and Hope Stevens.[51] While the opportunity to meet colonial officials was always welcomed, there was significantly more attention paid to visiting West Indian politicians and activists.

The visit and activities of Norman Manley, leader of the PNP in Jamaica, in the United States in the fall of 1945 offers insight into what became routine exchanges between the West Indies and the broader black diaspora over the next several years. The *New York Amsterdam News* announced Manley's arrival and his upcoming public meeting, hosted by the WINC and JPL, on 7 October at the Abyssinian Church in Harlem. As the black communities prepared for this visit, so did the FBI for less altruistic reasons, in line with its apprehensions about transnational ties between African Americans, West Indians, and other colonial peoples. Speaking before a packed auditorium, Manley detailed the work of the PNP in Jamaica, described the need for federation, and urged closer ties between West Indians in the colonies and the United States. On federation Manley said, "I do not regard federation alone as a solution of the West Indian colonial problem but as a most essential step towards a solution of those problems." He received $2,500 in cash and pledges to support his work in the Caribbean.[52]

Although initial press coverage described Manley's visit as focused on the West Indian leaders and organizations in the area, he extended his attentions on 8 October 1945 to the board of directors of the NAACP, to whom he declared, "I have come to America to enlist the practical help of West Indian and progressive labor and colored organizations in our fight in Jamaica." Manley began by praising the work of the association in the United States, which he said was well known and respected in Jamaica. Invoking the common cause of colonial and subject peoples across the globe, he presented the work of the PNP and the need for a Caribbean federation as not only a West Indian or colonial issue but one that was particular important for all peoples of African descent, given the shared racial heritage of most West Indians. "Only by a federation can we achieve complete self-government and be able to build a cultural society predominantly West Indian and a project of men of African descent." Connecting the pursuit of federation not only to colonial peoples but also more explicitly to black peoples, Manley believed the creation of a federation would have ramifications for other peoples of African descent. "African advance is in the air, but African colonial advance is going to be considerably affected by the results of the West Indian experiment. The status of colored people the world over must be affected by the achievement of the West Indian people and by their success or failure as a people on the threshold of the possibility of self-government." He closed with a plea for his fellow West Indians to remember their close ties to their African American brethren, and seemingly the black freedom movement in the United States too. "I hope that they themselves may realize that any tendency they may show in America to treat themselves as a minority within a minority rather than to become interested in the larger organizations of America would in itself be a fatal mistake for them and for the West Indian cause which they are so willing to help."[53]

Following Manley's meeting with the NAACP, the *New York Times* and several black newspapers relayed his message that creation of a self-governing Caribbean federation was "of interest to the Negroes of the United States" and "would have a salutary effect on the status of Negroes everywhere."[54] At a dinner sponsored by the WINC in his honor, Manley remarked to the gathered West Indian, African American, and black diaspora activists that West Indians must move beyond the assumption "You can't unite, you can't unite!" The federation must be created, he argued, and "that federation must be of own creation." Others in attendance, such as Walter White and Max Yergan, expressed their admiration for Manley's work as part of the "great upward and onward movement of the oppressed peoples" and larger struggles of self-determination.[55] At yet another luncheon with the NAACP, Manley once again drew connections between West Indians and African Americans. As Mabel Staupers recalled, "I was delighted that Mr. Manley pointed out the fact that the colonial system in the West Indies is the same as the feudal system of the [US] south."[56]

Manley returned to the United States for another round of meetings on Christmas Day 1945. Over the next few weeks, Manley visited Chicago, Detroit, and Philadelphia before returning to the New York area. In Chicago at the 31st General Convention of Alpha Phi Alpha on 30 December 1945 he delivered a speech, "To Unite in a Common Battle," that further addressed connections between African Americans, West Indians, and other colonial peoples. As reported in the *Chicago Defender*, Manley was introduced by Charles Wesley, president of Wilberforce University and a leading member of Alpha Phi Alpha, who noted the fraternity's aim to unify "Negroes in the West Indies, Africa and America in a solid phalanx to fight for equality and equal participation in those countries of which they are a part." Although

Manley called for African Americans to champion "the cause of minority and colonial groups all over the world," he focused primarily on the connections between peoples of African descent, including those of the British Caribbean, which he estimated at more than 90 percent of African descent. He argued African Americans "cannot hope to win genuine equality for Negroes in the United States until people of African descent in the West Indies and Africa enjoy freedom and self-government and take their place as equals among the nations of the world." Older ideas of "Back to Africa" should become "'Backing Africa.' Peoples of African descent whether in Africa or the West Indies . . . need your moral, spiritual and material support." In Chicago he also spoke to the American–West Indian Welfare Association before departing to meet with the West Indian Social League of Detroit.[57]

Back in New York, Manley spoke on Sunday, 13 January, at a Brooklyn church on the topic "Political Emancipation of the British West Indies in Relation to the Negro in the Post-War World." Two days later he gave the address "The West Indian Fight for Political Freedom" to a Harlem meeting cosponsored by the WINC, JPL, and NAACP, where he shared the stage with Roy Wilkins of the NAACP, among others.[58] Upon his return to the Caribbean, Manley noted with pride to T. A. Marryshow, "On the whole the tour was a great success. There is a tremendous amount of enthusiasm and interest in America about the whole West Indian scene as it exist[s] today."[59] Indeed, over the course of several months, Manley had undoubtedly convinced many in Black America of the significance of a Caribbean federation not only for the West Indies but for black peoples across the globe. And he did so through an explicitly racialized portrayal of federation as primarily a black nation-building project.

Seemingly to coincide with Manley's recent tour, the January edition of the NAACP's *Crisis* published a significant article titled "The Road to West Indian Federation" by Herman Osborne of the WINC. Osborne dismissed "England's generosity" as the reason for postwar reform efforts in the Caribbean. "If the West Indian masses are now swinging down the rugged road to federation and self-government, it is due more to their militancy, political awakening and preparedness, than to any other combination of historical circumstances." In his summation of imperial reform and West Indian activism during World War II, much of which focused on the work of the WINC, and praise for the PNP as "the party of all the West Indian people," Osborne described federation as the best means to achieve the long-sought freedom of the British Caribbean. Noting that the majority of

West Indians were of African descent, he highlighted the racial aspects of the nation-to-be, while assuring readers "this rule by the majority, when it comes, must be respectful of the rights and opinions of the minority within the new nation." He also solicited the aid of African Americans in building a West Indian federation where "the manhood and the womanhood of the area could quickly come to flower." This support would have reciprocal effects on African Americans who "could escape many of the withering blasts of national oppression with the conscious, reciprocal aid and fraternal affection of a united West Indian national community of free peoples."[60]

Manley's tours of the United States and Osborne's essay demonstrate the concerted effort of activists to strengthen the already considerable bonds between West Indians in and out of the colonies, as well as to connect the political activities and possibilities of the British Caribbean to the broader struggles of black peoples in the United States and elsewhere. Though the bonds existed in previous years, in the postwar world and with the opportunity for federation at hand, such activities proved particularly important. In these settings, Caribbean federation remained more than simply a West Indian project.

Following Manley's departure and Osborne's article in January, US-based supporters of federation worked to maintain the momentum. In January 1946, longtime federation supporter Charles Petioni urged West Indians to not only unite for their own advancement "but to join all their native-born brethren, the sons of Africa, the world over in the common struggle for the common cause. Since the problem is one of color . . . the race everywhere [should] use the common bond of color as the lever of salvation."[61] A. M. Wendell Malliet continued to use his columns in the *New York Amsterdam News* to keep the matter before the public. In February 1946, following the announcement of the Malayan Union, he offered a cynical commentary on the slow progress of federation plans in the Caribbean. Malliet pondered whether the fear of black majority rule was one of the primary reasons for the slow progress in the West Indies compared to Southeast Asia. "It is difficult to understand how the Malayan federation came about. Is it that His Majesty's Government is so deeply concerned about the desires and wishes of the ruling class minority in the Caribbean that it would not dare attempt to 'enforce' federation in the West Indies but at the same time bring about federation in Malaya?" Malliet warned that progress toward federation and dominion status in the Commonwealth must move more swiftly, or the region might choose to break its historical ties with the British once and for all.[62]

In conjunction with the second session of the Anglo-American Caribbean Commission's "West Indian Conference," hosted in the US Virgin Islands in late February and early March 1946, a series of articles in the black press offered coverage and criticism of the meeting. This conference brought together delegates from US, British, French, and Dutch Caribbean colonies, with only minuscule representation of the black majorities or even elected officials in the Caribbean.[63] Charles Taussig, chairman of the US section, offered an optimistic tone in his speech by calling for the adoption of human rights and human obligations charters, which he and others believed could create a strong basis for development. Unfortunately, his proposal did not carry. The meeting continued with its agenda, including an assessment of progress made by the AACC in recent years, identification of the basic problems of West Indian economies and societies, and recommendations for further reform in the region.[64] As with previous official conferences, many West Indians and their allies doubted if anything beneficial would come from the recommendations at meetings in which representatives and voices of West Indians themselves remained small, and in many cases muted.

Shortly after its launch, a *New York Amsterdam News* editorial attached an alternative significance to the West Indian conference in St. Thomas. "More important than these rather 'social-workerish' items [is] the implication of solidifying bonds among the Negro populations of the Western Hemisphere."[65] Though most delegates and observers at the conference shied away from the racial aspects of West Indian reform efforts, others continued to read these matters through racialized lenses. As Malliet argued from the United States, "Race and the color line are more important in world affairs than most people are willing to admit."[66] Indeed, some in attendance noted an increase in Jim Crow–style racism in the islands and pushed for the adoption of antidiscriminatory policies in the various colonies. Other observers to official delegations, such as T. A. Marryshow of Grenada and Grantley Adams of Barbados, noted the problems inherent in the conference, where the overwhelmingly white delegates represented the governing powers in place of duly elected delegates speaking for West Indians themselves, which would invariably bring far more Afro-Caribbean delegates and voices from the region to the table.[67] By the close of the conference, little progress had been made. Much like the AACC itself, the West Indian conference was only an advisory body with no power to introduce policy. Still, many hoped more would come of it. As Ralph Bunche, who attended as part of the US delegation, noted, "It is now a solemn obligation of the governments here represented to insure that your words are translated into effective, beneficial action."[68] Nevertheless, many remained skeptical of the AACC, and its activities in the Caribbean.[69]

Ties between Caribbean nation building and black diaspora politics continued throughout 1946. From London, the LCP pressed demands to the Crown for a Caribbean federation. In the spring of 1946, the majority of attendees at an LCP-sponsored debate on federation supported the motion "Federation is an immediate necessity."[70] Back in the United States, Paul Robeson requested a statement from Manley on the West Indies, which was to be presented at another mass rally of the CAA at Madison Square Garden. Robeson claimed it would be "the mightiest demonstration on behalf of independence of colonial peoples, especially of Africa and the West Indies, which America has ever had." Though much of the meeting would demonstrate the CAA's particular focus on South Africa at this time, once again the future of the West Indies remained clearly intertwined with African and African American struggles.[71]

Strengthening the already close bonds between West Indian nationalists and African Americans, in May 1946 Howard University awarded Norman Manley an honorary doctorate in recognition of his work "to set the common people of Jamaica and the West Indies fully free and to make them competent to manage their own affairs in a truly democratic fashion." Although Manley was initially hesitant to accept the award, as he had personal qualms about receiving individual recognition for his efforts within the broader movement, he agreed to accept the honor so as not to alienate African American allies who supported his and others' work in the Caribbean. In a letter to Eric Williams, Manley said, "I so fully understand the broad motives that underlie the thing that Howard has done and its significance as a policy stand that I feel I would be guilty of betrayal if I did not sink the feelings that arise from this somewhat personal instinct."[72]

Manley relayed similar sentiments in letters to the editor of the *Gleaner* and a published letter thanking all of those who had congratulated him on his award from Howard. He claimed the award exemplified Black America's "interest in the Political and Social Movements of the West Indies . . . and the interests of coloured America with the progress of coloured people in the British Empire." In his estimation, "It is the work, not myself, that receives the honour and it would be easy for you to understand that in America, as I discovered, they are able to take a much broader historical perspective of what is going on in the West Indies than we who in our concerns with the day to day struggle sometimes fail to see our own horizons."[73] It is reasonable to assume his latter comment displayed not only recognition of a stronger sense of West Indianness outside the region, but also the overt role of race in garnering support for West Indian self-determination and federation.

In late 1946 various West Indian and black diaspora organizations continued their push for federation. In September, Petioni, Malliet, Ethelred Brown, and others held a roundtable sponsored by the Institute of Caribbean Affairs to discuss their proposals for federation and other connected issues, such as the forthcoming University of the West Indies and the need to train "native leaders" to administer the new West Indian governments under federation. The latter clearly indicates many diaspora activists believed firmly that those outside the West Indies would continue to play an important role within federation.[74] Around the same time, a new organization named the West Indies Conference Committee (WICC) was created under the slogan "For a Federated, Free and Independent West Indies." The WICC, which included activists such as Herman Osborne, Ethelred Brown, and Mabel Staupers, worked to coordinate the activities of West Indians in the United States on a national scale, fight what they believed was the intertwined struggle against lynching in the United States and colonialism in the Caribbean, for the political emancipation of West Indian women at home, and for the immediate realization of federation and self-government.[75] Though it gave the Caribbean priority focus, like many previous organizations, the WICC exemplified connections between US and West Indian struggles within the broader black diaspora activism of the era. Following communication between the WICC and the Barbados Progressive League on the matter of lynching in the United States, Grantley Adams wrote Walter White to express the BPL's support of the NAACP. "We stand together with you and all others who are engaged in the struggle against the common foe."[76] While there was undoubtedly similar support between numerous West Indian groups and a wide array of anticolonial activists and organizations, not just those of African descent, it is difficult to dismiss or diminish the ways in which race strengthened the bonds between African American, West Indian, and African struggles, despite periodic tensions and differences among some with each group.

The Watershed of 1947

The year 1947 was a watershed for decolonization within the British Empire, and for federation in the British Caribbean. At the imperial level, the end of the British Raj and the inauguration of India and Pakistan as independent nations in August was momentous. Despite the significant strife and loss of life attending the partition of India, the creation of these new nations proved a blow to the continuity of the empire and bolstered the hopes of anticolonial activists across the globe. As for the West Indies, the seemingly slow progress toward federation since the Stanley Dispatch received a boost early in the new year.

In February 1947 the new secretary of state for the colonies, Creech Jones, issued a new dispatch on the matter. Jones argued federation was the means through which to create a sizeable West Indian nation capable of standing on its own.

> It is clearly impossible in the modern world for the present separate communities, small or isolated as most of them are, to achieve and maintain full self-government on their own. . . . On the other hand a community of well over two million people in the Caribbean area, with much that is homogeneous in their culture, could reasonably hope to achieve real self-government and be strong enough to stand against economic and cultural pressure and to formulate and carry through a policy and way of life on its own.[77]

He called for the convening of a formal conference in Montego Bay, Jamaica, during September 1947 to discuss closer union between the various West Indian colonies. Jones suggested colonial legislatures nominate three delegates, to be accompanied by their colonies' legal and financial advisors, and joined by four observers from the Caribbean Commission to meet with British officials.[78]

As plans for this Conference on the Closer Association of the British West Indian Colonies, better known as the Montego Bay Conference, took shape, a new wave of fervor for federation emerged in the Caribbean and Harlem. Reminiscing on these days, Grantley Adams, future prime minister of the West Indies Federation, claimed, "We were now about to take practical steps toward a West Indian Federation and I honestly believed that such a federation would prove to be the greatest thing in the lives of West Indians—a phenomenon that would prove to be of importance second only to the great historic event of emancipation."[79]

Once again, various West Indian and black diaspora activists, with support and coverage from the black press, mobilized to prepare their visions of and support for federation. During a tour of the United States in early 1947 designed to "give American citizens a clear view of the tremendous importance of events unfolding so close to America's shore," Dr. Ivan Lloyd of Jamaica's PNP described and promoted the plans for a Caribbean federation as the "second Negro nation in the Western Hemisphere."[80] Malliet also continued to characterize the creation of federation as a black nation-building project in various articles and editorials. Writing in March, for instance, Malliet emphasized the need for Afro-Caribbeans to unite in the cause of West Indian self-determination. "Even if the spirit of a Toussaint L'Ouverture, Dessalines and Christophe, the greatest leaders of the African race, must be invoked to unite the black men of the West Indies, and the wrath and flames of all that is hateful in the hearts and souls of men fanned, a united Caribbean nation must arise and take its place in the world."[81] Such appeals to support for federation as part of a general program of racial uplift proved compelling and beneficial.

In March 1947, plans for a discussion of federation at an all–West Indian conference emerged. With costs estimated at $15,000 and only $3,000 likely available from the islands themselves, West Indians appealed to the transnational West Indian, African American, and other black organizations in the United States for the remaining funds.[82] In June, Norman Manley and Grantley Adams returned to the United States to speak to these organizations to continue their fund-raising efforts, and to push for greater cooperation between African Americans and West Indians in what was perceived as a cause affecting both groups as peoples of African descent. On 7 June approximately four hundred African Americans and West Indians attended a conference on West Indian federation at the Abyssinian Baptist Church in Harlem, where Manley and Adams spoke alongside West Indian activists, such as Bindley Cyrus of the Chicago-based American West Indian Association (AWIA), and even African nationalist Nnamdi Azikiwe. The speakers called for the creation of a nationwide organization of West Indians and African Americans to support the goal of federation, arguing, "The inclusion of American Negroes in [the] new organization will strengthen it financially and politically and will increase [the] chances of obtaining federation for [the] West Indies."[83] A few days later, on 10 June, Manley and Adams met with the NAACP to discuss similar ideas for "closer integration activities [between] West Indian and American Negroes." On 13 June a preliminary meeting of an ad hoc committee for closer relations between these groups and a Caribbean federation took place at the NAACP's New York office. The organization would be cochaired by real estate mogul A. A. Austin, a longtime Jamaican resident of New York, and Walter White of the

NAACP, and supported by "a central committee composed of representative persons of both groups from all over the country."[84]

By July, plans for the all–West Indian conference became more concrete. This meeting was to take place in Kingston, shortly before the official Montego Bay Conference, under the auspices of the CLC (thereby leading to its unofficial moniker as the CLC Conference). There the CLC planned to draft proposals for federation, which would be presented to official delegates at the later conference. In July the West Indian–African American ad hoc committee became official with the launch of the American Association for Caribbean Advancement (AACA). For the moment, it aimed to raise $10,000 for the upcoming CLC Conference.[85]

Although the AACA included African American and West Indian support, upon its formal founding, Channing Tobias, chairman of the NAACP and a member of the AACA, said the committee should clarify that while the AACA was cooperating with the CLC, this did not constitute formal endorsement of the CLC's entire program. He was presumably acknowledging the US government's continued suspicions of international connections between these black populations and a desire to not alienate their support of the NAACP. Nevertheless, while he likely shared some of Tobias's concerns, Walter White noted his hopes that the funds raised would keep supporters' eyes on the goals at hand and that the recent divisions between West Indians would be set aside.[86]

There were indeed long-standing differences of opinion between many West Indians in New York, but other than periodic elevated tensions, they had largely been able to sink their ideological differences in order to work together for the common cause of West Indian liberation. However, with progress toward federation, divisions along ideological lines became more prominent among West Indians abroad. Some of this, as hinted by Tobias, may have been connected to rising Cold War politics in the United States. However, much was analogous to divisions and power struggles between West Indian political parties within the islands, such as in the contentious rivalry of Jamaica's two primary political leaders and parties—Alexander Bustamante, leader of the Bustamante Industrial Trades Union and the Jamaica Labour Party (JLP), and Norman Manley, leader of the Peoples' National Party in Jamaica. In June 1947 Malliet, who increasingly drifted to the right in these years, resumed his criticism of some former WINC members, several of whom stood ready to play a significant role in other organizations following the demise of the WINC. Malliet warned that poor leadership could sidetrack the agreed-upon purpose and goals of groups such as the AACA.[87] Still, he continued to work with some WINC members like Richard B. Moore, and an increasingly loose united West Indian front maintained among most expatriate West Indian activists and their allies.

Around the same time, Herman Osborne, a former WINC member and now spokesman for the West Indies Conference Committee (WICC), wrote to Manley in late July complaining that Austin, who worked increasingly closely with Osborne's former WINC colleagues, including Charles Petioni, Richard B. Moore, and Hope Stevens, had pushed the WICC aside during the creation of the previously planned West Indian–African American organization (which became the AACA).[88] The specifics of this dispute remain unclear, but by August little else was heard from the WICC and Osborne, while Austin's organization pushed on with its fund-raising efforts. Although tensions between West Indian activists were often confined to verbal sparring, in some cases they did escalate. In August 1947, for instance, Malliet and the recently returned W. A. Domingo, who had maintained a lower public profile following his internment in Jamaica, engaged in a physical confrontation in Richard B. Moore's Harlem bookstore.[89]

Despite some discord among West Indians activists in the United States, in August the CLC received $10,000 from expatriate West Indians and African Americans "to help carry on the brilliant and effective fight for West Indian independence and federation which the Congress has led since it was organized in September 1945."[90] These funds represented more than simply transnational support by West Indians for their homelands. They demonstrated the ways in which race motivated support for federation among expatriate West Indians and African Americans. As Alexander Bustamante commented resentfully on this support for the CLC, with its close association with his political rivals the Manley-led PNP, "I am cognizant that Americans and West Indians love to feel they are fighting for the betterment of their race."[91] Shortly after these communities raised the $10,000 to help fund the CLC Conference in Kingston, a *New York Amsterdam News* article noted the commonly held belief that a Caribbean federation could help the domestic struggles of African Americans. "It is not too much to assume, perhaps, that the UN representative of a federated West Indies will concern themselves with the plight of disfranchised Negro Americans. When we aid the people of the West Indies in their independence fight today, we aid our fight for freedom in America tomorrow."[92]

Hopes remained high that the CLC Conference would stimulate and solidify unity among West Indians in their pursuit of federation. Days before the conference, Malliet offered an optimistic, yet cautious, assessment of what the upcoming CLC and Montego Bay Conferences, as well as federation, could produce. "These two conferences are important and should succeed in laying solid foundations for the building of a united Caribbean nation in the future." He cautioned, however, "Federation [alone] will not solve the many problems which keep the West Indies among the backward areas of the world. . . . As we see it, federation is one of the first and basic steps to be taken to launch a program of national reconstruction" from which a modern and thriving West Indian nation could emerge. Noting that many in the West Indies had not been properly prepared by the British, he also hinted that federation and self-government might not be instituted together, and claimed that the "success or failure of any plan of federation will depend almost entirely upon Britain's attitude and assistance."[93]

Delegates and observers of the CLC Conference met on 2–9 September 1947 in Kingston, Jamaica. Attendees included a blend of old and new West Indian labor and political leaders from the region, including T. A. Marryshow (president of the CLC), Grantley Adams, Hugh Springer, Norman Manley, Albert Gomes, and Herbert Critchlow. Here the CLC reiterated demands for a federation and "internal responsible government" for the member territories. "This Conference declares in favour of the establishment of a federation of the British Caribbean territories and of the immediate initiation of all practical steps that must be taken to secure that end." Delegates argued that no barriers to this goal existed that could not be overcome by "the united will and the combined statesmanship and leadership of the peoples of our lands." On the matter of federation, they stipulated two key components: (1) each territory must be granted a new constitution that provided internal self-government immediately upon the creation of the federal structure, and (2) the federal constitution must provide for responsible government—that is, dominion status. The CLC Conference also offered extensive proposals for the various components of the federation itself, including the federal constitution and the powers and structure of the federal government, including executive officers, federal parliament, and judiciary.[94]

The delegates to the CLC Conference planned to share their proposals with delegates at the official Montego Bay Conference, and those scheduled to attend both meetings were expected to support the resolutions of the

CLC at the latter meeting. Given that Colonial Secretary Creech Jones also spoke at the CLC conference, where he offered praise to the CLC for its "historical contribution to the common life of the people in the West Indies," many were optimistic their goals might be achieved in the very near future.[95]

Although the role of expatriate West Indians and African Americans in raising money for the CLC Conference was crucial, they did more than simply fund-raise. A. A. Austin and Bindley Cyrus attended the conference as representatives of the American Committee for West Indian Federation (ACWIF), which was apparently the recently organized AACA under a revised name.[96] In Kingston, Austin shared with attendees a "Memorandum on Federation and Self-Government of the West Indies" prepared for the ACWIF by Richard B. Moore. The presentation of this memo continued the tradition of expatriate and black diaspora organizations' support for Caribbean federation. However, while in many previous efforts these West Indian and black diaspora activists spoke for the region, this exchange differed. As Joyce Moore Turner notes in her recent study of expatriate West Indian activism, "This was a change—the document was not submitted on behalf of the Caribbean peoples, but directly to Caribbean representatives in support of their efforts."[97]

The ACWIF's memorandum and three appendices addressed various aspects of Caribbean federation. It noted, "In such a momentous hour, our Committee feels it to be an inescapable duty to address your Conference." The ACWIF claimed the memo represented "another tangible expression of the deep and abiding interests of West Indians" who have migrated to the United States but not forsaken their homelands. "Along with their devotion to the best traditions and highest interests of the country of their adoption, they have never lost their feeling of solidarity with their brothers in the Caribbean, nor their sense of obligation to render every possible aid toward the development and advancement" of them. It also recognized the "growing interest and solidarity of persons of African descent born in [the United States], who are increasingly conscious of the ties of common interest which link their destiny with that of their brothers in the West Indies."[98] Austin echoed the latter sentiments to Jamaica's *Daily Gleaner* when he claimed "that federation would have a psychological effect on Negroes' own status in the great republic."[99] On the issue of federation, the memorandum detailed the ACWIF's support for it, the need to push for a definite date for its creation, and the organization's insistence that a federation be composed of sovereign states, rather than a collection of colonies. During his presentation of the memorandum at the conference, Austin also announced plans for another New York–based organization, the American Association for West Indian Advancement (AAWIA), which aimed to "further the aims of federation in the West Indies."[100]

A few days after the close of the CLC Conference, the Montego Bay Conference opened on 11 September 1947. Twenty-two delegates from the colonies met alongside representatives from the British section of the Caribbean Commission, legal and economic advisors, and British officials "to consider the formulation of proposals for closer association." The colonies' delegates, nominated by the respective colonial legislatures, included some of the key leaders associated with island and regional political movements in the West Indies—Grantley Adams and W. A. Crawford of Barbados, Bustamante and Manley of Jamaica, V. C. Bird of Antigua, and Albert Gomes of Trinidad—but they were only a minority of the overall conference participants. Over the course of the next week, numerous committees and subcommittees debated the possibilities of federation, its structure, costs, and possible benefits, which exposed the disparate views on federation and its purpose and demonstrated the ongoing tensions between the islandism of some, such as the misgivings and at times outright opposition to federation among a few delegates from Jamaica (particularly Bustamante) and British Guiana, and the more overt regionalism of others.

In spite of these sometimes contentious debates, by the close of the Montego Bay Conference, all the colonial representatives except British Guiana's delegation accepted the principle of a federation in which each unit would retain control over all matters not specifically given to the federal government. Among the most important recommendations of the conference was the proposal for a Standing Closer Association Committee (SCAC) "to report on the most suitable form of [a] federal constitution and judiciary, and the means of financing federal service" within the next two years. Other proposals included increasing "responsible government" in most colonies (though no timetable was established), and the creation of various committees for further investigation of economic conditions and opportunities in the British Caribbean colonies, particularly as they related to joint efforts between the colonies in these matters. Overall, many delegates and onlookers believed the resolutions of the conference to be a successful first step toward the goal of federation, although all understood much work remained.[101]

Many West Indian and black diaspora activists in the United States, who followed the events of the CLC and Montego Bay Conferences closely, cel-

ebrated these actions as bringing the long-sought West Indian nation closer
to reality. Some assumed it could come about within just a few years. During the early days of the Montego Bay Conference, one *Pittsburgh Courier*
article noted that while the British were concerned with improving social
and economic conditions in hopes of "developing a larger measure of self-
government, the native delegates . . . are interested in going much further in
the direction of dominion status or even independence." It emphasized the
practicality of a federation between the islands, given their many similarities, including race, and questioned how the more diverse India was able to
achieve its freedom before the West Indies. "There is no more reason why
India should have her freedom than there is for the British West Indies
to have their freedom. Indeed there is less."[102] A few weeks later, an Associated Negro Press article claimed that the British stood ready to grant
self-government in the West Indies, but that while most delegates accepted
"federation in principle," they differed on "how and when."[103] Upon his return to Chicago, Bindley Cyrus of the ACWIF and the American West Indian Association, who along with A. A. Austin attended both the CLC and
Montego Bay Conferences, optimistically claimed the West Indies would
have dominion status within the British Commonwealth by 1949, when the
SCAC's proposal on the federal constitution and structure was expected.[104]
Similarly, under a banner proclaiming "New Nation Born," the *Pittsburgh
Courier*'s brief summary of the Montego Bay Conference incorrectly reported the conference resolved to grant dominion status to the British Ca-
ribbean within two years.[105]

Richard B. Moore, secretary of the ACWIF, offered one of the more
substantial reflections on the CLC and Montego Bay Conferences. Moore
described the agreement reached at Montego Bay as "official recognition
to the popular demands for a united West Indian nation." He claimed little
surprise at the support there for federation, given the actions of the CLC
Conference the previous week. "The age old demand of the West Indian
people for voluntary federation with full self-government attained to such
clear expression and challenging power at that epoch making conference
that the results of the Montego Bay conference were almost a foregone
conclusion." Moore recalled the crucial support of federation by some key
delegates such as Gomes, Crawford, Adams, and Manley, while also decrying the opposition of some like Bustamante, who instead pushed for
Jamaican self-government before ultimately supporting further discussion.
The opportunity for a federation, "born at the Kingston conference and
swaddled at Montego Bay," was at hand. To ensure that opponents, such as

the "planter and big merchant classes," did not sidetrack the project, Moore pleaded with West Indians and their allies to continue the push for federation, including support from the US-based advocates.[106]

In conjunction with these various proclamations on what was perceived as a significant step forward in the federation movement, many stressed the importance of these actions in diasporic terms. Speaking around the time of the CLC and Montego Bay Conferences in 1947, Paul Robeson noted the "tremendous significance" of Caribbean federation "to colored people throughout the world," and called for "stronger support by American negroes" for federation and independence.[107] He said, "At this moment in world history nothing could be more important than the establishment of an independent Negro country to the south of us," which could "help show the way to Negro peoples in Africa."[108]

Richard B. Moore's reflection on these conferences also highlighted connections to the broader black diaspora struggles of this era. Caribbean federation, he maintained, would "hasten the day of full equality and self-determination for the millions of African descent in the United States, for the African and all other colonial peoples, and for all working and oppressed people everywhere regardless of race, color or creed."[109]

Still another editorial celebrated the importance of the Montego Bay Conference to Black America.

> This event is of extraordinary interest to all liberty-loving Americans, especially to the fifteen million citizens of African descent in this republic. For it signifies another great historic triumph for genuine democracy. Since the overwhelming majority of these Caribbean people are of African origin, this recognition by [the] British of their right of self-determination and self-rule constitutes an important international setback to the pernicious theory and practice of "white supremacy." The rising free Caribbean Commonwealth will thus be greeted with enthusiasm and acclaim.[110]

These and other reflections in the wake of the Montego Bay Conference demonstrate the continued characterization by some of West Indian nation building as a racialized, black nation-building project. Writing in January 1948, Horace R. Cayton claimed the Montego Bay Conference resolutions were the "most decisive step on the steep climb from chattel slavery toward self-government and nationhood." Although Cayton connected Caribbean federation with the broader anticolonial struggles of India, Burma, and Palestine, he argued those were "brown people," while the efforts for the West

Indies was "the first time a group of black people within the British Empire have set their sights on complete freedom and have some chance of obtaining it."[111] Cayton's comments demonstrate what one US official referred to as "a strong movement on the part of certain colored peoples in the United States to press federation of the British West Indies for the prime purpose of seeing a colored independent entity composed of the British West Indian islands."[112]

Despite the excitement of many in the immediate aftermath of the Montego Bay Conference, others tempered this enthusiasm. Manley demonstrated a more reserved hopefulness in communications with black diaspora activists in New York and London. Writing to W. A. Domingo in October, Manley recalled the great success of the CLC Conference, but said he did "not take the Montego Bay decisions at their face value. The fact is that every important decision has been referred for further study and the important elements whose final decisions would be decisive have not really committed themselves to anything." Nevertheless, he believed that with continued effort from their US supporters, the CLC could continue "the business of building up a mass opinion."[113] In reply to a November letter from George Padmore, who had recently announced preliminary discussions for the creation of a London-based organization "for the purpose of propagandising West Indian Federation," Manley responded, "I am afraid we are further away from Federation than a superficial glance at the Federation Conference might suggest. The real gain is that the idea is now in the open. If the Caribbean Labour Congress can develop its work and if [the PNP] could win through in Jamaica the thing might go forward but there is a lot of work yet to be done."[114] Malliet, who had expressed doubts on the effectiveness of the conferences beforehand, announced his dismay that the West Indian delegates at Montego Bay had not presented a "more united and encouraging front," which could have produced greater and more concrete gains for federation.[115]

From Montego Bay to the Rance Report

From late 1947 through late 1949, official debates over federation, as defined by the Montego Bay resolutions, continued among the British and various colonial governments. In December 1947 the secretary of state for the colonies issued another dispatch to the colonial governors of the British Caribbean regarding the Montego Bay resolutions. Maintaining official colonial policy not to force the colonies into federation, he instructed the various colonial legislatures to debate the conference resolutions, including the creation of the Standing Closer Association Committee. By the late spring of 1948, all the colonial legislatures represented at the Montego Bay Conference—including British Guiana, which had not accepted federation at that meeting—agreed to participate in the SCAC. Over the next year and a half, the SCAC met four times to create proposals for the federal constitution and structure: Barbados (November 1948), Trinidad (March 1949), Barbados (June 1949), and Jamaica (October 1949).[116]

During these years, the initial excitement following the Montego Bay Conference appeared to wane, especially within the region itself. As Gordon Lewis describes it, "The hammering out of the federal constitution—optimistically assumed by the Montego Bay conference to be the work of a brief period only—became, in fact, a tedious process." Lewis also claimed that much of the ongoing planning for the proposed federation became confined to the work of West Indian politicians and British officials, with little input from the West Indian masses. While true, is it surprising that official planning took shape among these groups and not the masses? Was this not the case in past and present nation-building endeavors in most other locales? A more valid criticism, and one that Lewis also makes, is that there remained little evidence of "enthusiastic popular opinion" among the masses in the colonies for federation—nor, more important, any "serious effort to educate the West Indian peoples" about it.[117]

Although true for much of the region at times, this overlooks the continued activism of expatriate West Indians and their allies outside the region. Indeed, as in many previous years, their efforts to rally mass support for federation matched, if not outdistanced, efforts within the Caribbean colonies themselves. Even as further intra-regional debates over the Montego Bay resolutions ensued in 1948, Caribbean federation continued to receive significant coverage and support in the US black press. Despite some shared disillusionment at the slow pace of official discussions, there remained a commitment to maintain the momentum toward federation, lest it wither away into another lost dream or broken promise.

A. M. Wendell Malliet, as much as any other activist in this era, kept federation before his West Indian and African American readers in the *New York Amsterdam News*. Inspired by the independence of Burma in early 1948, which he claimed "should serve as an inspiration to the people of the British Caribbean," Malliet argued, "Federation is not a dream of an idealist lost in the clouds of wishful dreaming and hopeful thinking," and "nationality and self-government are the stepping stones to progress and respect among the peoples of the earth."[118] Over the next several months, Malliet routinely criticized the Montego Bay Conference for its failure to devise definitive plans for federation, which he believed was "a matter for immediate realization; not a project for some time in the future." Caribbean federation, he insisted, must include responsible government and dominion status with control over its own foreign and domestic policies, and a sound economic plan (including British financial support) when launched. Moreover, like many of his colleagues, he maintained that US-based activists must maintain their vigorous support for federation.[119] Malliet's repeated calls to sustain the momentum and demands for federation while awaiting the SCAC report stressed not only the duty of West Indians in the United States to advance the cause of federation but also the support of African Americans, because "a sovereign and independent commonwealth in the Caribbean will be an achievement of which [African Americans], too, should and will be proud."[120]

Other expatriate West Indian and black diaspora activists and organizations also kept the pursuit of Caribbean federation before the public. The various ad hoc committees created before and after the CLC and Montego Bay Conferences presented and pushed the cause of Caribbean federation as a matter of much importance. A. A. Austin and his colleagues presented reports on these conferences to supporters and interested parties in the New York area.[121] Despite some tensions between Austin's organization and the NAACP following the Montego Bay Conference, the NAACP, which helped raise funds for many of these endeavors and continued to garner praise from the Caribbean for its racial activism, maintained its support for Caribbean federation.[122] Richard B. Moore presented the plight of Caribbean peoples, especially those from the British West Indies, before the U.S. Progressive Party's national convention in mid-1948.[123] A Harlem meeting that summer marking the 113th anniversary of Emancipation noted with excitement "the new Emancipation which looks forward to federation of the Caribbean with full political sovereignty."[124]

While there had been some indications of its presence in previous years, in the fall of 1948 the simmering Cold War thrust itself further into debates over Caribbean federation. Similar to increased tensions and schisms within the African American freedom movement, philosophical differences fractured some Caribbean political movements at this time. The CLC, which had risen to prominence only three years earlier, soon found itself crippled by ideological "left-wing" and "right-wing" divisions among its members. In October 1948, around the same time that DuBois was forced from the NAACP for pushing a human rights agenda before the UN, two events displayed these divisions within the CLC. Albert Gomes, vice president of the CLC, who had been aligned with Manley and other more socialist activists as late as Montego Bay, announced his support of Bustamante due to concerns that the PNP and allied groups were communist.[125] The following week, Grantley Adams's defense of British colonial policies before a UN meeting in Paris, which he attended as a member of the British delegation, created much consternation among more progressive Caribbean and diaspora activists. Colleagues within the CLC, such as Richard Hart, as well as a variety of others throughout the diaspora, including Nnamdi Azikiwe in Africa, George Padmore in London, and Richard B. Moore in New York, denounced Adams for betraying the anticolonial cause.[126] While both Gomes and Adams defended themselves against their critics and dismissed allegations that their actions set back the push for Caribbean liberation and federation, the fallout from these events severely fractured the CLC and foreshadowed future divisions within West Indian political movements resulting from the Cold War.[127]

Support for federation remained steady through 1949 as federation advocates in and out of the Caribbean anxiously awaited the SCAC report. Among transnational West Indian and black diaspora organizations in the United States, this excitement continued to be associated primarily with what many viewed as the pending creation of a new black nation. Over the course of the year, the issues of federation became tied to ongoing debates regarding new restrictions on West Indian immigration to the United States. In March the US House of Representatives passed HR 199, a bill that would restrict immigration from the British West Indies to one hundred persons a year by removing the right of colonial peoples to enter under the larger numbers of their "mother country." As the bill awaited debate in the US Senate, familiar West Indian and African American activists and organizations—A. A. Austin, Wendell Malliet, Reginald Pierrepointe, Richard B. Moore, the NAACP, newly created ad hoc committees such as the Queens Committee on Antillean Immigration and the United Caribbean American Council (UCAC), and others—rallied against its "unwarranted and discriminatory" language.[128]

Under the chairmanship of Austin, with Moore as secretary, the UCAC claimed to represent thirty organizations of "native born and foreign born citizens and residents of the United States" and sought to "unite Caribbeans and Americans for mutual protection and common advancement," including protest against the restrictions of HR 199.[129] Although British officials claimed initially that the UCAC was a communist organization, further investigation by the FBI showed this was not the case.[130] The UCAC organized public rallies in the New York area and protested the discriminatory language of the pending immigration bill. They and allied organizations like the AWIA presented the possible restrictions on West Indian immigration as but another attack on black peoples, and connected it to the fight for civil rights and equal employment and to anti-lynching and anti–poll tax efforts in the United States. At a rally in May 1949 that included Austin, Moore, and Adam Clayton Powell, speakers noted, "The Caribbean Peoples are almost all of African descent and would be the only peoples in this hemisphere subjected to such injurious restriction. . . . In view of the number of Europeans now being admitted, this discrimination is vicious and reflects directly against American citizens of African descent as well as upon the democratic status of all Americans."[131]

Protests against the possible immigration restrictions were also presented directly to the US and British governments. In a joint statement by the UCAC and AWIA before a US Senate subcommittee in July 1949, the groups argued, "It appears that this restrictive provision is aimed also at discouraging and deterring peoples of African descent from the United States. This reflects adversely upon the fifteen million Americans of African descent who constitute the largest single minority in this nation of minorities."[132] As for federation, the UCAC noted its connections to this particular struggle before the British Embassy, when Moore said that the creation of a "free Federate Caribbean Commonwealth" would "remove these Caribbean people from the dire disabilities and searing stigma inseparable from colonial status and entitle them . . . to equal treatment in respect to immigration and other vital questions."[133] In this sense, federation would create the nation that would in turn allow West Indians to take their place as equal peoples, not subject to the immigration restrictions as colonial peoples, and also aid in the larger struggles of black people in the United States.

In the months prior to the release of the SCAC report in the spring of 1950, there remained much excitement about the possible launch of the federation and its ramifications beyond the Caribbean. In late 1949 a *Pittsburgh Courier* editorial characterized federation as "the dream of the three million colored people of the British West Indies." Although some could argue the use of "colored" was not restricted to only those of African descent, any ambiguity was removed when the same article predicted, "Before long British imperialism will cease in the Caribbean, and a new Negro nation will be born."[134]

In January–February 1950, Robert Adams, a West Indian barrister, actor, lecturer, and singer based in London, penned a series of articles on "the color and race problem in Britain and the Empire" for the *New York Amsterdam News*. While relaying to readers the continued problems of racism and discrimination in the Caribbean and in Britain, Adams registered skepticism of the recent official Crown support for federation. He claimed, given that "In the West Indies . . . where the majority of the population is black and where federation and dominion status would mean political domination by the black majority . . . it is reasonable that people of African descent should be suspicious as to the reasons of the apparent generosity of the British Government."[135] In his last article Adams argued federation would empower the black masses, and for that reason "the plantocracy of the colonies will always oppose federation in the West Indies, because after federation, their stranglehold on the political, economic and social life of the area will be broken."[136] Suspicions aside, Adams's presentation of federation as a new black nation, as well as description of the worries and opposition to federation by the white minorities and other nonblack groups within the West Indies, further tied the creation of a Caribbean federation to notions of black empowerment and self-determination in this era.

A similar attitude was relayed by T. A. Marryshow on his visits to the United States in late 1949 and early 1950. During his stay in December for medical treatment, Marryshow spoke to various interested West Indian and African American parties on the possibilities of federation. On 2 December, at a small meeting of West Indians attended by NAACP public relations director Henry Moon, Marryshow detailed the work of the CLC to bring about federation and dominion status for the West Indian colonies.[137] In the following weeks, at a reception held in his honor by local West Indian activists including Petioni, Austin, Stevens, and Moore, Marryshow said that "federation of the Caribbean with self-government is the basic essential for providing the means of solving [poverty] and other vital questions which adversely affect the future of the area." He argued, "We cannot accept any kind of federation which will not give us full self-government."[138] On their own, Marryshow's statements appear to present efforts to create federation as a national (or regional) struggle of West Indians. However, as he had done for many decades, Marryshow saw federation as far more.

In a February 1950 speech at the UCAC-sponsored Caribbean American Folk Festival in New York, Marryshow dismissed allegations of a growing "anti-British feeling" in the Caribbean, and instead presented federation as a struggle against colonialism and imperialism. He did not, however, shy away from emphasizing the racial aspects of this struggle and of a federation. "Speaking to an audience he termed Americans of African descent," Marryshow encouraged the crowd to make their contributions to both Black America and the Caribbean. "Be good Americans, continuing to make worthy contributions to the country of your adoption." At the same time, he reminded them, "Your destiny is one with your brothers in the Caribbean and a free nation there will [redound] to your prestige and advancement."[139]

During this same visit, Marryshow shared similar ideas in a presentation to the Grenada Mutual Association. Over the course of his hour-long address, he claimed that federation was within the grasp of its supporters and encouraged those in the United States to maintain and bolster their support of their homelands by uniting their various West Indian organizations. Emphasizing the need for federation, self-government, and dominion status, Marryshow urged listeners, "Be more than arm-chair admirers or arm-chair critics of what goes on at home. Just as Irish independence was won right here in New York by the vision, the efforts and sacrifices of remembering Irishmen abroad, so you too, as remembering men, even though with different methods, may help us win national recognition for our West Indies." He said the time for meetings, petitions, resolutions, and investigative commissions had passed. "It is for us, we in the West Indies in combination with West Indians here, to act as real students of the situation and chart our own road of progress."

Marryshow's speech also addressed the need to further build racial solidarity between West Indians and African Americans and to connect their respective racialized struggles for mutual benefit.

> Prove yourselves reliable and worthy in offices of trust and so act that your native brothers in blood will be bound to admit that it is good that you are here and that others like you should come and dwell among them. . . . Stand up with others in America for great principles, associate yourselves with fine and noble causes, for as "native-sons" of a West indies old in the struggle for freedom, you should have a distinct contribution to make in building race solidarity here and everywhere as the one and only basis for a self-discovered pride and dignity in Negro life and being.

As for the connections between race and federation, Marryshow noted the role race had possibly played in its delay, as well as the positive impact of federation on struggles of the black diaspora.

A Dominion of the West Indies should have existed long ago and with due ceremony have taken part in calling up Ceylon to equal sisterhood in the Commonwealth. Is it because the West Indies are preponderantly peopled by blacks? For the time being, with India and Ceylon in the fold, a browning down process has taken place in the common complexion of Commonwealth statesmen. We must see to it that the West Indies, Negro America and Africa do their own blackening up of the United Nations before long.[140]

In March 1950 the SCAC released its long-awaited report. Commonly known as the Rance Report, it recommended creation of a British Caribbean Federation including Barbados, British Guiana, British Honduras, Jamaica, Antigua, St. Kitts–Nevis, Montserrat, Trinidad and Tobago, Grenada, St. Vincent, St. Lucia, and Dominica. The committee described this project as the quickest path *to* self-government for these West Indian colonies and described the project as an "economic and political necessity." They proposed a federal government composed of a bicameral legislature with a wholly elected House of Assembly and fully nominated Senate; a federal executive consisting of a governor-general (representing the Crown), an advisory Council of State, and a prime minster elected by the House of Assembly; and a federal supreme court. The constitution followed the Australian model, with the federal government's powers restricted only to those specifically given to it, and all other power residing in the individual colonial governments of the participating islands. It suggested the Crown provide financial assistance for the first two years. As for the issue of self-government (dominion status) for the federation, the committee did not recommend it at this time.[141]

The SCAC's proposal for a weak-centered federation with limited powers and continued colonial status was hardly the self-governing federation that many West Indians or their black diaspora allies had envisioned. Not surprisingly, it received mixed reactions from federation supporters in the Caribbean and the wider black diaspora. In the United States, Malliet offered an extensive summary of the Rance Report to readers in early March, with little indication of his own personal opinion.[142] The following month, a *New York Amsterdam News* article argued that although it was difficult to predict what would come of the SCAC's report in the Caribbean, "viewed from any angle, the Report and Recommendations constitute a far reaching step not only in the British Caribbean but also in the history of worldwide colonialism."[143]

Between mid-April and early May, a four-part series by Malliet appeared in the *New York Amsterdam News*. While his previous article had simply summarized the Rance Report, this series demonstrated Malliet's mixed reactions. He claimed the SCAC would bring federation and independence closer to reality if it was able to get through local debates in the Caribbean. In defense of what some considered the inaction of the report, Malliet reminded readers the committee was only charged to make recommendations. Malliet displayed some concern over the proposed reserved powers of the governor-general and the financial structure of federation. Still, in spite of some "grave shortcomings," he believed the proposed federation was a step in the right direction. Surprisingly, given his long-standing arguments on the critical role of West Indians in the United States on matters regarding their Caribbean homelands, he argued that the acceptance or rejection of the report was a matter for Caribbean peoples—implicitly limited to those in the West Indian colonies—to decide for themselves.[144] Moreover, unlike most of Malliet's writings on federation, these articles appear to de-emphasize the diasporic and racialized dimensions of federation, instead portraying it primarily as an intra-regional project.

Among organizations, the UCAC proved one of the most active involving discussions of the Rance Report. In March it organized a Good Neighbor Anniversary program designed to "foster closer relations between Americans and West Indians and to aid the Caribbean Labour Congress in its striving for economic and social advancement and federation and self-government." The gathering also planned to analyze and discuss the SCAC's report.[145] Although no record of this meeting's discussion of the report can be found, the following month UCAC secretary Richard B. Moore noted to CLC secretary Richard Hart,

> Our immediate reaction is that this [proposed constitution] is neither a plan for federation nor self-government. It seems to us also that there is grave danger that this "glorified crown colony government" (to use the apt phrase of Mr. Marryshow) will be foisted upon the Caribbean people unless there is a clear and firm stand of the leaders of the people's organizations and of the broad masses of the people themselves.[146]

Around the same time, the Women's Committee of the UCAC hosted multiple meetings on the Rance Report and federation during April and May. These included public discussions such as "Is Federation the Path to Self-

Government for the Caribbean People?" "Federal Caribbean Constitution," and "Should British Guiana Be Included in a Caribbean Federation?"[147]

Amid the various discussions of the recently released SCAC report and plans for federation, African Americans and West Indians continued to highlight the ties between these groups and the benefit of a self-governing West Indian nation to Black America. In April 1950 a group of West Indians and African Americans met to discuss plans for the creation of a permanent "West Indian-American organization to aid the people of the British Caribbean in their fight for federation and self-government," including financial and moral support of the CLC in the Caribbean. "The speakers endorsed the project as necessary in the over-all development of the African peoples in the United States and abroad: they saw in the forward movement of the people in the Caribbean a raising of the world-wide level of Negro advancement, which was essential to the 15,000,000 Negroes in the United States."[148]

The following week, a *New York Amsterdam News* editorial applauded the "local efforts" of West Indians in the cause of Caribbean federation, including their efforts with the CLC, at the Montego Bay Conference, and in the SCAC meetings. It also reminded readers that the joint efforts of West Indians and African Americans in the United States should not be forgotten in the building of federation.

> The Amsterdam News welcomes the spirit of cooperation which would extend its effectiveness into the Caribbean; it looks upon all efforts to unite and strengthen the forces of the African peoples in the United States and the world at large as a great contribution to racial pride and achievement, to democracy and national solidarity, to the recognition of human rights and responsibilities.[149]

West Indian nation building, therefore, remained for many far more than simply a West Indian project.

One could argue over the extent to which these sentiments seeped into the consciousness of Black America as a whole, particularly in regions where black communities lacked the multinational population found in other areas. However, we must remember that while many of the organizations that supported federation in this era may have been centered in the New York area, the black press undoubtedly took their messages, as well as their own perspectives, well beyond simply New York and other large metropolitan areas. Indeed, if one of the criticisms *within* the West Indies was that there was not an effort to educate the masses on the benefits of federation or to rally support for it, the same cannot be said of transnational West Indian, African American, and other black diaspora activists and organizations in the United States. Here the reasons to support federation were quite defined—and quite racialized—not only as expressed by US-based supporters but also as emphasized and played to by visiting West Indian politicians in much more explicit ways than one finds in their activities within the colonies.

As the long-standing dream of a united West Indian nation moved closer to reality, with greater commitment from the Crown and greater participation of local political parties in the mid-late 1940s, the project undoubtedly became increasingly perceived and promoted by some as an intra-regional endeavor. Nevertheless, as had been the case for much of the twentieth century, expatriate West Indians, African Americans, and other black diaspora activists (particularly, though not solely, in the United States) remained important in the transnational and diasporic efforts to forge a Caribbean federation. More than just vocal outsiders who lacked a clear understanding of what was transpiring within the region, these "insiders outside" continued to maintain close contacts with Caribbean leaders and movements within the Caribbean, and offered crucial moral and material support, even as they transitioned from their vanguard roles of previous decades to more auxiliary supportive roles.

Unfortunately, in the years after the Rance Report, there would be significant difficulty in translating ideas into action within the West Indies. Racialized diasporic perceptions of federation shared by many outside and some inside the Caribbean had rarely caused problems up to this time, coexisting alongside transracial and multiracial views of the region. Similarly, islandist and regionalist perspectives had also long coexisted. However, as plans for federation took final shape in the 1950s, these and other issues would become increasingly scrutinized as the very notion of a unifying West Indianness was put to the test.

4

Finalizing, Defining, and Welcoming the New Nation, 1950–1958

As the 1950s began, the British Caribbean colonies stood on the verge of nationhood. The final steps to its attainment and the particular form it would take, however, remained uncertain. There continued to be divided opinions within almost all groups involved—West Indian politicians and the general population, British colonial officials, and other interested parties outside the region—on whether the different colonies would (and should) proceed individually or together toward nationhood, as well as various questions related to the degree and achievement of self-government.

The release of the Rance Report in March 1950 by the Standing Closer Association Committee offered some clarity on these issues when it established that British Caribbean colonies would move together in a federation toward, rather than with, self-government. This marked an important milestone in the history of Caribbean federation. Over the course of several decades, the wide-ranging efforts of federation supporters, in and out of the Caribbean, had laid crucial groundwork for the creation of a united West Indian nation. More recently, regional meetings such as the CLC and Montego Bay conferences of 1947 promoted discussions of the issue, with the latter securing a commitment from the colonial governments to explore the matter of federation further. Without diminishing the crucial role of these prior actions, while various federation plans had been proposed and debated for years, concrete planning between West Indians and Britain (the colonized and colonizer) for the actual formation of a federation had not taken place. With the release and approval of the Rance Report, discussions moved from debates over the possibility of federation to formal discussions over its specific structure.

The Rance Report initiated a series of official conferences at which final negotiations for a Caribbean federation took place between West Indian political leaders and the British government. The series of official meetings on federation in the 1950s have been well documented in the existing historiography. The progress and final steps toward federation certainly excited some supporters, even as the slow process and internal debates proved taxing and troubling for some delegates and onlookers who wondered when, if, and how federation would be achieved. As these conferences and their subsequent agreements established the structures and powers of the formal West Indies Federation, they are indeed important to understand, especially if one's focus is that particular federal scheme. With that said, they remain only part of the larger history of federation.

As the previous chapters established, the idea of a Caribbean federation long existed as both an intra-regional endeavor within the British Empire similar to the advancement of other former colonies toward self-government—a process in which colonies typically gained responsible government and eventually dominion status in the British Commonwealth—and a racialized, black nation-building project seeking nationhood in or out of the empire. During these official conferences and the ongoing negotiations between the Crown and West Indian colonies, the idea of federation became more firmly centered on the former. The islandist and regionalist motivations for the pursuit of federation—which had coexisted for the past several decades, at times easily and at other times with more contention—became more pressing during this era as conference delegates and their associated West Indian political parties struggled over the prioritization of and their commitment to their respective colonies or the region as a whole. With the move from the pursuit of an idea to formal planning of a federation, the tensions between islandist and regionalist loyalties could no longer be ignored. In fact, these issues would have a significant impact during the official conferences and in the early years of the actual West Indies Federation.

Despite the increased intra-regional orientation of federation in the 1950s, support for it among transnational West Indian and black diaspora activists and organizations remained significant. While some within the West Indies viewed these activists as outsiders disconnected from the realities of the contemporary West Indies because of long absence, many expatriates remained vigilant in their support of federation even as their roles receded from the vanguard positions of previous years. Ironically, despite their marginalization by some West Indian political leaders, they remained more conscious of, and more practiced in dealing with, many of the very issues that the West Indian populations of the colonies faced during the planning and actual years of federation—particularly the elusive establishment of greater bonds of regional unity to counter islandist insularity.

This chapter explores the final steps in the creation of a Caribbean federation in the 1950s, culminating in the inauguration of the West Indies Federation in 1958. Discussions of the official meetings that formalized the federation are noted. However, given the numerous studies that have interrogated these events, such issues are not the sole or even the primary focus. Instead, this chapter examines the continued support for, and in some cases opposition to, a federation among transnational West Indian and black diaspora activists and organizations outside the region, their relationships with political parties and leaders within the colonies, and federation's place within black diaspora politics in this era. In doing so, it also investigates the place of race within "West Indianness," and the coexisting and competing conceptualizations of the pending nation—intra-regional and diasporic, racialized and transracial characterizations—all of which would be applied to the West Indies Federation upon its creation.

The Final Negotiations

Following the release of the Rance Report, one of the first matters to be addressed was its formal approval or rejection by the colonial legislatures of the various West Indian colonies. Much like some supporters in the United States, many West Indians in the colonies expressed their disappointment at the report's suggestion for a federation without self-government and dominion status.

From 1950 to 1951, the vast majority of the West Indian colonies that considered the Rance Report approved it. In Trinidad, while there was some opposition by politicians such as Patrick Solomon who expressed concern over the cost of federation, the lack of independence, the undemocratic nature of a nominated Senate, and the governor-general's reserved powers, the measure was passed by the legislative council. In Jamaica, whose place within a federation had long been unsettled, given that many Jamaicans assumed they could achieve dominion status on their own, both Manley and Bustamante declared support for the report, albeit with reservations, as best for the region as a whole, and the report was supported in that colony as well. In Barbados the House of Assembly voted in favor of the report, though some worried the federation might come to be dominated by Jamaicans and disagreed with the location of the federal capital in Trinidad. Grantley Adams also echoed T. A. Marryshow's sentiment that the federation described in the Rance Report was little more than a "glorified crown colony." The Windward and Leeward Islands likewise approved the report, although Marryshow continued to voice his opposition due to the lack of self-government. Finally, the legislatures of the British Virgin Islands, British Guiana, and British Honduras rejected the proposal.[1]

The insular islandism of the colonies that rejected the Rance Report is evident. However, one should not conclude that all who voted in its favor did not also maintain a significant islandist perspective. While each of the colonies that supported the Rance Report obviously embraced some level of regionalism, several also displayed islandist sentiments through their expressed concerns over how federation would affect their particular colony.

Following the voting on the Rance Report in the Caribbean, additional meetings were planned to address several concerns that appeared during the legislative debates of the participating colonies, as well as additional reports concerning other matters related to unification. The latter included publication of the Public Service Commission's report (March 1950) and the Customs Union Commission's report (February 1951) and the creation of a unified currency for Eastern Caribbean colonies (1951) and of a Regional Economic Committee (May 1951).[2]

While the matter of federation was now in the hands of West Indian politicians, international factors such as British and American fears of communism in West Indian colonies also influenced discussions of federation and West Indian political advancement. As discussed in chapter 3, tensions between "left-wing" and "right-wing" factions splintered and weakened the CLC in the late 1940s. In 1952 the PNP, in an effort to disassociate the party from any charges of communism, expelled the "4Hs" (Richard Hart, Arthur Henry, Frank Hill, and Ken Hill) who were considered the leading left-wing activists in the party. The following year, fears of communist infiltration also fueled British intervention in British Guiana, during which the recently ratified constitution was suspended and the democratically elected government of Cheddi Jagan forced from office.[3] Although these events occurred in individual colonies, they spoke to the broader political atmosphere of the area and era. Thus the negotiations between the Crown and West Indian leaders in the Caribbean in the 1950s took place under the watchful eyes of British and United States officials determined to see the creation of an anticommunist ally in the forthcoming Caribbean federation.

At the 1953 London Conference, delegates from the colonies that ratified the Rance Report, as well as observers from British Guiana and British Honduras, which rejected it, met to discuss the report further. This meeting differed from previous conferences in that for the first time all the West Indian delegates were elected by universal suffrage. Over the course of the meeting, the delegates agreed upon various modifications to the report. These included minor revisions of language in the proposed constitution and changes in the location of the federal capital, the number of representatives in the House of Representatives (formerly referred to as the House of Assembly), some legislative procedures, the composition of the federal executive, and various financial matters, including the power of the federal government to raise loans and the amount of assistance from the Crown during the early years of federation. While most delegates agreed on the broad principle of federation, additional meetings were still necessary to finalize the federal structure and settle remaining obstacles to federation.[4]

The 1953 conference's revised *Plan for a British Caribbean Federation* was returned to the participating West Indian governments for approval.[5] During the ensuing months, all agreed to the plan, even as some criticized it as too colonial, especially because the 1953 plan, like the Rance Report upon which it was based, did not concede self-government and dominion status to the proposed federation. Eric Williams, who rose to power in Trinidad in the mid-1950s, was among the most fervent supporters of federation, yet also one of the chief critics of the 1953 plans. In Jamaica, Manley accepted the plan, though he considered it far from settled or ideal, particularly in regard to self-government. Bustamante also remained in favor of federation at this time.[6]

One of the most pressing, lingering issues following the 1953 London Conference was freedom of movement between islands. This was a matter of great importance for overcrowded islands, as well as those less populated areas that feared being overrun. Moreover, the support or opposition to this issue spoke to the larger challenges of forging a collective sense of West Indianness beyond the insular island identifications many continued to prioritize. In 1955, at a conference on interterritorial migration in Trinidad, delegates came up with a rather ambiguous agreement that purportedly preserved "the principle of freedom of movement" while allaying "the fears of any territory concerning the effects of its immediate application."[7]

In February 1956 another London Conference was held to finalize the plans for the West Indies Federation based upon the 1953 plans. While some deemed it necessary to have all the intricacies solved, others believed that the fine points could be formalized later. Speaking a few days before the conference, Marryshow, the well-known "Father of Federation" from Grenada, proclaimed that the federation was for future generations. It was more important to launch it and let it evolve than to create a rigidly fixed plan. In some regards this was a surprising concession by Marryshow, whose dedication to federation with self-government had been so long-standing. At the same time, it speaks to his and others' ultimate decision to get what they could rather than prolong what had already been protracted negotiations since the 1947 Montego Bay Conference. At numerous times during these meetings, it appeared a final agreement would be prevented by attendees who wanted the resolution of issues ranging from establishment of a customs union to other financial and constitutional contentions. Eventually the representatives fell into line with Marryshow's plea, and after approximately a decade of continuous debate, the federation was formalized.[8]

On 23 February 1956, "leaders of the British West Indian colonies signed an agreement . . . merging the 1000-mile chain of islands into a new nation."[9] The matter was submitted to the British Parliament, which on 2 August 1956 passed the British Caribbean Act. This established a federation incorporating ten territories: Antigua, Barbados, Dominica, Grenada, Jamaica, Montserrat, St. Kitts–Nevis–Anguilla, St. Lucia, St. Vincent, and Trinidad and Tobago. Thereafter, in August 1957, Parliament approved an order-in-council establishing the newly named West Indies Federation, which would be formally established in 1958. While the particular structure of this new federal government was set, many constitutional and financial questions remained. Nevertheless, it was decided these could be settled during the early years of the Federation, rather than indefinitely delaying its creation.

Throughout these final federation negotiations, expatriate West Indian and black diaspora activists, as well as the black press, monitored the events and offered their assessments. As the legislative bodies of the colonies debated the Rance Report, the skepticism expressed abroad following its release continued.

At a January 1951 meeting in the offices of the *New York Amsterdam News*, Malliet brought together various West Indian leaders to discuss the matter, and to push Jamaica's colonial government to support the SCAC as some other West Indian colonies had already done. Although the gathered audience understood they possessed no official standing in the various colonial governments' debates over the Rance Report, they felt determined and obligated to have their voices heard. Malliet claimed "he had received word from responsible sources in Jamaica that supporters of federation would welcome the assistance of West Indians in the U.S. and that some competent representatives of the group here should be sent to Jamaica to 'lobby' for federation before it comes up for consideration in the current session of the House of Representatives." Several in attendance noted familiar shortcomings in the structure of the proposed federation. Nevertheless, Malliet and most others remained convinced that federation was desirable "as an end to persisting insularity, poverty, illiteracy, and social frustration." The group also created another temporary committee, the West Indies Emergency Committee for Federation.[10]

In February 1953, two months prior to the London Conference, Malliet organized a luncheon for Lord Listowel, a visiting British official, at the Hotel Theresa in New York. Here Listowel and various West Indian activists in the area discussed the ongoing negotiations. Richard B. Moore spoke of the need for the federation to be self-governing, which, he argued, peoples of African descent had been for centuries before the rise of European colonialism. Malliet's speech focused on the need for accelerated finalization of federation and for "Britain [to] discharge her [financial] obligations to us honorably and without undue delay." Hope Stevens asked Listowel if it would be advisable for West Indians to send representatives to the upcoming conference. Although Listowel did not agree, he did think "some good would come from the support of West Indians in this country."[11]

Between the 1953 and 1956 London Conferences, Caribbean federation remained an important matter to interested parties in the United States. Although there appeared to be less public discussion of the meetings than in previous decades, there was steady coverage of federation planning in the Caribbean, and of events such as the 1953 and 1956 London Conferences, in the black press. Much of the space was devoted specifically to the debates and actions of these meetings, rather than the passionate editorials of previous years.[12]

At the same time, various West Indian politicians and activists continued to visit both West Indian and African American audiences during their periodic trips abroad. In early 1954 Manley undertook another US tour, which included speeches in New York, Detroit, Chicago, and Boston. In New York his theme was "The Tremendous Task Ahead of Us," which likely addressed the official negotiations for federation, as well as more specifically Jamaican issues.[13] During the summer, Bustamante attended a New York rally sponsored by Malliet's Caribbean Associates organization, which sought to highlight the achievements of Bustamante and the JLP, and their support of federation and independence. Presumably Malliet, who had officially became the JLP's US representative a few years earlier, hoped to counter the overwhelming support of Manley and the PNP by both expatriate West Indians and African Americans.[14] The following spring, Grantley Adams undertook a tour of the United States, while it appears Marryshow returned to New York during the summer months.[15]

Although there was still significant support for Caribbean federation within the multinational black communities of the United States, particularly in Harlem and surrounding New York City areas where much of the activism on its behalf had been centered, there was not, nor had there ever been, complete consensus on the matter. The Jamaica Progressive League's stance on federation remained convoluted and perplexing. As in previous years, the JPL was dedicated to and focused on self-government and dominion status for Jamaica. Nevertheless, many of the members worked in other transnational West Indian and black diaspora organizations. On the question of federation, the membership included both staunch supporters and critics in the 1950s as before.

From the release of the Rance Report in 1950 through the 1956 London Conference and after, W. A. Domingo and W. Adolphe Roberts campaigned vigorously against the ongoing negotiations. While neither had been advocates of most proposals for federation previously, especially if Jamaica was to be included, the evolution of federation from an idea to a pending reality—one that would include Jamaica—made the matter pressing. Speaking more as individual members of the JPL than for the JPL, both Domingo in New York and Roberts in Jamaica maintained that federation would be a mistake, especially for Jamaica. As the various conferences, reports, and votes took place in the early-mid 1950s, Domingo and Roberts exchanged numerous letters with each other and with others, while contributing frequent articles and opinion pieces to Jamaican newspapers like the *Daily Gleaner* criticizing the federation.

The release and subsequent debates over the Rance Report offered opportunities to voice their opposition. After sending letters to several leaders of the PNP with no reply, Domingo wrote to Roberts concerning the PNP's recent acceptance of the Rance Report. He was particularly dumbfounded that the PNP had set aside the demand for self-government and was supporting a federation without it, which he believed would essentially prolong Jamaica's colonial status. Roberts replied with his own denouncements of federation. Like Domingo, he thought a federation without self-government would inevitably delay Jamaica's progression to dominion status. However, whereas Domingo appeared opposed to any form of federation, Roberts maintained that, while Jamaica should gain its own independence first, should a federation come about, it should hew to the idea of two federations that he had detailed at the 1943 Howard University conference "The Economic Future of the Caribbean."[16]

During and after the 1953 London Conference, Domingo and Roberts voiced their opposition to federation through the *Daily Gleaner*. In an April 1953 article, Roberts argued that Jamaica's participation in a federation would only serve to prolong Jamaica's existence as a British colony. Likewise, he claimed that a single federation was impractical and suggested that if a federation was to be created, there needed to be two: Eastern Caribbean and Western Caribbean. Domingo proved more agitated than Roberts in his May 1953 article. After stating the reasons for his opposition to the federation currently being negotiated, Domingo directly criticized federation supporters, including the PNP, for putting a vague notion of "West Indian unity" ahead of their own national interests as Jamaicans. Overall, he maintained that Jamaican supporters of federation had failed to show the benefits to Jamaica.[17]

In addition to his collaborative efforts with Roberts, in 1956 Domingo published a booklet, *British West Indian Federation: A Critique*, which summarized his opposition. Within its sixteen pages, Domingo argued there had been little public debate in Jamaica on the issue of federation, or indication of its support among the Jamaican population. He also criticized what he deemed the vague benefits for Jamaicans in a federation. He claimed there was no evidence of economic benefits to be gained in federation, and that Jamaica did not need federation to gain self-government. Moreover, he questioned the extent of any real connections between the different islands other than a shared colonialism. Instead of pursuing what he believed was an inherently flawed project, Jamaicans should focus on their own achievement of dominion status, which would provide definite benefits for their own population and pave the way for similar achievements by other West Indian colonies.[18]

The extent of Domingo's islandism and his stance against federation undoubtedly shocked many, particularly given his long involvement in multiple black diaspora organizations. Indeed, it would be some of his colleagues from those, many of whom were still working hard for federation, who would be the most troubled.

Defining a Nation and a People

"We were—indeed we are still—unsure of ourselves, still feeling our way to Nationhood—still trying to discover what we are like—what makes us characteristically West Indian or, if you like, what is the essence of our West Indianness." Writing in 1953, H. W. Springer, a Barbadian labor leader and politician serving as registrar and chief administration officer at the University College of the West Indies (UCWI) in Jamaica, poignantly noted the ongoing debates over and construction of a shared West Indian consciousness, which many people believed to be a basis or prerequisite for a successful federation.[19] Although the Roseau Conference in 1932 had offered a working definition of "West Indian," much time and many events had passed between that meeting and Springer's reflection, with few finding it necessary to offer a definitive definition. Nevertheless, numerous activists and organizations in and out of the region routinely appealed to the notion of a common West Indianness within discussions of Caribbean federation. As the pending West Indian nation took shape in the post–World War II era, the defining of West Indians and West Indianness *within* the colonies themselves became a more pressing issue, or at least one more openly debated. As famed West Indian historian Elsa Goveia noted at the onset of the West Indies Federation in 1958,

> Changes in government will be meaningless until we have settled the fundamental question of our national identity. In the earlier struggle for our political rights, it was perhaps enough to be anti-British. Now that we face Independence, and the immense problems which it will bring, it has become absolutely essential that we should know whether we are West Indians.[20]

One of the most vital questions was whether or not such a regional consciousness existed, and if so, how its importance ranked among the various identifications of the region's peoples. Some dismissed the reality and logic of a shared West Indianness. Writing in January 1955, *Daily Gleaner* columnist Thomas Wright noted many were still struggling to develop their respective island-based outlooks, much less a prioritized regional consciousness. "You cannot develop a West Indian outlook until the component parts have first developed a Jamaican, or a Trinidadian, or a Barbadian outlook."[21] In an August column, Wright offered a facetious suggestion to supporters of federation, who he felt were trying to build a nation on rather weak notions of commonalties.

May I suggest to the champions of Federation that they endeavor to include Hong Kong and the Falkland Islands into the scheme. After all, they are only a few thousand miles further away than Trinidad, and communications by sea and air are excellent. . . . Then, having done that, I further suggest we incorporate the whole lot into the City of Birmingham (thus gaining industrial potential) and then apply to become the 49th state of America, along with Great Britain. We could then call the whole thing the Federation of English-speaking peoples and live in peace and happiness for ever after.[22]

Although aware of the weaknesses of a collective West Indianness, especially in relation to the various insular identifications, many supporters of federation emphasized the recent progress and potential in forging a regional nationalism. Written around the time of the 1956 London Conference, an article in the *Port-of-Spain Gazette* argued, "Scattered as we are over a million square miles of sea, it was difficult for a long time . . . to cultivate a sufficient identity of thought & interest which could remove such strong insular prejudices as arose from the fact that our people of each island were accustomed to live unto themselves as self contained units." The writer claimed, however, that "within recent years there has been a great change of heart. We have become more self-conscious of the need for united action and more nation-conscious of our aspirations."[23] Indeed, the ability of the various West Indian delegates to even agree to plans for the creation of a federation in the 1950s marked an important step.

While the official negotiations had successfully created a structure for the Federation, there remained much to be done in the promotion and adoption of West Indianness within the colonies. Prior to the 1956 London Conference, a columnist in Trinidad commented, "The flash of pens across paper . . . does not really create a new nation. Tangibly, of course, it does not and cannot create anything. . . . For them to become a new nation—for them to become one nation at all—the West Indian people have got to learn to live and act like one nation."[24] Following the final approval of the federation, one Jamaican minister declared, "Today we rejoice not so much for what has been achieved, but rather for the opportunity for what can be achieved in the future. For surely, it would be idle to pretend that a West Indian nation already exists—that, West Indians already think as West Indians, and not as Jamaicans, or Barbadians, or Trinidadians."[25]

Many contemporary scholars questioned the existence and appeal of this regional consciousness, particularly among the West Indian masses and above other identifications. Writing in the latter part of 1956, sociologist Lloyd Braithwaite argued that "West Indianism" was weak and largely confined to the elites of these colonial societies. In his overview of federal associations and institutions in the years prior to the creation of the actual West Indies Federation, Braithwaite noted that regional collaborations based on shared West Indian interests included economic groups such as the Associated Chambers of Commerce of the West Indies, professional organizations like the Federation of the Civil Servants of the West Indies, Caribbean Bar Association, and Caribbean Union of Teachers, and regional institutions such as the Imperial College of Tropical Agriculture and the newly created University College of the West Indies. While he did acknowledge the existence of regional labor organizations, which somewhat challenges his argument of an elite basis for West Indianness, his message was clear—the vast majority of West Indians did not assert a regional consciousness above their other identifications.[26] Writing a few years later, David Lowenthal made similar criticisms. "To be sure, there are West Indian cricket teams; there are West Indian students in Montreal, West Indian businessmen in New York, West Indian emigrants in London and Birmingham. There are even West Indian political parties, a prime minister, and a cabinet. But most of these are only superficially or intermittently West Indian." Like Braithwaite, he noted, "Most of the people who are consciously West Indian . . . are among or close to the elite."[27]

Among those who believed such a regional consciousness could and did exist, there remained questions of what was the "essence" of it. On one hand, the regional bond between the West Indian colonies centered on the supposed shared history and status of the various groups of colonial peoples in the region as part of the British Empire.[28] Some who emphasized these bonds accentuated the racial and ethnic diversity of West Indian colonies and promoted a regional, creole multiracial (or transracial) nationalism. Imagined in this de-racialized manner, as an inclusive West Indian community beyond racial and ethnic divisions, their new nation would showcase the region as an area to be emulated the world over. Federation would be a symbol of hope for the world, and a source of pride that the West Indies had shown this was possible. It would also provide a striking challenge to white supremacist notions of "inferior peoples" and their ability to govern themselves. At the same time, Caribbean federation existed as a more explicitly racialized, black nation-building project, with similar power and potential in world affairs. In some cases, such a characterization was intentional and spoke to diasporic notions of racial unity and empowerment via the creation of a black homeland, while in others it was presented more matter-of-factly based upon the demographics of the region and ideas of majority rule. Interestingly, many West Indian nationalists played to all of these visions by emphasizing and deemphasizing race, depending upon their intended audience and locale.

Numerous examples of multiracial and transracial conceptualizations existed amid the efforts to create the West Indies Federation in the mid-1950s. In a call for unity among West Indians in 1955, Manley declared that "peoples of diverse races and colour working together . . . could make the West Indies Federation an example to the world."[29] In this case, Manley's explicit appeal to a transracial vision of federation is quite different from the rhetoric he routinely employed when speaking to audiences beyond the West Indies. Another 1955 *Daily Gleaner* article said federation was "going to be the only full-fledged, multi-racial, self-governing country in the world."[30] At the end of the 1956 London Conference, Marryshow described federation as "a fascinating prospect, the new Caribbean nation, with its melting pot of races and creeds, producing a common British Caribbean spirit and devoted to the dreams of democratic freedom and Christian peace."[31] Much like Manley's comment above, this characterization appears quite distinct from his frequent presentation beyond the West Indies, as well some of his earlier work within the colonies.

In the ensuing months, several others underscored these ideas and opportunities. Although the West Indies did not have "a common land, not much of common culture or customs, apart from the common apron-strings of British rule . . . [nor] a common blood . . . it can be one of their greatest glories, that they can weld men of different blood, different race and different colour into one family."[32] Gordon Lewis's 1957 article on the background to the federation closed by saying the federation had "the opportunity to terminate the long and evil history of colour warfare, both in the Caribbean and, through Caribbean example, in the world outside."[33] In the opinion of Jamaican governor Sir Hugh Foot, "The islands represented a microcosm of the whole racial problem in the British Commonwealth, and inter-racial relations there 'are better than anywhere else in the world.'"[34]

These multiracial and transracial visions of federation proved both popular and powerful, but they were not the only views of the West Indian nation and its associated West Indianness. Some did not see race as an issue to move beyond, but instead continued to view both West Indians and West Indianness more explicitly as a racialized project connected to the struggles within Africa and other locations of the broader black diaspora. With peoples of African descent making up the vast majority of the West Indians as a whole (approximately 2.5 million of the 3 million people in the planned federation), many people believed that the federation was to be "a Negro republic to a predominant degree," and looked forward to its creation.[35] In the words of C. G. Walker, a former mayor of Kingston, "Federation of the British West Indies and the 'new and proud nation' that will spring from it will mean much to the Negro peoples of the World." In reference to Black America particularly, he claimed, "Millions of colored Americans suffering under Jim Crowism could look to us for guidance and at least moral support."[36]

Opponents of federation recognized the historical differences between the various island populations, and believed it was preposterous to simply expect them to federate on commonalties such as race, religion, region, language, history, and culture. W. A. Domingo—notwithstanding his previous activism and leadership in transnational West Indian and black diaspora organizations, close association with federation supporters, recognition of regional connections between West Indians, and, at times, characterization of nation building in Jamaica and other West Indian colonies as black nation-building endeavors linked to other black diasporic struggles—became one of the chief critics of the proposed federation in the 1950s and rejected ideas of a regional West Indianness. In fact, the different islands' distinctions were a major reason to oppose a federation. Domingo now considered ideas of a common West Indianness absurd, especially if based on race. "If being of Negro descent in the Caribbean is justification for federation, Haiti and the French West Indies with their heavy Negro population, eminently qualify for inclusion in such a union." Even a shared territory did not necessarily denote similarities, he argued. "The French, Germans, Italians, Poles, and Spaniards occupy the same European land mass and are of the same race . . . but this 'oneness' is not regarded by Europeans as a compelling reason for federating their nations." Ultimately, Domingo now believed, no matter how homogeneous its proponents made the peoples of the English-speaking Caribbean, it was a "superficial unity—an artificial oneness."[37]

Despite such contentions, the pursuit and promotion of West Indianness remained prominent as the region marched toward federation in the 1950s. In the postwar era through the formal creation of the West Indies Federation, one of the most important issues confronting an inclusive West Indianness *within* the British Caribbean was the question of its Indo-Caribbean populations. "East Indians," as they were popularly known in the West Indian colonies, were not the only other "minority" group, but they were especially prominent in Trinidad and British Guiana, which had received nearly 400,000 Indian indentured servants (89 percent of the overall Indian migration to the region) between emancipation and the early twentieth century, and where by the mid-twentieth century they composed a sizeable portion of both colonies' population.[38]

From the 1930s to the 1950s, Indo-Caribbean activists and organizations in Trinidad and British Guiana increased their political activism. Like their Afro-Caribbean counterparts, many Indians used the Moyne Commission of the late 1930s as a venue through which to address a variety of economic, social, political, and cultural issues. Although some British officials assumed Indo-Caribbeans might seek repatriation to India, many of the memoranda and testimonies submitted to the Moyne Commission represented Indo-Caribbean efforts to secure their place *within* the British Caribbean, while maintaining their cultural traditions and ties to India.[39] Such desires did not prevent some level of cooperation, at times, between black and Indian communities in these West Indies, especially Trinidad.[40] Nevertheless, just as it can be precarious to argue there was no interracial cooperation, it can be equally problematic to overstate its extent.

Acknowledgement of the Indo-Caribbean population was limited in the larger realm of black diaspora politics. Many black diaspora organizations supported independence for India, but their prioritized anticolonialism in the early-mid twentieth century often muted and overlooked the place of Indo-Caribbeans within the West Indies. There were exceptions, especially among Black Marxist and other "race and class" conscious groups. For instance, the IASB's 1938 "Open Letter to the Workers of the West Indies and British Guiana" showed some level of commitment to the welfare of all West Indian workers and not just Afro-Caribbeans. Of course, even those organizations primarily described the West Indies and West Indians as a black region and identification. In other cases, the lack of recognition of the Indo-Caribbean population was more conspicuous. For instance, as discussed in previous chapters, despite their significant numbers in British Guiana, the presence of the Indo-Caribbeans had been completely ignored by some expatriate and black diaspora activists who had seen British Guiana as a black homeland and potential site for immigration.[41]

In the post–World War II era, tensions between Afro- and Indo-Caribbeans escalated. Following India's independence in 1947 many Indo-Caribbeans asserted their "Indianness" at the same time that others in the

Caribbean were advocating a federation and a collective, regional West Indianness. As the region proceeded toward federation, these tensions increased, especially in colonies with large Indo-Caribbean communities where efforts to maintain a distinctive Indianness was viewed by some with ever greater suspicion. In Trinidad and British Guiana, competition and disdain grew between Afro-Caribbean and Indo-Caribbean communities—both of which sought to stake their claims in the colonies as they moved toward self-government.[42]

At the same time, there was a widespread belief within the region that most Indo-Caribbeans opposed federation. These perceptions—to some degree warranted—made them a target for both justified and unjustified criticism from supporters of federation. Two matters were particularly troubling for Indo-Caribbeans. First, while they were obviously excluded from being considered "West Indians" by those who openly saw this as a regional black identification, even within purportedly inclusive and de-racialized ideas of "West Indian" there remained a particular Afro-Caribbean hegemony. As David Lowenthal argues, "Black and colored West Indians sometimes [did] express solidarity in a phrase like 'we West Indians,' or, in Trinidad, 'we Creoles.' In the local context, both terms ordinarily [left] out whites, whether native-born, metropolitan, or foreign, and persons of all other races."[43] Also, the region's unbalanced demographics undoubtedly worried those Indians who stood ready to stake a greater claim politically in the postcolonial West Indies, particularly in colonies like British Guiana and Trinidad. The Indo-Caribbean population in Trinidad and Tobago alone was "greater than the total population of any of the other British Caribbean islands except Jamaica." However, if Trinidad and British Guiana joined the federation, they would be "only about one-tenth of the population of the entire area to be federated."[44] In fact, some West Indians (and others) believed that one reason British Guiana refused to join the federation was because the Indian majority in that colony refused to have their power curtailed under a black-majority federation.[45]

Anti-federation attitudes among many—though not all—Indians, inspired charges of separatism and racism against the Indo-Caribbean population, including the rather preposterous notion that Indians were trying to take over those colonies and make them part of a Greater India. As David Lowenthal argues, "East Indian hesitations about federation tend[ed] to be construed by Creoles as a lack of loyalty, if not a positive disloyalty, both to the West Indies and to Great Britain."[46] As early as the spring of 1947, a CLC message to the Inter-Asian Conference in India requested the "leaders of the peoples of Asia" to make a "forthright declaration to RACIAL minorities of Asiatic extraction wherever they may be in the Caribbean area that their future hopes and aspirations necessitate full support for and brotherhood in the NATIONAL movements of the territories in which they have their homes."[47] Following the 1953 London Conference, at which the SCAC proposals for federation were agreed upon and submitted to the various legislatures in the colonies, many Indo-Caribbean politicians and organizations did openly oppose federation.[48]

Despite an alleged "deep-seated hostility" among many Indo-Caribbeans to federation, many supporters of federation believed the Indo-Caribbean population should merge themselves into the larger West Indian community. As Eric Williams noted in 1955, "Indians are, for better or worse, an integral part" of the West Indian community in Trinidad and British Guiana.[49] Likewise, Sir Hubert Rance, governor of Trinidad, argued that Indo-Caribbeans "must show undivided loyalty to their new homelands and identify themselves fully with other sections of the population in the plans for the progress and prosperity" of the West Indies. This meant they should "consider themselves West Indians in the first place, then Trinidadians, and lastly East Indians."[50]

Although the extent of Indo-Caribbean opposition to federation is debatable, many West Indians, particularly among the Afro-Caribbean majorities, undoubtedly shared Rance's attitude.[51] As one article in the *Trinidad Guardian* argued, East Indian cultural retention in itself was not a problem. However, if these actions should "lead to an intensification of racial feeling, and of the desire to draw apart and preserve a separate identity instead of uniting with the general population as part of a West Indian society, those who foster or support them may do a disservice to Trinidad and to the West Indies in general."[52] What many West Indians viewed as efforts to bring together all communities in the colonies, many Indo-Caribbeans viewed as calls for their assimilation into a largely Afro-Caribbean-defined West Indianness.

In addition to their purported opposition to federation, Indo-Caribbeans' efforts to maintain their cultural distinctiveness caused some West Indians to question their loyalty and their place within the emerging West Indian nation. In the mid-1950s, some criticized Indians for failure to embrace and contribute to the emerging West Indianness that formed the basis of federation, while others questioned Indian cultural separation and called for their assimilation. In a 1955 article in the *Port-of-Spain Gazette*, Harold Julien claimed Indians had remained unassimilated because of improper British colonial policies that "provided and permitted for them special and exclusive institutions and privileges," such as "a special Indian commissioner in the colony." These policies had hindered the absorption of the Indian population, which Julien appears to have believed was necessary.[53] Some Indo-Caribbeans read this as a call for their assimilation. One respondent believed that Julien's plan for the absorption of Indians was essentially advocating the obliteration of the group.[54]

In October 1955, a debate over the teaching and use of Hindi in Trinidad ensued in the *Trinidad Guardian*. In a letter that set off a string of angry responses, "Scarlet Ibis" cheered the return of an Indian commissioner to India from Trinidad because he believed the commissioner had encouraged the use of Hindi, which was "the best medium of spreading racial issues for political propaganda."[55] One respondent argued "that if speaking different languages in one's own home was somehow subversive then Trinidad would have long been in a chaotic situation because of its multiple languages and people."[56] Indraprakash Bann was not so calm in his rebuttal. He asked, "Now what would the 'Ibis' type of people want Indians to do? First, they must destroy the Hindi language; then they must cut off all cultural and religious relationship with India. After that, if they still persist, they must be wiped off." He went on to say that "there is so much hatred in the minds of this type of people against things Indian that they put fear into our minds, forcing us to hate a Federation of the West Indies where Indians will be in a minority."[57]

If the "Indian question" highlighted the difficulties of achieving an inclusive West Indianness beyond race, West Indian students in and out of the region purported to demonstrate it. Although the College of Tropical Agriculture in Trinidad had existed since 1921, the establishing of the University College of the West Indies in 1948 was an important development. Created to provide university-level education with an eye to future political development in the West Indies, the UCWI would, some assumed, play a crucial role in "fostering West Indian nationalism and sentiment."[58] Speaking a few years prior to its formal creation, Norman Manley claimed, "The West Indian University is likely to be the most powerful agent to make federation of the British West Indies a practical possibility."[59] By the mid-1950s there was widespread belief that the UCWI was "the symbol and promise of a West Indian Federation," demonstrated that West Indians could "work together and play together," and formed a "core of Federation."[60] In 1962 Hugh Springer declared, "The University College has indeed made a considerable contribution to the growth of a truly West Indian feeling."[61]

While West Indian students at UCWI proved to be an important symbol of West Indianness in the late 1940s and 1950s, West Indian student populations outside the Caribbean were likewise influential and significant in this era, as in previous decades. Well before the advent of the UCWI, West Indian students—mostly of African descent—at British, American, and Canadian universities constituted some of the most recognizable "West Indian" groups in the early-mid twentieth century. In areas of Britain, they actually formed one of the key segments of the small black population prior to World War II, whereas in the United States they joined with thousands of other West Indian migrants within multinational black communities. Like other diaspora-based West Indians, despite the maintenance of island-based identifications, as well as class and color issues among themselves, these students often underwent familiar processes of regionalization and racialization during their time abroad. Prior to the growing emphasis on regional consciousness and identification in the post–World War II era, their racialization was particularly prevalent among these students.

Outside the Caribbean, many West Indian students lived and faced discrimination as both colonial subjects and racial minorities. In Great Britain, before the creation of their own student organizations in the postwar era, many West Indian students associated—either by choice or because discrimination limited their options—with a variety of African student groups. For much of the early twentieth century, the experience of Afro-Caribbean students in Britain was intricately intertwined with African students, which further forged racial consciousness and activism. In addition to the Ethiopian Progressive Association, West African Christian Union (associated with the Student Christian Movement), the Union of Students of African Descent, the West African Students' Union, and other student organizations, West Indian students were actively involved in various racial uplift and anticolonial movements including the African Association, African Progress Union, Society of Peoples of African Origin, League of Coloured Peoples, International African Service Bureau, and Pan-African Federation.[62] In the United States, West Indian students attended various historically black colleges and universities (HBCUs), joined black fraternities and sororities, and participated in a variety of West Indian, African American, and diaspora-focused activist organizations. In such settings, race proved to be a prominent issue in the daily life of the majority of these students, both as a crux of their discrimination and as a basis of their support for, and association with, organizations and movements involved in various forms of black diaspora politics.

In the postwar era, alongside the formal planning of the federation, numerous West Indian student organizations appeared throughout Great Britain, the United States, and Canada.[63] While this did not terminate the association with African and African American students and the engagement in black diaspora politics, the advent of various West Indian student organizations in the 1940s reflected a markedly more focused West Indian nationalist agenda. In Britain these groups included the West Indian Students' Union and the Oxford University West Indian Society, in the United States the West Indian Students' Association and the Caribbean Association of Howard University, in Canada the British West Indian Society at McGill University in Montreal and the West Indian Student Society at the University of Toronto. Subtle differences aside, they all promoted a supposedly inclusive regional West Indian identification, as well as a spirit of West Indian nationalism—that is, regionalism. In many of these student organizations, one of the strongest manifestations of West Indianness was support for federation, which would create a West Indian nation and confer upon them recognition as a national, independent people rather than colonial subjects.

One of the most prominent groups in Britain was the West Indian Students' Union (WISU). Formed in 1945, WISU aimed to "to unite in *one* organization *all* West Indian students in *all* the Universities and other institutions in the United Kingdom and Eire." WISU organized itself on an inclusive "West Indian" definition that included peoples of the British West Indies and adjacent American, French, and Dutch colonies, as well as the independent nations of Cuba, Haiti, and the Dominican Republic. Its aims and objectives included (a) promotion of fellowship between and encouragement for West Indian students; (b) concern for the general well-being of West Indian students in the United Kingdom; (c) stimulating interest in the cultural, political, and economic development of the West Indies; (d) promotion of higher education in the West Indies and the growth of a university in the West Indies; and (e) establishing contacts with similar organizations in other parts of the world. It also sought to unite West Indian students beyond island parochialism and racial prejudices. Ordinary membership was open to all West Indians studying in the United Kingdom, with associate membership open to all West Indians and others interested in the aims and objectives of the union.[64]

Although some British officials expressed concern about the politicization and radicalization of colonial students during their stay in Britain, especially racial activism or communist activities, WISU was generally commended for bringing West Indian students together, arranging lectures and discussions on West Indian subjects, and helping build a regional consciousness that would undoubtedly aid the ongoing efforts to build a Caribbean federation.[65] One colonial official recognized WISU as "keenly interested in Federation" and praised it for "good work in bringing West Indians over here together and in breaking down parochialism among them."[66]

Many colonial officials and West Indian students and activists believed support for federation went hand in hand with the assertion of West Indian identification, and that students could not properly call themselves West Indians if they did not support federation—a common claim by many West Indian nationalists in this era.[67] In line with this philosophy, WISU proclaimed support of the endeavor, hosted guest speakers on the subject, and held discussions on such topics as "Social Aspects of Federation" and "Political Aspects of Federation."[68] Prior to the release of the SCAC Report in 1950, WISU noted the desire of students to unite as West Indians and play their part in the West Indian future, and argued their activities and efforts in recent years displayed their commitment to federation.

> Our Students Union [is] doing our small bit towards making it come true, for we [are] gathering together and uniting the students of our various islands, breaking down the walls of isolation by distance, finding common points. . . . We were and are learning to be West Indians, so that when asked where we come from we now automatically reply the West Indies. We are also learning by experiment in our own Union how to organize, how to work together for a common goal, how to sink personal differences and ambitions in trying to build an organization of which we can be proud, feeling sure that it will survive us.[69]

In a similar tone, another WISU circular bragged that social events such as WISU-sponsored dances created the "the atmosphere that makes the idea of federation a real and reasonable prospect instead of a remote and abstract topic for conversation."[70] In the coming years, visiting West Indian politicians routinely praised WISU and spoke to students on the political scene in their homelands.

Similar organizations and activities flourished in the United States and Canada during these years. Much as they did in the United Kingdom, officials voiced concern over the radicalization and racialization of African and West Indian students during their sojourn in the United States. Some expressed bafflement that the overt racism in the United States actually raised the racial consciousness and anti-British sentiments of colonial black students, rather than forging greater allegiance to the empire.[71]

While West Indian students in North America maintained association with a variety of organizations, several West Indian student organizations came about during and after World War II. As with their counterparts in Britain, support for Caribbean federation became not only a goal but the very idea on which various student associations organized. For example, in 1940–41 the British West Indian Society was created at McGill University to "foster a spirit of co-operation and understanding, between the representatives of the various islands, and between representatives of the various persuasions."[72] A few years later at Howard University, which had long been popular with West Indian students and activists, the Caribbean Association was formed "to foster and promote cooperation among students from the Caribbean area, irrespective of nationality, in view of the current official policies of federation and regionalism."[73] In 1945–46 the Caribbean Association hosted a range of lectures and discussions on West Indian topics, including federation.[74]

In 1950, at one of the first meetings of the recently formed West Indian Students Association of New York, its president stated that "the aim of the new group, in view of the forthcoming West Indian Federation, was to encourage West Indian students to make the best of any educational opportunities offered them so that they could prepare themselves for leadership." This meeting also featured two lectures, "The Future of the West Indian University" and "The Role of Students in West Indian Federation."[75]

Judging from such proclamations by these various student organizations, West Indian students outside the Caribbean were one of the best symbols of an inclusive regional West Indianness. They were doing their part, as West Indians, to promote and build a nation of their own. Most of the activities and rhetoric within these student unions did not explicitly evoke race or ties to larger black diaspora struggles, and therefore appeared to support federation as a transracial, intra-regional nation-building project. Nonetheless, upon closer examination, there remained a clear racial consciousness among many West Indian students that strained notions of an inclusive West Indianness within these unions. As one student noted in regard to the complex place of race within the West Indies, "I found that I sometimes presented two separate pictures of the West Indies in my conversations with friends: when we talked about the racial situation in the world the West Indies was an area of hope; when we talked about the West Indies in isolation it was a hot-bed of racial neuroses."[76]

While these associations organized and operated on a nonracial basis, and undoubtedly included small numbers of Indian, Chinese, and white students from the Caribbean, like many expressions of West Indianness, they showed a clear Afro-Caribbean hegemony. Several instances illustrate how Afro-Caribbean students, much like the general Afro-Caribbean population, often considered themselves more legitimate or the "real West Indians," and maintained a striking racial consciousness and recognition of themselves as the vast majority of the Caribbean. As Lloyd Braithwaite recounts in his study of colonial West Indian students in Britain, during the first elections of the West Indian Students' Union, a Trinidadian was chosen as president despite the proportional dominance of Jamaican students. Braithwaite contends that a white Jamaican student who had been active in organizing the union and was "the obvious choice for the presidency" lost Jamaican support because several "members were opposed to the idea that a white person, who lorded it over them in their homeland should now, through the assertion of West Indian nationality in London, continue to lord it over them."[77] Seemingly ignoring his own perceptive point, Braithwaite summarizes this election as embodying the assertion of a West Indian consciousness beyond insular island loyalties. While true, this also clearly shows the assertion of a racial consciousness—not necessarily beyond West Indian identification but rather in conjunction with it.

Race issues and the development of an Afro-Caribbean hegemony among West Indian students were not the result of diabolical or separatist agendas, nor were they always the fault of Afro-Caribbeans themselves. As noted by WISU's Commission on the Social Scene in the West Indies,

> the achievement of political independence in India and China had emphasized the minority problem in the West Indies, because owing to the fact that the West Indies had not yet achieved similar status there was a tendency for West Indians of Indian extraction to consider themselves as Indians rather than West Indians. Unless the West Indies could achieve Dominion Status, we would have nothing to offer these minority groups which would equate with the dignity of being an Indian or Chinese *citizen*.[78]

In another case, despite the objective of McGill's British West Indian Society (BWIS) to promote cooperation, there was apparently some racial discord among the Caribbean students of African, Indian, and Chinese descent. In a series of letters between the BWIS and Eric Williams in 1945, one of the key issues was conflict between the Afro-Caribbean leadership of the organization and some of the Indo-Caribbean students. Writing to one Indo-Trinidadian student at McGill, Williams stressed the need for these issues to be solved.

THE PRESENT BREACH IN THE B.W.I. SOCIETY MUST BE HEALED. I do not give a rambling damn about the whites. If they wish to come in, well and good. But if coming in means the principle of white supremacy, then to hell with them. The Indians are an entirely different problem. No organisation of students in Montreal, claiming to be a West Indian organisation, is possible without the Indian element. They must come in. That is your job. You enjoy a triple advantage: you are an excellent West Indian student, you are Indian, and you enjoy great respect among the coloured students. That places upon you three times the responsibility that would fall to any other Indian. You positively must encourage the Indians to join the Society.

Without assigning blame, it appears the Indians either were not made as welcome by some of the black students or had chosen not to be part of a group dominated by black students.[79] In hindsight, it was likely a little of both.

Overall, West Indian students, like many West Indian migrants in previous decades, clearly demonstrated the development of a regional and racial consciousness during their time outside the Caribbean. Students from the West Indies often realized their regional identification while studying abroad; however, this did not always translate to an inclusive West Indianness beyond all racial and ethnic tensions. While recognizing that some notions of West Indianness were indeed transracial, students faced with overt racism abroad and surrounded by anticolonial activities also developed an increased racial awareness that was intertwined with their identification and activities as West Indians.

On the eve of federation there remained considerable debate over the extent and basis of regional unity among the constituent units of the planned nation. Not surprisingly, given the historical construction of West Indianness beyond the region, there was far less ambiguity on what it meant to be West Indian in those areas than within the islands themselves. Yet even abroad, as displayed in the experiences of West Indian students, the issue was far from settled. Of course, race was hardly the only obstacle to or basis for unity. Still, given its ubiquitous ties to the West Indian future since the post-emancipation era, its relevance, good or bad, should not be discounted. Beyond the Caribbean, race remained a useful tool with which to rally support for federation, whereas in the islands, increasing numbers viewed it as the crux of disunity. As the West Indies sped toward nationhood, the nation and its West Indianness remained not *either* racial or transracial but more appropriately both racial *and* transracial, depending upon the context.

Final Preparations

The final preparations for federation demonstrated the elusive nature of an overriding West Indianness within the region—and, in the opinions of some, the divisive nature of race within the British Caribbean. A prime instance was the selection of the capital's location in 1957. As David Lowenthal noted in his study of the federal capital, "If West Indian parochialism made federation difficult, physical insularity made it still harder to agree on the capital site, for the choice of any island would deprive all the others of direct contact with the seat of power."[80] Discussions had taken place at all of the previous federal planning meetings and in their respective reports, including the SCAC sessions and Rance Report, 1953 London Conference, 1955 conference on interterritorial migration, and 1956 London Conference.

Most of these meetings made tentative recommendations, later overturned. Trinidad was named preliminary capital by the SCAC in October 1949, but then the 1953 London Conference decided in favor of Grenada before going back to Trinidad, which was dropped again later. By the 1955 migration conference, many representatives believed that Barbados was the leading candidate.[81] Finally, delegates at the 1956 London Conference proposed a Federal Capital Sites Fact-Finding Commission. The three members undertook a tour of all thirteen islands that summer in an effort to recommend a site that was "as broadly representative as possible of the diverse elements in the Federation" and a "place which will draw people from all the islands and foster the growth of that West Indian patriotism which is essential if the Federation is to be a success."[82] Their investigation and report initiated a controversy threatening the already tenuous notion of West Indianness.

On 2 January 1957 the Fact-Finding Commission announced its top three choices for the capital site: (1) Barbados, (2) Jamaica, and (3) Trinidad. As if prepared for the backlash from the islands that were not chosen, the commission offered several reasons for the rankings. Explanations for the lower placement of Trinidad, an early favorite, included the supposed instability of Trinidad's political scene and a low standard in public life characterized by "widespread reports of corruption." The commission also noted "a disturbing element in the public life of Trinidad to which importance is attached in the other islands." In their investigation, the committee heard allegations that the large Indian population that comprised approximately one-third of Trinidad held "ideals and loyalties differing from those to be found elsewhere in the Federation and they exercise a disruptive influence on social and political life in Trinidad."[83] Though the commission claimed "to pass no judgment on these allegations" (which were included in the formal findings), it did say that "the existence of such a large minority, differing in so many ways from the rest of the people of the island, is bound to introduce complications" which would make the "growth of healthy political traditions in Trinidad" even more difficult. These sentiments mirrored earlier commentary describing the fears of some in the region that if Indians were ever able to get political power in Trinidad, they could wreck or endanger the federal process by taking the country out of the federation.[84]

Reaction was swift, as Trinidadians and other federation supporters joined to voice disapproval of the way ethnic differences and racial hearsay were used to damn Trinidad as the federal capital. Mass meetings were held in the Indian communities, and leaders expressed their outrage at being used as scapegoats in the Fact-Finding Committee's decision to pass over Trinidad as the capital site. They demanded an apology for antagonizing the Indian community, which some Indians claimed "had taught the world that harmonious relationships could exist between different races."[85] Protests quickly appeared in Trinidadian newspapers to defend the Indian population and Trinidadian society against these charges. Many of these reiterated that Indians had been misconstrued as anti-federation, and even disloyal to Trinidad. One letter said that the Indian population was not anti-federation, and that it was "a very great nation in the West Indies." Another called the Indian population the "backbone of agriculture in Trinidad" and "loyal to Her Majesty's Government." Even the chief minister, Eric Williams, lectured that the Indian population was not an alien population but an integral part of West Indian society.[86] Thus it appeared for a moment that Trinidadian society had rallied beyond race, as Trinidadians, as West Indians, for the regional good of the federation.

The claim of a "disruptive" Indo-Caribbean population was not the only controversy involving race that came from the Fact-Finding Commission's report. There was also a backlash against Barbados as the top nominee for the capital site. While the committee gave various reasons, many of those upset by its choice focused on the island's race problems. As early as 1956, some representatives noted the extent of racial discrimination in Barbados and implied this should prevent Barbados from being the federal capital. If the federation intended to portray an inclusive West Indianness and fuel West Indian patriotism, this was a horrible choice. An article in the *Trinidad Guardian* asserted that if the "national capital would be a showcase to the world in human relations . . . Barbados is certainly the least qualified spot to build such a showcase."[87] A letter from Antigua claimed the commission had "ignored the obnoxious colour and class question in Barbados." It went on to say that the choice of Barbados "would be like moving the capital of the United States to Jim Crow Dixie land."[88] Gordon Lewis submitted that it was hard to stay in Barbados for an extended period without feeling the "prejudices of a golf club in Outer London."[89]

In addition to decrying the segregation of Barbados, it appears that many sought to discredit Barbados as a way of showing that racial problems in Trinidad were not as bad as in other islands. Some wondered how the "very English" and "squirearchic Barbados with its social separation of races" would be an ideal site for a West Indian capital compared to Trinidad "with its plurality of races" which had "gone further than the others in evolving a cultural solidarity."[90] In response, some Barbadians maintained that the taint of segregation extended into almost all West Indian societies, and that it was no worse in Barbados.[91] An article written by an Indo-Trinidadian, who was not on speaking terms with his family since he married a black woman, concluded "what was wrong with Commissioner's report? Nothing. It should teach us to behave differently."[92]

The concept of West Indianness emerged from the capital controversy with mixed results. On one hand, the rallying in support of Trinidad produced an optimistic outlook of an inclusive regionalism. At the same time, the initial critique of the Indo-Caribbean population, which even some of the defenders of Trinidad had expressed themselves at different times, demonstrated the lingering "problems" of race in the Caribbean despite premature pronouncement of its irrelevance by some. Eventually, in February 1957, Trinidad was selected as the location of the federal capital.

The following year, the first federal elections in the West Indian colonies also revealed the struggles of the region to bring claims of racial harmony and unity to reality. Scheduled for March, between the start of the Federation in January and the inauguration of the full federal government in April, the election pitted the West Indies Federal Labour Party (WI-

FLP) against the Federal Democratic Labour Party (FDLP).[93] Organized
in 1956, the socialist-oriented WIFLP incorporated the ruling parties in
each territory except St. Vincent, and included some of the most powerful
political leaders in the region: Norman Manley and the People's National
Party (PNP) in Jamaica, Eric Williams and the People's National Movement (PNM) in Trinidad, and Grantley Adams and the Barbados Labour
Party (BLP) in Barbados. The FDLP included Alexander Bustamante and
the Jamaica Labour Party, the recently formed Democratic Labour Party in
Trinidad (DLP), which was a largely anti-PNM party in opposition to Eric
Williams, and various opposition parties in other colonies.[94] Given the size
and power of Jamaica and Trinidad, which included approximately 78 percent of the Federation's population, the federal elections in those colonies
were particularly important.

Moving beyond the specific political aspects of these federal elections,
the various charges of racial politics within the campaigns demonstrate
the continued political uses and relevance of race in the region. In the year
before the 1958 election, many in Jamaica promoted the idea of a transracial
society where people had been amalgamated into a "Jamaican race." Bustamante, for instance, proclaimed that "all races should think of each other
as brothers . . . in Jamaica we don't know any difference of races. We all live
as one people." Some went so far as to say Jamaicans had moved beyond
race and racism altogether. Here the people of Jamaica were "all Jamaicans."
The Lord Bishop of Jamaica even declared that the terms "colour bar" and
"segregation" were "meaningless in Jamaica."[95] Despite these claims, this
was simply not true. Indians in Trinidad protested (possibly in place of
their Indian brethren who wielded far less power in Jamaica) against "Anti-
Indian Jamaican laws" such as discriminatory contract procedures, restrictions on non-Christian Indian rights of marriage, and anti-cremation laws
that were still in force in this era. Norman Manley's statement during the
1956 London Conference that the "opposition to the idea of a Caribbean
Federation comes largely from British Guiana and Trinidad where the East
Indian communities believe they are about to attain political dominance
on a communal level" alarmed many in the region.[96] Racial controversies,
therefore, were not absent from Jamaica at this time.

The competition between Bustamante's JLP and Manley's PNP in Jamaica
during the federal elections further highlighted issues of race and politics.
Although both parties were "multiracial" (and at the same time composed
largely of Afro-Jamaicans due to the island's overwhelming black majority),
the JLP contained many of the former "white Jamaican" politicians stand-

ing for election. In this era of decolonization, white skin was in some cases a political liability of sorts, with white politicians an easy target for black politicians and candidates dedicated to decolonization.

In the months leading up to the elections, charges of race-baiting from the JLP against the PNP began to appear. Early in 1958, letters from JLP supporters claimed the PNP had made the coming election a "Colour War" by advocating "colour for colour and skin for skin." Vivian Blake, a PNP candidate in one of the parishes, was accused of referring to JLP candidate Lionel Densham's color as a reason to reject him. In response, Blake claimed to have only noted Densham's connections with "that group of employers and planters" who made a mockery of the concept of labor politics. "If mischievous people choose to mis-represent this as an attack of race and colour: he was not to blame." Others contended that this exchange was nothing to caterwaul about, as the idea of "colour for colour" had been used by the JLP in previous elections.[97]

In March a similar incident occurred with Morris Cargill, another white JLP candidate who claimed the PNP attacked him on the basis of his race. Letters to the *Daily Gleaner* questioned wondered why the PNP resorted to introducing race into the elections.[98] PNP supporters, however, were quick to note that the "PNP is, as it has always been, unalterably opposed to racial or class prejudice in politics."[99] Another letter claimed that this form of campaigning was the norm, as politicians appealed to crowds by making "wise cracks at a candidate who comes from a minority group." This editorial went on to argue that minorities should come out of their shells and assert that they were Jamaicans too.[100]

In the actual election, the JLP stunned the PNP by winning the majority of Jamaica's seats in the new federal House of Representatives. The defeat of the PNP cannot be attributed solely to racial politics, as the JLP victory actually spoke to some Jamaicans' uneasiness with the federation. Nevertheless, some believed this victory was more than a defeat of PNP policies—it was a defeat of racial divisions and the manipulation of them. One JLP supporter claimed the victories of Lionel Densham and Morris Cargill over the PNP's "open colour attacks" proved that white skin was not a political liability.[101]

In Trinidad, the 1958 federal election followed closely on the heels of the 1956 national elections in which Eric Williams's PNM had swept to power over opposition from weaker political groups such as the Party of Political Progress and Trinidad Labour Party, and the People's Democratic Party, which represented the expanding participation of Indo-Caribbeans in

Trinidadian and West Indian politics.[102] The PNM was a rather new party itself, created largely upon Williams's calls for a truly national party that would "appeal to all classes, all colours, all races, all religions." Williams envisioned a party where members felt secure and pledged to "oppose racial discrimination in all shapes and forms."[103]

Williams's idea of a multiracial party was realized to some extent, as the PNM claimed representatives from all racial groups. However, it was predominately black (or Creole in local terminology). For this reason the PNM still confronted the historical animosities between the black and Indian populations in both Trinidadian and federal politics. Some Indians believed the PNM, referred to by some opponents as the Popular Negro Movement, was a "black nationalist and racist movement" that only used Indian and other minority members for "the necessary window-dressing to give the PNM a 'national' appearance." H. P. Singh, a leading Indo-Caribbean nationalist, declared that Williams was "an Indian hater . . . [and] hates white people." He also claimed that Williams's scholarship on the black experience in the Caribbean and his anticolonial speeches (which Singh believed were essentially antiwhite) were nothing more than appeals to raise racial discord in Trinidad.[104]

Many of these issues predated the 1958 elections, and spoke more specifically to Trinidadian rather than federal politics, but they came to play a major role in the federal campaign too. The campaign lines were drawn: it was Williams and the PNM versus an anti-PNM coalition in the Democratic Labour Party that included the parties the PNM defeated in 1956. This alliance combined a large number of Indo-Caribbean nationalists and former colonial politicians pursuing the common goal of defeating Williams and the PNM. Even Albert Gomes, a white politician whom some Indians had described as anti-Indian in prior decades, was welcomed by many Indo-Trinidadians in their fight against Williams and the purported threat of a "black neo-colonialism."[105]

Charges of race-baiting and the manipulation of multiracialism by both parties characterized the federal elections in Trinidad. Though fewer than in Jamaica, there were claims of racist campaigning before the election. For instance, in late March 1958 a letter from a "Democrat" in the *Trinidad Guardian* questioned why Dr. Winston Mahabir, an Indian supporter of the PNM, had attacked Albert Gomes and openly said that he should not be elected since he was not black or Indian. The writer claimed that Trinidadians "were dwelling together in unity until" Mahabir and the PNM entered the political scene.[106] While the campaigns saw such minor squabbles, it was in the aftermath of the election that the better-known controversy arose.

The recent momentous rise of the PNM suffered a severe blow when the DLP won a majority of Trinidad's federal seats. Just as in Jamaica, the ruling party in the WIFLP camp experienced a shocking setback. However, the ensuing controversy was not so much over the results of the election as over how those results came about. In the following month the PNM and DLP exchanged accusations of racism, while both purported to uphold the federation's multiracial motto of "dwelling together in unity." The postelection disputes began with Eric Williams's accusations that the "East Indians" of the DLP used racial propaganda to win the election. He based this claim an anti-PNM letter supposedly circulated by DLP supporters directed to "My Dear Indian Brothers" and signed "Yours Truly, Indian." Williams alleged this was the action not of the respectable "Indian nation" but of a "recalcitrant and hostile minority" within it. Some believed it was meant to scare the Indians, and it appeared to work, as the PNM was beaten convincingly in the rural areas dominated by Indians. Williams charged this "deliberate attempt of our opponents to exploit race as the basis of political power" was a threat to Trinidad and Tobago and the federation.[107]

DLP supporters quickly voiced their outrage. To some Indians, it was "plain as daylight that the advent of [the] PNM in this colony started this race feeling," and they demanded an apology.[108] The *Trinidad Guardian* published various responses: Williams was just making excuses; he was attacking Indians since he was scared of the white society; he was ruining the harmony and understanding of previous years. Furthermore, some claimed, it was Williams who brought up racial issues when they would have been better left alone—including the alleged racist history lessons some claimed he preached in many of his speeches. Gomes and others even likened Williams to Hitler. Was "the Doctor, like Hitler and the Jews, looking for a scapegoat and finding the Indians a good target?"[109] Others argued that Williams provided "a very rude shock" to the federation's motto. Even Bustamante voiced the opinion that Williams's allegations were "vulgar" coming from such an educated man, and that anyone "who attempted to set up race against race in any country should be thrown out of the country."[110]

Williams and the PNM defended themselves and responded with their own accusations. The PNM resolved "that the multi-racial ship of the PNM" would not succumb to the "fascist flood of racial conflict." PNM supporters penned replies to clarify that Williams had not attacked all Indians, only those leaders who introduced race and misled the "illiterate Indians" of the rural areas.[111] Their case gained some validity with confirmation of DLP political rallies where promises were made to largely Indian audiences that an Indian would be appointed prime minister if the DLP won. Further support can be discerned in the letter of one disgruntled DLP supporter who complained about rumors that the white Albert Gomes might be made prime minister of the West Indies Federation. The writer asserted that this "would be a complete betrayal of the East Indian community as the elections in the rural area were fought to the bitter end on the ground that if the [DLP] won, the first Prime Minister would be an East Indian."[112] Thus it appeared that the DLP had indeed used race and the fear of black domination over Indians in its campaigns.

These debates in the press continued for some time. Both sides pushed their assumptions and denied their opponents' allegations. Yet neither party could honestly claim that it had not simultaneously employed race as a political tool. As one PNM Indian noted in defiance of his own party, "if the DLP is racial in that Indians voted for their candidate, then the PNM is equally racial in another direction."[113] By May 1958 many of the daily salvos on the issue of race in the election calmed to a few weekly lingering complaints. Most were renewed cries for an end to these racial controversies. They wanted the "Government heads and political leaders to whatever party they may belong to teach and preach racial unity." Others insisted that race must cease to be an issue or it would ruin the West Indies. What was needed was the reestablishment of West Indian cooperation, as had been presented in the capital site struggle. Only then could federation be strong and successful.[114]

As West Indians in the region finalized the formation of federation, West Indians and their allies operating beyond the region also prepared for the arrival of the new nation. In New York, London, and other locales outside the Caribbean, activists and supporters observed and analyzed the final preparations for federation. Given the struggles within the region, some abroad undoubtedly pondered why West Indianness could not seem to take root in the islands themselves. Of course, the fact was that those actually planning the Caribbean federation found it difficult at times to translate what some considered romanticized ideals of West Indianness into the concrete aspects of nation building. Nevertheless, those in the broader diaspora, who by now had largely settled into auxiliary roles of support, maintained their determination to do just that—support the Federation for which they too had worked so hard.

As the date of the Federation drew closer, many expatriate West Indians, African Americans, and other black diaspora activists anxiously awaited its arrival. In Britain, particularly London, the West Indian population was growing dramatically. Many "returned home" to the mother country in search of economic opportunity, especially as immigration restrictions in the United States took shape. From a few thousand before the war to a few hundred thousand in the postwar years, this migration made a considerable impact on British society. Although these West Indians, as well as other black and Asian immigrants, focused primarily on their lives in Britain, where they faced widespread discrimination and racism from reactionary white citizens, they did support and look forward to the start of federation.

Many of these new West Indian arrivals, like those before them, and like other colonial populations in Britain whose homelands were involved in similar nation-building endeavors, believed the creation of a West Indian nation would have positive ramifications for them wherever they resided. In Britain, West Indian activists led by figures such as Claudia Jones worked to improve West Indians' (and at times even other black and colonial peoples') lives in the face of white British racism and for the development of their homelands.[115]

Black America also continued to lend support. Amid the various preexisting West Indian and black diaspora organizations that supported federation from abroad, West Indian activists in New York created the Caribbean League of America (CLA) in January 1957. Headquartered in New York, the CLA hoped to expand through the creation of additional branches in other US cities with sizeable West Indian populations in the near future. Prominent members included familiar activists such as Richard B. Moore, Reginald Pierrepointe, Hope Stevens, and A. A. Austin, who brought to the CLA not only decades of activism on behalf of federation but also black diaspora activism. CLA objectives included (1) service as a liaison between peoples of the Caribbean and the United States so as to promote closer relationships and better understanding between these groups; (2) encouragement to "movements and tendencies" in the Caribbean promoting political, social, and economic democracy within the Caribbean or in relation to the Caribbean and other countries; (3) encouragement to "movements and tendencies" in the Caribbean seeking to advance the national independence of Caribbean; and (4) advocating for maximum freedom of movement and communication between the Caribbean and the United States.[116]

The CLA tried to balance supportive and activist roles on behalf of West Indians in the islands and the United States. They asserted, "West Indians living in the United States should accept certain responsibilities towards their Caribbean homeland . . . [including] the development of the area wherever and whenever possible." At the same time, the organization stressed its unreserved loyalty and service to the United States. In fact, the CLA sponsored a Caribbean-American Friendship Week (initially planned for March but taking place in April 1957) proclaimed by Governor Averell Harriman, which celebrated the enrichment of "the life, culture, and industry of New York State and our Nation" by Caribbean peoples, who had proved themselves "alert to the duties, responsibilities and privileges of citizenship, and have contributed much to our development sharing with us a love of freedom and democracy."[117]

As for federation, in the words of CLA president Dr. Gerald A. Spencer, "Our purpose is to co-ordinate the virtually unanimous spirit of approval behind Caribbean Federation. Nationhood for the West Indies is a long-cherished dream. We must prepare ourselves to meet and solve the various problems that will arise with this new status."[118] This included being an example of West Indian unity for the region itself. The CLA proclaimed:

> The Island units that comprise the West Indies are being unified into a federated whole. We hope that this will include eventually two large sections which are not now committed to the plan [British Guiana and British Honduras]. The unification of the area however, can succeed only if there is unification (of aims and efforts). West Indians must stop thinking as Jamaicans, Barbadians and Trinidadians,—Indians and Chinese etc.
>
> We who have lived in America are fortunate in having close association one with the other. We have learned to work together and we enjoy each other thoroughly. It is our responsibility to set an example in Unity for all our people in the Caribbean. We must be prepared to take the broad view of the affairs which concern the whole region. We must see the Caribbean as one unit within which our kith and kin are struggling with common problems towards a common destiny.[119]

Other supporters of federation eagerly awaited its arrival. Many of these continued to stress and trumpet the national and racial aspects of federation. Written at the same time that West Indian representatives in the Caribbean met to choose the site of the federal capital, a February 1957 *Chicago Defender* editorial argued,

This step [federation] is of great significance not only to the native West Indians but as well to American Negroes whose ingenuity, resourcefulness and talents have been bottled up by American race prejudice. Great avenues of opportunity for commerce, for industrial expansion and for cultural interchange will open up, broadening with enduring benefits the horizon on both sides of the blue Caribbean.

Although the author praised the West Indies for solving "the delicate problem of race relations within their own geography" and the growing "sense of oneness" among the various islanders, there remained an unquestioned tie between federation and the racial uplift of black peoples. "There is a bright future awaiting the citizens of the new nation whose sovereignty will heighten the prestige of the Negro people the world over."[120]

At an American West Indian Association meeting in Chicago in July, Bindley Cyrus described the forthcoming Federation as the "first time a non-white nation has been set up in the Western hemisphere by the British." He proposed a $25,000 gift to the scholarship fund of the UCWI in Jamaica. Cyrus also addressed the disappointment expressed by some in attendance at the appointment as governor-general of Lord Hailes, a white Englishman, instead of a "colored man." Cyrus suggested Hailes's appointment could be beneficial to the federation during its early stages, and that the prime minister "will definitely be a colored man."[121]

Throughout the final years of negotiations, as before, notions of West Indianness upon which the federation was to be based remained fluid, ambiguous, and in many ways elusive. The decades of debate over federation had done little to confirm a particular vision of the forthcoming West Indian nation and its associated West Indianness. Thus the birth of the nation in 1958 came to mean diverse (but connected) things to different peoples in and out of the West Indies.

Welcoming the West Indies

The West Indies Federation came into existence on 3 January 1958. Some local celebrations took place in Port-of-Spain, Trinidad, the capital of the Federation, but the larger celebrations were reserved for the inauguration of the federal legislature in April 1958. For now, the events included the inauguration of the governor-general, Lord Hailes, who would lead an interim advisory council until the full federal government was installed, and speeches by the leaders of the various delegations in attendance.

As John Mordecai remembered, "But for two or three points made, the series of speeches by heads of Government merely embroidered the well-known clichés of the Federation's position." Several focused on the future possibilities of the Federation, while noting the work that remained to see the new nation beyond its infancy. Norman Manley claimed that it was up to the West Indian leaders themselves, and not the governor-general, to make both political and economic progress. He warned, however, that the Federation would have to proceed "cautiously and slowly. The first years will largely be years of planning and laying foundations."[122] In his inaugural address, Governor-General Hailes emphasized the need for the various units to think in terms of themselves as united West Indians. "I know that the far-flung West Indian territories have their own individualities: there are the rivalries, perhaps even jealousies . . . but surely the people are West Indians."[123]

The formal creation of the West Indies Federation has been well documented within official narratives of the new nation. Given the overwhelming focus of those works on federation as the culmination of an intra-regional struggle for nationhood, the reactions recounted have largely been drawn from the West Indies themselves. However, what about the responses of West Indians, African Americans, and black diaspora activists and movements outside the Caribbean that had worked tirelessly, and in previous years even led at times, the efforts to create the West Indian nation? How did they welcome and define the new nation?

In early January 1958, multiple articles appeared in the black American press regarding the recent launch of the Federation. As in the Caribbean, more elaborate coverage and celebrations were reserved for the inauguration of the federal legislature in April. At this time, rather general recognitions of the Federation appeared. The *Pittsburgh Courier* referred to the creation of the West Indies Federation as the product of "over 20 years of agitation, advocacy and discussion" by West Indians and others in the Caribbean and the United States—a new nation with "high hopes but many handicaps."[124] An article in the *Afro-American* offered a summary of the recent events in Port-of-Spain, highlighted a US State Department telegram offering "good wishes and greetings from the American people and the President," and detailed the upcoming elections in the "multi-racial federation."[125] Surprisingly, given its location, the *New York Amsterdam News* offered little coverage of the January launch. Instead, a column on the upcoming year as one likely to be marked by "a great many crucially important events, whether in the field of international, domestic, or race relations" described the forthcoming April inauguration of the West Indies Federation (when the federal legislature would be seated) as an event representing "all three kinds of relations." The author claimed this new nation would increase the dignity and pride of West Indians in the Caribbean and the United States, as well as other black and nonwhite peoples.[126]

Despite the rather subdued initial coverage within the black press, many supporters demonstrated their delight at the creation of the Federation. In the preceding months, several US-based groups began preparations for the April ceremonies, which were widely regarded as the more formal inauguration of the new nation. In November 1957, for instance, even before the installation of the governor-general, the AWIA and *Chicago Defender* began efforts to organize a national committee of West Indians and African Americans to create a Salute to the British Caribbean Federation. This program proposed to arrange travel for five hundred people to attend the inauguration ceremonies in Trinidad in April, publish a special supplement in the *Chicago Defender* to mark the occasion, and raise $25,000 for the UCWI "as a token of American friendship for the new Federation."[127] In February 1958, advertisements offering travel arrangements and tours of the West Indies for those interested in attending the ceremonies in April appeared in both the *Chicago Defender* and *New York Amsterdam News*.[128]

While it is possible that expatriate West Indians and black Americans of Caribbean descent held greater sentiment for the Federation, the venture remained important for African Americans too. As one *Pittsburgh Courier* article on the federal elections in April noted, "Most American Negroes will join us in hoping for every success for the new Federation of English-speaking people."[129] The creation of the American Friends of the West Indies Federation (AFWIF) in early April exemplified this interest.

The idea for the AFWIF came from Mrs. Una Morrison Staples, a Jamaican living in the United States, who recommended that "native West Indians living in this country and their well-wishers should organize themselves in an effort to support the newly formed federation." Further support of the idea came from, among others, Congressman Adam Clayton Powell of New York, Congressman Charles C. Diggs of Michigan, and Rayford Logan of Howard University, all of whom had long-standing interest and ties in the West Indies. A national committee lead by Rayford Logan was formed to plan a mass meeting following the inauguration ceremonies in Trinidad later in the month, where they hoped to hear reports from those who attended, including Powell and Diggs. Local branches of the AFWIF also formed. Rayford Logan became the temporary chairman of a District of Columbia chapter, while Powell established a New York branch soon after the initial formation of the national organization. Diggs, who introduced a motion in the US House of Representatives in March that produced a concurrent resolution from the US House and Senate extending cordial greetings and best wishes to the new Federation, also announced his goal to create a Detroit branch of the AFWIF. Congressman William L. Dawson expressed a desire for a Chicago branch.[130] Although the impact of such moral support is debatable, as Zachery R. Williams notes in his study of black public intellectuals at Howard, "The formation of the [AFWIF] was significant . . . because it demonstrated the support offered and concern felt by black American scholars and political leaders for the affairs of the West Indies in particular, and for the Caribbean in general."[131]

Much as some black activists viewed all black struggles against racism and for self-determination as portions of a larger struggle for peoples of African descent across the globe, black achievements in different locations also came to be viewed and celebrated as a victory for "the race" as a whole. At a time of multiple anticolonial and nationalist movements among black colonial populations, it was not uncommon for black populations to celebrate the successful attainment of nationhood in one area as but one victory in the overall struggle for self-determination. During the 1950s, when the majority of the world's black population remained under colonial control, the creation of new black nations was something to be celebrated beyond the bounds of just that nation.

In the postwar era, as independent African nations emerged and the West Indies Federation stood ready to do so, black diasporic celebrations of their achievements expressed such attitudes. To many, the creation of the West Indies Federation in 1958, on the heels of Ghanaian independence in 1957, was one more achievement in these diaspora struggles. It is not unreasonable to assume the members of the AWIA who attended festivities in Chicago connected to Ghana's independence in March 1957, including a Ghana Ball and a Salute to Ghana, drew inspiration for their own Salute to the British Caribbean Federation the following year. As a March 1957 *New York Amsterdam News* editorial urged, "While we rejoice at the celebration of the independence of Ghana we must not lose sight of events of importance closer to our shores. . . . Independent Ghana today—a federated West Indies tomorrow!"[132] In London, Claudia Jones and the *West Indian Gazette* made similar comparisons. Jones, who supported the West Indies Federation and viewed its initial creation "as a first, halting but unfailing step towards national independence for the Federation and a complete self-government for its units," also noted the connections between the independence of Ghana in 1957 and the launch of the West Indies Federation in 1958.[133]

In the weeks prior to the formal inauguration of the Federation on 22 April 1958, various US-based groups organized celebrations to mark the occasion. In Chicago the Associated West Indian Clubs of America, which included the AWIA, sponsored a gala reception and ball on 20 April connected to its Salute to the West Indies and attended by West Indian and African American supporters.[134] The West Indian Federation Celebration Committee of Boston organized a banquet and ball in that city for 22 April.[135] Some historically black colleges planned similar events, including Morgan State and Howard, which hosted events in Baltimore and the Washington, DC, area.[136]

In New York, home to the largest expatriate West Indian communities and a black diaspora center for decades, a series of events occurred in the week prior to the Federation events in Trinidad. City Councilman Earl Brown introduced a resolution requesting the mayor to declare 22 April "West Indies Federation Day." The American-Caribbean Friendship Week, originally planned for March as the Caribbean-American Friendship Week, was celebrated on 20–27 April. Many of these events were sponsored by the Caribbean League of America, but numerous other groups undoubtedly collaborated, given the shared constituency of many organizations. The schedule included a West Indian art exhibit at the Countee Cullen Branch of the New York Public Library, a church service, a public rally, and a Federation Dance (sponsored by the West Indian Students Association). The week was capped with a dinner and ball.[137]

Back in Trinidad, a week of festivities planned by all the member states of the Federation marked the inauguration of the federal parliament on 22 April 1958. Events included West Indian historical exhibitions and an array of performing arts presentations highlighting West Indian drama, music, dance, and painting. The inauguration hosted Princess Margaret, representatives from all the new federal states, foreign dignitaries from all the Commonwealth nations and the United States, West Indian activists from the West Indies and the broader diaspora, and an array of other regional and international guests who made their way to Trinidad to greet the new nation. As John Mordecai described the events, "The local public could almost choose a list of legendary personalities, and find them there in the flesh." He went on, "The maturity of the whole spectacle led many visitors to assume that a new Member's entry to the Dominion family was being celebrated."[138]

Pomp and circumstance dominated inauguration day: a procession to the legislative building, the installation of the federal legislature, another procession to Governor's House, cocktail parties, a state dinner, and a large fireworks display. The speeches of the day downplayed, or outright ignored, the issues and problems that many knew the Federation faced in its infancy. Instead, most stressed the success of bringing the various units together, the need to continue forging regional bonds, and that this was but the beginning of what would soon enough be a self-governing member of the British Commonwealth. In acknowledgement of the Federation's national motto, a message from the queen said, "May the people of the West Indies, indeed, 'Dwell Together in Unity.'" Princess Margaret's address highlighted the hard work of the West Indians (and their British supporters) that brought the Federation into existence. "Today . . . the Federation of the West Indies for so long a dream, [becomes] a living reality." She reminded the gathered West Indian leaders, "You will no doubt be confronted by many problems and difficulties, your path may not be easy and you may have many obstacles to surmount, but at least you will know that the burden that you bear is an honorable one." In response, Grantley Adams, who had recently and somewhat surprisingly been chosen prime minister of the Federation following the decisions of Norman Manley and Eric Williams not to run for federal office, said, "We set our steps on the new road in sober confidence with high hopes."[139] This may not have been the federation that many had envisioned and worked for since the late nineteenth century, but it was celebrated nonetheless.

The responses to the final arrival of federation further highlight the disparate visions of the new West Indian nation. Within the region, the arrival of the Federation was celebrated by many political leaders and activists as the culmination of an intra-regional nation-building project. The West Indies' diverse but connected peoples had come together beyond race for the good of the region, and set an example for the world to admire and possibly emulate. As Hugh Springer remarked, in the past the racial diversity of the West Indian population "has been a source of weakness, a great dividing force, but we believe that in the future that very weakness may become our greatest strength."[140] The Crown had long been more comfortable with these visions of the Federation than more racialized ones, and its praise for the region mirrored those views. As John Drummond, Earl of Perth, minister of state for colonial affairs, noted in an interview with the *Jamaica Times* in the weeks following the inauguration events,

> The population of the West Indies has come from the United King-
> dom, from Ireland, from Spain and Portugal, from France and Hol-
> land, from India, from Africa and from China. But all these people
> have settled in together and are first and foremost West Indians.
> Racial feeling at times rises high, but this is more like antagonisms
> between Scots and English than anything else. And in their general
> good humour, outspoken and energetic ways, they lead the way in the
> world in showing that racial problems are eminently soluble and are
> perhaps no problem at all. Here is a lesson for many to learn.[141]

Reactions from Black America to the final birth of the new West Indian nation continued the celebratory tone of the previous few weeks with rec-ognition of both the national and diasporic dimensions of this undertak-ing. The CLA published *A Salute to the Federated West Indies*, a booklet that included a variety of well-wishes from local businesses, African Ameri-can and US-based West Indian groups, local, state, and federal politicians, United Nations representatives, and even political leaders from the broader black diaspora, including Ghana. There were also a variety of short essays detailing the past, present, and possible future of the Federation. Surpris-ingly, given the involvement of figures like Richard B. Moore, Reginald Pierrepointe, and Hope Stevens, several of these articles did not address the diasporic significance of the new nation. As for the place of race in the new nation, which had been such an important issue for much diaspora activ-ism on behalf of federation, the booklet's materials demonstrated the coex-istence of multiracial and racialized visions of the new nation. H. D. Hug-gins, a UCWI professor in a visiting position at Yale, claimed in his essay on the significance of the new nation, "Perhaps in no part of the world are the complications which are associated with differences in class, colour and creed regarded with more tolerance and treated with more maturity than in the West Indies." At the same time, others noted the new nation's ties to black diasporic struggles. Roy Wilkins's resolution on behalf of the NAACP said, "May you demonstrate for all the world to behold, the capacity of the Negro for self-rule," and also "uphold and protect the basic human rights of the white minority which dwells among you and thereby set an example for older and stronger nations." Even Langston Hughes penned a poem, "Salute, Federation," which noted the bonds between African Americans and West Indians.[142]

In the weeks that followed the inauguration ceremonies, the black press also carried numerous editorials and articles on the Federation. Black businesses placed congratulatory ads welcoming the new nation in the *New York Amsterdam News*. From beauty shops and ballrooms to cafes, bars, and lounges, the Federation was celebrated by the black community.[143] Many ads and articles emphasized its arrival as the culmination of the building of a black nation. Carver Federal Savings and Loan Association, a joint West Indian–African American financial center in the community, said, "British West Indians and American born Negroes are bound together by a common heritage and common ancestry. . . . Indeed, the American Negro has toiled side by side with his West Indian brother here and on the Islands in tireless effort to bring to realization the events now taking place in the Caribbean." The text continued, "The advent of the Federation of the West Indies marks another milestone in the continued emergence of the people of African descent all over the world into positions of leadership and authority." It could serve as a "dynamic force in bringing to West Indians and Americans of African descent a new awareness of kinship and similarity of racial ambitions."[144]

Although the New York area may have been called the Capital of the Caribbean, like the diaspora activism that helped forge it, praise for the Federation appeared in other parts of Black America too. An *Afro-American* editorial in May congratulated the three million citizens of the West Indies on the "birth of the second colored republic in the Western Hemisphere."[145] In the *Chicago Defender*, a local resident of nearby Evanston asserted,

> The Federation of the West Indies was cause for celebration by Negroes everywhere. For it adds one more star to the growing circle of free nations ruled by black people. West Indians need no longer boast of their being British subjects. They have carved out a nation of their own and it is only a matter of time before complete independence will come to these islands. We in America should make every effort to establish a closer relationship with the people in the Caribbean. . . . Besides, there are tremendous possibilities of commercial exchange and extension of our constricted Negro market. Many of our commodities could find a ready outlet in those islands. So a prosperous West Indies may have many rewarding implications to Negro America. Besides enlarging the scope of our cultural and commercial activities, the new Federation also heightens the prestige of the Negro world. We should thank God for this new blessing.[146]

All of these articles demonstrate that the Federation remained viewed by many as a victory for black peoples in their global struggle for self-determination and empowerment. However, such views did not belie or undermine multiracial and transracial views of the nation. Few black supporters conceived of the Federation as an exclusively black nation where no other races were welcomed. Still, as in previous decades, whether by design or default, many conceptualized federation as inherently a black nation-building project with connections to black diaspora struggles, and not simply a nation *of* black peoples.

Such views can also be found among some Africans. During a visit to Jamaica in May, William Van Lare, Senior Justice of Appeal in the Supreme Court of Ghana, who represented Ghana at the inauguration ceremonies, said "he hoped the time would come when there would be interchanges on a much higher scale between Africans at home and those abroad." He also shared Kwame Nkrumah's wish "to see all black peoples of the world have a voice in running their own affairs," and "praise for leaders of the West Indies Federation" in seeing this take shape in the Caribbean.[147] Despite his opposition to regional federations in Africa, where such ideas were promoted as a means to protect white settler populations and power, Kwame Nkrumah said, "I must confess that my ultimate interest in the establishment of a united West Indies stems also from the fact that a strong and powerful nation of peoples of African descent in the West Indies would . . . give a strong fillip to the efforts we in Africa have been making towards the creation of a united Africa." In Nkrumah's estimation, the Federation was an important site for his dreams of black self-determination throughout the diaspora. "Success in the establishment of a powerful West Indian nation would substantially assist the efforts we are making in Africa to redeem Africa's reputation in world affairs and to re-establish the personality of the African and people of African descent everywhere."[148]

In June a *New York Amsterdam News* editorial emphasized a sense of a growing momentum in the fight for black self-determination.

> All over the world today we are surrounded by bigotry, hate and malice and at the core of the world's trouble is the caste and class erected against the black man. But the picture is changing so rapidly there is scarcely time to celebrate the independence of a Ghana before the fires on the hilltops signal the start of a new upheaval which may lead to the independence of an Algeria or the Federation of the West Indies. Black people are on the march.[149]

In these views, a Federation was to be a powerful symbol of black political power, rather than a multiracial lesson for the world to witness.

Even those who recognized that the Federation was not populated exclusively by peoples of African descent described it as likely to be overwhelmingly under black political control. An article in the May 1958 edition of *Ebony* claimed, "Down in the sugar-coated islands of the Caribbean a colored nation has been born." While the article noted that this would include some East Indians in areas like Trinidad, it presented the federation as a nation to be led by people of African descent primarily.[150] Stated more directly in a *New York Times* article, in the Federation "the black man rules."[151]

Although many in Black America celebrated the arrival of federation through the sometimes overly optimistic lens of racial romanticism, it would be careless to assume there was no critical reflection and analysis of the new Federation. Like their counterparts in the Caribbean, US-based supporters of federation also noted some of its shortcomings and problems. As the title of one article stated, "Federation Starts on a 'Sticky Wicket.'"[152] During the euphoric days following the ceremonies in Trinidad, a rather even-toned editorial appeared in the *Chicago Defender* detailing some of the financial challenges of the federation, while also noting its potential. "While Federation will not at once bring wealth to the islands, it fashions a political unity and regional planning that bodes well for the future of the West Indies."[153] A more critical article appeared in the *New York Amsterdam News* a few days later. "After all the preliminary letting off of political hot air and passing of the buck by the leaders of the people, all the parties have now settled down to the grim economic and political reality of the West Indies Federation."[154]

Unfortunately, these more critical reflections on the Federation proved far more prophetic than those that trumpeted a bright future for it. Nevertheless, despite the many shortcomings that would cripple the new nation almost immediately upon its inauguration, the actual creation of the Federation still proved quite an achievement, demonstrating not only the success of West Indian nation building but also the close links of such a project to black diaspora politics in the twentieth century. Even if *this* Federation was not the federation that many had imagined, a West Indian nation was born. That nation, however, would be short-lived.

Epilogue

Many within and beyond the Caribbean celebrated the birth of the West Indies Federation in 1958 even as a variety of problems simmered just beneath its gilded surface. Yet despite the festivities that accompanied its launch, the fervor for federation had undoubtedly dipped compared to previous years. As Hugh Springer recalled, between the 1947 CLC and Montego Bay Conferences and the formal agreement to federate in 1956, "enthusiasm for the federal idea diminished from the high pitch of 1947 to the level of mere acceptance of the decision that there was to be a federal center."[1] Given that it was still a crown colony, the West Indies Federation appeared to be more the "foul federation" that T. A. Marryshow warned about in 1919 than the achievement of West Indian nationhood many supporters had long sought.[2] Indeed, the limited power and unsettled financial questions of the new federal government led one observer to refer to it as a "ghost federation," while Secretary of State for the Colonies Alan Lennox-Boyd claimed the "Federal government is hardly worth the name."[3]

In addition to the waning enthusiasm among some supporters, the Federation faced a series of contentious issues soon after its creation. Officials at the London Conference of 1956 agreed to move forward with the Federation despite several unresolved issues, lest the project be indefinitely delayed. They also adopted what Sir John Mordecai called the "strategy of 1956"—an agreement that the "Federal constitution should not be reconsidered for five years" following the inauguration of the new nation.[4] They hoped this would provide the new nation an opportunity to gain more solid footing before tackling important and highly divisive subjects that could possibly fracture the tenuous unity among its members. Unfortunately, this strategy proved short-lived, as the spirit of compromise that helped prevent any further delays in the creation of the Federation was not maintained in the early years of its actual existence. There would be no honeymoon period for the West Indies Federation.

Stumbling from the Start

Soon after the inauguration of the Federation, some West Indian politicians within the federal and various unit governments quickly demanded more concrete decisions regarding the structure and powers of the federal government, with an eye to uncluttering the still uncertain future of the West Indies Federation. During the first session of the federal legislature in 1958, some pushed for a conference to review various aspects of the Federation's constitution no later than 1959. These included key questions related to the relationship between the Federation and the individual island units. Although the original constitution included a provision that delegates from the Federation, member units, and the Crown should convene a conference no later than the fifth anniversary to review the constitution, this more immediate demand for constitutional review at the 1959 Intergovernmental Conference showed the urgency some felt to address a range of issues and interests.[5]

Over the course of the next year, West Indian officials and political parties at the federal and local levels, as well as general supporters and opponents, presented their views on possible constitutional revisions. Most agreed the Federation needed to be reformed. The problem was that many of the matters to be resolved involved diametrically opposed opinions, several of which confirmed the prevalent problem of insular islandisms which continued to thwart efforts to bind the nation via a prioritized sense of West Indianness.

Numerous issues proved troublesome. The colonial character of the federal constitution, which reserved many powers to the Crown, left much to be desired. West Indian officials had begrudgingly accepted federation without independence during the last stages of the negotiations of the 1950s. Nevertheless, the lack of a firm commitment from the Crown on when the Federation would achieve its independence troubled many who believed West Indians were ready to rule themselves, as well as those who worried the current Federation had extended rather than ended colonial rule. The financial state of the Federation was also disconcerting. Considering the wealth the West Indies produced for the empire during their extended colonial status, many considered the financial aid initially offered by the British insufficient. Others believed that relationships between the Federation's members were more important. Key internal disagreements involved debates over federal taxation, a customs union, tariff rates, the movement of goods and people between the islands, and federal representation. While some sought greater interisland cooperation, others continued to prioritize their respective islands over the region.

Debates on these issues came to be exemplified in the struggle between those who favored a strong federal government, with extensive powers over the unit members, and those who preferred a weaker, loose federation with most powers reserved to the individual island's government.[6] The often oppositional views between the political leaders of the Federation's two largest members, Jamaica and Trinidad, exemplified many of these debates. Several studies of Federation have noted the differences of opinion between Eric Williams (chief minister and then first premier of Trinidad and Tobago), Norman Manley (chief minister and then first premier of Jamaica), and Alexander Bustamante (leader of the opposition in Jamaica), and the conflict between a resurgent Jamaican nationalism and regional West Indianness. As Williams remembered,

> The Federal Government immediately became a battle-ground for two major issues: Independence, with Trinidad and Tobago as the champion; and the powers of the Federal Government . . . with Jamaican insisting on non-interference with its right to its own conception and practice of economic development . . . against Trinidad and Tobago insisting on a strong centralised Federation with extensive powers.

As for the other island units, "the smaller territories, like the Federal Government, wobbled indecisively in this struggle between the two major territories."[7]

In Jamaica, the desire for a weak federal government exhibited the continued relevance of islandism in the Federation. Within the current federal structure, some argued that Jamaica already carried an excessive load and was being forced to care for the less developed "small islands" of the eastern Caribbean, all while lacking representation in the federal government commensurate with the island's geographic and demographic dominance in the region. Thus they felt significant trepidation concerning the creation of a strong federal center with extensive powers over the individual unit governments, which they believed could sidetrack Jamaica's recent economic boom or place additional undue burdens on them.

These sentiments were shared by both supporters and opponents of the Federation in Jamaica, including key political leaders. Although Bustamante still supported federation in the late 1950s, his fluid stance on the idea had already begun to shift and would soon become more solidified in opposition to its existence—or at least Jamaica's place within it. Manley, despite his long-standing support of federation, struggled in these years to juggle his own regionalism and islandism. In most cases it appears the former was tempered by the latter. Manley continued to insist the Federation was crucial for the future of Jamaica and the other West Indian colonies, but he tended to favor a more gradual approach to cooperation between the islands. In the case of Jamaica, he preferred a weaker federal government that would not hinder Jamaica's development.[8]

On 27 May 1959 the demands for a weak federal center and the protection of local (island) interests and power were put forth in Jamaica's Ministry Paper no. 18. This called for a loose federation with representation based upon the population of each federal unit, thereby ensuring a Jamaican majority within the Federation. Furthermore, it maintained that the Federation's taxation powers and the introduction of a customs union should be limited so that each unit could protect its own markets. While it was unanimously supported within Jamaica's legislature as a means to ensure the Federation would not derail Jamaica's development, it was met with much skepticism and criticism by others in the Federation. As John Mordecai recalled, "A Federation in which the promised income tax powers were withdrawn, the existing alternative access to commodities levies cancelled, the Concurrent List of powers pruned, and each Unit left to decide what it would reserve for its own control, seemed, as the Minister of Finance repeatedly termed it, 'a headless and bodiless Federation.'"[9]

Whereas some in Jamaica found the current Federation too intrusive, others, especially in the eastern Caribbean islands, sought to strengthen the Federation's power within the region and over the individual units. In Trinidad, Eric Williams, who had long supported the creation of a strong, independent federation, remained one of the most outspoken West Indian leaders in favor of independence as soon as possible.[10] On 24 May 1959, a few days prior to Jamaica's Ministry Paper no. 18, Williams and the PNM called for a stronger Federation with full independence by 22 April 1960 (the second anniversary of the inauguration of the Federation's legislature). They supported the revision of the federal constitution in order to secure, among other things, independence, a national spirit, and the economic development and integration of the region.[11]

These demands were published in the fall of 1959 as *The Economics of Nationhood*. This booklet offered a definitive statement in support of a powerful and independent Federation. Williams argued the Federation should have total control over such issues as defense, external affairs, immigration and emigration, exchange control and currency, and customs.[12] He argued it was only through a powerful federal government that the islands could move beyond their long history of insularity. "Only a powerful and centrally directed economic coordination and interdependence can create the true foundations of a nation. . . . [The units] will be knit together only through their common allegiance to a Central Government. Anything else will discredit the conception of Federation, and in the end leave the islands more divided than before."[13]

It is somewhat ironic that while Jamaica sought a weaker Federation to protect its own economic interests, Trinidad, the wealthiest unit of the Federation, supported a stronger Federation and greater financial cooperation between the islands. In many ways, it was a powerful gesture of regional unity over insularity. Nonetheless, the Trinidadians did not sacrifice all of their local concerns for the good of the region. Their stance against the freedom of movement of federal citizens between colonies, as well as their opposition to Jamaica's development of an oil refinery, exposed the realities of insularism even within the Federation's champion.

By the time of the first Intergovernmental Conference in September 1959, tensions were high, especially between Jamaica and Trinidad. Manley and the Jamaican delegation arrived determined to press the issue of federal representation by population, and refused to consider any other issues until the matter was settled. As the conference became a showdown between Jamaica's Ministry Paper no. 18 and Trinidad's *Economics of Nationhood*, Prime Minister Adams suggested that all of the issues be examined by ministerial committees that would report back to the federal and unit governments. By the end of this conference, the delegates had done little more than tentatively agree on federal representation based on population.[14]

A Vigilant Watch

As the various political leaders and parties *within* the West Indies struggled to hold the new nation together in the face of contentious internal debates over the scale and scope of the Federation's power and its relationship with the individual unit members, expatriate West Indian and black diaspora activists watched from abroad. Despite their diminished influence in the region over the previous decade, they remained resolved, given their prominent role in the pursuit of West Indian self-government and federation, to be heard regarding the nation many knew they helped create. This included both support for and criticism of the Federation and the ongoing struggles to settle the various problems incurred during the first two years of its existence.

A particularly critical assessment of the Federation came from W. A. Domingo, who by the late 1950s was established as one of the most vocal critics of Jamaica's participation in the Federation. As previously discussed, members of the Jamaica Progressive League (JPL) had been divided among themselves over the issue for several years. Despite the strong opposition of some members, many in the organization seemingly accepted the impending reality of the Federation shortly before its launch.[15] Domingo was not one of them. He continued his assault on Federation from New York in March 1958 with the publication of another anti-federation booklet, *Federation—Jamaica's Folly*.

Written between the creation of the Federation in January and the inauguration of the federal government in April, it presented Domingo's "strong conviction that Jamaica . . . has infinitely more to lose than to gain from the alliance."[16] Much of *Jamaica's Folly* aimed to discredit the idea that federation was necessary or even desired in the West Indies, particularly for Jamaica and by Jamaicans. He declared the creation of the Federation had been a decision of misinformed political leaders and not the West Indian populations themselves, most of whom still did not have a real understanding of federation.[17] While he had already dismissed many pro-federation arguments for Jamaica in his previous *Critique*, he recounted many of them here as well with a focus on Jamaica.

Domingo insisted, "Jamaican proponents of federation offered and still offer no worthwhile evidence that their island will derive any real, measurable benefits" from the Federation. He rejected the idea that federation was a necessary step for Jamaica (and other West Indian colonies) to obtain independence, and argued that Jamaica was on its way to dominion status on its own before the Federation. Domingo noted the recent achievement of dominion status and independence by several nations in Africa and Asia—including Sudan, Ghana, India, Pakistan, Ceylon, Burma, and Malaya—as examples that Jamaica could and should follow.[18]

Domingo also dismissed the potential economic benefits of federation for Jamaica and other West Indian colonies. He argued that intra-regional trade among unit members would not prove beneficial, especially given the common products of many colonies, and a federation was not necessary to attract foreign capital. Moreover, despite its size and population within the Federation, given its official representation in the federal government, Jamaica could be "out-voted" and see "federal interference in purely Jamaican matters to the detriment of Jamaica and Jamaicans." Overall, Domingo claimed, as had other opponents of federation, that the British had pushed the Federation on the region "as a means of relieving themselves of further financial responsibility for the Caribbean colonies," rather than for the benefit of those colonies.[19]

Jamaica's Folly also refuted the notion that the Federation would improve Jamaica's, or any other West Indian islands,' international prestige. Domingo acknowledged it could "serve to correct some of [the] flagrant racial disabilities and disadvantages" that the region had suffered under colonial rule if its leaders were "courageous and determined." It might even become "an example of racial tolerance in a world sorely beset by conflicts of race and colour," as some supporters suggested. Nonetheless, in Domingo's opinion, multiple independent West Indian nations could provide the same prestige. They would also provide the region greater influence on the international level because each would hold a vote in the United Nations, compared to the one vote the Federation would receive whenever it achieved independence. Domingo charged the British knew this, and pushed for a federation in the West Indies so as to limit "the political influence of coloured people in the world" in the future. He concluded that the British "out-witted" Jamaicans and other West Indians into accepting a federation that "will not promote the national interests of Jamaica, in particular, nor of the West Indian peoples as a whole."[20]

While supporters of the Federation also found faults in the new nation, their critiques most often focused on solidifying, rather than dismantling, the Federation. C.L.R. James's *Lecture on Federation* offers a prominent example from an expatriate West Indian. From the 1930s to the 1950s, James became a major figure within black diaspora politics in Great Britain and the United States through his involvement with various Black Marxist, Black Internationalist, and Pan-African organizations. Like many others in these movements, James had long supported self-government and a federation for the West Indian colonies as part of the larger freedom struggles of colonial peoples, but especially those of African descent. As Kent Worcester notes in his biography of James, "His call for a political and economic federation of the new nations of the West Indies had a Pan-African flavor and was designed, in part, to inspire similar initiatives in Africa and elsewhere." James viewed federation "as essential to the development of black unity and as the only plausible solution to the problem of underdevelopment" in the Caribbean.[21]

In 1958, after approximately twenty-five years abroad, James returned to his native West Indies for the inauguration of the Federation's legislature at the invitation of Governor General Hailes. James initially intended to stay in the region for only a few months. Instead he quickly became involved in both Trinidadian and West Indian politics through his association with Eric Williams, the PNM, and the West Indian Federal Labour Party. These movements offered James avenues through which to apply his long-standing support for the idea of federation to the actual West Indies Federation, before his acrimonious split with Williams in 1960.[22]

In June 1958, James gave a public lecture on the Federation at Queen's College in British Guiana. James dismissed the criticisms of some within the colony who were displeased at his presence. Likely in response to those who viewed him as a "stranger" in British Guiana and indeed the entire region, given his many years abroad, James began his lecture by noting he, like other West Indians in the United States and England, had long discussed a Caribbean federation—one with British Guiana—well before the recent events leading to the inauguration of the West Indies Federation. While James recognized that those in the West Indies "experience and see much that escapes [those] who live abroad," he countered that their time outside the region allowed them to interact with each other and other colonials. They were "in a position to see the general trends of development, to mark the stages, to see each problem [of colonials] as part of a whole."[23] Therefore he and his fellow expatriates were able to view the struggles of the West Indies as part of the broader anticolonial struggle, and not just an intra-regional nation-building project. Given this perspective, his lecture represents the views of an expatriate West Indian, despite his recent return to the region and official participation in federal politics.

Over the course of his talk, James discussed his support for the Federation, some of its current shortcomings, and the need for British Guiana to join the other West Indian colonies. Like Domingo, he dismissed pro-federation arguments that emphasized financial gains for the colonies, which could be achieved without a federation. Instead James underscored what he believed to be the bigger issue of federation as a transformative venture that would help usher the West Indian colonies into a new era. "Federation offers a way out"—a path from the old world of imperialism and colonialism and into a new world for which the West Indies must be prepared. "Federation is the means and the only means whereby the West Indies and British Guiana can accomplish the transition from colonialism to national independence, can create the basis of a new nation; and by reorganising the economic system and the national life, give us our place in the modern community of nations." Without Federation, he thought this could not be done.[24]

James agreed "the West Indian Federation [was] not a very exciting Federation, nor did it come into the world with vigorous screams as a healthy baby should." Nevertheless, he maintained its shortcomings could be fixed, including the Federation's constitution and the lack of independence. "The last Constitution came like a thief in the night. Some people went abroad and some experts wrote and then suddenly the people were told, 'This is the Federal Constitution.'" Given this process, James agreed the lack of enthusiasm for *this* federation among some in the general population was understandable. To address this grievous error, he called for a constituent assembly through which the West Indian public might be more included in the revision of the federal constitution and the achievement of its independence.[25]

James's lecture did not solely aim to convince British Guiana to join the Federation, but he obviously hoped to use the opportunity to counter several of the arguments against it. Many of his points did just that. He also made some direct appeals for the colony's political leaders to take a stand on the Federation. While James sarcastically noted that a plebiscite was not needed in Trinidad, Barbados, or Jamaica regarding participation in the Federation, he argued that if Cheddi Jagan believed one was needed to determine British Guiana's possible late entry into the Federation, then he should state his position on the matter. If not, Jagan would only allow the current racial rivalries over the issue, such as widespread assumptions of Indo-Caribbean opposition to British Guiana joining the Federation, to continue. Although he was sympathetic with Jagan's disillusionment over other West Indian leaders' lack of support for him in his struggles with the British in the preceding years, James said if Jagan were to lead British Guiana into the Federation, he would find those leaders willing to support him and, in the process, also help the Federation's pursuit of dominion status by demanding it as a condition of the colony's entry.[26]

The Federation's lack of independence became the focal point of a meeting in New York in September 1958 between Manley, expatriate West Indians, and other US-based supporters of federation. Manley spoke about the recent racial violence against West Indians in London during the Notting Hill race riots, as well as the ongoing development of the Federation. Following his talk, Manley addressed several questions from the audience, particularly concerning the latter. When asked what prevented West Indian leaders from forcing the British to grant the Federation independence,

Manley responded, "Perhaps the timidity of West Indians." His answer seemed to surprise many, and prompted a follow-up question from another audience member that criticized the current status of the Federation as much as it requested a formal reply.

> Since what has been established as a federal structure for the Caribbean Federation is obviously totally inadequate, being a temporary hodge-podge makeshift which if maintained can only discredit the very idea of genuine federation and self-government, when will a serious drive be made to achieve full Commonwealth status and to build a free, united Caribbean nation?[27]

Manley dismissed the notion of the current Federation as a "hodge-podge makeshift," given the provision for a constitutional conference in five years. He also said the British were not withholding self-government. "We can have full self-government whenever we ask for it, and we West Indians alone will decide when to ask for it." Additional questions asked Manley about his decision not to hold office in the federal government (a decision he defended and said he would make again), the issue of a customs union in the Federation (to which he replied the matter was not yet settled), on why British Guiana had not joined the Federation (which he said was a decision of its political leaders, who would not join without independence and satisfactory representation), and the possible liquidation of the governor's office in the federal units as a means to save money (an idea he admitted he had not considered but dismissed as not saving enough money to run the Federation for six hours).[28]

Richard B. Moore wrote a lengthy article on this meeting for the *Gleaner* a few months later. He claimed, "The nature of these questions clearly shows the vital interest and specific thought being given here in the United States to the situation and strivings of the Caribbean people." After recounting the actions of the WINEC/WINC at the Pan-American Conference in Havana (1940) and the UNCIO in San Francisco (1945), and the role of expatriate West Indians and African Americans in raising $10,000 for the CLC Conference in 1947, Moore said, "Such fraternal interest and financial support for the advancement and freedom of the Caribbean people will doubtless be carried forward in the future, despite discouraging expressions of apparent lack of care on the part of a particular leader." He then proceeded to detail twenty-one observations in response to Manley's answers to the questions posed to him at the New York meeting.[29]

Moore's "observations" presented his, and very likely many of his colleagues,' critiques of the current Federation and its leadership. He criticized West Indian leaders for failing to secure independence, especially since other former colonies such as Malaya had successfully done so in recent years. As for Manley's claim that the West Indies could have self-government when they wanted it, Moore noted previous demands for a self-governing federation by the CLC and many other groups, as well as meetings and conferences where Manley himself had supported the idea. "From all these and still other forthright demands of representative leaders and groups, it is logically concluded by us here that the West Indian people had already [asked] for self-government and indeed had entrusted their political leaders with a sacred mandate to secure precisely that." The failure to achieve self-government, therefore, fell upon leaders such as Manley, Adams, and others.[30]

Moore also condemned various other aspects of the Federation. He criticized the current structure and constitution which failed to provide "Responsible Government equivalent to Dominion Status," a customs union, free movement of people between the units, and appropriate economic planning and power for the Federation to be successful. If these issues were addressed, "Thousands of the Caribbean people would not then be forced to leave their healthful and sunny shores and to migrate to England and other lands, where they have to face racist hostility." Without full self-government, a customs union, and freedom of movement, the Federation was a "proclaimed nation without freedom and a flag without sovereignty—all are woefully inadequate for the achievement of freedom, statehood, national dignity, and vital economic advancement." Moore said such a nation would inevitably collapse, and when it did, some would assume that Caribbean people were not ready for self-government. Therefore, a "genuine federation with full self-government" was required so that the West Indies could "achieve its rightful place among the nations of the Americas and of the world."[31]

Moore concluded with what can be regarded as a defense, not only of West Indians' right to ask such questions and make demands of their leaders, but also of the right of expatriate West Indians to speak for and to the region concerning the current circumstances of the British Caribbean.

May we not be permitted to warn the political physicians presiding over the birth of the Caribbean nation that too long delayed birth throes must imperil the lives of both mother and child? Is it not our bounden duty to cry out to those who now appear to have become like gods and who testily tell us in effect to await their own good time? Aid the delivery now before it is too late. Let the Caribbean Nation come forth into the world and breathe the invigorating air of freedom.[32]

Moore and other longtime supporters of a federation were not the only ones within Black America watching and advocating for the Federation in this era. In January 1959 the *West Indian–American* began publication. The paper strove to "encourage warm relationship between the West Indies and America, focus attention on the new nation—The West Indies, help raise the living standard of the new nation, influence changes in the immigration laws, be the voice of West Indians everywhere, and spotlight the progress of [West Indian] organizations."[33] Federation was routinely covered in the newspaper, including a May 1959 edition with multiple articles and well-wishes marking the one-year anniversary of the nation. Following a trip to the West Indies that summer, Oliver Bert Walker, the publisher of the newspaper, noted the ongoing efforts by West Indians to see the Federation succeed and drew parallels to similar struggles in Africa.

> The struggle that West Indians are making to be self-ruled; the desire to pool their resources to make out of a few scattered islands a nation, and the elimination of insularity. All of this is the ingredient necessary to propel, if not stabilize, a strong feeling of nationhood. The West Indies, like the African nations who have either shed blood or won with words part of what is rightfully theirs, has embarked upon a project and they are ardently trying to get the most returns from what they are putting into it.[34]

In April 1959 the Caribbean League of America (CLA), which included many of the more prominent supporters of the Federation—Moore, Hope Stevens, Reginald Pierrepointe, A. A. Austin—organized a conference on Caribbean-American economic, social, and cultural affairs to coincide with the first anniversary of the Federation. The conference sought familiar goals such as the fostering of closer relations between American and Caribbean peoples, exploration of greater trade possibilities, reevaluation of US restrictions on Caribbean immigration, development of a scholarship aid program, and a search for sources of technical and financial aid for the Federation. Delegates at this conference also expressed their desire for the

Federation to move forward toward independence as quickly as possible and hoped British Guiana would also soon join.[35] Similar meetings took place periodically over the next few years, and West Indian politicians continued to meet with these organizations during visits to the United States.[36]

The impact of these activities within the West Indies themselves during these early years of the Federation is debatable. They are, nonetheless, enlightening. The attitude of Manley during his visit to New York in September 1958, as well as Adams in his visit to the city in October 1959 (as detailed in the introduction), displayed far more contempt for US-based supporters of federation than in previous years. It appears Manley and Adams felt these people now lacked a comprehensive understanding of the internal struggles within the Federation and, at times, resented their questioning of West Indian leaders about the problems of the new nation. Nevertheless, many of these supporters undoubtedly assumed they continued to hold a mandate to speak to and for the region, especially given their many years of service to the cause of West Indian nationhood and self-government. As the region became embroiled in debates over the structure of the Federation and struggles between the respective units, their activism and interest in the West Indies represented the continued support for West Indian nationhood from abroad. It also displayed the very West Indianness that seemed so elusive within the region itself.

The Demise of Federation

While the first two years of the West Indies Federation (1958–59) revealed the many obstacles the young nation faced to survive its infancy, the next two years (1960–61) demonstrated the ultimate failure to overcome them. Despite continued efforts to unite the region upon a shared West Indianness and to revive a spirit of compromise in these years, the contentious relationships among West Indian leaders, as well as general supporters and opponents of federation, persisted. Ultimately, the inability to solve the ongoing problems that beset the Federation in prior years—many of which centered on the unrelenting struggle between advocates of a strong federation and a loose one—set the Federation on a path to dissolution.

While the Federation faced many internal issues in these years, there were also external matters such as the ongoing struggle over control of the Chaguaramas area in northwestern Trinidad. US control of this land became a point of contention in 1957 when Trinidad was chosen as the location of the Federation's capital. Some West Indian leaders suggested Chaguaramas as the site for the new capital. Unfortunately, the area was home to one of the United States' most important military installations in the Caribbean. Driven by its Cold War security concerns, the US government sought to preserve its ninety-nine-year lease of the area (gained through the Bases-for-Destroyers Deal) and refused to release it to the Federation.

The ensuing struggle over Chaguaramas became an opportunity for the fledgling Federation to challenge the continued colonialism under which it existed. Eric Williams, who supported a Federation with more extensive powers over its own destiny, led the charge for the return of Chaguaramas in the late 1950s and early 1960s. Williams maintained the lease was null and void since it had been made between the United States and Great Britain. He believed the Federation should now have the final say in the matter. One of the most famous moments of Williams's campaign for the return of Chaguaramas took place on 22 April 1960, the date Williams and the PNM had previously suggested for the independence of the Federation. Following the "March in the Rain" by several thousand supporters in Port-of-Spain, Eric Williams gave a fiery anticolonial speech that condemned the "seven deadly sins" that plagued Trinidad and the wider Federation and demanded, among other things, an independent Federation.[37]

The Chaguaramas crisis produced mixed results. It certainly rallied anticolonial sentiment among some. However, others did not support Williams's position or consider the issue to be as significant, so it furthered tensions between some leaders within the Federation as well as political rivalries in Trinidad. The dispute over Chaguaramas also resulted in increased friction between the Federation, Great Britain, and the United States during these years.[38]

As Williams led the struggle for Chaguaramas in 1960, Manley contemplated the future of Jamaica in the Federation. Like Bustamante, Manley maintained Jamaica would not stay in the Federation without guarantees that its interests would be protected. The 1959 Intergovernmental Conference had given Manley a preliminary victory on the matter of federal representation based on population, but with the ministerial committees yet to report on the other matters, many issues remained unsettled. Moreover, the ongoing opposition of some West Indian leaders to Jamaican demands for a loose federation, and growing disillusionment with the Federation in Jamaica, even among some within the PNP, pushed Manley to begin exploring alternatives to the Federation.

In January 1960, Manley led a delegation to London to discuss Jamaica's place in the Federation with the secretary of state for the colonies and other colonial officials. The delegation expressed their concerns regarding possible revisions to the federal constitution, particularly the creation of a strong federal government. They sought clarification on whether a loosely structured federation with limited powers—as proposed by Jamaica's Ministry Paper no. 18—would meet the Crown's "requirements of effective sovereignty" and dominion status. The Colonial Office's list of general requirements for the Federation to become independent convinced Manley and the delegation that a strong federal government with extensive powers over the units, such as proposed by Williams, was not needed in order to achieve independence.[39]

Considering the ongoing debates within the Federation, the delegation also inquired about Jamaica's possible secession and the attainment of dominion status on their own. Colonial officials responded that should Jamaica secede from the Federation, it would be a "severe disappointment to all those who had hoped" the Federation would "take its proper place as both an independent nation and member of the Commonwealth"—but that Jamaica did possess, albeit marginally, the size, population, and resources to achieve independence on its own. Manley construed from this response, as well as subsequent "semi-official discussions," that should Jamaica choose to leave the Federation, the Crown would not force the island to stay or place any obstacles in its path to obtaining dominion status.[40]

Encouraged by what he believed to be the Colonial Office's affirmation of Jamaica's perspectives on the structure and powers of the Federation, as well as the possibility of Jamaica's own independence, Manley returned to the West Indies with renewed determination to press Jamaica's demands. Although he remained committed to negotiate with the other federal units, Manley warned that if a satisfactory agreement could not be reached, then Jamaica would leave the Federation and seek dominion status on its own. "We have given our unqualified pledge to make an honest and determined effort to reach agreement with the other units . . . and it is only if we fail in that effort that we will feel compelled and entitled to part company."[41] Predictably, the delegation's trip to London and the Colonial Office's responses to its inquiries annoyed many in the eastern Caribbean and exacerbated tensions between the Federation's members.

Several months later, the events of 31 May 1960 sowed additional seeds of discontent that would shape the future of Jamaica in the Federation and the very existence of the union. Encouraged by what some assumed to be confirmation from London that Jamaica could seek and achieve dominion status on its own, Bustamante and the JLP announced their formal opposition to the Federation. With one of the two major Jamaican political parties now officially against Federation, Manley, as premier of Jamaica, made the fateful decision just a few hours later that a referendum would be held to decide if Jamaica would remain in the Federation.[42]

For the next year and a half, the Jamaican referendum lingered over discussions of the Federation's future and possible constitutional revisions. As Colin Palmer notes, "With a referendum in Jamaica imminent, Williams, Manley, and Adams all realized that Jamaica and Trinidad had to resolve their differences if the federation were to survive."[43] In a series of meetings between Manley and Williams in 1960, including a secret meeting in Antigua in August, Williams and Manley worked to negotiate a middle ground between their disparate views on Federation. Manley maintained his support for a loose federation, but agreed that it would not be weaker than the current one. He also agreed to support Williams's position on restricted freedom of movement. At the same time, Williams showed a more appeasing position toward Jamaican demands for a weaker federal government now, which could grow in power over time, because he believed Jamaica's secession would destroy the Federation. Their actions temporarily improved their relationship, and reduced the distance between the Trinidadian and Jamaican positions on the Federation. However, their private discussions drew the ire of other Caribbean political leaders.[44]

Despite some revived desires and willingness to compromise, disputes over possible reforms to the Federation remained prominent, as shown during the October 1960 and May 1961 Intergovernmental Conferences. Since the actions of these meetings could have a direct effect on the outcome of the pending Jamaican referendum, some delegates approached them more willing to accede to many of Jamaica's demands. Both conferences, however, included significant disagreements between delegates, including Williams and Manley, over such issues as freedom of movement within the Federation, Jamaica's veto power, and federal taxation. By the end of the 1961 Intergovernmental Conference, Manley and the Jamaican delegation had secured majority support for almost all of their demands for a loose federation with limited powers over the member units.[45]

In May and June 1961, West Indian delegates met at Lancaster House in London for the West Indies Constitutional Conference to discuss with the Colonial Office the recent Intergovernmental Conference agreements and unresolved matters. Despite the continued differences of opinion between the delegates on many of the same issues (weak or strong-centered federation, freedom of movement, and veto power), the delegates ultimately agreed on a new constitution for the Federation, which was to be presented to the various legislatures of the West Indies for approval. They also secured an agreement from the Colonial Office that if the new constitution was ratified, the Federation would achieve its long-sought independence on 31 May 1962.[46]

Following these series of conferences, from which the Federation emerged with some renewed hope for its future, attention returned to the Jamaican referendum. Having initially announced it in May 1960, Manley intentionally delayed a formal vote until discussions of the federal constitution's revision concluded. With the Intergovernmental Conferences and West Indies Constitutional Conference meetings completed, Manley announced in August 1961 that the referendum vote would take place on 19 September.[47] The referendum asked whether Jamaica should remain in the Federation, but given the general population's limited familiarity with and understanding of the Federation, it essentially became a showdown between Jamaica's two major political parties, pitting Manley, the PNP, and Federation against Bustamante, the JLP, and secession. In the months leading to the formal vote, Manley was confident, though somewhat cautiously, that the Jamaican electorate would support remaining in the Federation. He and others, however, underestimated the extent of the opposition's campaign.

By the time the PNP began to rally support for Federation in the upcoming referendum, the anti-Federation movement had been in motion for some time. While the JLP led the call for Jamaica's withdrawal from the Federation, it was not alone. Additional support came from disillusioned supporters of the PNP such as W. A. Domingo and W. Adolphe Roberts, who continued to be among the leading critics of the Federation, and had even called for a referendum as early as 1959. Given the current possibility of secession, Roberts's 1955 declaration that "if Jamaica accepts a foolish [federal] structure, she will someday secede from Federation in disgust" appeared somewhat prophetic. Bustamante and the JLP also found support from smaller Jamaican political parties such as Millard Johnson's Peoples Political Party (PPP). Overall, the anti-federation campaign proved more extensive than its pro-federation counterpart. It also employed more direct campaign slogans that appealed to the rural masses in Jamaica, including claims that the Federation meant the domination of Jamaica by the small-islanders.[48]

Voter turnout for the referendum was dishearteningly low. Of the registered voters in Jamaica, only approximately 60 percent cast ballots. When the votes were tallied, 54 percent of the voters opposed remaining in the Federation and 46 percent were in favor. Manley's gamble on a referendum had backfired. Subsequent analysis of the results showed the JLP campaign had rallied significant support in the rural areas, while many in the urban areas did not vote at all. Given that 40 percent of Jamaica's voters did not even participate, John Mordecai remarked, "The federation was killed not by active hostility, but merely by indifference." While some opponents of the Federation celebrated its defeat as a victory for Jamaican nationalism over West Indian nationalism, as Trevor Munroe notes, the results "hardly suggested great enthusiasm for Jamaican nationhood" either.[49]

With Jamaica's secession pending, many wondered what would happen to the Federation. Following the Jamaican referendum, Eric Williams famously quipped that "one from ten leaves nought," which underlined his belief that the withdrawal of Jamaica from the Federation denoted the union's end. Despite Williams's initial observation, in the aftermath of the referendum there was some brief discussion of preserving the Federation between the remaining units that were concentrated in the eastern Caribbean. Given the long-held belief that this area, within the region, held the strongest support for a West Indian federation, it seemed a logical suggestion. Some colonial officials even hoped British Guiana might join a revised Federation, noting that the secession of Jamaica might alleviate some Indo-Caribbean apprehensions of being engulfed by the overwhelming Afro-Caribbean population of the other islands. Although all of the remaining Federation's members were also, with the exception of Trinidad, overwhelmingly black, their combined populations were smaller than Jamaica's. In the end, formal plans for a nine-member Federation led by Trinidad or the addition of British Guiana as the tenth member never materialized. By January 1962, Trinidad and Tobago also left the federation, believing that they too would be better off "going it alone." Subsequent discussions of a federation among the "Little Eight" of the eastern Caribbean failed as well.[50]

In an ironic twist, the date recently set for the independence of the West Indies Federation, 31 May 1962, became the date of its formal dissolution. The West India Dissolution Bill, introduced in the House of Lords on 1 March 1962, was passed by the House of Commons on 2 April 1962 and followed by the formal dissolution act.[51] In the aftermath of the Federation's collapse, both Jamaica and Trinidad gained their independence in August 1962. As for the remaining West Indian colonies, most would gain their independence gradually over the next twenty years. Out of one (attempted) nation would come many.

Reasons for and Reactions to the Dissolution of Federation

In the aftermath of the Federation, West Indian officials, activists, and others offered numerous reasons for its demise. The multiple articles, essays, memoirs, and formal studies of the subject that appeared soon after the collapse of the new nation cast blame on multiple culprits for the Federation's failure. As with the various problems encountered during its brief existence, the causes were both external and internal.

Many of the external explanations for the shortcomings of the Federation noted the flawed structure and implementation of the union. Although West Indian officials who negotiated the parameters of the federal system must undoubtedly shoulder some blame, the cumbersome and weak federation presented by British colonial officials during the formal planning conferences impeded the creation of the united West Indian nation many sought. As Amanda Sives notes, "The failure on behalf of all participants (British and West Indian) to create a strong institutional federal framework" was one of the key problems. R. L. Watts cites similar structural issues as the root of the Federation's downfall. "The scope of central authority was so restricted, its function so limited, and its budget so minute, that to most West Indians the federation appeared to involve additional expenditure to no effective purpose."[52]

Other problems emerged from the negotiations with the British in the 1950s. The Crown's failure to provide dominion status (independence), which most West Indian supporters of federation believed was key to the success of any regional association, proved particularly disconcerting and hampered the new nation from the start. To many, a federation without self-government represented the continuation of colonialism, rather than a decisive step forward. The prolonged negotiations between West Indian political leaders and British colonial officials were also problematic. The eleven-year delay between the 1947 CLC and Montego Bay Conferences, "the high point of West Indian nationalist feeling," and the actual launch of the Federation included four conferences, two standing committees, and six commissions. This resulted in diminished enthusiasm for the federal project and the erosion of regional West Indian nationalism.[53] As Hugh Springer remembered,

The West Indian political leaders, instead of being united in demanding independence from Britain, now found themselves engaged in long drawn out negotiations with one another about the terms of a federal constitution and the structure of political and economic institutions for the proposed federal system. Negotiations of this kind, which involve bargaining and the safeguarding of self-interests, are divisive rather than unifying, and by January 1958, when the federal constitution came into effect, the West Indian spirit was at a very low ebb.[54]

The fact that these official negotiations took place primarily in London after 1947 distanced the project of federation from the West Indian populations.[55] Finally, the different stages of political development among the federal units, including Jamaica and eventually Trinidad and Tobago with internal self-government while the rest of the West Indian colonies lacked it, further complicated the operations of the federal government and the relationships between unit members.[56] Some of these matters may appear trivial in light of the internal squabbling that undoubtedly occurred. But one cannot know how the unit members would have interacted with each other as equals within a self-governing federation.

Internal explanations for the failure of the Federation often focus on the inability of the participants to agree on key constitutional matters, particularly the assigned powers of the federal government and various financial issues. The decision to review these questions so soon after the initial launch of the Federation, rather than waiting five years as originally agreed, undoubtedly led to the confrontation the initial agreement sought to avoid. The subsequent turmoil became a "clash of nationalisms" in which the strong islandism of some West Indian politicians and federal units challenged, undermined, and impeded the spirit of regional West Indianness that supporters of the Federation believed necessary for success.

As previously discussed, support for federation and regional West Indian nationalism had long been considered stronger in the eastern Caribbean, whereas Jamaican nationalism had long existed as one of the most prominent islandisms in the region. Although many Jamaicans embraced regional nationalism and the purported benefits of federation, especially from the era of the Montego Bay Conference in the late 1940s, the vigorous reemergence of Jamaican nationalism in the late 1950s fueled many of the contentious attitudes toward the Federation. By the end of the union, the development of Trinidadian nationalism also thwarted the continuation of the Federation.[57]

Jamaica was hardly the only colony with islandist sentiments, but because its secession essentially terminated the Federation, it has received much of the blame within the region for the collapse. Whereas the insular concerns of British Honduras, British Guiana, the British Virgin Islands, and the Bahamas had kept those colonies from joining the Federation, Jamaica and its leaders (both Manley and Bustamante) had voluntarily led the colony into the Federation. To do so, only to take antagonistic stances on constitutional reforms, particularly the powers of the federal government, in order to protect local interests, certainly annoyed many. As famed calypsonian Mighty Sparrow argued in his calypso "Federation," if Jamaicans knew they did not want to unite with the other islands in the Federation, "why didn't they speak before? This is no time to say you eh federating no more. . . . Don't behave like a blasted traitor. How the devil you mean you ain't federating no more?" The Jamaican delegation's discussions with the Colonial Office on possible secession reinforced the image of Jamaica as a divisive force within the Federation, though some placed equal blame on the British for their affirmation of Manley's query. Still others were surprised and troubled by Manley's call for the referendum, particularly since he had dismissed the idea just seven months earlier as unnecessary and a betrayal of the responsibility given to political leaders by the people. Even if Manley felt a referendum on Jamaica's place in the Federation was necessary, some believed it needlessly placed the larger federation at risk for the sake of one unit's internal politics.[58]

While it is true that Jamaica chose to join the Federation and participated in the official negotiations in the late 1940s and 1950s, attitudes within Jamaica evolved during these years. During the actual existence of the Federation, there were increased doubts regarding the benefits for Jamaica. To some it represented a step backwards, since Jamaica had gained internal self-government in 1957, only to join a federation without it a year later. Moreover, given Jamaica's strengthening economy in this era, some saw a need to protect the colony's own economic interest.[59] These issues certainly shaped Manley's actions during discussions of federal reforms, but he was far from the only West Indian leader whose actions in the Federation were shaped by the concerns of his home colony.

Following the collapse of the Federation, W. Arthur Lewis, the principal and vice-chancellor of the University College of the West Indies during the

West Indies Federation, created a list of "strategic errors" often cited as the reason for its failure only four short years "after forty years of popular agitation and a dozen years of careful preparation." Lewis claimed that many West Indians assumed the Federation would have survived if:

(1) the Colonial Office had moved quicker in the planning and implementation of the Federation, rather than waiting until 1958 when some came to view it as an obstacle to self-government as opposed to the path to it;

(2) the federal capital had been placed in Jamaica, which would have strengthened support for the Federation within that colony;

(3) the original agreement to delay any review of the federal constitution had been adhered to, so as to give the new nation a chance to settle and strengthen;

(4) Manley had agreed to be prime minister of the Federation rather than forgoing federal office to focus on Jamaican politics in 1958;

(5) Manley and Williams had discussed their respective views on internal free trade instead of letting them become a divisive issue in the early years of the Federation;

(6) Prime Minister Grantley Adams had been a more tactful politician in his dealings with fellow West Indian leaders and others;

(7) Manley had not pursued a weaker federation in 1959 and instead given its current structure a chance to win over critics, especially in Jamaica;

(8) Williams had not published *The Economics of Nationhood* in 1959, which exacerbated tensions with Jamaica to the benefit of Bustamante and the anti-federation movement;

(9) Secretary of State for the Colonies Iain Macleod had told Manley that Jamaican secession was impossible;

(10) Manley had not proposed a referendum—or, once he called the referendum, had made a more immediate appeal in favor of the Federation rather than holding the vote more than a year later;

(11) Adams had recognized, as Williams did, that Manley could lose the referendum, and accordingly worked to help him instead of making his situation more difficult.[60]

Lewis argued this was a list of avoidable errors, and he offered additional reasons. Despite the commitment to federation by Adams, Manley, and Williams, who Lewis noted were all outstanding and Oxford-educated men, these leaders did not understand the nature of a federation, lacked willingness to compromise, and failed to communicate with each other in an appropriate manner. In fact, economic obstacles and tensions that appeared in the Federation were exacerbated by poor relations between West Indian leaders. Lewis also wondered if including Jamaica in the Federation was a mistake, though he recognized the reasons the Colonial Office included the island and how opposition to the Federation in Jamaica came later. Overall, Lewis argued, "The Federation was destroyed by poor leadership rather than by the intractability of its own internal problems."[61]

The failure of the Federation pained many. Despite their unceasing differences of opinion and strained relations, Adams, Manley, and Williams were dismayed at the Federation's collapse. Throughout the final Intergovernmental Conferences in 1960–61, Grantley Adams expressed his disappointment at the weakened Federation being created by concessions to Manley and the Jamaican demands for a loose structure. Following the Jamaican referendum, Adams quickly moved to champion the continuation of the Federation among the remaining members and eventually the Little Eight without Trinidad. In the final days of the West Indies Federation, Adams referred to its dissolution as a "shattering blow . . . to the idea of West Indian Unity."[62] In later years Adams wrote, "I have often wondered how the course of West Indian history might have been changed if the Federation could have been launched at such a time when the feeling of West Indian national consciousness was riding the crest of West Indian mass approval."[63] Nevertheless, many contend his ineffectual leadership of the Federation was one of the many reasons for its downfall.

Norman Manley also expressed his disappointment at the loss of the referendum and the collapse of the Federation. On the night of the referendum, when his granddaughter asked if they won, Manley replied, "We didn't win, everybody lost."[64] While this remark exhibits Manley's longstanding support for a Caribbean federation, many of his actions during the Federation call into question his commitment to regional unification—at least compared to his commitment to Jamaica. Even if his uncompromising stance on many issues during the Federation reflects the contentious politics in Jamaica during these years, which few other West Indian leaders faced, his attitude and actions during the formal West Indies Federation undoubtedly shocked many and call some aspects of his legacy into question. As F.S.J. Ledgister notes in his study of creole nationalism in the British Caribbean, "In spite of his strong public commitment to the federation . . . the outcome though not desirable cannot have been altogether unwelcome to him."[65]

Unlike Adams and Manley, who were in the twilight of their political careers by the time of the Federation, Eric Williams was still in the early years of his. Although a relative newcomer to public office, Williams had long supported the idea of a Caribbean federation. Despite his post-referendum remark that "one from ten leaves nought" and his ultimate decision that Trinidad should join Jamaica in seeking independence in 1962, Williams remained supportive of the idea of regional association in one form or another. In fact, upon announcing Trinidad's exit from the Federation, Williams invited other eastern Caribbean islands to join Trinidad in a unitary state.[66]

Expatriate West Indians and black diaspora activists outside the Caribbean had also been watching the ongoing struggles and debates over the future of the West Indies Federation. In the aftermath of the Jamaican referendum and the Federation's demise, both supporters and critics offered their own reasons for and reactions to the dissolution of the West Indian nation.

W. A. Domingo played an active if not prominent role in the campaign against the West Indies Federation. In addition to his anti-federation publications of the late 1950s, Domingo also participated in the referendum campaign in Jamaica from New York, particularly via letters to the *Daily Gleaner*. While his colleague W. A. Roberts undertook a six-part radio broadcast in Jamaica to rally opposition to the Federation, Domingo participated in his own radio broadcast from New York. When the results of the referendum were announced, Domingo proudly noted to Roberts, "Jamaica can now march forward to achieve the independence that you, O'Meally, and myself dreamt of and worked for."[67]

C.L.R. James remained in the Caribbean following the collapse of the Federation, but his views were still largely those of an expatriate West Indian. Writing to a colleague in October 1961 following the Jamaican referendum, James called the current situation in the West Indies "the most desperate" era the West Indies "have faced since the emancipation from slavery." While he argued that "the idea of a West Indian nation cannot dissolve," he admitted that "it is now infinitely harder to establish than ever before." James feared the very idea of a West Indian nation had been "destroyed or corrupted" by the recent failure of the Federation. "Jamaica is not only out, but the whole political atmosphere" in the West Indies "has been poisoned, thus preparing the way for further organizational and political demoralisation, confusion and disorder." He continued, "What we need is a political programme that is based upon the idea of a genuine

Federation. We have not got it. . . . there is no profound and comprehensive Federal programme before the public now. We shall have to find one or perish."[68] Like many others, James believed that the flawed structure of this particular federation, as well as a lack of leadership from the West Indian politicians, doomed the project and possibly even future discussions of a regional union, which he maintained was necessary for the successful development and progress of the region.

Others were equally distressed. Kwame Nkrumah, prominent Pan-Africanist and the first prime minister and first president of Ghana, who had expressed his support for the newborn West Indies Federation as the creation of "a strong and powerful nation of peoples of African descent in the West Indies" that could aid efforts to build a united Africa on that continent, sent letters to the various government leaders of the West Indies in June 1962, shortly before Jamaica and Trinidad were to become independent, in hopes of convincing them it was "not too late to save the islands from disintegration in the separate and competitive existence which will result from their failure to federate now." He warned that disunity would make them "easy prey to far greater dangers than the evils which they suffered under imperialism and colonialism." While he sympathized with the difficulties of bringing together the various islands into one nation, Nkrumah said this was "the price the present generation of West Indians must pay for building a nation conceived in harmony and deserving the pride and admiration of all." He noted the success of Indonesia, with its hundreds of islands joined in one nation, as an example that this could be accomplished. "Federation is the surest means of establishing security in the West Indies against the dangers of colonialism and imperialism, and for ensuring that a new basis for creating a strong nation can be found." Independence, Nkrumah argued, will create "new vistas of development and new horizons . . . for our people." He closed, "I hope that you will agree that the time has come for all Africans and peoples of African descent to work together as a team, not only for the total liquidation of colonialism but also for creating a strong identity of interests so that the voice of Africa, the true voice of Africa, can make its just impact upon the counsels of the world." While some supporters of the Federation had ignored or downplayed the racial dimensions of the West Indian nation in recent years, for Nkrumah and others, Caribbean nation-building remained part of the ongoing black freedom struggles in Africa and the diaspora.[69]

Some of the most reflective assessments on the failure of the West Indies Federation came from Richard B. Moore, who by the 1960s had supported a Caribbean federation for approximately forty years.[70] Following the dissolution of the Federation, Moore penned multiple articles that highlighted his disappointment with West Indian leadership and the recent federal experiment. In 1962 his "Independent Caribbean Nationhood—Has It Been Achieved or Set Back?" began by noting that he and some of his colleagues (presumably fellow "Awaymen" in the United States) could not rejoice at the recent independence celebrations of Jamaica and Trinidad in August 1962, given that just as many West Indians remained under colonialism without self-determination and self-government. He recalled the celebrations for the Federation just four years before, which deceived many by creating not a true federation but only the "farce of a flag without sovereignty." Moore also pondered the fate of the small-islanders in the remaining West Indian colonies. Would there be independence, unity, or fragmentation?

Following an overview of the Caribbean liberation movements led from the region and the broader black diaspora in previous decades, Moore condemned the flawed planning and negotiations of the West Indies Federation in the 1950s by British and West Indian officials. He was especially critical of the weak federal constitution, which from the outset of the Federation failed to provide all of the requirements for true nationhood, including independence, a customs union, and free movement of people between the islands. Moore also criticized the lack of any effort to educate the masses of the West Indies on the vital issues of federation, or to create an economic development plan for the region.

All of these issues resulted in the creation of a flawed federation, which was only exacerbated by the weak leadership of West Indians in the Federation. Setting aside the matter of Indo-Caribbean opposition to the Federation in British Guiana, Moore claimed that criticism by Adams, Manley, and Bustamante of Cheddi Jagan's democratically elected government earlier in the 1950s had also robbed the Federation of that colony's crucial inclusion. Reflecting upon the visits to New York by Manley in 1958 and Adams in 1959, Moore decried the "discouraging expressions" of the two leaders in these meetings, which blamed the people of the West Indies for the failure of the Federation to achieve independence, or at least make greater strides toward it, rather than accepting their own failures as leaders of West Indian peoples.

Moore also condemned the Jamaican referendum, which paved the way for the secession of Jamaica and the collapse of the Federation. He argued that Manley "retreated from every principle of federation" until there was little difference between him and Bustamante. Like others, Moore questioned the logic of Manley in calling for a referendum, given the previous support for the Federation by the PNP, JLP, and Jamaican legislature. As for the anti-federation campaign that came to flourish in Jamaica, he criticized his onetime colleague Domingo—who he maintained had formerly been a progressive advocate for federation—for his anti-federation activism in recent years. Moore concluded that the national liberation movement of the Caribbean people was incomplete, since not all West Indians were free, independent, or united, and that the withdrawal of Jamaica from the Federation was a serious setback to those aspirations.

In 1964 Moore published another article on the topic, "Caribbean Unity and Freedom." Following a broad overview of the wider Caribbean's history, Moore addressed the "movement toward unity" between British West Indian colonies in the twentieth century. He recalled the efforts of activists and organizations within the region, such as Cipriani, Marryshow, and the CLC, and of those based in Harlem, including himself, Pierrepointe, the WIDC, and the WINC.[71]

As for the Federation, Moore argued, "Despite all counsel, warnings, and entreaties, the chief political Caribbean leaders, together with their imperial tutors . . . launched the ill-planned and ill-fated West Indies Federation." Reflecting on the secession of Jamaica and Trinidad, and the ultimate collapse of the Federation, Moore once again blamed not only the flawed planning and structures of the union but poor West Indian leadership. He also pointed to the role of insularity in the disputes within the Federation, noting the failure of those West Indian leaders to embrace the West Indianness that he and other expatriates upheld and embodied outside the West Indies.

> Those of us who by enforced economic exile, or through some enlightening experience, have managed to overcome narrow insularity, petty provincialism, purblind prejudice, and smug satisfaction, ought to exercise care lest we stir the smoldering embers of disastrous discord. This, then, is hardly the time to identify personalities responsible for the miserable petty demagogy, strange intellectual weakness, cupidity, insularity, and titled ineptitude, unexplained insistence upon unitary association as yet unrealized, self-centered leadership and opportunist opposition . . . Let us then simply say now that all the chief Caribbean political leaders of that period together bear responsibility, in varying degrees, for the miserable debacle and the distressing setback of the Caribbean liberation movement.[72]

While many long-standing activists offered extensive reflections on the collapse of the West Indies Federation, there was significantly less coverage and discussion than in previous decades among the multinational black communities of the United States. Many in Black America, including black newspapers, were now focused on the ongoing civil rights movement of the early 1960s, although the failure of the Federation did receive some minimal attention. In the days following the referendum vote in Jamaica, a *New York Amsterdam News* article reported on Jamaicans' rejection of the Federation, while a similar article appeared in the *Chicago Defender*.[73] Unlike many of the more passionate reflections noted above, or even the numerous editorials and articles that would have likely appeared in previous years, these articles neither made mention of the Federation's place within ongoing black diaspora struggles (including connections to Black America) nor considered the fallout from Federation's failure. Instead they gave little more than a brief summary of the referendum's outcome.

There are numerous possible reasons for this decline in coverage and interest in the West Indies Federation. Just four years earlier, several West Indians and African Americans in the United States celebrated the birth of the Federation as not only a regional nation-building project but also one with diasporic importance for black peoples across the globe. Such conceptualizations of the West Indian nation were undoubtedly maintained during the actual Federation by many, particularly among longtime expatriate West Indian and black diaspora activists. For other US-based West Indians and African Americans who were less familiar with diasporic visions of a West Indian nation—including a younger generation who came of age as expatriate West Indian and black diaspora activism took on more auxiliary roles in the 1950s and as the Federation was increasingly promoted within the West Indies as primarily a regional endeavor with little overt connection to black diaspora politics, even by visiting West Indian leaders who just a few years earlier had promoted the racial dimensions of such an endeavor—Federation's importance beyond the Caribbean certainly appears to have declined.

Given the successful use of race in previous years to rally support for a Caribbean federation, it would be unwise to underestimate the extent to which the "de-racialization" of federation by some proponents undermined the basis of interest and support. And, again, many West Indians and their descendants in the United States may have found the ongoing civil rights movement, which expanded significantly in the era of the Federation, more pressing for their everyday lives as black people in America.

Even among those who viewed the West Indies Federation as the creation of a black nation that could wield international influence for black struggles in Africa and the diaspora, the replacement of one West Indian nation by two independent West Indian nations (Jamaica and Trinidad) was not necessarily a loss. As Domingo argued in his *Jamaica's Folly* in 1958, the creation of multiple West Indian nations in place of the Federation could result in greater representation for black peoples within international bodies such as the United Nations. From this perspective, the failure of the Federation may have been less distressing. Moreover, one could argue that by 1962 the emphasis on large or supra-nations had passed. The numerous nations of Africa and Asia that gained their independence shortly before and during the West Indies Federation's brief existence (including "small nations") demonstrated a shift in, or at the very least less commitment to, the Colonial Office's previous perspectives regarding the size of colonies and their ability to achieve independence. In turn, these events altered the perspectives of some activists.

Some certainly continued to assume larger nations were more prepared for and able to sustain their independence. For many black activists long active in African, Caribbean, and other black liberation movements, the creation of larger nations, such as the Federation was supposed to be, had also exemplified ideas of racial unity. Nevertheless, by the early 1960s, the prospect of independence for small nations appeared less problematic for many than in previous years.

While an examination of the reasons for the failure of the West Indies Federation is not of primary concern in this study, the preceding chapters do provide some insight. Many of the explanations offered from within and beyond the West Indies undoubtedly played a role. The flawed structure of the Federation with members at different stages of political advancement inherently undermined the view of the Federation as a nation of equals and increased tensions between the different federal units. It also allowed competing islandisms in more "advanced" colonies to view their own advancement as being impeded by the other colonies, if not by the Federation itself. The lack of dominion status for the new nation certainly tempered the enthusiasm for the Federation, particularly since the most prominent proponents of a united West Indian nation had long maintained this as one of the most crucial aspects of any such nation. Criticism of the West Indies Federation as a "glorified crown colony" was justified in many ways. Given these factors, one could make an argument that a true federation in the West Indies was never even undertaken.

Insular islandisms certainly wreaked havoc within the young Federation, as they undermined the showcasing—or forging—of a regional West Indianness. Although some have argued that the lack of a "powerful spirit of West Indianism" was irrelevant to the failure of the Federation, it could have fostered a greater willingness to compromise for the good of the region during the contentious debates of the brief federal years.[74] Thus the failure to develop or prioritize such identification among both West Indian leaders and the masses undoubtedly played some role as the West Indian nation tried to work through its tumultuous beginning. At the same time, while it is possible that an overriding West Indianness among all the federal units could have saved the Federation, or that a federation among only the eastern Caribbean colonies with longer and stronger ties to the idea might have proved more workable, it is precarious to assume that problems of insularity would have been overcome merely with the exclusion of Jamaica from the West Indies Federation. Insularity was not confined to Jamaica, even if islandism proved most prominent there during the years of the Federation.

As for assertions that the Federation undertook contentious debates over the scope and scale of the federal government's power without allowing proper time for the young nation to develop, even if these matters had been deferred for the first five years of the Federation, as originally agreed, there is no guarantee this would have secured the ascendency of a powerful regionalism within and between the different units. Those who noted other successful federations as evidence that internal divisions could be overcome often overlooked or underestimated the time it took to achieve such allegiances and the uncertain nature of them even after decades, and in the case of the United States almost a century, of existence.[75] While a delay in these discussions might have proved useful, there was no guarantee insularity would have disappeared during or after these first few years. Moreover, as Kwame Nkrumah noted, the success of the Federation was a task *this* generation of West Indians had to be willing to undertake for the good of future generations, and that was not to be the case. Of course, efforts to attain a greater and enduring commitment to the Federation might have been bolstered if the West Indian masses had been more involved, but there remain many questions about the extent of the efforts to educate and sell the masses on the benefits of federation—particularly the attempt launched in 1958.

The failure of creole multiracial nationalism, upon which many West Indian leaders came to base their appeals for regional unity, to rally the region in support of the Federation may have also been one of the most significant flaws. As discussed earlier, this form of nationalism had long existed alongside racialized, black nationalist and black internationalist visions of the region and associated nation-building endeavors. Beyond the region, where West Indianness was far more identifiable, racial appeals were a proven means to rally support for a Caribbean federation, as they did at times within the region itself. However, as the idea of federation moved from a dream to pending reality, creole multiracial nationalism became increasingly promoted at the expense of more overt racial appeals.

Although seemingly displeasing and disconcerting to some West Indian leaders by the 1950s, and certainly to the British officials overseeing negotiations of the Federation, the continuation of such racialized appeals in a region overwhelmingly composed of peoples of African descent might have rallied many within the West Indian masses, which most observers agreed had little understanding of or attachment to the Federation. Race, which had often been used at home and abroad to damn Afro-Caribbean populations, like other populations of African descent, was embraced by many as the basis for their respective liberation and empowerment. While West Indians had often come to adopt insular identifications in recent years, this did not eradicate their racial consciousness or its place within these island identifications. Therefore, racial appeals to Afro-Caribbean populations, particularly the black working masses of many West Indian colonies, could have been extended to regional identifications, as many West Indian migrants and immigrants had done for decades prior to the Federation. As Lara Putnam argues, "Not only did race-based nationalism echo the nativist populism that across the hemisphere had proved the most reliable route for working classes to claim social citizenship; but Caribbeans facing a political system in flux might well believe it was all they had."[76]

What if Norman Manley had appealed to Jamaicans during the Federation, especially in the referendum campaigns, in the same manner as he did to expatriate West Indians and African Americans in the United States in previous decades? Would descriptions of a Caribbean federation based upon appeals to and emphasis on racial unity and empowerment within the region and for the good of other black peoples in Africa and other parts of the diaspora have changed perceptions of the Federation? Could this approach have rallied some support for the Federation among the Jamaican masses, especially in rural areas, where "Africanisms" (creole cultural practices derived from African traditions) and racial identification remained prominent, and where movements such as Rastafarianism had begun to take root despite official government opposition? Would Millard Johnson's race-conscious Peoples Political Party (PPP) have been swayed from support of the anti-federation campaign? It is quite possible that such activities could have rallied support for the Federation, or at least provided a better understanding of its purpose and, from that, potential support soon after, although it would certainly have exacerbated racial tensions in some colonies.

Whether or not racial appeals would have rallied West Indians, the middle classes or the masses, to the cause of Federation given its aforementioned structural and financial flaws, there were clearly inherent shortcomings of creole multiracial nationalism within the Federation. For West Indian leaders who maintained that racial appeals could lead to discord, there is little indication that the lack of them produced racial harmony and unity in the region. Eric Williams, for example, repeatedly appealed to creole multiracial nationalism in Trinidad in the early years of the PNM, and yet these efforts proved largely fruitless in overcoming Indian and white opposition, or black and Indian divisions during the Federation and in subsequent years.

The possible misstep of West Indian leaders in dismissing the persuasive power of race in calls for regional unity must at least be considered among the reasons proposed for the ultimate failure of the West Indies Federation. It is certainly true that race had (and has) limitations as a nation-building tool. However, the same could be said of imperial or state power, or appeals to multiracialism, a common colonial heritage, language, or geographical location. While racialized appeals might have undermined views of the Federation as the symbol of multiracial cooperation that some desired, it could have created a Federation that symbolized the racial unity and empowerment that many others had long envisioned as a central component of a West Indian nation.

Legacy and Lessons of the Federation

The reasons for the collapse of the West Indies Federation remain debated today. On some level, C.L.R. James, Richard B. Moore, and others were correct in saying that the failure of that particular federation diminished the interest in and possibility of future attempts to forge a united West Indies nation. Nevertheless, as had been the case for decades, visions of British Caribbean unity took many forms, and despite the dismal legacy of the

West Indies Federation, new visions and projects for regional unity (or at least regional association) emerged in the aftermath of the failed federation.

In his 1966 study of nationalisms in the West Indies Federation, Samuel J. Hurwitz noted:

> The concept of a West Indian federation has been killed, but it refuses to be buried and may, phoenix-like, rise out of the ashes at some future date. Perhaps this is the case because it is so much more difficult to bury ideals than it is to kill off their immediate results. As a factual reality, the Federation of the West Indies expired almost at the very moment of its birth. The funeral rites were without ceremony. Friends of the deceased grieved, while others grinned, and all shared in the paltry inheritance. Yet, as an ideal, it is enshrined in the hearts of many West Indians who continue to look beyond their very narrow geographical limits for a bond that will unite them with others for the greater glory of the entire West Indian community.[77]

Hurwitz's reflection on Caribbean federation captures the legacy of this undying idea in the region. The West Indies Federation failed, but the idea of regional unity lived on in the Caribbean in the years to follow.

The continuation of a political union between the remaining federation members that was contemplated shortly after the Jamaican referendum sealed the secession of that colony in 1961 included, as previously noted, ideas of a Trinidad-led nine-member federation, the possible inclusion of British Guiana to replace Jamaica as the tenth member, an offer from Trinidad to merge with eastern Caribbean colonies in a unitary state, and a scaled-down federation between the Little Eight of the eastern Caribbean.[78] While nothing came of these proposals, they spoke to the initial refusal of some in the Caribbean to abandon the idea of a federation. W. Arthur Lewis argued in the mid-1960s that there remained several reasons for a federation: (1) an emotional tie between people with a common heritage; (2) the need for cooperation in various areas such as education, shipping, and currency; (3) the need for competent administration; and (4) the need to preserve political freedom. In his estimation, at that time, "The case for a West Indian federation [was] as strong as ever."[79]

Although there may have been some interest in the continuation of political federation in the immediate aftermath of the collapse, the idea became largely taboo among West Indian leaders in the ensuing years. In its place, various other attempts at "regional integration" between newly independent West Indian nations took shape in the 1960s, 1970s, 1980s, and beyond. These projects were not the "political federations" that many West Indians pursued in previous decades. Instead, they focused largely on economic cooperation between the various West Indian nations similar to some of the earliest ideas of regional cooperation among the colonial power brokers of the late nineteenth and early twentieth century. Prominent examples of such projects include the Caribbean Free Trade Association (CARIFTA, 1965–72) and the successive Caribbean Community (CARICOM, 1973–present).[80] Still, even these endeavors faced the specter of the failed West Indies Federation as members carefully considered the motivations and benefits of these collaborations. As Cheddi Jagan noted during the years of CARIFTA, "Caribbean Unity is once again in focus. The question which now must be posed is what kind of unity? Here we come immediately to a clash of interests—what the people want, what the governments want, what the Chamber of commerce want and what the imperialists want.[81]

Despite the failure to revive a political federation, ideas for political unions of various West Indian nations were periodically discussed, some more formally than others, in the 1970s, 1980s, and 1990s. Thus the dream did not disappear, especially among those who saw both the need and the potential for regional unification beyond just economic cooperation. These sentiments have continued into the twenty-first century. In 2006 historian Colin Palmer called for the region to revisit the idea of a federation, beyond CARICOM. Palmer argued, as Eric Williams did as early as the 1940s, "some form of a federation is demanded at least by common sense."[82] As recently as 2012, Rachel Manley, granddaughter of Norman Manley and daughter of Michael Manley, called for the British Caribbean to reexamine the possibilities of a federation, which she claimed was "compelling [for more] than economics or trade, foreign policy and regional defense, the centralizing and economizing of government. That subterranean urge that invisibly links the archipelago behind [sic] the years and beneath the seas— it is simply that instinct of family. History made siblings of us. Why would we resist a union so compelling?"[83]

Rachel Manley's allusion to the proverbial "West Indian family" embracing the various nations of the region invariably returns to lingering questions of who and what is West Indian, and what are the bonds that bind them together. This has long been a matter of debate. There is no single correct answer. Nevertheless, the long history of Caribbean federation and its legacies does provide some insight on this issue, particularly within the more immediate postcolonial years of the 1960s and 1970s.

As the preceding chapters have shown, the history of Caribbean federation consists of far more than an account of the official West Indies Federation's creation, troubles, and ultimate failure in the late 1950s and early 1960s. Among other things, it also provides a lens through which to examine the place of race within West Indian identifications and struggles, and their connections to the broader black diaspora politics of the twentieth century. In this regard, the legacy of Caribbean federation encompasses not only the various attempts at regional integration following the Federation but also the continuing debates over issues of "race and nation" (and "race and region" in this case) and the connections between the British Caribbean, Africa, Black America, and the broader black diaspora in the postcolonial Caribbean of the 1960s, 1970s, and beyond.

Given the failure of West Indian leaders within the Federation to consider the shortcomings of their nationalist appeals within that ill-fated endeavor, many who came to lead the independent West Indian nations that emerged from the ashes of the Federation in the 1960s and 1970s continued to promote the creole multiracial nationalism of previous decades. The national mottos of some of the earliest independent West Indian nations that appeared in the 1960s reflected this ideology: Jamaica's "Out of Many, One People," Trinidad's "Together We Aspire, Together We Achieve," and Guyana's "One People, One Nation, One Destiny." These mottos spoke far more to aspirations of, rather than the reality of, multiracial unity. Still, the leaders who promoted such aphorisms hoped they would appeal to the various populations of their respective nations and showcase them as symbols of racial harmony. Creole multiracial nationalism, however, would be confronted by familiar, alternative nationalisms and visions of the West Indian future in the postcolonial era.

These aspirations met resistance in many colonies, among them Jamaica, Trinidad, and Guyana. Many Indo-Caribbeans, especially in Guyana and Trinidad, continued to view ideas of creole multiracialism as largely insincere and a continuation of the previous social order in which they felt marginalized or excluded. Afro-Caribbeans who embraced black nationalism and internationalism also criticized these appeals as the promotion of a multiracial myth at the expense of more concrete and prominent acceptance of the African heritage of most West Indians.[84] This was especially the case in Jamaica, where the national motto has been described as "an

aspirational slogan that nevertheless reproduce[d] colonial social hierarchies ... pushing out the possibility of a hegemonic blackness within the
public sphere."[85]

Issues of "race and nation" in the West Indies during the 1960s and 1970s
would not be confined to intellectual critiques of national mottos. Racial
conflict was rare, but it did occur occasionally, as in the anti-Chinese riots
of Kingston, Jamaica, in August–September 1965. Tensions between Afro-
and Indo-Caribbean communities also remained, especially in Trinidad
and Guyana, throughout the postcolonial era. Discord also arose between
proponents of creole multiracial nationalism and advocates of black nationalism and black internationalism, exemplified in the rise of race- and
class-conscious Black Power movements within the Caribbean in the 1960s
and 1970s and their ideological struggles with the ruling West Indian political parties. While most West Indian governments were led primarily
by Afro-Caribbeans in these years, Black Power adherents mockingly referred to such leaders as "Afro-Saxons" and charged that they represented
the continuation of "white capitalist imperialist society" in the postcolonial
Caribbean. The Rodney Riots in Jamaica in 1968 and the Black Power Revolution (or February Revolution) in Trinidad in 1970 are two of the most
prominent examples of such confrontations.[86]

In the 1970s and beyond, the creole multiracial nationalism of West Indian governments continued to confront the black consciousness of many
of their citizens. In conjunction with the growing popularity of reggae and
Rastafarianism in Jamaica, Michael Manley did what his father had not and
appealed directly to the black masses of Jamaica for support in the early-
1970s national elections. This included the presentation of Manley as the
biblical figure of Joshua wielding the "rod of correction" given to him by
Haile Selassie.[87]

The provocative 1979 calypso "Caribbean Unity" by Black Stalin also
challenged perspectives of an inclusive, multiracial West Indianness. Its
chorus, which referenced "one race" from the "same place" who made the
"same trip" on the "same ship," presented a shared history among Caribbean (West Indian) people—at least some of them—as the basis of regional
unity.

Reactions to the calypso varied. Some charged that the song was racist
and offensive to "other races" in the region who had arrived on "different
ships and from different places." Others contended that his description of
the Caribbean man had not explicitly excluded those groups. Still others
defended the calypsonian's apparent focus on the Afro-Caribbean majori-

ties of the region, given that they were "more integrally Caribbean than any other group." Any ambiguity was dismissed when Black Stalin answered directly that the song was only about Afro-Caribbeans—"Africans were the ones who developed the Caribbean. . . . they were the only ones concerned with Caribbean unity." His response characterized the long-standing assumption among many in the region who continued to view Afro-Caribbeans as the "real" West Indians.[88]

Black Stalin's calypso also criticized previous and contemporary failures of well-educated West Indian politicians to unite the region, and suggested the basis of regional unity was quite apparent—a shared racial heritage. He included explicit references to the failure of the West Indies Federation and the struggles of subsequent attempts at regional integration such as CARIFTA and CARICOM, and implied that official attempts to forge regional unity were misguided and overlooked popular expressions of a regional West Indianness. In the closing verses of the calypso, Black Stalin noted the spread of Rastafarianism throughout the Caribbean while formal regional associations like CARIFTA struggled. He claimed this showed there was something the Rastas understood about the bonds between the region's populations that politicians did not. By evoking the success and growth of the race-conscious Rastafarian movement, Black Stalin once again drew attention to the persuasive power and place of race in identifying a basis for Caribbean unity that politicians either failed to recognize or ignored.

These are but a few examples of the continuing struggles to define the relationship between race and region in the West Indies, as well as the connections between the Caribbean, Africa, and other parts of the black diaspora in the postcolonial era. In subsequent years, through the close of the twentieth century and into the twenty-first, racial politics and divisions did not cease. While not dismissing the reality of amicable and cooperative relationships in many cases, tensions between Indo- and Afro-Caribbean populations in Trinidad and Guyana persisted. Likewise, debates concerning the place of race, particularly blackness, within Jamaica and many other West Indian nations also remained commonplace beneath the veneer of multiracialism that continued (and continues) to be promoted by many. Although these debates existed before and outside of the lengthy push for a united West Indian nation via federation in the early-mid twentieth century, continued discussions of these matters in the postcolonial era were in many ways also a part of the legacy of the numerous movements for and conceptualizations of federation.

The long history of support for and visions of a Caribbean federation—

beyond the limited scope of the official West Indies Federation and imperial and regional histories of these events, which are only part of a broader history rather than *the* history of the subject—offers significant insight into many questions related to West Indian nation building and its importance beyond the British Caribbean. The incorporation of the diasporic and transnational history of Caribbean federation, inclusive of black diaspora perspectives, provides numerous examples of West Indian involvement in and engagement with black diaspora politics (including the freedom struggles within the region itself), and the political dimensions of the diasporization of black populations and their respective struggles. Within *this* context, Caribbean federation came to embody a black nation-building project outside Africa and a focus and source of black diaspora activism connected to the struggles of Africa and Black America in the twentieth century.

Such visions of federation and the explicit connections to other black freedom struggles undoubtedly shaped and influenced more than discussions of nation building within the region. It also helped forge and further deliberations over "race and nation" (and "race and region") for many years leading to the Federation, as well as in its aftermath within the various independent West Indian nations that would emerge from its ashes. An understanding of the concurrent racial and multiracial appeals for a Caribbean federation in the early-mid twentieth century also demonstrates how the Anglophone Caribbean has long coexisted as both a transracial and racial region—a key site and symbol of multiracial cooperation, alongside an equally important site and symbol of black diaspora activism—a characteristic that continues in many ways to this day.

Race as a nation-building tool—be it black nationalism, black internationalism, multiracialism, or transracialism—ultimately failed to provide a strong enough base upon which to build and sustain a Caribbean federation. However, that should not diminish its importance. Before dismissing its relevance and the significant role it played in rallying and shaping support for a federation, we must also remember that a common geographical area and language, the shared experience of British colonialism, and even political support by the British and US governments also failed to establish the basis for a thriving united West Indian nation. Thus while the West Indies Federation may have failed, the long history of federation remains important to our understanding not only of the Anglophone Caribbean's past and present but also of the broader black diaspora.

Notes

Abbreviations

CLC-RHC	Caribbean Labour Congress—Richard Hart Collection
CO	Colonial Office Records
CPGB	Archive of the Communist Party of Great Britain
Demas Papers	William Demas Papers
DuBois Papers	W.E.B. DuBois Papers
EWMC	Eric Williams Memorial Collection
FCBR	Fabian Colonial Bureau Papers
FO	Foreign Office Records
James Collection	C.L.R. James Collection
James Papers	C.L.R. James Papers
JPL Collection	Jamaica Progressive League Collection
Logan Papers	Rayford Logan Papers
Manley Papers	Norman Manley Papers
MEPO	Metropolitan Police Records
Moore Papers	Richard B. Moore Papers
Moyne Papers	West India Royal Commission, Moyne Papers
NAACP Papers	National Association for the Advancement of Colored People Papers
PMOGA	Prime Minister's Office: General Administration
PMOIS	Prime Minister's Office: Information Service
RG 84	Record Group 84: Foreign Service Posts of the Department of State
RG 126	Record Group 126: Records of the Office of Territories
Roberts Papers	W. Adolphe Roberts Papers
Staupers Collection	Mabel Staupers Collection
WIC Records	Records of the West India Committee
WINC Collection	West Indies National Council Collection

NEWSPAPERS AND PERIODICALS

AA	*Afro-American* (Baltimore)
CD	*Chicago Defender*
DG	*Daily Gleaner*
IAO	*International African Opinion*
LCPN	*League of Coloured Peoples News Letter*
NYAN	*New York Amsterdam News*
NYASN	*New York Amsterdam Star News*
PC	*Pittsburgh Courier*
POSG	*Port-of-Spain Gazette*
TG	*Trinidad Guardian*
WI	*West Indian* (Grenada)
WIA	*West Indian-American*

Note on Terminology

1. My use of "islandism" here is drawn from Earl Gooding's *West Indies at the Cross-roads*. Although British Guiana and British Honduras were not islands, this term applies to local nationalisms in those colonies as well.

2. Putnam, *Radical Moves*, 6.

Introduction

1. "Sir Grantley in NYC For 5-Day Visit," *NYAN*, 17 October 1959, 2; "Adams: No Danger of Federation Breaking Up," *DG*, 20 October 1959, 1; "Adams and Federation," *DG*, 26 October 1959, 10; "Prime Minister Adams' Address in New York," West Indies News Service, 26 October 1959, box 10, folder 2, Moore Papers, SC.

2. "Prime Minister Adams' Address in New York," West Indies News Service, 26 October 1959, box 10, folder 2, Moore Papers, SC.

3. "Adams and Federation," *DG*, 26 October 1959, 10; "Prime Minister Adams' Address in New York," West Indies News Service, 26 October 1959, box 10, folder 2, Moore Papers, SC.

4. "Prime Minister Adams' Address in New York," West Indies News Service, 26 October 1959, box 10, folder 2, Moore Papers, SC.

5. Ibid. Criticism of Adams existed well before the creation of the West Indies Federation, and his position as prime minister only intensified the scrutiny by his detractors. In May 1959, Reginald Pierrepointe of the West Indies News Service, who was a member of multiple other expatriate West Indian and black diaspora organizations based in the Harlem area, sent a scathing rebuttal of a London newspaper's recently published article on Adams and his previous activism and leadership within Barbados and the broader Caribbean. See Pierrepointe, "Open Letter to the London Sunday Observer," 22 May 1959, box 10, folder 2, Moore Papers, SC.

6. "Dear Mr. Moore," *Barbados Recorder*, 2 November 1959, box 10, folder 2, Moore Papers, SC; "An Open Letter to the Editor of the *Barbados Recorder*," n.d., box 10, folder 2, Moore Papers, SC.

7. "An Open Letter to the Editor of the *Barbados Recorder*," n.d., box 10, folder 2, Moore Papers, SC. Moore was not alone in challenging some accounts of this New York meeting. In an editorial in Jamaica's *Daily Gleaner*, W. A. Domingo criticized a "misleading" Federal Information Office release that failed to mention Adams's offensive stereotypes of the different islanders. See "Adams and Federation," *DG*, 26 October 1959, 10.

8. The Harlem and wider New York City–based West Indian community was not unique. Similar expatriate communities existed in other multinational black communities of the United States, Great Britain (particularly London), and various locations in the broader Caribbean and circum-Caribbean during these years. Nevertheless, Harlem and greater New York City was particularly prominent as a center of black diaspora activism, and therefore one of the primary communities examined in this study.

9. W. James, *Banner of Ethiopia*, 71.

10. Like many other recent works on such issues, this study routinely employs "identification" in place of "identity." This includes both self- and other-identifications. On the limitations of "identity," see Brubaker and Cooper, "Beyond Identity."

11. On the process of diasporization, see Guridy, "Feeling Diaspora," 116.

12. Romo, *Brazil's Living Museum*, 2.

13. Franklin Knight in *Race, Ethnicity, and Class* defines these sugar revolutions as "a series of interconnected fundamental changes in agriculture, horticulture, landholding, demography, society, and economy . . . [which] began in Barbados in the 1640s, spread to Jamaica, Martinique, Guadeloupe, and Saint-Domingue by the 1740s, and to Cuba and Puerto Rico by 1800" (36–37).

14. Charles Wagley divided the Western Hemisphere into Meso-America, Euro-America, and Plantation-America. The term "Plantation-America" encompassed some coastal areas of South and Central America, the US South, and all the Caribbean islands. See Wagley, "Plantation-America," 3–13. On sugar cultivation in the British Caribbean, see Goveia, *Slave Society*; Dunn, *Sugar and Slaves*; Sheridan, *Sugar and Slavery*; Mintz, *Sweetness and Power*.

15. Blackburn, *New World Slavery*, 323–24. For a similar view on racial solidarity among whites, see Goveia, *Slave Society*.

16. Given the importance of slavery to the history of the Caribbean, there is an extensive historiography of slave resistance in the British Caribbean. For a general overview of resistance to slavery in the British West Indies, see Craton, *Testing the Chains*. Especially helpful is Craton's appendix "Chronology of Resistance, 1638–1837." For information on marronage, see Price, *Maroon Societies*; Zips, *Black Rebels*. For studies of slave women resistance, see Beckles, *Afro-Caribbean Women*; Beckles, *Natural Rebels*; Bush, *Slave Women*; Gaspar and Hine, *More Than Chattel*. For specific studies on plots and rebellions in the British West Indies, see Craton, *Testing the Chains*; Gaspar, *Bondmen and Rebels*; Costa, *Crowns of Glory*. For a discussion of the shift in the goals of slave resistance, from withdrawal to the overthrow of plantation slavery, see Genovese, *From Rebellion to Revolution*.

17. For a classic study of the rise of the abolitionist movement in Europe and the Americas, see Davis, *Problem of Slavery*. An abridged, chronological account of the rise of British abolitionism can be found in Davis, *Inhuman Bondage*, 234–38. On proslavery and antislavery ideology in the eighteenth- and nineteenth-century Caribbean, see G. Lewis, *Main Currents*, chaps. 3–4.

18. No fewer than three major slave rebellions occurred in the British West Indies between the end of the slave trade and the formal end of slavery: Barbados in 1816, Demerara in 1823, and Jamaica in 1831–32. See Heuman, "From Slavery to Freedom," 142–47. For more on these rebellions, see Craton, *Testing the Chains*, chaps. 19–22. On the Demerara Rebellion, see Costa, *Crowns of Glory*. On the so-called Baptist War in Jamaica (1831–32), see M. Turner, *Slaves and Missionaries*, chap. 6.

19. While the motivations for British abolitionism are not of primary concern for this study, the issue has long been a heated debate within the historiography of the British Empire, especially the West Indies. One popular belief was that the British Empire, heavily influenced by the broad reach of the abolitionist movement, made a humanitarian gesture to end their slave trade and slavery—a virtuous example that led the way for other European empires (and the United States) to abolish their slave trades and, eventually, the institution of slavery.

This idea has been critiqued by numerous scholars who noted the economic considerations embedded in the emancipation debates and procedures. Among the most famous is Eric Williams's *Capitalism and Slavery*. Williams dismissed the humanitarian basis of emancipation, and instead claimed that the rise of industrial capitalism and a decline in the profitability of West Indian slavery led the British Empire to abolish plantation slavery. Williams's historical treatise reflected a West Indian nationalist position challenging the British Empire's record as a faithful, paternalistic body that could be trusted to institute changes at the proper time. On the endorsement of the humanitarian basis of abolition among British historians in the nineteenth and twentieth centuries, see E. Williams, *British Historians*. For an overview of subsequent debates over the "Williams thesis," see Carrington, "State of the Debate."

20. Davis, *Inhuman Bondage*, 233.

21. Davis, *Inhuman Bondage*, 234; Heuman, "From Slavery to Freedom," 147–48.

22. Many of these questions were present in all post-emancipation societies. However, the situation in the British West Indies and some islands of the French West Indies, which remained colonies, differed somewhat from other Caribbean and Latin American post-abolition societies in which the end of slavery had occurred alongside the emergence of independent states. On Haiti, see Dubois, *Avengers of the New World*; C.L.R. James, *Black Jacobins*; Fick, *Making of Haiti*. On Latin America, see Andrews, *Afro-Latin America*; Ferrer, *Insurgent Cuba*; Blanchard, *Slavery and Abolition*; R. Scott, *Slave Emancipation in Cuba*; Rout, *African Experience in Spanish America*; Lombardi, *Decline and Abolition*.

23. Quoted in Holt, "Essence of the Contract," 34.

24. With few exceptions, this consisted of three institutions in each colony: a Crown-appointed governor (representing the king), a nominated executive council of twelve men (acting as an upper house), and a local assembly, ranging in number from a dozen in some smaller colonies to more than forty in Jamaica, elected by a limited number of freeholders. The local assemblies, originally designed to be subservient to the respective colonies' governors and executive councils, instead became formidable forces within the colonies, acting as a local House of Commons. Wrong, *Government of the West Indies*, 37–41.

25. G. Lewis, *Modern West Indies*, 95–96. Despite the supposed supreme position of the governor, under the Old Representative System he was often torn between his responsibilities to the Crown and the reality of a powerful local assembly, which on occasion forced governors out of office and in one case even led to a colonial governor's death. See Wrong, *Government of the West Indies*, 37–38.

26. Such worries were not completely fanciful. There were some challenges to the white monopoly of power, including a "coloured" majority in Dominica's assembly, and growing numbers of Afro-Caribbean representatives in Jamaica. See Heuman, "From Slavery to Freedom," 156.

27. Holt, "Essence of the Contract," 36.

28. For an overview of post-emancipation protests in the British West Indies, see Craton, *Empire, Enslavement, and Freedom*, 324–47. For a more specific focus on Jamaica in these years, see Holt, *Problem of Freedom*, chap. 8.

29. At its peak, an estimated 1,500–2,000 people were involved in the Morant Bay Rebellion. Holt, *Problem of Freedom*, chap. 8, gives a detailed account. A more exhaustive study, especially of its classification as a rebellion rather than simply a riot, is Heuman, *Killing Time*.

30. Wrong, *Government of the West Indies*, 75. These actions are further detailed in Heuman, *Killing Time*.

31. Exact tallies of the repression vary. See Holt, *Problem of Freedom*, 302; J. Smith, "Liberals, Race, and Political Reform," 135.

32. As James Patterson Smith notes in "Liberals, Race, and Political Reform," 134, "From the start Eyre viewed the situation in almost purely racial terms."

33. Crown Colony rule describes a system in which "all executive powers [were] in the hands of the Crown-appointed Governor . . . [as well as] control of general policy and legislation because the legislature consisted of officials, subordinates of the Governor plus some colonists nominated by the Governor." In a Crown Colony, the Crown abolished the local assembly. It was replaced by either an entirely nominated legislature (in a "pure Crown Colony") or a legislature with both nominated and elected members (in a "semi-representative Crown Colony"). The loss of a representative element was obvious in a "pure Crown Colony," while in a "semi-representative Crown Colony" the representative element was little more than window dressing, since the nominated members invariably outnumbered any elected numbers. See Ayearst, *British West Indies*, 18; Wrong, *Government of the West Indies*, 71.

Before the Morant Bay rebellion, the Crown had considered more direct colonial rule as a solution to an array of West Indian problems. In fact, Trinidad and St. Lucia, two late additions to the British West Indies, had been Crown Colonies since their acquisition. In some other colonies the Old Representative System had slowly evolved toward Crown Colony rule in the mid-nineteenth century, but the change in Jamaica was immediate after Morant Bay. Therefore Jamaica's transition is often remembered as the "beginning of the end" for the Old Representative Systems. From 1866 to 1898, most British West Indies became pure Crown Colonies under a wholly nominated legislature. Jamaica's status as a pure Crown Colony lasted less than two decades, with its transition to a semi-representative Crown Colony in 1884 when an elective element returned to the legislature. Yet the Crown was still assured of control due to the power of the governor. British Guiana maintained its Dutch-based semi-representative system until 1928, when it also became a pure Crown Colony, while Barbados and the Bahamas never lost their original local elected assemblies. On the early establishment of Crown Colony rule, see Millette, *Genesis of Crown Colony Government*. For more on the constitutional changes in the late nineteenth century, see Wrong, *Government of the West Indies*, chaps. 5–9; Will, *Constitutional Change*; Benn, *The Caribbean*, chap. 2.

34. Ayearst, *British West Indies*, 30.

35. Ibid., 26.

36. For discussions of the Haitian Revolution and its reverberations throughout the Americas, see C.L.R. James, *Black Jacobins*; Dubois, *Avengers of the New World*; Dubois, *Colony of Citizens*; J. Scott, "The Common Wind"; Blackburn, *Overthrow of Colonial Slavery*; Egerton, *Gabriel's Rebellion*; Gaspar and Geggus, *A Turbulent Time*; Ferrer, *Insurgent Cuba*. As will be shown later in this chapter and subsequently, the "specter of Haiti" loomed large in discussions of black self-rule, be that bad or good, well into the twentieth century.

37. For a discussion of the rise of scientific racism in the British Empire, see Stepan, *Idea of Race*.

38. Such notions of "fit to rule" were by no means confined to the British Empire. For a similar debate within the Spanish Caribbean, see Ferrer, *Insurgent Cuba*.

39. MacMaster, *Racism in Europe*, 65.

40. J. Smith, "Liberals, Race, and Political Reform," 135.

41. Bryan, *Jamaican People*, 11.

42. Brereton, *Race Relations*, 25.

43. C.L.R. James, "West Indian Intellectual," 24.

44. Holt, *Problem of Freedom*, 316.

45. Brereton, *Race Relations*, 25.

46. On Chinese and Indian migration to the Caribbean in this era, see Look Lai, *Indentured Labor, Caribbean Sugar*.

47. Carlyle, "The Nigger Question," 1.

48. These images are summarized in August's introduction to *The Nigger Question*, xviii–xix. Such stereotypes are similar to the happy "Sambo" image in the United States, and can be found in other Caribbean settings too.

49. C. Hall, "What Is a West Indian?" 43.

50. Carlyle, "The Nigger Question," 30.

51. Ibid., 29.

52. Mill, "The Negro Question," 45. Colonel Fortescue was one of the commanders-in-chief of Cromwell's army in Jamaica, and governor of Jamaica for a short time. Carlyle, "The Nigger Question," 30.

53. Mill, "The Negro Question," 45.

54. For discussion of such titles as Anthony Trollope's *The West Indies and the Spanish Main* (1859) and Charles Kingsley's *At Last: A Christmas in the West Indies* (1871), see C. Hall, "What Is a West Indian?" 44–46; F. Smith, *Creole Recitations*, chap. 4; Cudjoe, *Beyond Boundaries*, chap. 9; Ledgister, *Only West Indians*, chap. 2.

55. Quote from F. Smith, *Creole Recitations*, 70. Also see Holt, *Problem of Freedom*, 303–7. For a discussion of Carlyle and Mill in the Eyre controversy, see C. Hall, *White, Male, and Middle Class*, chap. 10.

56. Froude, *English in the West Indies*, 278–86. In this case Froude obviously denied the equality of black people; however, he seemingly believed they could be "civilized" with proper white, in this case British, guidance. Thus his ideas fall in line with the emerging notions of British imperialism in the late nineteenth century.

57. Ibid., 4.

58. Ibid., 333.

59. Ibid., 287.

60. E. Williams, *British Historians*, 176. In this work, first published in the 1960s, Williams provided a thorough critique of Froude. The work as a whole provides an insightful examination of the role of historians in justifying and popularizing British colonial expansion—a process "profoundly tainted with racialism" (168).

61. Cudjoe, *Beyond Boundaries*, 300–306.

62. Salmon's career included stints as president of Nevis (British West Indies), colonial secretary and administrator of the Gold Coast, and chief commissioner of the Seychelles Islands.

63. Salmon, *Caribbean Confederation*, 53, 134. James W. Green in "Culture and Colonialism" argues that Salmon "challenged what he saw as the unholy alliance of Colonial Office bureaucracy and West Indian planter-merchant interests" (490).

64. Salmon, *Caribbean Confederation*, preface.

65. Ibid., 54.

66. Ibid., 5, 44, 90–91.

67. C.L.R. James, "West Indian Intellectual," 26–27.

68. D. Wood, "Brief Biography," 20.

69. J. J. Thomas, *Froudacity*, 51, 57, 52–54, 146–49, 154. Ironically, Thomas does not give as spirited a defense of Haiti as Salmon does, instead saying that the British West Indies should be compared to Liberia. For a discussion, see F. Smith, "Man Who Knows His Roots," 4.

70. Ibid., 2. For further discussion of J. J. Thomas as a Pan-African figure, see F. Smith, "Man Who Knows His Roots" and *Creole Recitations*, chap. 2; R. Lewis, "J. J. Thomas."

71. F. Smith, "Man Who Knows His Roots," 6. A similar case can be found within the work of the "Jubilee Five" in Jamaica. In 1888 this group of black (not "coloured") men published *Jamaica's Jubilee; or, What We Are and What We Hope to Be*. This text was designed to show how far the formerly enslaved population had progressed since final emancipation. In arguing their case, the group present themselves as loyal to both their island of Jamaica and the larger British Empire, while also maintaining a crucial racial consciousness and diasporic interests. See D. Thomas, "Modern Blackness" and *Modern Blackness*, chap. 1.

72. On these numerous connections, see for instance Blackett, "The Hamic Connection"; W. James, "Wings of Ethiopia." For some of these figures' key writings, see Moses, *Classical Black Nationalism*.

73. As John McCartney notes in his discussion of black nationalist thought in the eighteenth and nineteenth centuries, Africa was not the only destination proposed for African American emigration. James T. Holly, among others, suggested black migration to the West Indies and Haiti in the nineteenth century. McCartney, *Black Power Ideologies*, 16. For a recent work on African American migration to Haiti in the nineteenth century, see Fanning, *Caribbean Crossing*.

74. Mathews, "Project for a Confederation," 71.

75. See for example Huggins, *Federation of the West Indies*; G. Lewis, "British Caribbean Federation"; Proctor, "Development of the Idea"; Hatch, *Dwell Together in Unity*; Ayearst, *British West Indies*; Ramphal, "Federalism in the West Indies"; Lowenthal, *West Indies Federation*; Mordecai, *Federation*. In more recent years, the few studies of federation within these fields have continued to bound it in similar ways. See for example Augier, "Federations"; Hart, "Federation: an Ill-Fated Design"; Killingray, "West Indian Federation."

76. For discussion of "overlapping" and "multiple diasporas" see W. James, "Wings of Ethiopia"; E. Lewis, "To Turn as on a Pivot."

77. Putnam, *Radical Moves*; Chambers, *Race, Nation, and West Indian Immigration*; Guridy, "'Enemies of the White Race.'" As early as 1927 one can find support for a Caribbean federation among some West Indians in Panama. See Putnam, *Radical Moves*, 202.

78. On the need to move beyond studies focused on New York City, see Baldwin and Makalani, *Escape from New York*.

79. See for example Watkins-Owens, *Blood Relations*; W. James, *Banner of Ethiopia*; J. Turner, *Caribbean Crusaders*.

80. See for example Plummer, *Rising Wind*; Von Eschen, *Race Against Empire*; Gallicchio, *African American Encounter*; Dudziak, *Cold War Civil Rights*; Meriwether, *Proudly*

We Can Be Africans; Gaines, *American Africans in Ghana*; Horne, *End of Empires*; Seigel, *Uneven Encounters*; Guridy, *Forging Diaspora*; Polyné, *From Douglass to Duvalier*; Makalani, *Cause of Freedom*.

Chapter 1. A Common Answer to Disparate Questions: Envisioning Caribbean Federation in the Late Nineteenth and Early Twentieth Centuries

Parts of this chapter were previously published, in slightly different form, in "The Diasporic Dimensions of Caribbean Federation in the Early Twentieth Century," *New West Indian Guide* 83, nos. 3–4 (2009): 219–48, used with permission of Koninklijke Brill NV.

1. DeLisser, "Negro as a Factor," 1.

2. Ashton and Killingray, *The West Indies*, xl.

3. Wrong, *Government of the West Indies*, 162.

4. Mathews, "Project for a Confederation," 71, 93–94.

5. Aspinall, "West Indian Federation," 58–59; Proctor, "Development of the Idea," 6.

6. This association included a common legislature and single governor for Antigua, Montserrat, St. Kitts, and Nevis. Although never officially dissolved, it "simply ceased to function" as insular interests developed between the islands. Augier, "Federations," 18–19.

7. Among the best overviews of these events are Ramphal, "Federalism in the West Indies," 210–29; Aspinall, "West Indian Federation"; Proctor, "Development of the Idea"; Augier, "Federations."

8. Prior to the twentieth century, "West Indian" identification was primarily associated with the white planters and merchants within the Caribbean and the metropole. See C. Hall, "What Is a West Indian?" 31–50. Associations representing such West Indian interests included the Society of West India Planters and Merchants and the West India Committee, both founded in the eighteenth century. The West India Committee remained important well into the twentieth century. For a history, see D. Hall, *West India Committee*. For a brief history of the Colonial Congress of 1831, see Higman, "Colonial Congress," 239–48.

9. For further information on the creation of British Guiana, see Augier and Gordon, *Sources*, 269–70.

10. Ramphal, "Federalism in the West Indies," 212, 216.

11. Franklyn, *Unit of Imperial Federation*. This book's subtitle, "A Solution of the Problem," reflects the idea that federation could be the "solution" to many problems in the empire.

12. The Leeward Islands Colony brought together the individual presidencies of Antigua, Montserrat, the Virgin Islands, and Dominica, with an additional presidency over St. Kitts and Nevis. There was a single governor for the federal colony and a general legislative council composed of members from the island legislatures. Proctor, "Development of the Idea," 7.

13. Ibid., 8. For further discussion of this failed proposal, as well as the vehement reactions of some in Barbados, see Augier and Gordon, *Sources*, 273–78; Levy, *Emancipation, Sugar, and Federalism*, chaps. 6–7; E. Williams, "Federation: Select Documents," 21–32.

14. Proctor, "Development of the Idea," 8–9.

15. E. Williams, "Federation: Select Documents," 38–39; Proctor, "Development of the Idea," 9.

16. E. Williams, "Federation: Select Documents," 39–41; Proctor, "Development of the Idea," 9–10.

17. Proctor, "Development of the Idea," 10.

18. Salmon's plan was to include Antigua (with Barbuda), the Bahamas, Barbados, Dominica, Grenada (with part of the Grenadines), Jamaica (with the Turks and Caicos Islands), St. Kitts and Nevis (with Anguilla), St. Lucia, Montserrat, Tobago, Trinidad, St. Vincent (with the remainder of the Grenadines), the Virgin Islands, British Guiana, and British Honduras. Salmon offers one of the most useful summaries of these colonies' various governments and economies, as they stood at the time of his proposal, in *Caribbean Confederation*, 131–32, 146–75.

19. Ibid., 137–38.

20. Ibid., 138.

21. James Froude, who, as described in the introduction, bemoaned any notion of black equality within the West Indies, believed federation would require the inclusion of the black population as full participating citizens, so it would become a black-dominated venture. If this occurred, he thought the inhabitants of white colonies like New Zealand and Australia would criticize the loss of the region for their white brothers. See Froude, *English in the West Indies*, 7–8; Salmon, *Caribbean Confederation*, 127–28.

22. Lamont, *Problems of the Antilles*, 42–43. Lord Cromer held colonial posts in Malta, India, and most famously as consul-general of Egypt at this time, while Lord Curzon, another famous colonial official, was viceroy of India. Lamont also called for "the best men we can send out," obviously asserting the need for continued appointment of colonial officials from outside the West Indies, rather than drawing them from the local populations.

23. Ibid., 104, 127–31. Lamont believed one of the main reasons the US would not welcome annexation of the West Indies was that the islands, which he assumed would become states at some point, had such a large black population.

24. Proctor, "Development of the Idea," 11.

25. G. B. Mason, "The Future of the West Indies," in Rippon, *Unification*, 21–25 (quote, 21).

26. Murray, *Scheme*, 30. Despite Murray's description of Rippon, Rippon generally avoided the terms "confederation" and "federation" because he, like many others in the era, believed such terms were reserved for a union of sovereign states, which the West Indian colonies were not. He preferred "unification" or "consolidation." See Rippon, *Unification*, 8.

27. Rippon, *Unification*, 8–13. This new government was to deal primarily with issues of common interest in the colonies, including trade, commerce, and communication matters among themselves and other countries. It is also important to note that Rippon included all of the British West Indian colonies, including the Bahamas, British Honduras, and British Guiana.

28. Unlike Rippon, R. H. McCarthy did not include Trinidad and Tobago, British Guiana, Jamaica, or British Honduras. See his "Notes on West Indian Federation," in Rippon, *Unification*, 26–33.

29. Ibid., 27.

30. D. S. DeFreitas, "Deliberative Convention," in Rippon, *Unification*, 43–45 (quotes, 44).

31. Ibid., 45. In the late 1910s DeFreitas would become a proponent of very limited constitutional reform through his work in the Representative Government Association in Grenada, but at this point such ideas are not obvious. See Emmanuel, *Crown Colony Politics*, 48–54.

32. These articles, originally published in the *West India Committee Circular*, are found in Rippon, *Unification*, 33–42.

33. A major difference in the constitutions of the West Indian colonies dated back to the nineteenth century, when several colonies including Jamaica were made Crown Colonies, while Barbados maintained its locally elected assembly. In a federation, either Barbados would have to surrender its assembly or the others would have to be given local representation, neither of which was an appealing option for the Committee.

34. Rippon, *Unification*, 34–36.

35. Murray, *Scheme*, 4–5.

36. Ibid., 7.

37. Ibid., 42.

38. Murray divided the region into two zones: North-Western West Indies (Jamaica, Bahamas, Turks & Caicos) and South-Eastern West Indies (Windwards, Leewards, Barbados, Trinidad & Tobago, and British Guiana). He left out British Honduras on the Central American coast. Ibid., 8–23.

39. Murray compared Jamaica to New Zealand, which chose not to join the Australian federation of the early twentieth century. He believed it was best to move on with a more "practical" federation than to wait for all colonies to want to join, much as Australia had done despite New Zealand's refusal. Ibid., 24–25.

40. Ibid., 28.

41. Ibid., 32–38; for a more complete list of these "common interests," 31.

42. Ibid., 30, 37. On necessary rearrangements for the Windward and Leeward Colonies, see 35–38. Also, Murray likely emphasized the limitations on the federal council to reassure the powerful interests of the West Indies that he did not wish to threaten their dominance. He did risk immediate opposition by noting that, unlike claims for some previous schemes, he did not think federation would necessarily lessen administrative costs. "The benefits gained by confederation should," he nevertheless argued, "as history teaches, out-balance any extra expenditure that may be incurred" (38–39).

43. As noted, Rippon considered terminology a major issue, preferring "unification" over "federation." Ibid., 47–49.

44. Ibid., 45–47. Rutherford's comment on the need for a "large enough leisure class" was obviously loaded with notions of race and class, with the wealthy white population viewed as the only responsible sector capable of ruling the region.

45. Ibid., 53–54.

46. Murray, *United West Indies*, 8.

47. "The West Indies and Federation: Obstacles to Union," *London Times*, 8 October 1913, 5. In this portion of the article, the author refers to the recent troubled negotiations between Canada and the West Indies. Murray, *Scheme*, 26, also cites this example, in which Canada refused to negotiate trade relations with individual colonies and expressed the need to be able to deal with the West Indian colonies as a whole.

48. "The West Indies and Federation: Obstacles to Union," *London Times*, 8 October

1913, 5. In this case the author's use of "coloured" included all people of African descent, black and coloured. His use of Haiti as a warning against black majority rule speaks to the continued stereotypical image of that black republic in the early twentieth century.

49. Davson had actually begun to organize this association before the war, with support from the West India Committee and all of the West Indian colonies except Jamaica. Braithwaite, "'Federal Associations and Institutions,'" 286.

50. "The West Indies and Federation," *London Times*, 16 December 1913, 7.

51. "The West Indies: Scheme of Modified Federation—Gradual Development," *London Times*, 31 January 1921, 6. Such intra-regional conferences were held sporadically in the late nineteenth and early twentieth centuries on such matters as quarantine, customs, communications, education, agriculture, and medicine. See Wrong, *Government of the West Indies*, 167–69.

52. Proctor, "Development of the Idea," 13–14.

53. Wood's contingent visited Jamaica, St. Kitts, Nevis, Antigua, Dominica, St. Lucia, St. Vincent, Barbados, Grenada, Trinidad, and British Guiana. The planned visit to British Honduras was cancelled due to a yellow fever scare, while trips to the Bahamas, Montserrat, Tobago, and the Virgin Islands could not be arranged in the limited time. E.F.L. Wood, *Report*, 1.

54. Ibid., 28–29.

55. Ibid., 32. As Ann Spackman notes in her study *Constitutional Development of the West Indies*, "There was a certain ambiguity . . . as to the identity of the public which was to express this opinion. Although it is not clearly stated one can nevertheless assume that it did not involve any attempt to ascertain the views of the mass of the West Indian population since they were expressly denied access to government by way of genuinely popular representation" (xxxiv–xxxv). Given the racial ideologies of British colonialism, it is obvious that many colonial officials, including the Wood Commission, believed that the oligarchy and other white elites were the responsible portion of the West Indian population from which regional opinions must be drawn. For further discussion of the Wood Commission's opinion on this matter, see Mordecai, *Federation*, 20; Wallace, *The British Caribbean*, 25–26.

56. E.F.L. Wood, *Report*, 32. The Wood Commission noted that they did hear some talk of a possible association between the Windward Islands and Trinidad, which some assumed would lead to financial savings and aid in the distribution of essential services. They believed, however, that would require both a demand and approval of all colonies involved. As a result of the Wood Commission's comments, the governor of the Windward Islands visited several of the colonies under his charge to gauge the interest in such a proposal, but nothing came of the idea. For details of the governor's address, see Windward Islands Governor, *Governor's Address to the Legislative Councils Relative to the Association of Those Islands with Trinidad*, 1922, archived in ICS Libraries Special Collections.

57. E.F.L. Wood, *Report*, 29–31.

58. H. Johnson, "British Caribbean from Demobilization," 602.

59. E.F.L. Wood, *Report*, 32.

60. At the time of the Wood Commission's visit, the majority of the West Indian colonies remained pure Crown Colonies with no elected members in their legislatures. Jamaica was a semi-representative Crown Colony with limited elected members. Barbados

and the Bahamas were the only West Indian colonies with representative assemblies, while British Guiana was soon to lose its semi-representative government and become a Crown Colony in 1928.

61. H. Johnson, "British Caribbean from Demobilization," 602–3.

62. "West Indian Conference in London," *London Times*, 28 April 1926, 15.

63. Davson, *Report of the West Indian Conference*, 4–5.

64. For the full record of this 1929 conference, see *Report of the First West Indies Conference*.

65. Despite repeated calls for federation by numerous West Indian leaders and organizations in the early twentieth century, they put forth surprisingly few concrete plans for the design and installation of federation. While the official colonial brokers debated the scale, scope, and practicality of federation, the West Indian nationalists do not appear to have concerned themselves with such details at this stage, other than their staunch demand for an end to Crown Colony rule and the establishment of representative self-government within the empire (i.e., dominion status).

66. Wrong, *Government of the West Indies*, 171.

67. C.L.R. James, *Cipriani*, 1–2, and "Self-Government," 53, 63. These works remain two of the most significant critiques of the Crown Colony system of rule in the British Caribbean. The latter, better known and more available, draws heavily and in some cases verbatim from the former.

68. C.L.R. James, *Cipriani*, 6, and "Self-Government," 52–53. James was especially critical of such policies given that he believed West Indians were "Western" (or British) in every sense. He drew a distinction between the colonial setting of the West Indies and Africa, which was more obviously tied to non-European culture. Nevertheless, this did not mean that James supported white colonial rule in Africa in any way, or that he separated the anticolonial struggles of the West Indies and Africa. See for example *Cipriani*, 52.

69. C.L.R. James, "Self-Government," 52–53. In many cases the coloured classes attempted to tie themselves to the white power structure in hopes of attaining better positions within the colonial setting. Some within the black middle class also tried to separate themselves from the black working class for similar reasons. For a brief discussion, see James's *Cipriani* and "Self-Government."

70. On Afro-Caribbean hegemony, see for example Lowenthal, "Social Background," 81.

71. Much like those centered in the British Caribbean, ideas of federation between other Caribbean islands confronted the "question of race." While a proposed Antillean Confederation between Cuba, Puerto Rico, and the Dominican Republic did not use race as the basis for unity, nor did Antenor Firmin of Haiti, who expressed more Pan-American visions of regional unity, others did. As noted, in the early nineteenth century Alexander von Humboldt believed the Caribbean could become an "African Confederation of the free states of the West Indies." In the early twentieth century Adolphe Lara of Guadeloupe called for a federation of Afro-Caribbeans from all islands of the region. See Mathews, "Project for a Confederation," 71, 93–94; Plummer, "Firmin and Martí," 217–18.

72. Though some scholars have argued that such activism preceded J. J. Thomas's eloquent rebuttal of Froude's polemical text, his *Froudacity*, as noted, is recognized by many

as a key moment in the development of West Indian nationalism. On such earlier activism, see Lumsden, "A Forgotten Generation," 112–22.

73. Bryan, *Jamaican People*, 242.

74. Lumsden, "A Forgotten Generation," 118. Lumsden's dissertation, "Robert Love and Jamaican Politics," unfortunately remains one of the few monographs on Dr. Love.

75. Bryan, *Jamaican People*, 261; Lumsden, "A Forgotten Generation," 120.

76. Lumsden, "A Forgotten Generation," 119. Jamaica was a semi-representative Crown Colony at this time. Therefore, although the work of Love and the People's Convention helped elect a few members to the Legislative Council, their power remained severely limited by the structure of Crown Colony rule, which ensured Crown control. Nevertheless, the symbolic importance of such elected officials should not be underestimated as a challenge to ideas about black inferiority.

77. Bryan, *Jamaican People*, 262; Bogues, "Nationalism and Jamaican Political Thought," 379. Given his political activism and race consciousness, "Love was particularly disturbed at efforts by Jamaican blacks to draw distinctions of superiority and inferiority between themselves and Africans." Quoted in Bryan, *Jamaican People*, 82.

78. Richards, "Race, Labour, and Politics," 508. Such phrases as "Jamaican white" were used in various British sources of the early twentieth century. While the phrase could simply be a way of noting that the "white" in question was born in Jamaica, it often implied a person was considered white in the islands but not necessarily white by British or US standards. The term "brown" was generally synonymous with "coloured" (mixed ancestry) in Jamaica.

79. Ibid., 508–11; Richards, "Race, Class, and Labour," 346–50. The National Club was one of the earliest political organizations in which Marcus Garvey participated.

80. *Our Own*, 1 July 1911, quoted in R. Lewis, *Marcus Garvey*, 44.

81. K. Singh, *Race and Class*, 1–13.

82. Cudjoe, *Beyond Boundaries*, 193–94.

83. Brereton, *Modern Trinidad*, 130.

84. Brereton, *Race Relations*, 96; Brereton, *Modern Trinidad*, 129.

85. Brereton, *Race Relations*, 96–97.

86. Cudjoe, *Beyond Boundaries*, 362–64.

87. This phrase is taken from W.E.B. DuBois, "The Color Line Belts the World," in D. Lewis, *W.E.B. DuBois: A Reader*, 42. For a more recent article on this topic, see Kelley, "'But a Local Phase of a World Problem.'" For a helpful discussion of Pan-Africanism in the Caribbean, see Martin, *Pan-African Connection*.

88. Wallace, *The British Caribbean*, 96.

89. Cox, "'Race Men,'" 75–76.

90. The original serial publication of J. J. Thomas's argument against Froude, later published as *Froudacity*, appeared in one of Donovan's earlier newspaper ventures. Ibid., 76. Also see Cox, "William Galwey Donovan."

91. Cox, "'Race Men,'" 75.

92. Ibid., 75–80, discussing of Donovan's specific Pan-African activities.

93. Meikle was educated at Howard University in Washington, DC, and spent some time teaching at the dental school there before going on to study medicine. He briefly worked for the US Public Health Service in Panama during the building of the Panama

Canal before returning to Jamaica. Hill, *Papers*, 22n7. For a discussion of the possible annexation of the British West Indies by the United States or Canada in these years, see DeLisser, *Twentieth Century Jamaica*.

94. Meikle, *Confederation*, 38–39, 200. Meikle used "confederation" and "federation" interchangeably.

95. Ibid., 6

96. Ibid., 43.

97. Although Meikle in the vast majority of *Confederation* describes "West Indians" as black, he occasionally defines the group in more multiracial terms. For instance, a footnote states the "term 'West Indians' is intended to mean the children of immigrants, both white and black, and their offspring born in the West Indies" (6). Yet the next page says, "The West Indian, as a negro, is not wanted in the United States" (7). In one of his last chapters Meikle declares his "hope that every West Indian who reads this book, be he white, black, or of mixed blood," will come to support a confederation of the British West Indies (255). Still, given his argument for federation and his description of West Indians throughout most of *Confederation*, it seems obvious that Meikle believed people of African descent to be the "real West Indians" because of their numerical superiority as well as their historical contributions to the region's development.

98. Ibid., 254.

99. However, Meikle repeatedly states (for example, ibid., 250–55) that whites have no reason to fear black majority rule.

100. Ibid., 89. For additional examples of Meikle's discussion of the region as "the assets of the coloured man," and the West Indies as a sort of black homeland, see 85–89, 254–55.

101. Ibid., 183. Also see 18–21, 38–39.

102. These "British West Indies Regiments" should not be confused with previous black regiments from the British West Indies, the "West India Regiment." Those regiments served against France in the 1790s in Martinique and Guadeloupe, in the suppression of the Morant Bay Rebellion in 1865 in Jamaica, and in West Africa during the Ashanti wars in the 1870s. See Joseph, "British West Indies Regiment," 94.

103. Catherine Hall in "What Is a West Indian" claims, "The naming of black regiments as West Indian fractured the prevailing image of West Indian as an exclusively white identity" (41). While I agree, I think it more appropriate to say such action *further* fractured whiteness from West Indianness, which, as noted, had been ongoing since the late nineteenth century.

104. Military service has long served as a means through which peoples of African descent have fought for and earned inclusion within the "nation" or "empire." Examples can be found throughout the Caribbean and Latin America (see Howe, *Race, War and Nationalism*; Ferrer, *Insurgent Cuba*; Beattie, *Tribute of Blood*) and the United States.

105. "The Kaiser's Protests Against Coloured Troops," *Dominica Guardian*, 28 October 1915, 2.

106. *Dominica Guardian*, 2 March 1916, 3.

107. *Daily Telegraph*, 8 November 1915, in "Album of Press Cuttings BWIR, 1915–1919," ICS 96/2/3, WIC Records, ICS.

108. For examples of such conditions, see Howe, *Race, War and Nationalism*; Joseph,

"British West Indies Regiment," 94–124; R. Smith, *Jamaican Volunteers*, chaps. 5–6; Elkins, "Black Nationalism," 99–103; C.L.R. James, *Cipriani*, chap. 3.

109. Ashdown, "Black Consciousness," 2.

110. C.L.R. James, *Cipriani*, 34.

111. Elkins, "Black Nationalism," 100.

112. Howe, *Race, War and Nationalism*, 165.

113. Major Maxwell Smith to G.O.C. Troops Taranto, 27 December 1918, CO 318/350, PRO. A similar description of the Caribbean League as a radical, racial organization noted, "The Caribbean League, which is a sort of secret society among negroes, is reported now to be whispering about a negro uprising to begin in Jamaica and to spread towards the Islands, the policy being the old one of falling upon the Whites and murdering them. The local authorities in each Island ought to watch the proceedings of this Society very carefully." See Directorate of Intelligence (Home Office), 18 June 1919, CO 318/349, PRO.

114. Strikes occurred in St. Lucia, Grenada, Barbados, Antigua, St. Kitts, Trinidad, Jamaica, and British Guiana. See H. Johnson, "British Caribbean from Demobilization," 600; Howe, *Race, War, and Nationalism*, 178.

115. Sylvester Williams's Pan-African Association had several branches in the British Caribbean in the early twentieth century, but by the time of the war it had largely given way to the UNIA. On Garveyism in Trinidad in this era, see Martin, *Pan-African Connection*, chap. 5. For an example of the UNIA in British Honduras, see Ashdown, "Marcus Garvey" and "Black Consciousness."

116. Quoted in Ashdown, "Black Consciousness," 4. On the debates over the controversial Seditious Publications Ordinance, through which some colonial administrators called for a ban of the *Negro World* in the immediate postwar years, see Elkins, "Marcus Garvey"; Ashdown, "Black Consciousness," 3–4.

117. Quoted in Ashdown, "Race Riot, Class Warfare," 11. Ashdown discusses the background of this riot, including the influence of the local UNIA, in two other articles, "Marcus Garvey" and "Black Consciousness."

118. Elkins, "Black Power," 71–75; Martin, *Pan-African Connection*, chap. 3.

119. "For Representative Government," *Dominica Guardian*, 6 February 1919, 2.

120. These included groups such as the Representative Government Association (Grenada), the Trinidad Workingmen's Association, the Jamaica Reform Club, and the Democratic League (Barbados). H. Johnson, "British Caribbean from Demobilization," 603–4.

121. A. Hinds, "Federation and Political Representation." Hinds argues that federation was not the primary goal for these activists, but rather the best means of attaining increased representation and self-government. Although true for some, it was certainly not for others.

122. Marryshow and Cipriani were similar in many regards. Both men decried the colonial policies of the British Empire that choked the aspirations of West Indians, and both sought significant reforms of the existing economic, social, and political systems for the benefit of the majorities. While both were socialists who called for reform of the colonial system, neither man could be broadly labeled "anti-British," as their activism in this era did not call for a break from the empire or British political models.

123. D. Thomas, *Modern Blackness*, chap. 1. In this text Thomas discusses the coexistence of "creole multiracial nationalism" and "black nationalism" in Jamaica. Anthony

Bogues makes similar distinctions in his study of Jamaican nationalism, which he says includes "brown creole nationalism" and "black nationalism"; see "Nationalism and Jamaican Political Thought," 373–74.

124. C.L.R. James, *Cipriani*, 20–22.

125. Ibid., 22–26, details Cipriani's role in the recruitment of the BWIR in Trinidad.

126. Ibid., 30, 35.

127. Ibid., 37.

128. Ibid., 103. Nigel Bolland, among others, argues that despite the expansion of the TWA, its "activities as a trade union declined under Cipriani's leadership" because of the captain's focus on reform politics. In fact, in the 1930s when trade unions were legalized, the TWA changed its name to the Trinidad Labour Party, with obvious connections to the British Labour Party with which Cipriani and numerous other Caribbean socialists were allied. Bolland, *Politics of Labour*, 203–4.

129. C.L.R. James, *Cipriani*, 66–68. For more on Cipriani in Trinidad during this era, see Ryan, *Race and Nationalism*, chap. 2.

130. C.L.R. James, *Cipriani*, 103.

131. See for example "Speech Delivered at the British Guiana and West Indian Labour Conference," 12–14 January 1926, and "Speech Delivered at the Labour Commonwealth Conference," July 1928, in Cipriani, *His Best Orations*, 91–95, 67–72.

132. Throughout its early existence, the TWA was associated primarily with black laborers. In fact, much of the leadership below Cipriani was composed of Garveyites, or at least advocates of racial unity and Pan-African policies. For example, William Howard-Bishop Jr., the TWA's general secretary, clearly linked industrial unity to issues of racial unity and consciousness; see K. Singh, *Race and Class*, 131–33. Moreover, Cipriani's leadership of the TWA should not be assumed to indicate a diminished or absent racial consciousness by black members. While that may have been true for some, the decision to appoint a white man as leader was also a political calculation by many of the TWA's membership, who knew that the colonial governments and planter-merchant oligarchy that they were dealing with were more likely to listen to a white man. See Richards, "Race, Labour, and Politics."

133. Minutes of the Proceedings of a Special Meeting of the Legislative Council held at the Council Chamber York House, 30 March 1955, ICS 40/Item D.6, James Papers, ICS.

134. Marryshow later anglicized his name to Theophilus Albert Marryshow. Sheppard, *Marryshow of Grenada*, 1–7. This title, though brief, remains the only biography of Marryshow. See Emmanuel, *Crown Colony Politics*, which Sheppard's work utilizes, for more on Marryshow's career, particularly in Grenada.

135. Marryshow was not unique in this regard, but rather a prominent example of the ways in which many journalists of the region called for and led reform movements with often overt racial motivations. This includes Love, Cox, and Donovan, as well as a new generation of racially conscious West Indian journalists in the 1920s. For example, see Martin, "Pan-Africanist in Dominica."

136. In this manner Marryshow carried on Donovan's legacy in Grenada, the West Indies, and the broader black diaspora (and in many ways the legacies of Love and Cox). For a comparative study of Marryshow and Donovan, see Cox, "'Race Men.'" Marryshow later became the godfather of Eric Williams; see Palmer, *Eric Williams*, 7. These relation-

ships show an important connection between some of the most prominent West Indian nationalists, diaspora activists, and federation supporters.

137. *WI*, 1 January 1915 quoted in Sheppard, *Marryshow of Grenada*, 10; "West Indian Prize Competition," *WI*, 10 January 1915, 1.

138. "West Indians and the West Indies," *WI*, 20 February 1915, 2.

139. "A Nearer West Indian," *WI*, 23 November 1916, 2; "The West Indies and the Empire Parliament," *WI*, 31 August 1917, 2–3.

140. "News and Topics," *WI*, 18 March 1917, 2; "Annexation of the West Indies to the USA a Danger," *WI*, 26 September 1919, 1; "No Yankee Rule for Us Negro British West Indians," *WI*, 7 November 1919, 1; "A New West Indian Consciousness: The Call of 1920," *WI*, 19 January 1920, 1.

141. "The Future of the West Indies," *WI*, 2 August 1918, 1.

142. "Foul Federation," *WI*, 17 January 1919, 1.

143. "The New West Indies," *WI*, 27 February 1920, 2.

144. Marryshow's letter to a Barbadian newspaper editor, published in the *West Indian* in February 1920, said, "There is a flight of stairs, a ladder, or a steep road leading to this Federation. Federation is a summit. . . . The flight of stairs, the ladder, the steep road, or whatever condition we are likely to find in getting to the summit, is Representation. . . . Without Representation, the Federation of the West Indies will never be reached in virtue and in fact." Marryshow's statement challenges assumptions that federation was simply a means to gain representative government, rather than the ultimate goal of the black and coloured intelligentsia of the Easter Caribbean in the 1920s and 1930s. Here representative government is a key step in attaining the ultimate goal of a federation. Such a debate speaks to multiple, simultaneous visions and goals of a possible Caribbean federation. "Steps to Federation," *WI*, 27 February 1920, 2.

145. T. Albert Marryshow to W.E.B. DuBois, 3 November 1932, DuBois Papers, UMass.

146. "Prejudice Follows the American Flag in the West Indies," *WI*, 3 August 1917, 3.

147. "Trinidad's 'White' Private Contingent," *WI*, 23 November 1915, 2; "The Black Soldier in the United States," *WI*, 22 June 1917, 2; "Execution of Negro Soldiers in America," *WI*, 4 March 1918, 7. Various letters and editorials on and from the BWIR can be found in the *West Indian* throughout World War I.

148. "Shall It Be," *WI*, 24 October 1919, 1; "Coloured Subjects—Not Citizens of Empire," *WI*, 24 October 1919, 3; "Shutting Out the Dawn with a Scrap of Paper," *WI*, 24 October 1919, 2; "St. Vincent Prohibits the 'Negro World,'" *WI*, 3; "The Negro and the Peace Conference," *WI*, 3 January 1919, 1; "The A.P.U. Telegram," *WI*, 3 January 1919, 1; "To Frederick Douglass," *WI*, 9 April 1920, 3. The exact relationship between Marryshow and Garvey remains unknown. In Surjit Mansingh's study of the failure of the West Indies Federation, she claims that Marryshow was at one time the president of Grenada's UNIA branch; see "Background to Failure," 173–74. Marryshow's biographer Jill Sheppard noted in *Marryshow of Grenada*, 12, that Garvey was "a man after Marryshow's own heart," and said that Marryshow had a photograph of Garvey in his home. Thus, while Marryshow may not have agreed wholeheartedly with Garvey, he and many other West Indians respected his work and agreed with many aspects such as race pride and unity, as well as the demand for self-determination for the region.

149. "The Horizon," *Crisis*, December 1922, 74.

150. Marryshow, *Cycles of Civilisation*, 1–2, 19–20.

151. Ibid., 2–3.

152. In a particularly telling passage in *Cycles of Civilisation*, Marryshow wrote, "The Virgin Mary, should she come back to earth, would never be able to recognise the son born of her womb in the current paintings and pictures" (7). This, along with his parallel discussion of the accomplishments and great history of Africa when Europe was in a primitive state (12–18), echoes sentiments found in many black nationalist ideologies in the late nineteenth and early twentieth centuries.

153. Ibid., 3.

154. Marryshow believed that not only were many European nations in decline, but many were never powerful or influential—here he named Austria, the Balkan states, and Scandinavian countries—while Russia was the only European nation with a bright future. Ibid., 9–10.

155. Ibid., 3–4.

156. Marryshow said this should not "be regarded as Cassandric prophesy . . . but a considered view of the revolution of the cycles of civilisation, and the rise and fall of nations and peoples" (ibid., 11–12).

157. Marryshow was especially impressed with the rise of Japan, which in fifty years went "from a nation of half-blind, insular and self-centered hermits, with no voice in the world, to a great enterprising and vigorous power—a force in international affairs." Japan was likely of particular interest to Marryshow both because it had been heralded as the "Champion of the Darker Races" in the early twentieth century after its defeat of Russia in 1905 and because it was a nation of islands, much as a united West Indies would be. He also argued that the opening of the Panama Canal would be a great boost to all nations of the Americas and the Caribbean, not just North America. Ibid., 4–6.

158. Ibid., 23.

159. Ibid., 48.

160. Ibid., 7.

161. Ibid., 1–2.

162. Ibid.

163. "A Call to Larger Fields," *WI*, 20 June 1919, 1. This decision should not be read as a rejection or downplaying of diaspora politics; instead it speaks to his belief that his work in the West Indies was important and also part of the broader struggle for peoples of African descent. In many ways this parallels a similar decision made by Eric Williams in the 1950s.

164. *WI*, 12 March 1920, as cited in Cox, "'Race Men,'" 98; Sheppard, *Marryshow of Grenada*, 13. Sheppard claims that the attention Marryshow received for *Cycles* was the basis for his invitation to the Second Pan-African Congress.

165. DuBois to Marryshow, 12 April 1923, 11 September 1923, 17 October 1923, 4 April 1924, and 10 March 1927, DuBois Papers, UMass.

166. Marryshow to DuBois, 27 June 1926; DuBois to Marryshow, 12 July 1926, DuBois Papers, UMass. For further discussion of the actual Sweet case, see Boyle, *Arc of Justice*; Wolcott, *Remaking Respectability*, chap. 4.

167. Unfortunately, in many studies of Marryshow his significant racial consciousness and its connection to his reform efforts in the West Indies have been overlooked. For instance, Emmanuel in his study of Grenada claims that a 1931 editorial by Marryshow

contrasted with his "previous emphasis on the notion of racial harmony." In this editorial Marryshow asserted West Indians "must be prepared to see 'black' in season and out
of season. . . . we must see the good in our own people and worship race as a religion.
. . . We should no more desire to be black Englishmen than Englishmen desire to be . . .
white negroes." "Along Life's Way," *WI*, 31 March 1931, cited in Emmanuel, *Crown Colony
Politics*, 91. However, as noted, Marryshow's racial consciousness was present in the 1910s
and 1920s too in his work for the *West Indian* and in *Cycles of Civilisation*. In a tone similar
to Emmanuel's, Surjit Mansingh's study "Background to Failure" notes that such a quote
by Marryshow was limited, as he "did not dwell on matters of race, but took up the cause
of West Indian labor's forming trade unions and demanding less unfavorable legislation"
(173–74). This depiction of Marryshow also tries to find some sort of clear divide between
Marryshow's racial and transracial activism when in fact they seemingly coexisted for the
bulk of his life. Particularly distressing is the notion that somehow his role in the labor
movements precluded a racial consciousness or commitment to racial uplift, especially
since the vast majority of the West Indian working class were black, and many of them
and their leaders held a stout racial consciousness throughout much of the first half of the
twentieth century.

168. It is imperative to acknowledge the variety of approaches and tactics employed
by black activists in the fight against white supremacy and for self-determination. For
instance, black internationalists collaborated with and supported the struggles of various
other colonial peoples who suffered similarly under white domination. Nevertheless, a
shared antiracist agenda did not necessarily diminish or preclude the racial consciousness
of such black activists. As noted, black nationalism and internationalism were not mutually exclusive, with some activists advocating or participating in both simultaneously at
times.

169. Winston James in "Wings of Ethiopia," 124–25, notes that United States corporate
interests in the Americas in this era--locales in the Hispanophone Caribbean, Central
America, and South America—preferred English-speaking laborers, a demand the British
Caribbean population largely filled. West Indians were also able, as "subjects" of the British
Empire, to migrate to regions of Africa and Europe.

170. Ibid., 123.

171. See for instance Putnam, *Radical Moves*.

172. Such recollections are abundant in memoirs of West Indian immigrants of this era.
For especially good overviews of these events, see W. James, *Banner of Ethiopia*, chaps. 3–4.

173. The regionalization and racialization of Caribbean immigrants was not confined
to the British Caribbean migrant experience. Such events can also be seen in other areas
of the Caribbean. However, scholars such as Winston James have noted distinctions between Hispanic and non-Hispanic Caribbeans, arguing the latter were much more likely
to embrace black diaspora politics, and noting stronger cross-racial nationalisms in the
Hispanic Caribbean than in the British, French, Dutch, and Danish Caribbean. See James,
Banner of Ethiopia, 108; also, for additional discussion of this issue, see James's comparison
of these Caribbean areas, and of Arturo Schomburg and Jesús Colón, in chaps. 4, 7.

174. Parascandola, *Look for Me*, 4.

175. Domingo, "The Tropics in New York," 648. Domingo himself was an immigrant
who, throughout his long career as one of the most important Black Marxist intellec-

tuals and activists, participated in various Jamaican, West Indian, and black diaspora organizations.

176. See Watkins-Owens, *Blood Relations*, chaps. 4–5.

177. Ibid., 73–74.

178. Difficulties between African Americans and West Indians included economic competition as well as different political strategies and philosophies. For instance, in *Holding Aloft the Banner of Ethiopia*, Winston James convincingly details the disproportionate overrepresentation of West Indians within black radical politics of this era, but he dismisses simplistic portrayals of African Americans as overwhelmingly conservative and West Indians as radical. For a contemporary account of these divisions, see Domingo, "The Tropics in New York," 648–50. Domingo notes many issues and misunderstandings between African Americans and West Indians, but he argues that such divisions can also be found within subsections of Harlem's black community. For instance, while some African Americans claimed Garvey represented all West Indian opinions on how to solve race problems, Domingo responded that Garvey no more represented all West Indians than the NAACP did all African Americans. His point was especially poignant given the internal divisions among African Americans in this era, as well as the fact that many of Garvey's most critical opponents were themselves West Indians, including many fellow Jamaicans.

179. Harrison, *When Africa Awakes*, 40. Similar calls are found throughout his numerous writings. For recent and extensive studies of Harrison, see J. Perry, *Hubert Harrison*; J. Perry, *Hubert Harrison Reader*; J. Perry, "Introduction"; W. James, *Banner of Ethiopia*, chap. 5. Other useful collections of his writings are in Harrison, *When Africa Awakes*; Parascandola, *Look for Me*, 131–62.

180. For helpful overviews of Briggs, the *Crusader*, and the African Blood Brotherhood, see Hill, *Crusader*, 1: v–lxxiii; W. James, *Banner of Ethiopia*, chap. 5; Makalani, *Cause of Freedom*, chap. 3; Parascandola, *Look for Me*, 199–226. Unless otherwise noted, all subsequent citations from the *Crusader* are taken from Hill's three-volume collection of this magazine, although I use the original publication dates and page numbers.

181. "Race Catechism," *Crusader*, September 1918, 11.

182. "Sowing Dissension," *Crusader*, September 1918, 30–31.

183. "West Indian and American Negroes," *NYAN*, 28 February 1923, 2; "No West Indian Problem," NYAN, 4 April 1923, 1. The presentations of Chandler Owen and W. A. Domingo took place around the same time that their working relationship on the *Messenger* dissolved, with Domingo quitting over a supposed anti–West Indian bias by the periodical's editors, Owen and A. Philip Randolph. See the *Messenger*, March 1923.

184. "All for One—One for All," *WIA*, 15 October 1927, 6.

185. "The Black Man's Burden," *Crusader*, October 1918, 9–10; "The African Knows," *Crusader*, October 1919; "V.P.M. Langston," *Crusader*, July 1920, 30.

186. For example, the *Negro World* ran Hubert Harrison's column "West Indian News Notes" from 1920 to 1922. J. Perry, *Hubert Harrison Reader*, 234. In the *Messenger*, popular historian J. A. Rogers, a Jamaican immigrant in Harlem, penned a series of articles on political, social, and economic conditions titled "The West Indies" (September 1922, 483–85; October 1922, 506–8; November 1922, 526–28) and "The Future of West Indians" (December 1922, 543–45).

187. Marcus Garvey and the UNIA have spawned numerous studies over the years,

for example Martin, *Race First*; Hill, *Papers*; Garvey, *Philosophy and Opinions*; R. Lewis, *Marcus Garvey*; Stein, *World of Marcus Garvey*. Additional studies that look at the role of the UNIA beyond Harlem, including more regional and local studies, as well as studies of other leaders within the UNIA, include Martin, *Pan-African Connection*; Lewis and Bryan, *Garvey: His Work and Impact*; Taylor, *Veiled Garvey*; Harold, *Garvey Movement in the Urban South*.

188. For an example of Garvey's supposed disinterest in Caribbean federation, see Mansingh, "Background to Failure," 218. Here Mansingh claims that Garvey "was more concerned with the fate of the entire Negro race and its connection with Africa than he was with the West Indies. The idea of federating the British Caribbean as a possible solution to some of the problems of the Negro in the Western Hemisphere did not seem to have occurred to him."

189. Garvey, *Philosophy and Opinions*, 53.

190. Hill, "First England Years," 47.

191. "The British West Indies in the Mirror of Civilization," *African Times and Orient Review*, October 1913, in Clarke, *Marcus Garvey*, 82. Such an idea predates but is seemingly connected to T. A. Marryshow's view of federation and the rise and fall of nations throughout history.

192. Garvey argued that a federation would give the West Indies a greater voice and representation within the empire, particularly among colonial officials in London. He opposed the recent federal proposal by Gideon Murray and maintained that Jamaica and British Honduras should be included because "if the people of the West Indies are to reach out to a higher destiny they must all move together." "West Indian Federation," *Gleaner*, 26 August 1914, quoted in Hill, *Papers*, 50–51.

193. Martin, *Pan-African Connection*, 61, 115–16.

194. "Summary of the Program and Aims of the African Blood Brotherhood," in Hill, *Crusader*, 1: lxvii. The ABB's objectives led them to seek a federation of all black diaspora organizations in the early 1920s. The ABB were particularly interested in joining with the UNIA, but Garvey rejected their efforts. On this failed proposal, see Stephens, *Black Empire*, 116–25. As the ABB embraced revolutionary socialism, its members became some of the chief critics of Garvey's black nationalism.

195. "Aims of the Crusader," *Crusader*, September 1918, 4.

196. "Crown Colony Government in the West Indies," *Crusader*, October 1919, 19; "British Seditious Laws," *Crusader*, July 1920, 22.

197. "A Race of Cry Babies," *Crusader*, December 1920, 9.

198. "The Fight for Freedom," *Crusader*, October 1919, 16.

199. While this editorial does not note the particular group, it is quite possible that the ABB correctly ascertained their objectives, given the presence of pan-African activism in Dominica, including the activities of J. R. Ralph Casimir and local UNIA branches. See Martin, *Pan-African Connection*; Martin, "Pan-Africanist in Dominica."

200. W. James, "Black Experience," 347.

201. For a helpful overview of the black experience in Britain at this time, see W. James, "Black Experience," 347–62.

202. Quoted in Elkins, "Hercules," 55. Also see W. James, "Black Experience," 358–60.

203. It is not the intent of this study to provide overviews for each of these historical meetings. For summaries see Geiss, *Pan-African Movement*, chaps. 11, 13.

204. D. Lewis, *W.E.B. DuBois: A Reader*, 640.

205. "Resolution Passed by Pan-African Congress," 26 August 1927, 8; D. Lewis, *W.E.B. DuBois: A Reader*, 674. The request to "begin" a movement for Caribbean federation demonstrates how some participants seemingly (and surprisingly) ignored the movements for federation ongoing for some time within the West Indies, as well as in New York where this Pan-African Congress convened.

206. J. Perry, *Hubert Harrison Reader*, 234.

207. "The Rise of the West Indian," *Crisis*, September 1920, 214–15; DuBois, "The Negro Mind Reaches Out," 401.

208. "Statement at the Congress of the League Against Imperialism and for National Independence, Brussels, February 1927," in Turner and Turner, *Richard B. Moore*, 143–46. Originally published as "Proceedings of the Congress," *Crisis*, July 1927, 126–30.

209. "A Federated West Indies," *Negro Champion*, 8 August 1928, 12.

210. "Demand Federated West Indies," *Liberator*, 7 December 1929, 4.

211. For examples of Black Marxists' focus on class and race issues, see Robinson, *Black Marxism*; Naison, *Communists in Harlem*; Solomon, *The Cry Was Unity*; Kelley, *Hammer and Hoe*.

212. "West Indians are Organizing in Harlem," *PC*, 21 January 1928, 4; "Purposes of Island Committee Told," *NYAN*, 1 February 1928, 2; "West Indians Hold Harlem Mass Meet," *PC*, 4 February 1928, 8. In Watkins-Owens, *Blood Relations*, 82, the WICA is labeled incorrectly as the West Indian Committee. It is apparent, however, that these are the same organizations. On the matter of naturalization, some likely believed one of the advantages of American citizenship would be the right to vote, which provided some voice in the formal political systems under which their communities resided. For an excellent discussion on the issue of naturalization among West Indians at this time, see *Blood Relations*, chap. 5.

213. "West Indian Tells 'Why I Cannot Become Americanized,'" *PC*, 9 July 1927, 2; "Segregation Race's Greatest Menace Says West Indian Writer," *PC*, 23 July 1927, A7; "West Indian Quotes Harvard Authority—'Jamaica Has Solved Race Problem,'" *PC*, 30 July 1927, 5; "Malliet Closes, Still Crying 'I Cannot Become Americanized,'" *PC*, 13 August 1927, 5. On the West Indian presence in the United States, see also Malliet's earlier article "Some Prominent West Indians."

214. Malliet, *Destiny of the West Indies*, 2.

215. Ibid., 8–15.

216. Ibid., 20.

217. Ibid., 14–15.

Chapter 2. Moving Toward the Crossroads of Our Destiny: Black Diaspora Politics and the Pursuit of West Indian Nationhood, 1930–1945

1. For a brief discussion of these acts and the growth of the British Commonwealth, see McIntyre, *British Decolonization*, chap. 1; Kitchen, *Empire and Commonwealth*.

2. On the rise of antiblack legislation aimed at West Indian workers in the circum-Caribbean in the 1920s and 1930s, the impact on West Indian communities in these areas, and Afro-Caribbean reactions, see Putnam, *Radical Moves*, chap. 3.

3. Given the rise of these political parties, many scholars have proposed the late 1930s as the genesis of West Indian nationalist movements, though this ignores the extensive activism in the late nineteenth and early twentieth century.

4. Wallace, *The British Caribbean*, 93.

5. Mordecai, *Federation*, 22; Mansingh, "Background to Failure," 18; Richards, "Race, Labour, and Politics," 512.

6. CUC, *Report,* iv–v.

7. Cipriani proved to be one of the major figures of the conference, and despite being a "white man," he was already well established as a leader who had "given his life to the cause of West Indian Nationalism and to the work of uplifting the lower classes of the West Indies." *Proceedings . . . at Roseau*, 20. Marryshow was unable to attend, as he was in London with a delegation making similar pleas directly to the Crown, but was in full support of the Roseau Conference and in communication with those in attendance and others (in and beyond the region).

8. *Proceedings . . . at Roseau*, 9–17; "Conference Considers Federation Desirable," *Voice of St. Lucia*, 1 November 1932, 2. Interestingly, Jamaica was not included in this specific call for a federation, nor was British Guiana. As detailed in chapter 1 and later here, Jamaica's place within a federation of Eastern Caribbean islands was a commonly debated topic. Nonetheless, delegates did leave the door open for this and other West Indian colonies to join later.

9. *Proceedings . . . at Roseau*, 2.

10. Ibid., 19.

11. "West Indies Demand Advance to Self-Government," *New Daily Chronicle*, 1 November 1932, 8.

12. "Minutes of Proceedings of the West Indian Conference held at Roseau, Dominica," CO 318/411/6, PRO.

13. CUC, *Report*, iv–vi.

14. CUC, *Report*; "West Indies: Closer Union Proposals," *London Times*, 19 August 1933, 7; Wallace, *The British Caribbean*, 94–95.

15. Luke Memo, 31 January 1933, CO 318/411/6, PRO.

16. Lockhart to CUC, 22 December 1932, CO 318/411/6, PRO.

17. Ibid.

18. Ibid. Throughout this memo, Lockhart's use of "West Indians" appears primarily associated with the Afro-Caribbean majorities.

19. Ibid.

20. Campbell to Beckett, 24 December 1932, CO 318/411/6, PRO.

21. W. James, *Banner of Ethiopia*, 12; Parker, "'Capital of the Caribbean,'" 98–99, and *Brother's Keeper*, esp. chap. 1. Though Parker's work emphasizes these connections in the late 1930s and 1940s, this support existed in the early 1930s and prior decades too.

22. Though the NAACP expanded its diasporic focus later in the decade, coverage of the Caribbean could be found regularly in the "Foreign News" or "Along the Color Line" sections of the *Crisis* in earlier years.

23. "Marryshow," *Crisis*, November 1932, 251; "Conference," *Crisis*, January 1933, 19.

24. Dominica Taxpayers' Reform Association to W.E.B. DuBois, 21 April 1933, DuBois Papers, UMass.

25. One of the most comprehensive reviews of Black Communist activities in Harlem is Naison, *Communists in Harlem.*

26. "World Aspects of the Negro Question," *Communist*, February 1930. For further information on the career of Otto Huiswoud, see J. Turner, *Caribbean Crusaders.*

27. "Imperialism in the West Indies," *Negro Worker*, January 1931, 16–20.

28. "'Negro Worker' Banned by Imperialists," *Negro Worker*, 15 June 1932, 14–15.

29. Despite restrictive immigration quotas that saw a dramatic decrease in immigration from the West Indies after 1924, West Indian immigration to the United States continued with some arriving under the "British quota." Kasinitz, *Caribbean New York*, 24.

30. Studies that do include brief mention of Petioni include Turner and Turner, *Richard B. Moore*; W. James, *Banner of Ethiopia*; Martin, "Eric Williams." My noting of a minor mention is in no way intended to dismiss the importance of these excellent works, as Petioni is not the focus of their specific studies.

31. "Civic Leader Sparked Many Local Drives," *NYAN*, 20 October 1951, 1; Obituaries, *Journal of the National Medical Association*, January 1952, 74; Gilbert Holliday (British Consulate General, NY) to George Middleton (British Embassy, Washington, DC), 9 May 1945, CO 968/121/4, PRO; Watkins-Owens, *Blood Relations*, 50.

32. "Dr. Petioni Quits Post Under Fire," *NYAN*, 26 February 1930, 1; "North Harlem Medical Society," *NYAN*, 28 May 1930, 2; "Petioni New Leader of Howard Doctors," *NYAN*, 10 January 1934, 16.

33. "Civic Leader Sparked Many Local Drives," *NYAN*, 20 October 1951, 1; "West Indians Hold Harlem Mass Meet," *PC*, 4 February 1928, 8.

34. Though it can be problematic to assume that the opinions of one member of an organization speak for the entire group, the opinions of Petioni, who is mentioned as speaking on behalf of the CU in the vast majority of the limited sources on the group, make this less treacherous.

35. "Caribbean Union Scope Enlarged," *NYAN*, 13 June 1936, 3. Though this article was written six years after the CU's founding, Petioni is clearly describing the current goals of the union, before moving on to suggest an expansion of these goals. As for naturalization, it was not pushed for all West Indians, but rather for those West Indians who intended to make the United States their home.

36. "Groups Seek Jobs in N. Y. Subway," *CD*, 23 July 1932, 13.

37. "Physician Urges All to Register On Time," *NYAN*, 4 October 1933, 4. In regard to potential political power, in August 1936 Petioni noted that some local political offices "which could have been won . . . if there had been united action were lost to the race" because of intra-racial jealousy. "Urges Closer Link Between Negro Groups," *NYAN*, 29 August 1936, 2.

38. West Indies National Council—Subversive Activities in the West Indies (FBI Report), 23 May 1944, box 1, folder 5 (WINC), WINC Collection, SC.

39. "Better Times in the West Indies," *NYAN*, 28 September 1935, 2A.

40. "Black Man's Paradise," *NYAN*, 5 October 1935, 2A.

41. "West Indian Group Launches Program," *NYAN*, 5 July 1933, 2; "West Indian Federation," *Crisis*, September 1933, 211. The extended quote is from the *Crisis* article. Interestingly, in the last line "group" is singular, further indicating a sense of racial unity between African Americans and Afro-Caribbeans.

42. Such meetings would not have seemed odd to African Americans, who had a long history of celebrating their own emancipation, including the anniversary of the Emancipation Proclamation on New Year's Day or Juneteenth in some areas of the country. Emancipation celebrations were also common in the British West Indies, and remain so to this day. For an example of the political uses of "golden jubilee" (1888) in Jamaica, see D. Thomas, *Modern Blackness*, chap. 1. On emancipation celebrations, see Brereton, "Birthday of Our Race"; Brereton, "Jubilees"; Higman, "Remembering Slavery." In all of these settings, it was common for participants to celebrate how far the race had come, assess where they stood presently, and establish plans for the near future.

43. "Judge Urges Group Amity," *NYAN*, 9 August 1933, 2. The organizers use 1834 as the date of emancipation, rather than the final abolition of slavery in 1838.

44. "Significant Event," *NYAN*, 11 August 1934, 8.

45. "To Celebrate Emancipation," *NYAN*, 28 July 1934, 2; "Emancipation Anniversary Observed by West Indians," *CD*, 11 August 1934, 13.

46. "100 Years of Freedom," *NYAN*, 18 August 1934, 8.

47. "Nationalistic Spirit Seen as Basic Need of the West Indies by American Federation," *NYAN*, 8 November 1933, 1.

48. "Indies Report Will Be Discussed Here," *NYAN*, 16 June 1934, 6.

49. "New Deal in B.W.I. Sought," *NYAN*, 4 August 1934, 16. It does not appear such an organization or congress was ever formally created.

50. For example, see Yelvington, "War in Ethiopia and Trinidad," 190.

51. On the long history of Ethiopia as a site of significant importance among black peoples in the diaspora, see Gebrekidan, *Bond Without Blood*.

52. As Kevin Yelvington argues in "War in Ethiopia and Trinidad," 189–90, scholars should not assume there was simply a preexisting "black consciousness" waiting to be awakened. While the Italian invasion of Ethiopia may have increased such a consciousness among those who already professed to hold it, the invasion also helped create and define black racial consciousness in these years.

53. Gebrekidan, *Bond Without Blood*, 51.

54. "My Husband's Back to Africa Idea Was Right," *DG*, 15 October 1935, 17.

55. Resolutions Passed by the Friends of Ethiopia [St. Lucia], 31 July 1935, CO 318/418/4, PRO.

56. Resolution of Universal Negro Improvement Association and African Communities League, 31 July 1935, CO 318/418/4, PRO.

57. A. E. James to Colonial Secretary, 9 August 1935, CO 318/418/4, PRO.

58. Weisbord, "British West Indian Reaction," 34.

59. Casimir to Dr. Azaj Martin, 17 October 1935, Box 1-Folder 13, Casimir Papers, SC.

60. Petition of Loyal Coloured Jamaicans to the Secretary of State for the Colonies, 8 October 1935, CO 318/418/4, PRO.

61. Resolution of the Spanish Town Branch of the UNIA, 9 October 1935, CO 318/418/4, PRO.

62. Petition of the Kingston Division of the UNIA to King George V, October 1935, CO 318/418/4, PRO.

63. Governor (Jamaica) to Secretary of State for the Colonies, 3 November 1935, CO 318/418/4, PRO.

64. Extract from S. O. letter to H. H. Beckett, 16 October 1935, CO 318/418/4, PRO.

65. Extract from S. O. letter to Sir C. Parkinson from Sir S. Grier, 26 October 1935, CO 318/418/4, PRO.

66. Telegram, Governor of British Guiana to Secretary of State for the Colonies, 17 October 1935, CO 318/418/4, PRO; Telegram, Governor of British Guiana to Secretary of State for the Colonies, 23 October 1935, CO 318/418/4, PRO.

67. Telegram, Governor of Windward Islands to Secretary of State for the Colonies, 26 October 1935, CO 318/418/4, PRO.

68. Acting Governor (Leeward Islands, Antigua) to Secretary of State for the Colonies, 26 October 1935, CO 318/414/4.

69. J. L. Maffey to Secretary (Admiralty), 29 October 1935, CO 318/418/4, PRO.

70. For an overview and key example of black newspaper coverage of these events, see Muhammad, "What Is Africa to Us?" chap. 5.

71. "Ethiopia and World Politics," *Crisis*, May 1935, 138–39, 156–57.

72. The historiography on African American reactions to the invasion of Ethiopia is rich. See for example W. Scott, *Sons of Sheba's Race*; J. Harris, *African-American Reactions*; Meriwether, *Proudly We Can Be Africans*, chap. 1.

73. "West Indians to Aim at England's Aid to Ethiopia," *AA*, 27 July 1935, 16; "Britishers in N. Y. Rap Embargo on Arms to Ethiopia," *AA*, 3 August 1935, 12.

74. "Will March Today Protesting War in Ethiopia," *NYAN*, 3 August 1935, 3. Of course, it is important to note that support for Ethiopia was not confined to black communities. In the march mentioned in this article, organizers hoped to symbolically organize black and Italian workers in protest of Mussolini's action. As Penny Von Eschen notes in her study of African American anticolonialism, *Race Against Empire*, communists such as those in the Provisional Committee for the Defense of Ethiopia "attempted to redirect antiwhite sentiment toward a critique of fascism" (11). This does not, however, preclude the leading role of race in cementing much of the action by African Americans and West Indians.

75. "Two Groups Hit England's Move," *NYAN*, 4 July 1936, 1.

76. For a discussion of London's black diaspora politics in the 1930s, see Adi, *West Africans in Britain*, chap. 3; Matera, "Black Intellectuals"; Matera, "Black Internationalism"; Makalani, *Cause of Freedom*, chap. 7.

77. Radical black activists sometimes chastised Moody and the LCP for this limited agenda, especially those involved in Marxist organizations that focused on revolutionary change. Moody was even labeled an Uncle Tom in 1933 in the *Negro Worker*. Nonetheless, there was some conversation and cooperation between them. See Killingray, "'To Do Something for the Race,'" 51. Killingray's is one of the best recent studies of Moody and the LCP. Also see Rush, "Imperial Identity in Colonial Minds."

78. As Imanuel Geiss notes in his classic study *The Pan-African Movement*, to Moody "'coloured' was to a large extent synonymous with 'negro'" (344).

79. Ann Rush notes in *Bonds of Empire*, "From the outset [Moody] made it clear that the organization would be run by people of color, and throughout its existence there were no white members included in its executive committee" (105). While true, her use of the general term "people of color" diminishes the leadership and dominant focus on people of African descent. For a brief discussion of internal LCP debates over the focus on Africa and the African diaspora, see ibid., 109–10.

292 · Notes to Pages 99–103

80. "League of Coloured Peoples—Seventh Annual Report (Year 1937–38) as presented to the Seventh Annual General Meeting," 11 March 1938, CO 3108/432/2, PRO.

81. Adi, *West Africans in Britain*, 67–70.

82. J. M. Kenyatta, "Hands Off Abyssinia," *Labour Monthly*, September 1935, 532, as quoted in Makalani, *Cause of Freedom*, 203. For a discussion of the IAFE and the subsequent development of connected black diaspora movements in London, see *Cause of Freedom*, 197–210.

83. On Afro-Caribbeans and the issue of British citizenship, see Putnam, "Citizenship from the Margins." On Afro-Caribbean views of themselves as British citizens, antiblack immigration legislation in the circum-Caribbean, and the responses (or lack thereof) by the empire, see Putnam, *Radical Moves*, chaps. 3, 6; Chambers, *Race, Nation, and West Indian Immigration*, chaps. 5–6.

84. Fraser, "Twilight of Colonial Rule." In view of these developments, some historians of the British Caribbean have identified this era as the genesis of West Indian nationalist movements—some islandist, some regionalist—that would lead these colonies to independence in the 1960s and beyond. Given the prior creation of various labor organizations, as well as both islandist and regionalist political movements, it is perhaps more correct to designate the new groups as the continuation of prior nationalist movements. Yet it would be equally problematic to dismiss the importance of these rebellions as a key moment within West Indian political development in the colonies and within the ever-expanding black diaspora politics (including direct links between black diaspora activism and both island and regional political movements).

85. Given the rich historiography of these labor rebellions, this chapter does not offer extensive coverage of the events themselves. Among the best and most extensive studies are works of O. Nigel Bolland; see for instance *On the March*, esp. chap. 5, and *Politics of Labour*. W. Arthur Lewis produced one of the most substantial contemporary studies, *Labour in the West Indies*. Official inquiries include Orde Browne, *Labour Conditions*; CO, *West India Royal Commission Report*.

86. In Trinidad there were various political movements associated with labor. By 1937 they included Cipriani's Trinidad Labour Party (which by this era proved more focused on politics than labor), Uriah Butler's Negro Welfare Cultural and Social Association, and Adrian Cola Rienzi's Oilfield Workers Trade Union. Butler and Rienzi undoubtedly worked together and in support of each other at times, but this alone did not equate to the removal of race as an important dimension of these rebellions. On Trinidadian labor movements in this era, see Basdeo, *Labour Organisation and Labour Reform*; Brereton, *Modern Trinidad*; K. Singh, *Race and Class*; R. Thomas, *Trinidad Labour Riots*. For a personal reflection on race and racial tensions within Trinidad in this era, see Gomes, *Through a Maze of Colour*, 151–87.

87. "Our Aims," *Negro Worker*, January 1937.

88. See, for instance, *Negro Worker*, January 1937.

89. "1937—A New Year of Struggle for West Indian Masses," *Negro Worker*, March 1937, 10–11.

90. "West Indians to Celebrate with Affair," *NYAN*, 31 July 1937, 5.

91. While the JPL is mentioned in many accounts of both black diaspora and West Indian activism in this era, a definitive history of the group remains absent from the his-

toriography. However, the work of historian Birte Timm should soon fill this void. For a sample of her work on the JPL, see "Caribbean Leaven" and "Transnational Roots."

92. "Declaration" in W. A. Roberts, *Self-Government for Jamaica*, located in MS 353, box 20, Roberts Papers, NLJ.

93. Timm, "Caribbean Leaven," 88–89, 91; Dalleo, "Public Sphere," 58.

94. Jamaicans are indeed considered West Indian, and an organization such as the JPL is technically a "transnational West Indian organization." However, as I have tried to do throughout this study, I reserve the term "transnational West Indian [organization(s) or activist(s)]" for those embracing a regional identification over island (colony-specific) identifications.

95. This was especially the case for Brown and Domingo, both of whom were already well known and highly regarded for their long-standing regional (West Indian) and diaspora activism prior to the founding of the JPL and continuing through much of its existence.

96. Domingo to Editors, *Negro Worker*, January 1937, 15.

97. For examples of JPL demands on these issues, see W. A. Roberts, *Self-Government for Jamaica*; O'Meally, *Why We Demand Self-Government*.

98. Timm, "Transnational Roots," 98, 423.

99. On Domingo and other JPL members, see Domingo to Arnett, 24 January 1941, 4/60/2a/2, Manley Papers, JA; "Jamaicans Hold Meet in Boston," *CD*, 12 June 1943, 6.

100. Turner and Turner, *Richard B. Moore*, 73–74. The Manhattan Council of the New York State Federation of Councils, a special committee of the National Negro Congress, organized a similarly named American–West Indian Defense Committee. This group appears to have had much the same focus as the WIDC, even hosting speakers from the Caribbean, but should not be assumed to be the same organization. For an example of the confusion between these groups, see "To Banquet Editor," *NYAN*, 18 June 1938, 5; "Harlem West Indians Hear Militant Newspaper Editor," 25 June 1938, 11; "Correction," *NYAN*, 2 July 1938, 5.

101. "Display Ad No.4," *NYAN*, 30 October 1937, 2.

102. "Had to Murder," *NYAN*, 4 December 1937, 23. Richard B. Moore, representing the Scottsboro Defense Committee, Charles A. Petioni of the Caribbean Union, and Hope Stevens were among the speakers. Moore and Stevens were also members of the WIDC.

103. For Crawford's recollection of these meetings, see Marshall, *I Speak for the People*, 57–74. For subsequent recollections by WIDC members themselves, see "Prime Minister Adams' Address in New York," *West Indian News Service*, 26 October 1959, and "An Open Letter to the London Sunday Observer on its Profile of Sir Grantley Adams," 22 May 1959, box 10, folder 2, Moore Papers, SC.

104. See, for example, "Labour Unrest in the Colonies," *Keys*, October–December 1937, 45.

105. League of Coloured Peoples—Seventh Annual Report (Year 1937–38) as presented to the Seventh Annual General Meeting, 11 March 1938, CO 3108/432/2, PRO.

106. Resolution of the LCP on Jamaican Disturbances, 17 June 1938, CO 318/435/2, PRO.

107. Not surprisingly, among the initial meetings that established the IASB in April 1937 was one with African American activists in London, including black radical Max Yergan,

a leader within the National Negro Congress who had just established the International Committee on African Affairs with Paul Robeson. Yergan's and Robeson's group was later renamed the Council on African Affairs. Makalani, *Cause of Freedom*, 212.

108. IASB pamphlet, "The International African Service Bureau—for the Defence of Africans and Peoples of African Descent," n.d., MEPO 38/91, PRO.

109. Ibid.

110. "Our Policy," *African Sentinel*, October–November 1937, 1.

111. IASB pamphlet, "The International African Service Bureau—for the Defence of Africans and Peoples of African Descent," n.d., MEPO 38/91, PRO. The breakdown of membership categories is especially interesting because while the IASB was representative of a broad anticolonial movement that embraced all of the colonial struggles of the era, the reservation of "active membership" for "black peoples" speaks to its particular race-conscious focus. As will be shown, the anticolonial struggle often consisted of transracial cooperation, but one cannot dismiss the racial focus of these organizations either.

112. See for instance "Labour Unrest in the West Indies," *Africa and the World*, 27 July 1937, 9; "Strikes in West Indies," *Africa and the World*, 14 August 1937, 7; "Stemming the Tide," *African Sentinel*, October–November 1937, 10; special West Indian edition of *Africa and the World*, 1 September 1937, 1–13; "Facing the New Year—The West Indies," *IAO*, February–March 1939, 1. All of these periodicals were associated with the IASB.

113. "An Open Letter to the Workers of the West Indies and British Guiana," 1938, MEPO 38/91, PRO.

114. These investigations occurred on specific colonies and for the region as a whole. On individual colonies, see *Report of . . . Disturbances . . . in Barbados*; CO, *Trinidad and Tobago Disturbances, 1937*. For regional coverage, see Orde Browne, *Labour Conditions*.

115. CO, *West India Royal Commission*, xiii.

116. Fraser, "Twilight of Colonial Rule," 16.

117. La Guerre, "Moyne Commission," 135.

118. Ibid., 134–35.

119. See for instance the views of the Jamaica Imperial Association in ibid., 141.

120. Such opinions were obviously shaped by racist beliefs of white, and even some "coloured," residents of the West Indies. See for example A. E. Jeffrey to T.I.K. Lloyd, 11 October 1938, ICS 56/16, Moyne Papers, ICS; Domingo, "Fallacious Arguments Against Autonomy," *Public Opinion*, 7 January 1939, and "What Path Shall We Take," *Public Opinion*, 4 February 1939, in 4/60/2a/2, Manley Papers, JA.

121. No. 907 Memo by the Indian Evidence Committee on matters pertaining to the welfare of East Indians, n.d., ICS 56/44, Moyne Papers, ICS; Memorandum of the British Guiana East Indian Association to the Royal Commission, n.d. [1938–39]; Testimony of Maha Sabha and East Indian Association to Fifteenth Session of Moyne Commission held at Georgetown, British Guiana, 13 February 1939; Testimony of East Indian National Union (Jamaica), 30 November 1938, CO 950/673, PRO.

122. Memorandum on the need for Agricultural and Industrial Education submitted to the Commission to the West Indies by the Negro Progress Convention of British Guiana, n.d.; Transcript of Negro Progress Convention testimony to Moyne Commission, 7 February 1939, CO 950/667, PRO.

123. No. 906 Memo by elected members of the [Trinidad] legislative council on con-

stitutional reform, 20 January 1939, ICS 56/43, Moyne Papers, ICS. John La Guerre has noted that Trinidadian testimonies, in comparison with other colonies, "were far more concerned with political questions" ("Moyne Commission," 141–45).

124. No. 902 Memo by "The West Indian Pilot" official organ of the Trade Union Movement in Trinidad & Tobago on social, economic, and political conditions in the colony, n.d. [1939], ICS 56/39, Moyne Papers, ICS; West Indian Pilot Memo to Moyne Commission, n.d. [1939], CO 950/802, PRO.

125. La Guerre, "Moyne Commission," 145; No. 914 Memo by Committee for Industrial Organisation on Political, Social, and Economic Conditions, 24 January 1939, ICS 56/51, Moyne Papers, ICS; No. 892 Memo by [British] Guiana and West Indies Labour Congress on the Social, Political, and Economic Welfare of the British West Indies and Guiana, 17 January 1939, ICS 56/34, Moyne Papers, ICS. As noted in chapter 1, the BGWILC had issued a call for federation in 1926, and continued to support this goal in the 1930s.

126. There were also doubts within the region on what the Moyne Commission would be willing or able to do to better the conditions of the region. See for instance Oswald E. Anderson [Mayor of Kingston, Jamaica] to Harold Moody, 5 July 1938, CO 318/435/2, PRO.

127. Interestingly, the IASB noted a similar reservation about the Simon Commission to India in 1932 because it did not include an Indian. In drawing this comparison, it is important to note that the IASB obviously felt an Afro-Caribbean would best represent the region, further demonstrating their views of the West Indies as part of the black diaspora and the prioritization of Afro-Caribbean welfare within the region. "The West Indian Royal Commission," *IAO*, August 1938, 1.

128. "The West Indian Royal Commission," *IAO*, August 1938, 2.

129. "Barbados," *IAO*, February–March 1939, 9.

130. Domingo, "Fallacious Arguments Against Autonomy," *Public Opinion*, 7 January 1939, in 4/60/2a/2, Manley Papers, JA. Domingo's mention of Haiti is important. It relates directly to the ways in which the existence of Haiti had been used by many whites as "proof" that black peoples cannot rule themselves, and to discourage self-government for the British West Indies. However, like many black activists, Domingo looked to Haiti with pride and defended Haitians, who he claimed had been doing well in the face of great opposition from white countries since Haiti's creation. Also see Domingo, "What Path Shall We Take," *Public Opinion*, 4 February 1939, in 4/60/2a/2, Manley Papers, JA.

131. The League of Coloured Peoples proved to be one of the more resolute groups in claiming a mandate to represent "our people both in the West Indies and Africa" based upon letters and telegrams of support from both regions. See for example *LCPN* no. 3 (December 1939): 1; Copy of Cablegrams Sent to Dr. Moody from Jamaica, August 1938, CO 318/435/2 (among them telegrams from the Bustamante Labour Union, Jamaica United Barbers and Hairdressers Association, Union of Teachers, and Jamaica Progressive League). While some within the Colonial Office doubted the LCP held such a mandate, it was increasingly recognized as such in the late 1930s and into the 1940s. See Harold Moody to Rt. Hon. Lord Lloyd of Dolobran, 21 May 1940; Internal CO Memo, 10 June 1940, CO 318/445/47; "Extract from the President's Address to the A.G.M.," *LCPN* no. 7 (April 1940): 5–7.

132. Memorandum on the Economic, Political and Social Conditions in the West Indies

and British Guiana Presented by the International African Service Bureau, the League of Coloured Peoples and the Negro Welfare Association, 9 September 1938, CO 950/30, PRO.

133. Ibid. For further discussion of this memo, see La Guerre, "Moyne Commission," 136–37.

134. Oral Evidence Transcript of Moody (LCP) and Mr. Blackman (NWA) before the West India Royal Commission—Ninth Session, 29 September 1938, CO 950/30, PRO.

135. For an overview of the history of the NWA in Britain, see Adi, *Pan-Africanism and Communism*, chap. 7.

136. Memorandum from the Jamaica Progressive League of New York to The Royal Commission, n.d. [1938], CO 950/73, PRO.

137. La Guerre, "Moyne Commission," 141–42.

138. Memorandum from the Jamaica Progressive League of New York to The Royal Commission, n.d. [1938], CO 950/73, PRO.

139. "Group Puts Effort Behind Foreign Born," *NYAN*, 24 July 1937, 20; UAPAD, *Memorandum*. The UAPAD memo's silence on the Indo-Caribbean population speaks further to Afro-Caribbean hegemony within Caribbean nation-building efforts, and foreshadows racial tensions between Afro- and Indo-Caribbean populations in some colonies that became more pronounced in the 1950s and beyond. However, the UAPAD's reference to the surrender of British Guiana to "another race" in this memo likely refers to emigration schemes of Europeans and others to the colony as suggested by the Crown in prior and subsequent years. These issues are addressed later.

140. "Manhood for British West Indians," *PC*, 31 December 1938, 8.

141. "New Deal in the West Indies," *NYAN*, 24 June 1939, 7.

142. CO, *West India Royal Commission, 1938–1939, Recommendations*, 25–26.

143. LCP, "Memorandum on the Recommendations of the West India Royal Commission," CO 318/445/47, PRO.

144. Citing its distance from these colonies, the LCP claimed Jamaica might have to be excluded until "better steamship services, aviation, and wireless telephony are brought into existence" (ibid.).

145. Ibid.

146. See Horne, *End of Empires*; Slate, *Colored Cosmopolitanism*; Kelley and Esch, "Black Like Mao"; Makalani, *Cause of Freedom*; Gallicchio, *African American Encounter*.

147. IASB, *The West Indies To-Day*, 42.

148. Makonnen, "A Plea for Negro Self-Government," *IAO*, February–March 1939, 14.

149. Ibid., 15.

150. As Penny Von Eschen argues in *Race Against Empire*, 33–34, perhaps it would be more appropriate to label Black America's "Double V" campaign a "Triple V" campaign, given the prominent attention of many black activists to the anticolonial struggles of colonial peoples, alongside the fight against fascism abroad and racism at home.

151. IASB, "Manifesto," n.d. [January 1940], MEPO 38/91, PRO. Similar sentiments can be found in IASB, "A Warning to the Colonial Peoples," 29 August 1939, MEPO 38/91, PRO; George Padmore, "The Second World War and the Darker Races," *Crisis*, November 1939, 327–28.

152. IASB, "Manifesto Against War," 25 September 1938, MEPO 38/91, PRO.

153. For an example of British endeavors to rally support in this era, see "West Indians

Hear War Aim," *NYAN*, 2 December 1939, 22. In this Harlem meeting the British consul general spoke on British war aims and noted Hitler's antiblack policies. Nonetheless, the article claimed, New York's West Indians knew very well that Britain had practiced similar policies toward her nonwhite subjects long before Hitler was born.

154. "West Indies Dealt Cruel Blow by War," *NYAN*, 23 September 1939, 4.

155. JPL Resolution—Passed at Mass Meeting at YMCA, 24 September 1939, JPL Collection, NLJ. As noted, the JPL focused primarily on self-government and dominion status for Jamaica, but it also supported the broader cause of West Indian liberation, and some of its members supported a Caribbean federation (though some thought Jamaica would not be a part).

156. "European War, West Indians to Be Forum Topic," *NYAN*, 21 October 1939, 13; Domingo to Campbell, 20 October 1939, 4/60/2a/2, Manley Papers, JA; "Group Opposes Colonial Aid in Imperialist War," *AA*, 4 November 1939, 7. While the use of the phrase "colored peoples of the world" could very well include all nonwhite colonial peoples, the specific mention of Africa and the West Indies appears to note a focus on black colonials.

157. Domingo to Campbell, 21 November 1939, 4/60/2a/2, Manley Papers, JA. In reference to this meeting, Domingo later noted, "I am not the least bit concerned about the outcome of the war from the standpoint of Europe or Europeans. They and their continent and civilization would sink in the ocean without evoking a tear from me, but I must think of Africa and my people. They are what count to me."

158. These debates included events on 17 December 1939, 11 February 1940, 21 April 1940, and 27 June 1940. See "Debate Support of British in War," *NYAN*, 9 December 1939, 7; Domingo to Campbell, 18 December 1939; Domingo to Campbell, 29 December 1939; Domingo to Campbell, 29 December 1939; Evidence Submitted to Advisory Committee, 21 September 1941, 4/60/2a/2, Manley Papers, JA.

159. "War and Dictatorship," *Crisis*, July 1940, 211.

160. "Grab of West Indies Bad," *NYAN*, 2 December 1939, 8; "England Might Sell West Indies to US," *NYAN*, 13 January 1940, 5.

161. "U.S. Should Buy B.W.I." *NYAN*, 6 May 1939, 10.

162. "Not For Sale!" *NYAN*, 20 May 1939, 10.

163. "Views on Many Questions," *NYAN*, 10 June 1939, 6.

164. "Protest Transfer of West Indies," *NYAN*, 30 December 1939, 2A.

165. "Debate US Rule of West Indies," *NYAN*, 27 April 1940, 3.

166. "Plan to Debate on West Indies," *NYAN*, 4 May 1940, 2; "Totten Defends Islands' Transfer," *CD*, 18 May 1940, 4; "Totten Favors Isles Transfer," *NYAN*, 18 May 1940, 6; "Ridiculous to Hold Up British Flag With One Hand, Eat Uncle Sam's Food With the Other," *PC*, 25 May 1940, 4.

167. "Asks Help Against WI," *NYAN*, 22 June 1940, 10.

168. "Views on Many Questions," *NYAN*, 27 July 1940, 10.

169. This Havana Conference, as it came to be called, was one of multiple Pan-American Conferences between foreign ministers of the Americas in the late 1930s and early 1940s.

170. Domingo, "Selling the BWI Islands," *Public Opinion*, 22 June 1940, in 4/60/2a/2, Manley Papers, JA.

171. Domingo to Campbell, 5 July 1940, 4/60/2a/2, Manley Papers, JA.

172. W. D. to Padmore, 2 August 1940, CO 137/846/10, PRO.

173. West Indies National Council—Subversive Activities in the West Indies (FBI Report), 22 September 1941, box 1, folder 5 (WINC), WINC Collection, SC.

174. Despite their differences of opinion on supporting the empire in World War II, Domingo and Moore remained allies and continued to work together, as they had for many decades. Both have claimed or been credited as the primary author of the WINEC's "Declaration." See Domingo to Campbell, 8 August 1940, 4/60/2A/2, Manley Papers, JA; Turner and Turner, *Richard B. Moore*, 75.

175. "West Indians Seek Delegate to Pan-American Confab," *PC*, 20 July 1940, 2; "Ask B.W.I. 'Home Rule,'" *NYAN*, 20 July 1940, 1. A petition from the Jamaica Progressive League, also sent to the Havana Conference, spoke to specifically Jamaican concerns. "We are unalterably opposed to any plan that would transfer Jamaica from one sovereignty to another, even though the new sovereignty be Western, or which would place that Island under a trusteeship of any sort, without negotiation with Jamaica leaders and a plebiscite to determine the wishes of the electorate." Petition lodged by the Jamaica Progressive League at the Havana Conference—To the Delegates of the Pan-American Nations in Congress Assembled at Havana, Cuba, 2 July 1940, CO 137/846/10, PRO.

176. "Views on Many Questions," *NYAN*, 27 July 1940, 10.

177. WINEC, "Declaration of Rights of the Caribbean Peoples to Self-Determination and Self-Government," 1940; WINEC, Appendix II—Evidence of the Widespread and Urgent Character of the Demands of the Caribbean Peoples for Self-Government and Self-Determination, 1940, CO 137/846/10, PRO. Birte Timm in "Transnational Roots," 259–60, credits Domingo as the primary author of the WINEC's declaration and notes that the Pan-American position espoused within it reflects prior discussions between Domingo and his JPL colleague W. Adolphe Roberts. Roberts, she claims, had long believed the West Indies should be a part of the "Pan-American family of nations" as independent nations.

178. W. D. to Padmore, 2 August 1940, CO 137/846/10, PRO. Though Domingo and other WINEC officials were quite proud of garnering Melo's support, his position was also likely shaped by Argentina's stance on the Falkland Islands, which could be affected by the Havana Act. See, for example, "Seizure of West Indies Is Advocated," *CD*, 3 August 1940, 12; "West Indians Oppose Seizure of Islands," *CD*, 10 August 1940, 1.

179. "West Indians Oppose Seizure of Islands," *CD*, 10 August 1940, 1. As Jason Parker has noted, despite the United States' recent Good Neighbor Policy, the longer history of US interventionism in the Caribbean and its "odious racial regime" still shaped many negative perspectives on US presence in the region; see *Brother's Keeper*, 28.

180. Leopoldo Melo to Ethelred Brown, 28 September 1940, box A332, folder "Labor—British West Indies, 1940–1947," NAACP Papers, LOC; W. D. to Padmore, 2 August 1940, CO 137/846/10, PRO.

181. "Seizure of West Indies Is Advocated," *CD*, 3 August 1940, 12; "West Indians Oppose Seizure of Islands," *CD*, 10 August 1940, 1.

182. WINEC to Delegates of the PNP's Annual Conference (Kingston, Jamaica), 26 August 1940, 4/60/2a/2, Manley Papers, JA.

183. Domingo to Campbell, 8 August 1940, 4/60/2A/2, Manley Papers, JA.

184. Domingo to Campbell, 8 November 1940, 4/60/2A/2, Manley Papers, JA; Domingo to Walter White, 6 November 1940, box A332, folder "Labor—British West Indies, 1940–1947," NAACP Papers, LOC. Domingo and the WINC sent their materials to various

African Americans and organizations, but it seems these three were the only ones to reply by this time.

185. Domingo to Walter White, 6 November 1940, box A332, folder "Labor—British West Indies, 1940–1947," NAACP Papers, LOC.

186. West Indies National Council—Subversive Activities in the West Indies (FBI Report), 10 November 1942, box 1, folder 5 (WINC), WINC Collection, SC. While many WINC leaders were supporters of federation, the position of WINC president Domingo is less clear. As noted, Domingo appeared to have gone back and forth on federation, depending on its proposed structure, particularly if it was to include Jamaica. Birte Timm in "Transnational Roots," 258–60, offers the provocative and thought-provoking claim that by this time (foreshadowing his more prominent anti-federation stance in the mid-1940s and beyond), Domingo was already anti-federation but was not yet outspoken about it so as not to derail his relationship with colleagues who supported the idea. She also claims that Domingo assured his JPL colleague W. Adolphe Roberts that he would not advocate a political federation through his work in the WINEC/WINC.

187. "West Indians Plan Protest," NYAN, 20 October 1934, 4.

188. "West Indians Enraged Over England's Act," NYAN, 26 November 1938, 5.

189. UAPAD, Memorandum. Once again there seems to be an absence of "East Indian" opinions within the UAPAD's stance, despite their significant numbers within British Guiana.

190. Domingo, "Jamaica Seeks Its Freedom," 371.

191. Domingo to Campbell, 8 August 1940, 4/60/2a/2, Manley Papers, JA.

192. Domingo to Campbell, 8 November 1940, 4/60/2a/2, Manley Papers, JA. Domingo was particularly critical of the "coloured" class in Jamaica, who he believed would welcome these refugees but learn later how their own claims to whiteness would actually be challenged.

193. "Self-Government," NYAN, 10 August 1940, 8.

194. Parker, Brother's Keeper, 31. Parker's reference to the Havana Declaration is synonymous with the Havana Act.

195. For an excellent discussion of US presence and goals in the region during this time, see Parker, Brother's Keeper, chaps. 1–2.

196. "WINEC to Delegates of the PNP's Annual Conference (Kingston, Jamaica)," 26 August 1940, 4/60/2a/2, Manley Papers, JA.

197. "West Indians Endorse U.S.-British Agreement," NYAN, 14 September 1940, 5.

198. For an excellent study of the presence and impact of Americans and their bases on Caribbean societies, see Neptune, Caliban and the Yankees.

199. "WINEC to Delegates of the PNP's Annual Conference (Kingston, Jamaica)," 26 August 1940, 4/60/2a/2, Manley Papers, JA; VL Arnett (Secretary, PNP) to Colonial Secretary (Jamaica), 17 September 1940, box A332, folder "Labor—British West Indies, 1940–1947," NAACP Papers, LOC.

200. W. A. Domingo (President, WINC) to Franklin D. Roosevelt (President, USA), 26 December 1940, box A332, folder "Labor—British West Indies, 1940–1947," NAACP Papers, LOC.

201. H. P. Osborne (Secretary, WINC) to Lord Moyne (Secretary of State for the Colonies), 25 January 1941, box A332, folder "Labor—British West Indies, 1940–1947," NAACP

Papers, LOC; H. P. Osborne (Secretary, WINC) to Lord Moyne (Secretary of State for the Colonies), 21 February 1941, CO 971/1/8, PRO.

202. T. A. Marryshow, Legislative Council Motion, 14 March 1941, CO 971/1/8, PRO.

203. Walter White to Norman Manley, 24 March 1939; Norman Manley to Walter White, 11 April 1939; Walter White to Norman Manley, 21 April 1939, box L1, folder "American Committee for West Indian Federation, 1939," NAACP Papers, LOC.

204. Vivian Morris (Asst Secretary, Caribbean Union) to Walter White, 19 May 1939; Walter White to Vivian Morris, 26 May 1939, box L11, folder "British West Indies, 1939," NAACP Papers, LOC.

205. For instance, Taussig asked White for information concerning Cipriani in Trinidad. White asked Ira Reid of Atlanta University, who replied with details of Cipriani and other labor/political organizations in Trinidad, which was passed on to Taussig. Walter White to Ira Reid, 15 October 1940; Ira Reid to Walter White, 17 October 1940; Walter White to Charles Taussig, 23 October 1940, box A155, folder "British West Indies, 1940–1949," NAACP Papers, LOC.

206. For instance, in early 1941, L. Alphonso Roberts of Jamaica wrote to White expressing his appreciation for the NAACP's work on a recent rape case, and noting his desire to create an organization "along the lines" of the NAACP. Roberts to Walter White, 15 March 1941, box A155, folder "British West Indies, 1940–1949," NAACP Papers, LOC. For a summary of Taussig's tour, see Parker, *Brother's Keeper*, 31–38.

207. Domingo to Walter White, 7 February 1941, box A332, folder "Labor—British West Indies, 1940–1947," NAACP Papers, LOC.

208. Domingo to Walter White, 20 March 1941; Walter White to Cordell Hull, 25 April 1941; John Hickerson to Walter White, 1 May 1941; Domingo to Walter White, 13 May 1941; Walter White to President's Committee on Fair Employment Practice, 29 August 1941; Lawrence Cramer to Walter White, 15 September 1941, box A332, folder "Labor—British West Indies, 1940–1947," NAACP Papers, LOC.

209. For an excellent overview of the rise of "national parties" in the various colonies of the British Caribbean, see G. Lewis, *Modern West Indies*. For the role of Caribbean labor organizations in World War II, see Horne, *Cold War in a Hot Zone*, chap. 3.

210. For a critique of these constitutional reforms and the Atlantic Charter, see George Padmore, "Democracy for the West Indies," *Crisis*, June 1941, 188–89; Cunard and Padmore, *White Man's Duty*.

211. Domingo had noted the temporary suspension of the PNP's push for self-government and its reinstitution to Walter White in late 1940. Domingo to Walter White, 6 November 1940, box A332, folder "Labor—British West Indies, 1940–1947," NAACP Papers, LOC. On the detention of Domingo, see People's National Party, *The Case of Domingo*.

212. For details on the creation and aims of the AACC, see H. Johnson, "Extension" and "Establishment."

213. Jason Parker in *Brother's Keeper*, 47–48, has correctly noted this as demonstrating the limitations of race alone as the primary motivation within these anticolonial movements. He also views this as an example of intra-racial tensions between African American and West Indian activists who supported West Indian self-government. While the latter point is true to an extent, it is precarious to assume African Americans were united in their views and West Indians in theirs.

214. Among the AWIACA's stated goals were the appointment of an American of British Caribbean descent to the AACC or its advisory committees, and the opportunity to provide recommendations to the AACC regarding the West Indies. See West Indies National Council—Subversive Activities in the West Indies (FBI Report), 10 November 1942, box 1, folder 5 (WINC), WINC Collection, SC; AWIACA, *Caribbean Charter*, 3–4. Also, the AWIACA appears to be the organization Jason Parker notes in *Brother's Keeper*, 48, as the American West Indian Association. It is possible the name was shortened at times by the organization itself and by others.

215. AWIACA, *Caribbean Charter*, 6.

216. There are numerous examples of such disagreements and cooperation. See for instance Malliet's chastisement of Herman Osborne and the WINC. "World Fronts," *NYASN*, 3 October 1942, 7; "World Fronts," *NYASN*, 10 October 1942, 7; "World Fronts," *NYASN*, 17 October 1942, 7; "World Fronts," *NYASN*, 31 October 1942, 9. For Malliet's statement on the treatment of black people like children, see West Indies National Council—Subversive Activities in the West Indies (FBI Report), 10 November 1942, box 1, folder 5 (WINC), WINC Collection, SC.

217. West Indies National Council—Subversive Activities in the West Indies (FBI Report), 10 November 1942, box 1, folder 5 (WINC), WINC Collection, SC.

218. For a helpful discussion of these differences and this conference, see Whitham, *Bitter Rehearsal*, chap. 7.

219. For details of this conference, see Frazier and Williams, *Economic Future of the Caribbean*. An earlier conference, "The Negro in the Americas," took place in 1940. For details see Wesley, *Negro in the Americas*. For recent work on the role of Howard University and other historically black colleges and universities (HBCUs) in anticolonial struggles, see Parker, "'Made-in-America Revolutions'?"; Z. Williams, *Talented Tenth*.

220. "May Unite All of West Indies," *NYAN*, 27 July 1940, 8; "Federation of BWI Studied," *NYAN*, 19 July 1941, 1; "U.S.-British Partnership in Colonies Post-War Aim," *CD*, 25 September 1943, 13. Smuts's plan for the Caribbean was connected to the idea of grouping British colonies into federal units according to geography. Such federations would become part of British colonial policy in the postwar years.

221. See for instance "BWI Labor Meet Stresses Union," *AA*, 29 April 1944, 8; "West Indian Colonies May Form Federation," *AA*, 24 June 1944, 9; "Federation of West Indies," *CD*, 15 July 1944, 12.

222. "Most Negroes Dislike British Colonial Policy," *CD*, 27 January 1945, 9.

223. CO, *Closer Association*, app. 1, "Despatch Dated 14th March 1945."

Chapter 3. From Long-Standing Dream to Impending Reality: Caribbean Federation and the Mobilization of Black Diaspora Politics, 1945–1950

1. CO, *Closer Association*, app. 1, "Despatch Dated 14th March 1945."

2. "West Indian Federation," *London Times*, 18 June 1945.

3. George Padmore covers some of these reforms in Cunard and Padmore, *White Man's Duty*, 36–41, but Gordon K. Lewis offers one of the best overviews of these events in *Growth of the Modern West Indies*.

4. For a discussion of the idea of federation among British colonies, see Watts, *New*

Federations; Hicks, *Federalism*. For analysis of the general idea of federation, see Franck, *Why Federations Fail*.

5. For a discussion of this shift in US policy, see Parker, *Brother's Keeper*, chaps. 3–4.

6. For further insight into the UN founding conference as it relates to African American and Afro-Caribbean freedom struggles, see Anderson, *Eyes off the Prize*; Plummer, *Rising Wind*, chap. 4; Sherwood, "The United Nations."

7. On the NNC, see Gellman, *Death Blow to Jim Crow*. On the CAA, see Von Eschen, *Race Against Empire*.

8. The FBI's fears of the WINC exporting its program obviously overlooks the already established connections between some WINC and Caribbean leaders within the islands, as established in chapter 2. John Edgar Hoover to Attorney General, 30 May 1944, box 1, folder 1 (Charles Petioni), WINC Collection, SC.

9. D. M. Ladd to E. A. Tamm, 15 October 1945, box 1, folder 3 (Hope R. Stevens), WINC Collection, SC.

10. This phrase is taken from the actual file group released by the PRO in March 2003. CO 968/121/4, PRO.

11. H. G. Nicholas to Angus Malcolm, 10 February 1944, FO 371/38653, PRO.

12. John Harrington to Colonel VPT Vivian, 14 August 1944, CO 968/121/4, PRO.

13. Ibid.

14. Memo from P. Rogers, 9 August 1944, CO 968/121/4, PRO; Memo from John Harrington, 9 October 1944, CO 968/121/4, PRO.

15. The LCP sent invitations to the British, French, and Dutch to attend the conference from which this charter emanated, but all refused to send representatives. As for the actual charter, Oliver Stanley, Britain's secretary of state for the colonies, thanked the LCP for its input but argued against any sort of uniform policies within the British colonies in place of the "steady progress" dependent territories were making under the current policy. LCP, "Charter for Coloured Peoples," 1944; Stanley to Moody, 31 August 1944, CO 968/159/9, PRO.

16. "Manifesto on Africa in the Post-War World for Presentation to the United Nations Conference, San Francisco," April 1945, CO 968/159/9, PRO; "African Leaders Demand Voice at San Francisco Conference," *PC*, 28 April 1945, 12.

17. Sherwood, "The United Nations," 27–29; CAA, "The San Francisco Conference and the Colonial Issue," April 1945, box 14, folder 1, Moore Papers, SC.

18. Meriwether, *Proudly We Can Be Africans*, 61–62.

19. "Dr. DuBois to Be Observer at San Francisco Confab," *NYAN*, 24 March 1945, 7A; "Negro Opinion and the San Francisco Conference," n.d., CO 968/121/4, PRO.

20. DuBois, "Speakers at the Colonial Conference," 6 April 1945, DuBois Papers, UMass. West Indian representation at the Colonial Conference had been decided through a series of exchanges between DuBois and Herman Osborne, secretary of the WINC. DuBois originally sought representation for multiple West Indian colonies, including Bermuda, British Guiana, British Honduras, Bahamas, Barbados, Jamaica, Leeward Islands, Trinidad, Grenada, St. Vincent, and St. Lucia. When Osborne replied with an extensive list of suggestions for each colony, all of them persons based in the New York area, DuBois requested he limit his suggestions to only a few of the most qualified and informed. As a result, members of the WINC and JPL came to represent the West Indies, as well as Eric

Williams, who was requested specifically by DuBois. Osborne to DuBois, 6 February 1945; DuBois to Osborne, 7 March 1945; DuBois to Osborne, 8 March 1945; Osborne to DuBois, 14 March 1945; DuBois to Osborne, 21 March 1945, DuBois Papers, UMass.

21. "Logan Gives Plan for Colonial Trusteeship," *PC*, 14 April 1945, 28.

22. "Instant Freedom Planned at NAACP Colonial Parley," *AA*, 21 April 1945, 16; Du-Bois, Memorandum on the Colonial Conference, April 1945; WINC, Memorandum on the Colonial Conference, 14 April 1945, DuBois Papers, UMass.

23. Reginald Pierrepointe, "West Indies News Service Press Release," 30 March 1945, box 8, folder 1 (WINC), Moore Papers, SC; "West Indians Seek Seat at Frisco Confab," *NYAN*, 7 April 1945, 1.

24. WINC, "Program Adopted by the Conference Committee," n.d., box 8, folder 1 (WINC), Moore Papers, SC.

25. "West Indians Nominate Five Delegates to San Francisco," *NYAN*, 14 April 1945, 8A; "West Indians Ask Voice at World Security Meet," *AA*, 14 April 1945, 7.

26. West Indies National Council—Subversive Activities in the West Indies (FBI Report), 16 April 1945, box 1, folder 6 (WINC), WINC Collection, SC.

27. "Mr. H. P. Osborne's Address," n.d., CO 968/121/4, PRO.

28. Ibid.

29. Ibid.

30. Sherwood, "The United Nations," 38.

31. "Race Issue Raised at Frisco," *NYAN*, 5 May 1945, 1A.

32. In the case of US representation at the UNCIO, although several African Americans attended in some capacity, the NAACP was the only African American organization to serve as official consultants to conference delegates.

33. It is not the intent of the chapter to delve into the wide-ranging activities of these organizations at the UN. For more in-depth studies, see Sherwood, "The United Nations"; Anderson, *Eyes off the Prize*; Plummer, *Rising Wind*, chap. 4.

34. Appeal to the United Nations Conference on International Organization on Behalf of the Caribbean Peoples, 25 May 1945, box 8, folder 2 (WINC), Moore Papers, SC.

35. "Back from Frisco," *NYAN*, 19 May 1945, 2A.

36. For press coverage of Moore's activities, see "Islanders Plead for Independence," *AA*, 2 June 1945, 6; "West Indians Ask Colonial Freedom," *AA*, 30 June 1945, 3. Moore remained on the West Coast giving speeches to interested parties after the conference ended in June. Also see Turner and Turner, *Richard B. Moore*, 78–81.

37. "What Is the Pan-African Federation?" n.d., CO 968/164/5, PRO.

38. Yearwood also interestingly noted that 180,000 of the 200,000 people in Barbados were of African descent. G. Padmore, *Colonial and Coloured Unity*, 47. This title contains the minutes of the Manchester Conference.

39. Ibid., 49.

40. Ibid., 53.

41. Ibid., 62.

42. Ibid., 60.

43. CO, *Closer Association*, app. 1, "Despatch Dated 14th March 1945."

44. The question of the working masses' support for and understanding of federation

awaits further and more critical historical examination. However, it is not the focus of this study.

45. "Secretary's Memo on Draft Bill for Federation of the British West Indies and British Guiana," n.d., CLC-RHC, NLJ; G. Lewis, *Modern West Indies*, 116. For the origins of the CLC, see Bolland, *Politics of Labour*, 474–80.

46. Mordecai, *Federation*, 32–33.

47. Timm, "Transnational Roots," 428.

48. This is not to suggest that more restricted regional perspectives and transracial visions of the pending West Indian nation were absent in Black America or Black Britain. However, it does appear that in the immediate postwar years, as in many previous years, rhetoric that more explicitly emphasized the diasporic and racial features of federation and underscored its connections and importance to black peoples outside the Caribbean remained far more common.

49. "World Fronts," *NYAN*, 30 June 1945, 12. Malliet noted British Guiana was large and wealthy enough to be self-sufficient, though he believed it needed a larger population for large-scale development. This was in line with his and others' previous support of that colony as a possible site for the relocation of West Indians (particularly Afro-Caribbean populations in such appeals) from overcrowded islands. He also said that Jamaicans should look more to British Honduras, which had historical ties to Jamaica. The idea of Jamaican ties to the western Caribbean connects with Stanley's previous mention of two possible federations, in the eastern and western Caribbean.

50. "West Indies Federation Drive Gets British O. K.," *NYAN*, 21 July 1945, B12.

51. "Governor of the West Indies Here," *NYAN*, 27 October 1945, 5.

52. "Manley in NY," *NYAN*, 6 October 1945, 2; "Foresees BWI Federation—Calls on Aids from States," *NYAN*, 13 October 1945, 5; West Indies National Council—Subversive Activities in the West Indies (FBI Report), 10 October 1945, box 1, folder 4 (Norman W. Manley), WINC Collection, SC.

53. Remarks of Manley before the Board of Directors of the NAACP," 8 October 1945, box A356, folder "American Committee for West Indian Federation, 1945–1948," NAACP Papers, LOC.

54. Quotes from "Federation Urged for West Indies," *New York Times*, 11 October 1945, 10. For black press coverage of this rhetoric beyond the New York area, see "The World Today," *PC*, 20 October 1945, 13; "W.I. Leader Tells Federation Plan," *AA*, 20 October 1945, 18. The *Afro-American* claimed Manley said federation's "salutary effect on the status of colored people everywhere," but the use of "colored people" in this context appears synonymous with the *New York Times's* and *Pittsburgh Courier's* use of "Negro."

55. "Jamaica Leader Is Backed as Federate Head by Barbadian," *NYAN*, 27 October 1945, 24. Additional speakers at this gathering included Walter White (NAACP), Max Yergan (CAA), Charles Petioni (WINC), and W. A. Crawford (president of the West Indian National Congress Party and member of Barbados Colonial Parliament). Crawford gave his own talk, "The Destiny of the West Indies," alongside Richard B. Moore later in November. "Algernon Crawford Tells BWI Destiny," *NYAN*, 24 November 1945, 6.

56. Walter White to C. B. Powell, 11 October 1945; Mabel Staupers to Walter White, 29 October 1945, box A356, folder "American Committee for West Indian Federation, 1945–1948," NAACP Papers, LOC.

57. Manley to White, 6 November 1945, box A356, folder "American Committee for West Indian Federation, 1945–1948," NAACP Papers, LOC; "Jamaica Leader Seeks Pan-African Unity," *CD*, 5 January 1946, 9; "Norman Manley Speaker at Two Local Meetings," *NYAN*, 12 January 1946, 5.

58. "Norman Manley Speaker at Two Local Meetings," *NYAN*, 12 January 1946, 5.

59. Manley to Marryshow, 24 January 1946, 4/60/2b/11, Manley Papers, JA.

60. Herman P. Osborne, "The Road to West Indian Federation," *Crisis*, January 1946, 14–15, 27–28.

61. "Colored Races Demand Spot in Sun," *NYAN*, 12 January 1946, 10.

62. "World Fronts," *NYAN*, 2 February 1946, 10. The Malayan Union, a Crown Colony, became the Federation of Malaya in 1948.

63. When the Dutch and French were added, the Anglo-American Caribbean Commission was renamed the Caribbean Commission in October 1946.

64. Transcript of Taussig's Speech to Delegates of the West Indian Conference, n.d., RG 126, entry 33, box 1, NARA.

65. "Lift Up Your Eyes," *NYAN*, 23 February 1946, 8.

66. "World Fronts," *NYAN*, 2 March 1946, 10.

67. "Color Plagues Confab," *PC*, 9 March 1946, 1; "Charter for Colonials Too Hot for W.I. Conference," *AA*, 9 March 1946, 15; "Able, Factual Expose by Natives Wins Conference," *AA*, 9 March 1946, 17; "Action Pledged West Indians," *AA*, 23 March 1946, 1.

68. "Action Pledged West Indians," *AA*, 23 March 1946, 1.

69. During a talk before the WINC and associated bodies in April 1946, Albert Gomes, longtime political and labor activist from Trinidad, called the AACC "a sham; a dishonest attempt by two predatory nations to delude world opinion and themselves. It is a glamorous farce; a magnificent hoax; the arm of despotism in disguise." "Flays British Colonialism—Distrusts Caribbean Body," *NYAN*, 27 April 1946, 22.

70. *LCPN*, no. 79 (April 1946): 15.

71. Robeson to Manley, 1 May 1946, 4/60/2b/11, Manley Papers, JA. This rally was a continuation of similar events sponsored by the CAA during World War II.

72. Citation to Norman Washington Manley by Mordeaci Johnson (President of Howard University), n.d., 4/60/2b/11, Manley Papers, JA; Manley to Williams, 23 May 1946, 4/60/2b/11, Manley Papers, JA.

73. Manley to CR Crosswell, 20 June 1946; Manley to Editor of *Gleaner*, 5 July 1946, 4/60/2b/11, Manley Papers, JA.

74. "West Indies Round Table on Sept. 10," *NYAN*, 7 September 1946, 21.

75. "Group to Have Breakfast-Meet," *NYAN*, 2 November 1946, 8.

76. Adams to White, 21 October 1946, box A155, folder "British West Indies, 1940–1949," NAACP Papers, LOC.

77. Central Office of Information, *British Caribbean Federation*, 1.

78. CO, *Closer Association*, app. 1, "Despatch Dated 14th February 1947," 3–5.

79. Grantley Adams, "Reflections on Federation 6," n.d., box 2, folder 7, Demas Papers, UWISA.

80. "Tells Plans for a New Negro Nation," *PC*, 25 January 1947, 11; "2nd Caribbean Nation Planned, Jamaican Says," *AA*, 25 January 1947, 5A.

81. "World Fronts," *NYAN*, 1 March 1947, 10.

82. One of the first groups contacted was the American West Indian Association in Chicago. "West Indies Seeks Freedom," *CD*, 22 March 1947, 3.

83. FBI teletype, 7 June 1947; FBI Director to Assistant Attorney General Caudle, 10 June 1947, box 1-folder 4 (Norman W. Manley), WINC Collection, SC; British Consulate General (NY), "Calls for West Indian Unity," n.d., CO 537/2259, PRO. The PRO record incorrectly identifies the meeting date as 15 June, but other records confirm the meeting took place on 7 June. As for Azikiwe's presence, little is noted beyond his attendance and support for Caribbean federation.

84. Walter White telegram, 9 June 1947; Minutes of Special Meeting of the West Indian-American Group, 14 June 1947; Madison Jones (NAACP) to Lester Granger (National Urban League), 10 July 1947, box A356, folder "American Committee for West Indian Federation, 1945–1948," NAACP Papers, LOC. In an interview with the *Trinidad Evening News*, Grantley Adams said others invited to help establish this committee included Paul Robeson, Marion Anderson, and Max Yergan. Ellis A. Bonnet (American Consul) to US Secretary of State, 26 September 1947, Port-of-Spain (Trinidad, British West Indies) Consulate, RG 84, box 3, folder "Telegrams, Airgrams, Dispatches," NARA.

85. In a 1969 newspaper article Poppy Cannon White, wife of Walter White, wrote, "Norman Manley told me . . . that Walter White was the one who made the suggestion that, instead of an expensive national campaign, it would be wise to ask 'a hundred people to give a hundred dollars apiece toward a fund that would get the movement started.'" "Manley, the Mountain," *NYAN*, 20 September 1969, 17.

86. Meeting Minutes, 11 July 1947, box A356, folder "American Committee for West Indian Federation, 1945–1948," NAACP Papers, LOC. For US government reactions to the CLC, see Horne, *Cold War in a Hot Zone*.

87. "World Fronts," *NYAN*, 14 June 1947, 10.

88. Osborne to Manley, 31 July 1947, 4/60/2b/12, Manley Papers, JA.

89. "That Chick Carolyn Wisecracking Again," *NYAN*, 16 August 1947, 12; Domingo to Manley, 15 August 1947, 4/60/2b/12, Manley Papers, JA.

90. "Labor Forum," *NYAN*, 23 August 1947, 8.

91. "Busta Says U.S. Aid Injures Him," *NYAN*, 2 August 1947, 2. Bustamante was likely dumbfounded by this support for the PNP and connected movements, considering that his JLP was at times described as the "black man's party" in Jamaica, while the PNP was associated more with the so-called brown middle class.

92. "Labor Forum," *NYAN*, 30 August 1947, 8.

93. "World Fronts," *NYAN*, 30 August 1947, 8.

94. CLC, "Resolution, Statement and Draft Bill by the Caribbean Labour Congress," in CO, *Conference on the Closer Association*, 2: 121–31.

95. Telegram, n.d., CO 537/2259, PRO.

96. No clear reasons can be found for the apparent name change from AACA to ACWIF. Given the individuals involved, the focus and presentation of the document, and evidence referring to the ACWIF's fund-raising for the CLC Conference, it is reasonable to assume the two were the same organization. Unfortunately, renaming of such ad hoc groups was quite common in expatriate West Indian and black diaspora circles in this era.

97. J. Turner, "Caribbean 'Awaymen' Network," 82.

98. ACWIF, "Memorandum on Federation and Self-Government of the West Indies,"

1947, box A356, folder "American Committee for West Indian Federation, 1945–1948," NAACP Papers, LOC. A more accessible copy is in Turner and Turner, *Richard B. Moore*, 279–83.

99. *DG*, 2 September 1947, quoted in Horne, *Cold War in a Hot Zone*, 109.

100. "US West Indians Spur Solidarity," *CD*, 20 September 1947, 7; "Augustine A. Austin Visits West Indies," 13 September 1947, *NYAN*, 7; "A. A. Austin Cheered at Jamaican Conference," *PC*, 20 September 1947. There is little indication why Austin and associates created a new organization in light of the two in recent months. The activists may have felt another ad hoc committee would be needed following the CLC and Montego Bay Conferences. On the importance and use of ad hoc committees, see Turner and Turner, *Richard B. Moore*, 81.

101. Central Office of Information, *Towards a Federation*, 9–10; CO, *Conference on the Closer Association*, 1: 4, 12–13. While the Montego Bay Conference is remembered as a most significant example of regional West Indian cooperation in favor of federation, as Michele A. Johnson notes in her reexamination of the conference, there were clear signs within it that the federation would ultimately fail; see "Beginning and the End," 117–49.

102. "West Indies Federation," *PC*, 13 September 1947, 6. African American social critic and newspaperman George Schuyler noted similar sentiments on the commonalities between West Indian colonies compared to India. "The World Today," *PC*, 30 August 1947, 1.

103. "How and When Divide W.I. Federation Delegates," *PC*, 27 September 1947, 3.

104. "West Indians Place 2-Year Deadline on Dominion Status," *CD*, 4 October 1947, 13.

105. "West Indies Will Get Full Dominion Status," *PC*, 1 November 1947, 5.

106. "West Indies Federate for Nationhood," *NYAN*, 27 September 1947, 11.

107. Ellis A. Bonnet (American Consul) to US Secretary of State, 26 September 1947, Port-of-Spain (Trinidad, British West Indies) Consulate, RG 84, box 3, folder "Telegrams, Airgrams, Dispatches," NARA.

108. *DG*, 10 September 1947, quoted in Horne, *Cold War in a Hot Zone*, 4.

109. "West Indies Federate for Nationhood," *NYAN*, 27 September 1947, 11. Although he mentions the possible effects of federation on "all working and oppressed people," this does not negate Moore's longtime prioritization of the liberation of black peoples within the broader anticolonial movement.

110. "The Free Caribbean Commonwealth," *NYAN*, 27 September 1947, 10.

111. "Off Their Backs—West Indian Blacks Have Same Urge for Freedom as Peoples of Asia," *PC*, 24 January 1948, 7.

112. Henry L. Taylor (American Vice Consul) to US Secretary of State, 2 October 1947, American Consulate (Grenada, British West Indies), RG 84, box 3, folder "Telegrams, Airgrams, Dispatches," NARA.

113. Manley to Domingo, 2 October 1947, 4/60/2b/12, Manley Papers, JA. Manley's statement mirrors that of Ellis A. Bonnet, the American consul in Trinidad, who remarked, "Although the delegates have reason to be satisfied with the success of the exploratory conference at Montego Bay . . . the fact remains that little was done, in so far as eventual Federation is concerned, other than to exchange views and to agree that eventual federation appeared to be desirable if numerous and obvious obstacles could be overcome." Ellis A. Bonnet (American Consul) to US Secretary of State, 26 September 1947, Port-of-Spain (Trinidad, British West Indies) Consulate, RG 84, box 3, folder "Telegrams,

Airgrams, Dispatches," NARA. For discussion of growing divisions over federation within the JPL, within the PNP, and between the JPL and PNP after the Montego Bay Conference, see Timm, "Transnational Roots," 430–31.

114. Padmore to Manley, 5 November 1947, 4/60/2b/12, Manley Papers, JA; Manley to Padmore, 14 November 1947, 4/60/2b/12, Manley Papers, JA.

115. "Opinion Review," *PC*, 22 November 1947, 6.

116. Central Office of Information, *Towards a Federation*, 10; Wallace, *The British Caribbean*, 101.

117. G. Lewis, *Modern West Indies*, 351–52.

118. "World Fronts," *NYAN*, 10 January 1948, 8.

119. "World Fronts," *NYAN*, 27 March 1948, 10; "World Fronts," *NYAN*, 3 April 1948, 10; "World Fronts," *NYAN*, 3 July 1948, 10. In the 3 July article Malliet called for creation of another ad hoc committee—an "Emergency Committee for Caribbean Federation."

120. "World Fronts," *NYAN*, 10 July 1948, 10.

121. Austin to White, 19 March 1948; Memo to Walter White from Madison Jones, 22 March 1948, box A363, folder "Leagues—Anglo-American Caribbean Commission, 1946–1951," NAACP Papers, LOC.

122. As noted, the collaborative efforts of West Indians and African Americans to raise funds for the CLC Conference included the creation of an American Association for Caribbean Advancement (AACA). This organization seemingly also operated as the American Committee for West Indian Federation (ACWIF). Austin's presentation at the CLC Conference, where he also announced the creation of an American Association for West Indian Advancement (AAWIA), at other times referred to as the Committee on West Indian Freedom (CWIF), drew the ire of Channing Tobias and Walter White of the NAACP due to Austin's failure to submit the memorandum to the ACWIF's advisory board before its presentation. While the NAACP supported Caribbean federation as part of its anticolonial activities, especially within the black diaspora, both Tobias and White maintained a cautious approach to official NAACP links to many organizations. This was due largely to mounting Cold War tensions and NAACP efforts to avoid alienating themselves from the US government. See for example Tobias to White, 15 September 1947; Austin to White, 31 October 1947; White to Austin, 5 November 1947, box A356, folder "American Committee for West Indian Federation, 1945–1948," NAACP Papers, LOC. Regarding Caribbean support for the NAACP at this time, including expressed desires to create similar organizations within the colonies, see Felix Reid, 28 August 1948; Madison Jones to Felix Reid, 10 September 1948; Ted Reid to Walter White, September 1948, box A155, folder "British West Indies, 1940–1949," NAACP Papers, LOC.

123. Moore, "Statement Before the Platform Committee of the New Party," 21 July 1948, in Turner and Turner, *Richard B. Moore*, 283–87.

124. "BWI Freedom Is Theme of 'Gate' Meet," *NYAN*, 31 July 1948, 1.

125. "Political Shifts in West Indies," *NYAN*, 16 October 1948, 34.

126. "Adams' Blasting of Reds Brings Big Rebuke Here," *NYAN*, 23 October 1958, 1; "Representative Of West Indies Speaks at U.N.," *CD*, 23 October 1948, 7; "Score Caribbean Delegate at UN," *NYAN*, 6 November 1948, 1; "Carib Group Seen Split Over Speech," *NYAN*, 27 November 1948, 22; Horne, *Cold War in a Hot Zone*, 111–12.

127. For an excellent analysis of the Cold War on the CLC, see Horne, *Cold War in a Hot Zone*, chap. 5.

128. "West Indian Ban Biased Thurgood Marshall Says," NAACP Press Release, 3 March 1949, box A155, folder "British West Indies, 1940–1949," NAACP Papers, LOC; "Mass Meeting to Urge End of B.W.I. Ban," *NYAN*, 26 March 1949, 1; "Queens Fights Ban on BWI," *NYAN*, 16 April 1949, 17.

129. Joint Statement of UCAC and AWIA (Chicago), 20 July 1949, box 7, folder 8 (UCAC), Moore Papers, SC; Plan of Organization and Budget, n.d., box 7, folder 8 (UCAC), Moore Papers, SC; "Caribbeans, Americans Form New Organization," *NYAN*, 30 April 1949, 30; "Plan Under Way to Unite Caribbeans, Americans," *AA*, 30 April 1949, A1.

130. Helen McDonald to Public Relations Officer, 27 May 1949, CO 537/4314, PRO; FBI Report on Hope Stevens, 22 November 1950, box 1, folder 1 (Hope Stevens), WINC Collection, SC.

131. "Unite to Fight Discrimination Against West Indians," n.d., box A155, folder "British West Indies, 1950–1953," NAACP Papers, LOC; "Mass Meet to Protest West Indian Exclusion," *NYAN*, 7 May 1949, 3; "Harlem to Protest Immigration Bill," *AA*, 21 May 1949, 5.

132. Joint Statement of UCAC and AWIA (Chicago), 20 July 1949, box 7, folder 8 (UCAC), Moore Papers, SC.

133. Moore (UCAC) Statement to British Embassy, 24 March 1949, box 12, folder 2, Moore Papers, SC.

134. "A Nation Being Born," *PC*, 26 November 1949, 14.

135. "Expose on Race Prejudice in the Caribbean," *NYAN*, 14 January 1950, 1; "Inside Story of Britain's Race Problems," *NYAN*, 21 January 1950, 1; "Inside Dope on BWI, Federation," *NYAN*, 28 January 1950, 1. Quote taken from "Inside Dope."

136. "Pro and Con of BWI Federation," *NYAN*, 4 February 1950, 1.

137. Moon said he would sponsor a tour of the country for Marryshow but "made it clear that [he] could not commit the NAACP to support of the [CLC], explaining, however, [the NAACP's] long-standing and continuing interest in the problems of the Caribbean." Moon to Wilkins, 6 December 1949, box A363, folder "Leagues—Anglo-American Caribbean Commission, 1946–1951," NAACP Papers, LOC.

138. "Harlemites Hear of BWI Poverty," *NYAN*, 17 December 1949, 4.

139. "Desire for Freedom Rules W.I.—T. Marryshow Sees Link to Negro in US," *NYAN*, 4 February 1950, 5.

140. "Marryshow Speaks to His Grenadians Here," n.d., CO 321/428/4, PRO.

141. Central Office of Information, *West Indian Federation*, 4–5; British Caribbean SCAC, *Report*; Wallace, *The British Caribbean*, 101–3.

142. "Propose West Indies Unity as Step to Independence," *NYAN*, 11 March 1950, 1.

143. "BWI Moves Toward Independence," *NYAN*, 15 April 1950, 6.

144. "Analysis of Report for BWI Freedom," *NYAN*, 15 April 1950, 1; "Structure of WI Union," *NYAN*, 22 April 1950, 19; "Money Key to BWI Freedom," *NYAN*, 29 April 1950, 19; "Caribbean Union Waits Final Vote," *NYAN*, 6 May 1950, 4.

145. "Meet Sunday to Protest Move to Ban West Indians," *NYAN*, 25 March 1950, 2.

146. Moore to Hart, 26 April 1950, fiche #2, CLC-Microfiche, UF.

147. UCAC clippings, n.d., box 7, folder 8 (UCAC), Moore Papers, SC.

148. The financial goal of this organization was to raise $25,000 for the CLC. Members

of the steering committee included A. A. Austin, Charles Petioni, George Schuyler, and P.M.H. Savory, copublisher of the *NYAN*. The NAACP and the National Urban League also pledged support of the proposed organization. "Aid for Caribbean Planned by Group: Back from Indies," *NYAN*, 8 April 1950, 4; "BWI's and Americans Join Hands to Push 25G Drive," *NYAN*, 15 April 1950, 1.

149. "Americans Aid BWI Cause," *NYAN*, 15 April 1950, 6.

Chapter 4. Finalizing, Defining, and Welcoming the New Nation, 1950–1958

1. Wallace, *The British Caribbean*, 103–6; Mordecai, *Federation*, 41–42. For further discussion of the Rance Report's shortcomings, see G. Lewis, *Modern West Indies*, chap. XIV.

2. Central Office of Information, *West Indian Federation*, 5–6.

3. On Cold War politics in the Caribbean in this era, see Horne, *Cold War in a Hot Zone*, chap. 8; Parker, *Brother's Keeper*, esp. chap. 4. On Cheddi Jagan, see Palmer, *Cheddi Jagan*. For black American press coverage on the "communist threat" in British Guiana, see "Says West Indians View B.G. with 'Alarm,'" *NYAN*, 24 October 1953, 18; "The Reds in British Guiana," *NYAN*, 24 October 1953, 19.

4. CO, *Report by the Conference on West Indian Federation*, 4–9; Central Office of Information, *British Caribbean Federation*, 3–4; Wallace, *The British Caribbean*, 109–11; Mordecai, *Federation*, 44–47.

5. See CO, *Plan for a British Caribbean Federation*.

6. On the general debates within the Caribbean following the 1953 conference, see Mordecai, *Federation*, 51–74; G. Lewis, *Modern West Indies*, 351–67; Wallace, *The British Caribbean*, 109–11. On Jamaica and federation, see Munroe, *Constitutional Decolonization*, chap. 4. On Eric Williams and federation, see Williams, *Federation: Two Public Lectures*. For a brief example of Williams's support for federation in the 1940s, see his *Negro in the Caribbean*. In this text Williams called for both political and economic federation as a key step in the future of the British Caribbean.

7. CO, *Movement of Persons*; "Full Agreement on Migration: Conference Report to Be Signed Today," *TG*, 17 March 1955, 1 (quote); "Federation of W. Indies Becomes Reality at Parley," *AA*, 2 April 1955, 21.

8. Central Office of Information, *The West Indies*, 1–4; "Words of Wisdom," *POSG*, 4 February 1956, 4. For details of the 1956 London Conference, see CO, *Report by the Conference on British Caribbean Federation*.

9. "Federal Report Signed: Delegates Agree to Create a New Nation," *TG*, 24 February 1956, 1.

10. "News of the Caribbean—Meet Seeks Jamaica Federation Backing," *NYAN*, 20 January 1951, 4.

11. Moore, "Speech on Caribbean Federation at the Luncheon Meeting for Lord Listowel," 3 February 1953, in Turner and Turner, *Richard B. Moore*, 287–90; West Indies News Service press release, 14 February 1953, box 11, folder 11 (Federation Without Independence), Moore Papers, SC.

12. See for example "WI Federation Signed After Near Failure," *NYAN*, 16 May 1953, 36; "West Indies, Britain Agree on Federation," *CD*, 9 May 1953, 12; "Set Final BWI Parley," *PC*, 10 December 1955, 27; "Iron Out Details for 'New Nation,'" *CD*, 14 February 1956, 9.

13. "Norman Manley to Visit N.Y. Feb. 26," *NYAN*, 27 February 1954, 1.

14. Event flyer, 13 June 1954, 4/60/2b/16, Manley Papers, JA. On Malliet's position with the JLP, see "Judge Watson's Illness Worries B.W.I. Leaders," *NYAN*, 5 January 1952, 34.

15. "Premier Predicts Colonies Will Form Federation Soon," *AA*, 30 April 1955, 22; Moon to Wilkins, 19 July 1955, box A155, folder "British West Indies, 1950–1953," NAACP Papers, LOC.

16. Timm, "Transnational Roots," 432–33.

17. Ibid., 433–36.

18. Domingo, *British West Indian Federation*, 1–16.

19. Springer, "On Being a West Indian," 181. This study uses Springer's notion of "West Indianness" synonymously with other contemporary ideas such as "West Indianism."

20. Goveia, *Federation Day Exhibition*, 40, quoted in Springer, *Reflections*, 17–18.

21. "Get It Straight," *DG*, 5 January 1955, 8.

22. "Get It Straight," *DG*, 17 August 1955, 8.

23. "An Historic Day," *POSG*, 7 February 1956, 4.

24. "No Birth Yet," *POSG*, 25 February 1956, 4

25. "Federation—Day of Opportunity," *DG*, 13 August 1956, 8.

26. Braithwaite, "'Federal' Associations and Institutions," 286–94, 311–20.

27. Lowenthal, "Social Background," 67, 72.

28. On Britishness within the West Indies in the twentieth century, see Rush, *Bonds of Empire*.

29. "Complete Unity Call by Manley," *DG*, 18 March 1955, 1.

30. "Birth of a Nation," *DG*, 23 August 1955, 8.

31. "Marryshow's Triumph," *POSG*, 24 February 1956, 2.

32. "Federation—Day of Opportunity," *DG*, 13 August 1956, 8.

33. G. Lewis, "British Caribbean Federation," 65.

34. "Race Relations Seen Best in West Indies," *Canada–West Indies Magazine* 47, no. 11 (November 1957): 41.

35. "Fantastic Political Adventure," *DG*, 18 December 1956, 10; "Unity Develops in Caribbean," *DG*, 9 January 1957, 8.

36. "Off the Record," *CD*, 5 July 1956, 10.

37. Domingo, *British West Indian Federation*, 4–5, 9.

38. On the process and the extent of these migrations, see for instance Look Lai, *Indentured Labor, Caribbean Sugar*. The numbers and percentages are drawn from G. W. Roberts, "Some Demographic Considerations," 265.

39. For instance, the Maha Sabha and East Indian Association noted a willingness to cooperate economically and socially with other communities in the colonies, but also demonstrated a desire to "preserve [their] racial identity and religious precepts" in the West Indies. See Oral Evidence Transcript of Maha Sabha and East Indian Association before the West India Royal Commission—Fifteenth Session, 13 February 1939, CO 950/673, PRO (quote from p. 2 of testimony). Other Indo-Caribbean organizations asked for the appointment of an Indian Commissioner in colonies with substantial Indo-Caribbean populations, greater respect for Indian cultural traditions in the Caribbean, such as the teaching of Hindi and cremation, and help in their efforts to prevent complete assimilation. See, for example, Memorandum of the British Guiana East Indian Association to the Royal Commission, n.d., CO 950/673, PRO; Memorandum of the East Indian Intel-

ligentsia of British Guiana to the Members of the Royal Commission, n.d., CO 9550/676, PRO; Transcript of Evidence from East Indian National Union (Jamaica) to West India Royal Commission, 30 November 1938, CO 950/244, PRO; No. 907 Memo by the Indian Evidence Committee on matters pertaining to the welfare of East Indians, n.d., ICS 56/44, Moyne Papers, ICS. For a helpful overview of Indo-Caribbean testimony before the Royal Commission, see La Guerre, "Moyne Commission."

40. Prior to World War II, Indo-Caribbean leaders such as Adrian Cola Rienzi made a significant impact within the labor movement for the good of all Trinidadian workers. Rienzi's activism is well known, but there lacks a definitive biography on his work. For a helpful overview of Rienzi, see Samaroo, *East Indian–West Indian.*

41. "An Open Letter to the Workers of the West Indies and British Guiana," 1938, MEPO 38/91, PRO; UAPAD, *Memorandum.*

42. See for example Ryan, *Race and Nationalism*; Samaroo, "Politics and Afro-Indian Relations," 97; Cross, *East Indians of Guyana and Trinidad*, preface.

43. Lowenthal, "Social Background," 81. For a more recent discussion of Afro-Caribbean hegemony, in this case Afro-Creole hegemony within Trinidad's national narrative, see Brereton, "Contesting the Past."

44. Proctor, "East Indians and the Federation," 370–71. A 1956 article in the *Trinidad Guardian* recorded that the East Indian population in Trinidad (37 percent of total population) and British Guiana (43 percent of total population) would be only 12 percent of the federal population. "The Preference," *TG*, 1 September 1956, 6.

45. For example, see C.L.R. James, *Lecture on Federation.*

46. Lowenthal, "Social Background," 83.

47. "Caribbean Labour Congress: Secretariat's Report to 1947 Congress," n.d., CLC-RHC, NLJ.

48. For instance, in 1953 the British Guiana East Indian Association announced their intention to support both anticommunist and anti-federation candidates in upcoming elections. "West Indian Political Intelligence Report No. 1/53," January 1953, CO 1031/129, PRO. For a brief overview of these events in Trinidad, see Ryan, *Race and Nationalism*, 100.

49. "Celebrations in BWI Toned by Developments of 'Great Significance,'" *TG*, 26 January 1955, 6.

50. "Governor Tells Local Indians Be West Indians First," *POSG*, 27 January 1955, 1; "Governor Opens 'Crucial' BWI Conference," *TG*, 15 March 1955, 6.

51. Debates over Indo-Caribbean attitudes toward federation continued throughout 1955. See for example "Prospects for 1955 are Good," *DG*, 4 January 1955, 8; "Recent Attacks on Writers Who Defend Colony Resented," *TG*, 9 January 1955, 5; "Trinidad Should Be More Receptive," *DG*, 3 March 1955, 11; "Are East Indians a Problem?" *DG*, 30 August 1955, 8.

52. "Unity Is Essential," *TG*, 30 October 1955, 6.

53. "People Not Consulted on Federation Issue," *POSG*, 18 March 1955, 4. In the mid-1950s there was significant suspicion among some Afro-Caribbeans and British officials that the Indian Commissioner in the West Indies rallied Indo-Caribbeans "on a racial, cultural and religious basis" and against federation. See for example "Notes of a meeting . . . to discuss the activities of the Indian Commissioner to the West Indies," CO 1031/1954, PRO.

54. "Indians' Attitude to Problems," *POSG*, 30 March 1955, 4.

55. "Language Query," *TG*, 13 October 1955, 6.

56. "No Political Issues," *TG*, 28 October 1955, 8.

57. "Future of the Indians Tied Up in the West Indies," *TG*, 18 October 1955, 8.

58. Braithwaite, "'Federal' Associations and Institutions," 322.

59. "Foresees BWI Federation—Calls on Aids from States," *NYAN*, 13 October 1945, 5.

60. "Co-operation the Touchstone for Success," *DG*, 10 September 1955, 8; "Why Are We Afraid?" *DG*, 17 September 1955, 11; "Federation," *DG*, 15 November 1955, 8.

61. Springer, "Historical Development, Hopes and Aims," 11.

62. See Rich, "Black Diaspora in Britain"; Adi, *West Africans in Britain*, 6–88; Olusanya, *West African Students' Union*.

63. Although there had been some previous attempts to create specifically West Indian student associations, including an early West Indian Students' Union in 1924 and a West Indian Students' Association in the 1930s, it was in the postwar era that more lasting associations flourished. Clover, "Dispersed or Destroyed," 3.

64. West Indian Students' Union, News Bulletin, 4 February 1950; West Indian Students' Union News Bulletin, 20 May 1950, CP/CENT/CTTE/02/04, CPGB, LHASC; WISU Constitution in Memo to Eric Williams from Winifred Birbeck, 14 February 1946, EWMC, UWISA; WISU Constitution, n.d., CO 1028/69, PRO.

65. G. E. Mills to Mr. Stone, 27 February 1951, CO 876/156. On Colonial Office attitudes toward colonial students in this era, see Report on Colonial Students in the United Kingdom and Eire, n.d.; Confidential Report on Colonial Students' Political Problem, n.d.; Report on Political Significance of African Students in Great Britain, n.d., CO 537/2574, PRO.

66. J. L. Keith, Colonial Office memo, 2 November 1952, CO 876/155, PRO.

67. Braithwaite, *Colonial West Indian Students*, 155.

68. West Indian Students' Union, News Bulletin, 8 October 1949, CP/CENT/CTE, 02/04, CPGB, LHASC.

69. West Indian Students' Union, News Bulletin, 4 February 1950, CP/CENT/CTE, 02/04, CPGB, LHASC.

70. West Indian Students' Union circular, n.d., box 133/1/3, FCBR, RH, Oxford.

71. See for example G. Campbell (British Embassy, DC) to Alan Dudley (Foreign Office, London), 14 March 1944, FO 371/38654, PRO.

72. Ralph Hoyte to Eric Williams, 6 March 1943, folder 11, EWMC, UWISA.

73. Caribbean Association of Howard University pamphlet, 1945, folder 13, EWMC, UWISA. For examples of contemporary Caribbean praise for Howard University for its role in the broader development of racial consciousness and bonds among African American and West Indian students, see Eric Williams to Dean J. St. Clair Price, 26 April 1944; Eric Williams to Dr. Mordecai W. Johnson, 21 September 1944, folder 19, EWMC, UWISA.

74. Eric Williams to Dr. Walter Daniel, 27 November 1945, folder 13, EWMC, UWISA.

75. "Student Meet to Aid Indies," *NYAN*, 22 April 1950, 6.

76. Morris, "Feeling, Affection, Respect," 8.

77. Braithwaite, *Colonial West Indian Students*, 133.

78. Dudley Thompson, "Commission on the Social Scene in the West Indies," n.d., CP/CENT/CTE, 02/04, CPGB, LHASC.

79. Quote taken from Eric Williams to Winston [Mahabir], 16 April 1945, folder 11, EWMC, UWISA. Additional accounts of this strife are drawn from Eric Williams to Ralph

& Milton, 16 April 1945; Winston [Mahabir] to Eric Williams, 28 April 1945; Wilma Cameron to Eric Williams, 18 April 1945, folder 11, EWMC, UWISA.

80. Lowenthal, "The West Indies Chooses a Capital," 341.

81. "Christmas and Federation," *TG*, 25 December 1956, 8; "Barbados May Get Capital," *POSG*, 18 March 1955, 1.

82. "Jamaica, Trinidad Chosen Capital Prospects 2 and 3," *TG*, 3 January 1957, 1; "A Federal New Year," *TG*, 1 January 1957, 1; "Questions and Answers on the Capital," *TG*, 13 January 1957, 8. The Fact-Finding Commission consisted of three members: Sir Francis Mudie (former governor of West Punjab), Professor H. Myles Wright (Lever Professor of Civic Design at Liverpool University), and Mr. A. E. Cook (retired permanent secretary in the Ministry of Finance, East Nigeria). For the official report of this commission, see CO, *Report of the British Caribbean Federal Capital Commission*.

83. "Jamaica, Trinidad Chosen Capital Prospects 2 and 3," *TG*, 3 January 1957, 1; "Battle for WI Capital Must Go On," *TG*, 4 January 1957, 1; "Questions and Answers on the Capital," *TG*, 13 January 1957, 8.

84. "Capital Sites Commission Findings," *DG*, 3 January 1957, 13; "Distorting the Picture," *TG*, 13 July 1956, 8.

85. "Indians to Protest," *TG*, 6 January 1957, 1; "Leaders Call for an Apology, Demand Capital for Trinidad," *TG*, 8 January 1957, 2.

86. "East Indians Are Not Opposed to Federation," *TG*, 8 January 1957, 6; "Attack on Indians Wrong and Unfair," *TG*, 15 January 1957, 8; "Dr. Williams Says 'Indians Are Part of W.I. Society,'" *TG*, 8 February 1957, 10.

87. "Race Bar 'May Rob Barbados of Federal Capital,'" *TG*, 12 January 1956, 1; "Trinidad 'Obvious Choice,'" *TG*, 11 January 1957, 3.

88. "Antiguans Hurt—Choice of 'Dixie' Barbados Attacked," *TG*, 5 January 1957, 2.

89. "BWI Must Look to the New World," *DG*, 7 January 1957, 8.

90. "Suitable Island Wanted," *TG*, 6 January 1957, 8.

91. "Barbados Is Victim of Unfair Criticism," *TG*, 5 February 1957, 8; "Barbadians Never Stoop to Slander and Abuse," *TG*, 13 February 1957, 8.

92. "We Must All Live Together," *TG*, 16 January 1957, 6. On the issue of race in Barbados in the mid-twentieth century, see Chamberlain, *Empire and Nation-Building in the Caribbean*, chap. 5.

93. Despite taking place after the launch of the West Indies Federation in January, these elections can be considered one of the final steps in the actual creation of the new nation, since they would produce the formal federal legislature.

94. Wallace, *The British Caribbean*, 140–41; Mordecai, *Federation*, 80–86. The only ruling party associated with FDLP was the government in St. Vincent.

95. "I Am No Socialist—He Says," *TG*, 18 May 1957, 1; "Federation," *DG*, 22 July 1957, 8; "Bishop Gibson: 'Colour Bar' Meaningless in Jamaica," *DG*, 15 May 1957, 7.

96. "Maraj Hits Anti-Indian Jamaican Laws," *TG*, 5 February 1957, 1; "Get It Right," *DG*, 4 January 1958, 6; "Mitra Sinanan Calls Manley Statement 'Irresponsible,'" *POSG*, 18 February 1956, 1.

97. "Colour Question," *DG*, 28 January 1958, 8; "Colour in Politics," *DG*, 30 January 1958, 10; "Colour in Politics," *DG*, 1 February 1958, 6; "Race Politics," *DG*, 4 February 1958, 8.

98. "I Can't Help the Colour of My Skin," *DG*, 18 March 1958, 8; "PNP Fighting Election on Class and Colour," *DG*, 24 March 1958, 11.

99. "Colour in Politics," *DG*, 1 February 1958, 6; "Race Politics," *DG*, 4 February 1958, 8.

100. "So What," *DG*, 16 March 1958, 8.

101. "Political Myths Go by the Board," *DG*, 29 March 1958, 8.

102. "West Indies DLP," *DG*, 5 October 1957, 8; Ayearst, "West Indian Political Parties," 79.

103. E. Williams, *Historical Background of Race Relations,* 34; E. Williams, *Case for Party Politics*, 18–19.

104. Singh, *Indian Struggle*, xlvi–xlvii, xlix.

105. Ibid., xlvi–xlix.

106. "Hatred and Animosity Seen in Election Move," *TG*, 22 March 1958, 8.

107. "CM Claims—Dems Used Race," *TG*, 3 April 1958, 1, 13.

108. "Trinidadians Should Not Be Misled by Political Novices," *TG*, 14 April 1958, 6.

109. "Racially Speaking," *TG*, 3 April 1958, 8; "Dems Deny Using 'Race' in Federal Election Fight," *TG*, 8 April 1958, 7; "Trinidad Was Famous for Racial Harmony," *TG*, 13 April 1958, 8; "CM Seeking a Scapegoat," *TG*, 9 April 1958, 6.

110. "Williams Gives Rude Shock to 'Unity' Motto," *TG*, 9 April 1958, 6; "Busta Hits Back at CM," *TG*, 13 April 1958, 2; "Busta Warns About Ghost of Manley," *TG*, 21 April 1958, 2.

111. "Fight Racialism with Multi-Racialism: PNM Victory in Defeat," *TG*, 4 April 1958, 9; "PNM Stands for Unity," *TG*, 12 April 1958, 6; "East Indians Were Not Attacked by Williams," *TG*, 16 April 1958, 6.

112. "Trinidad DLP Stands Condemned," *TG*, 15 April 1958, 8; "False Impressions Given to Public About PNM," *TG*, 21 April 1958, 6; "East Indian Should Be Prime Minister," *TG*, 11 April 1958, 8.

113. "CM Seeking a Scapegoat," *TG*, 9 April 1958, 6.

114. "Preach WI Unity," *TG*, 25 April 1958, 8; "Forget Race or Ruin WI—Hopkin Says," *TG*, 8 May 1958, 7; "Unity Alone Can Give Federation Strength," *TG*, 9 May 1958, 8.

115. W. James, "Black Experience," 373–82. For further discussion of West Indian migration to London and general black experiences in Britain in the twentieth century, see Paul, *Whitewashing Britain*; Matera, "Black Intellectuals"; James and Harris, *Inside Babylon*; K. Perry, "'Little Rock' in Britain"; and the various works of Hakim Adi and Marika Sherwood, among others. On Claudia Jones, see Sherwood, *Claudia Jones*; Boyce-Davies, *Left of Karl Marx*; Schwarz, "Claudia Jones and the *West Indian Gazette*."

116. "Objectives of the League," *Caribbean League of America*, 6 March 1957, 4, in box 12, folder 10, Moore Papers, SC; "Role of the Caribbean League of America," *A Salute to the Federated West Indies*, 22 April 1958, box 12, folder 1 (West Indian Federation), Moore Papers, SC.

117. "Proclamation," *Caribbean League of America*, 6 March 1957, in box 12, folder 10, Moore Papers, SC.

118. "New Caribbean Unit Chartered," *NYAN*, 9 February 1957, 2.

119. Editorial, *Caribbean League of America*, 6 March 1957, 2, in box 12, folder 10, Moore Papers, SC.

120. "West Indian Dream," *CD*, 16 February 1957, 10.

121. "Bindley Cyrus Speaks to West Indian Group," *CD*, 6 July 1957, 3.

122. Mordecai, *Federation*, 75–76.

123. "Long Live the West Indies," *DG*, 4 January 1958, 6.

124. "British West Indian Federation," *PC*, 11 January 1958, A2.

125. "West Indies Federation Is Born in Trinidad," *AA*, 11 January 1958, 17.

126. "Manhattan and Beyond," *NYAN*, 11 January 1958, 4.

127. "Add Members to Caribbean Group," *CD*, 11 January 1958, 3; Bindley Cyrus to Rayford Logan, 22 November 1957; Rayford Logan to Bindley Cyrus, 4 December 1957, box 166-7, folder 3, Logan Papers, MSRC.

128. "Air Tours to Trinidad Leave Chicago April 20," *CD*, 1 February 1958, 12; "2-Week West Indies Tour Set for Federation Ceremonies," *NYAN*, 22 February 1958, 17.

129. "West Indies on the Way," *PC*, 5 April 1958, A8.

130. Z. Williams, *Talented Tenth*, 131; "Friends of West Indies Federation Set in D.C.," *AA*, 12 April 1958, 9; "Form WIF Chapter, *PC*, 12 April 1958, 17; H. Con. Res. 298, 25 March 1958; Rayford Logan to Frederick Stanton, 23 April 1958, box 166-7, folder 3, Logan Papers, MSRC.

131. Z. Williams, *Talented Tenth*, 131.

132. "Social Interlude in Chicago," *PC*, 9 March 1957, A15; "Windy City Smart Set Hails Forming of West Africa Republic," *CD*, 23 March 1957, 13; "Forward," *NYAN*, 9 March 1957, 6.

133. Boyce-Davies, *Left of Karl Marx*, 69, 87. For the importance of Ghanaian independence to Black America, the West Indies, and other parts of the black diaspora, see Gaines, *American Africans in Ghana*.

134. Untitled photo, *CD*, 15 April 1958, A14; untitled photo, *CD*, 24 April 1958, 14; "Local West Indians Salute Birth of Federation at Gala Reception," *CD*, 3 May 1958, 15.

135. Untitled photo, *CD*, 16 April 1958, 28; "Bostonians Mark Birth of Federation," *AA*, 26 April 1958, 10.

136. Invitation to Mabel Staupers, 22 April 1958, box 96-1-A, folder 6, Staupers Collection, MSRC; Caribbean Association Invitation to Dr. & Mrs. Logan for Inaugural Celebration of the West Indies Federation, 22 April 1958, box 166-24, folder 2, Logan Papers, MSRC; "Morgan College Salutes West Indies Federation," *AA*, 26 May 1958, 9.

137. "Brown Asks Mayor for WI Honors," *NYAN*, 19 April 1958, 1; "West Indian Art Exhibit at Library," *NYAN*, 19 April 1958, 13; "West Indies Celebrations April 20–27," *NYAN*, 19 April 1958, 5.

138. Mordecai, *Federation*, 94–95.

139. Ibid., 95; Alexander-Gooding, Beckles, and Griffin, *Photographic Journey*, 18. The messages and speeches quoted come from black American press coverage of these festivities. See "Princess' Federation Speech," *NYAN*, 3 May 1958, 1; "Inaugurate New Nation," *AA*, 3 May 1958, 1; "New WI Nation Born," *NYAN*, 26 April 1958, 13. On the decisions of Manley and Williams to concentrate on the "local" politics in Jamaica and Trinidad, where both felt they faced strong opposition that could possibly sidetrack the Federation, see Wallace, *The British Caribbean*, 143–45.

140. Springer made this claim in episode 2, "Weakness into Strength," of a four-part documentary series *New Nation in the West Indies*, produced by the National Film Board of Canada and aired in four consecutive weeks in April 1958.

141. "The West Indies Federation," *Jamaica Times*, 31 May 1958.

142. H. D. Huggins, "Significance of the New Nation"; Roy Wilkins, "Long Live the West Indies"; Langston Hughes, "Salute, Federation," all in *A Salute to the Federated West Indies* program, 22 April 1958, box 12, folder 1 (West Indian Federation), Moore Papers, SC.

143. House of Beauty ad, *NYAN*, 26 April 1958, 20; Savoy Ballroom ad, *NYAN*, 26 April 1958, 15; Palm Cafe, Keitt's Bar, Spot Lite Bar, Ebony Lounge, Teddy's Shanty ads, *NYAN*, 26 April 1958, 19.

144. "Carver Bank Shows WI-American Unity," *NYAN*, 26 April 1958, 18; Carver Federal Savings and Loan Association ad, *NYAN*, 26 April 1958, 18.

145. "Hope and Confidence," *AA*, 3 May 1958, 4. It is reasonable to assume the use of "colored" here is synonymous with "black" with the federation joining Haiti as a black republic in the Western Hemisphere.

146. "The People Speak," *CD*, 3 May 1958, 10.

147. "Ghana High Court Judge Visits Jamaica," *NYAN*, 24 May 1958, 20. In this case the Federation was invariably viewed as a black nation with importance and attachment to Africa and the broader black diaspora.

148. Nkrumah to West Indian Chief Ministers, 7 June 1962, 4/60/2B/27, Manley Papers, JA. Though written in 1962 shortly before the fall of the Federation, it is reasonable to assume his comments and racialized visions of the West Indies also applied to the Federation's arrival in 1958, particularly given William Van Lare's comments on behalf of Nkrumah in 1958.

149. "The Test," *NYAN*, 7 June 1958, 8. Given the inclusion of the "Arab" population of Algeria, one could see this piece as speaking to a broader idea of "colored races" (that is, nonwhites). However, the authors could also be assuming that all of Africa was indeed "black."

150. "West Indies Federation," *Ebony* 13, no. 7 (May 1958): 146–48.

151. "New Federation in the Sun," *New York Times*, 10 August 1958.

152. "Federation Starts on a 'Sticky Wicket,'" *NYAN*, 24 May 1958, 20.

153. "The West Indian Federation," *CD*, 24 April 1958, 11.

154. "Islands Settle Down to Federation Task," *NYAN*, 26 April 1958, 1.

Epilogue

1. Springer, *Reflections*, 8–9.

2. "Foul Federation," *WI*, 17 January 1919, 1.

3. Anglin, "Political Development of The West Indies," 54; Lennox-Boyd quoted in Killingray, "West Indian Federation," 75.

4. Mordecai, *Federation*, 155.

5. Springer, *Reflections*, 13–14.

6. Some have suggested that one of the reasons dominion status was withheld from the Federation was because the British wanted to judge the viability of such an arrangement in the region, especially in regard to the financial state of the British West Indies. For overviews of these and other issues Federation faced in its infancy, see Wallace, *The British Caribbean*, chap. 6; Mordecai, *Federation*, chap. V; Springer, *Reflections*, chap. 2. For a more recent work on the subject, see Killingray, "West Indian Federation."

7. E. Williams, *New Federation*, 6–7.

8. For a brief collection of Manley speeches on federation, see Nettleford, *Manley and the New Jamaica*, 162–84.

9. Mordecai, *Federation*, 159. On Ministry Paper no. 18, see Mordecai, *Federation*, 158–59; O. Padmore, "Demise of an Idea," 51–52.

10. Palmer, *Eric Williams*, 58–59.

11. Springer, *Reflections*, 15.

12. Mordecai, *Federation*, 161–62.

13. E. Williams, *Economics of Nationhood*, 11.

14. Mordecai, *Federation*, chap. IX.

15. Timm, "Transnational Roots," 442.

16. Domingo, *Federation—Jamaica's Folly*, 3.

17. Ibid., 8–9.

18. Ibid., 9–14, 19.

19. Ibid., 10, 14–16, 22.

20. Ibid., 17–24.

21. Worcester, *C.L.R. James*, 148, 156.

22. For a discussion of James's return to the West Indies in these years, see Worcester, *C.L.R. James*, chap. 6. For his own account of his initially amicable and then oppositional relationship with Williams and the PNM in Trinidad, see C.L.R. James, *Party Politics*.

23. C.L.R. James, *Lecture on Federation*, 2.

24. Ibid., 4–7.

25. Ibid., 13–14, 22.

26. Ibid., 18–21.

27. "Revelations and Reflections on West Indies Federation," 2 November 1958, *DG*, 8.

28. Ibid.

29. Ibid.

30. Ibid.

31. Ibid.

32. Ibid.

33. "Greetings," *WIA*, January–February 1959, 1. It is unclear what connection this *WIA* had with the *WIA* of the 1920s other than the name.

34. "The W.I. Is Gaining," *WIA*, September 1959, 11.

35. "Caribbean-American Conference in April," *NYAN*, 28 March 1959, 5; "West Indian-USA Racial Relations," *NYAN*, 4 April 1959, A4; "3-Point Program For West Indies," *NYAN*, 2 May 1959, 1.

36. See for instance "Sir Grantley Says US Helps Germany, But Not Federation," *NYAN*, 24 October 1959, 6; "Norman Manley to Speak," *NYAN*, 3 September 1960, 14; "Caribbean Women Hear Ghana Envoy," *NYAN*, 10 June 1961, 37; "Inauguration Banquet," *CD*, 28 April 1961, 10; "Caribbean Symposium" *NYAN*, 28 October 1961, 9.

37. Palmer, *Eric Williams*, 76–78.

38. The United States was not persuaded to surrender its claim to Chaguaramas, though it would eventually abandon the base and return it to an independent Trinidad a few years after the collapse of the Federation. For examinations of the Chaguaramas crisis as it relates to both US Cold War policy and West Indian nationalism, see Mordecai, *Federation*, chap. VI; Parker, *Brother's Keeper*, 109–18; Palmer, *Eric Williams*, chap. 3.

39. Mordecai, *Federation*, 198–200.

40. Ibid., 201–2.

41. *DG*, 19 January 1960, quoted in Mordecai, *Federation*, 201; O. Padmore, "Demise of an Idea," 53.

42. Although Bustamante and the JLP had been moving toward such a position, their announcement this day, which included a decision to not even put forth a candidate in an upcoming election for an open seat in the federal legislature, finalized their stance against Jamaica's participation in the Federation. Mordecai, *Federation*, 219.

43. Palmer, *Eric Williams*, 61.

44. W. A. Lewis, *Agony of the Eight*, 5–10.

45. Wallace, *The British Caribbean*, 183–85; Mordecai, *Federation*, chaps. XVII, XX.

46. Wallace, *The British Caribbean*, 185–90; Mordecai, *Federation*, chap. XXI.

47. Mordecai, *Federation*, 401.

48. Roberts quoted in Timm, "Transnational Roots," 437. On the referendum in general, see for example Wallace, *The British Caribbean*, 192–96; Mordecai, *Federation*, chap. XXIII; M. Johnson, "To Dwell Together in Unity"; Munroe, *Constitutional Decolonization*, 129–38; C.L.R. James, *Federation, "We Failed Miserably,"* 1–10. On Domingo and Roberts in the referendum campaign, see Timm, "Transnational Roots," 448–59. On PPP support for the anti-federation campaign, see: Mordecai, *Federation*, 404–7. For examples of the limited PNP pro-federation propaganda in this era, see People's National Party, *Federation Facts* and *Great Sayings on Federation*; Jamaica Premier Office, *Federation*.

49. Mordecai, *Federation*, 414; Munroe, *Constitutional Decolonization*, 135–38.

50. Palmer, *Eric Williams*, 179–181. On subsequent debates on these other possible continuations of the Federation among the other West Indian colonies, including firsthand perspectives, see W. A. Lewis, *Agony of the Eight*, 10–39. The so-called Little Eight were Antigua and Barbuda, Barbados, Dominica, Grenada, Montserrat, St. Kitts-Nevis-Anguilla, St. Lucia, and St. Vincent and the Grenadines.

51. Wallace, *The British Caribbean*, 208.

52. Sives, "Dwelling Separately," 30; Watts, *New Federations*, 36.

53. Watts, *New Federations*, 35; Springer, *Reflections*, 8.

54. Springer, *Reflections*, 42.

55. G. Lewis, *Modern West Indies*, 353.

56. Sives, "Dwelling Separately," 22–24.

57. Springer, *Reflections*, 36–37, 43–44.

58. Ibid., 28–30; Rohlehr, "Scuffling of Islands," 71–73. On Manley's logic for calling the referendum and reactions to it, see Mordecai, *Federation*, 223–35; Munroe, *Constitutional Decolonization*, 129–35. For an excellent examination of the idea of federation before, during, and after the Federation, see Rohlehr, "Scuffling of Islands."

59. Springer, *Reflections*, 18–19.

60. Mordecai, *Federation*, 455–56.

61. Ibid., 457–62.

62. Ibid., chap. XXIV. Quote from Wallace, *The British Caribbean*, 212.

63. Grantley Adams, "Reflections on Federation 6," n.d., box 2, folder 7, Demas Papers, UWISA.

64. Ramphal, *Glimpses*, 144.

65. Ledgister, *Only West Indians*, 111.

66. Springer, *Reflections*, 44; Palmer, *Eric Williams*, 181–182.

67. Timm, "Transnational Roots," 457–59.

68. CLR James to "My Dear Carl," 23 October 1961, box 5, folder 105, James Collection, UWISA.

69. Nkrumah to West Indian Chief Ministers, 7 June 1962; Nkrumah to Manley, 8 June 1962, 4/60/2B/27, Manley Papers, JA. Given that Nkrumah is writing on the eve of Jamaican and Trinidadian independence, following the dissolution of the West Indies Federation, it is unclear if he is appealing to current and former members of the Federation, or just the remaining units. In either case, his appeal for West Indian unity as a means of achieving racial unity and progress applies and displays his reaction to the recent disunity in the region and his belief in the need for the Federation to continue.

70. The information and quotations in this and the next three paragraphs are drawn from R. Moore, "Independent Caribbean Nationhood."

71. R. Moore, "Caribbean Unity and Freedom," 305–8.

72. Ibid., 308–9.

73. "Jamaicans Reject West Indian Federation," *NYAN*, 23 September 1961, 21; "Jamaica Votes to Leave West Indies Federation," *CD*, 21 September 1961, 3.

74. Gordon Lewis, for example, dismissed the idea that the lack of such a regional identification resulted in the failure of the Federation; see *Growth of the Modern West Indies*, 369. However, shortly before the launch of the Federation, even he had proclaimed the essentialness of this identification; see "Powerful West Indianism Necessary to Federation," *DG*, 3 January 1957, 7.

75. In the case of the United States, discussions of divisive issues such as the slave trade had been delayed for twenty years following the ratification of the federal constitution in 1787. This did not prevent the fracturing of the nation once these debates reemerged in the nineteenth century and the outbreak of the Civil War more than eighty years after the country's creation. In fact, regional divisions remained a prominent issue well into the twentieth century, and some may argue to the current day.

76. Putnam, *Radical Moves*, 228–29.

77. Hurwitz, "Study in Nationalism," 139.

78. W. A. Lewis, *Agony of the Eight*, 10–39; Palmer, *Eric Williams*, 179–81.

79. Mordecai, *Federation*, 461.

80. For a history of these efforts, see Payne, *Political History of CARICOM*.

81. Jagan, *Caribbean Unity and Carifta*, 26.

82. Palmer, "Continuing Challenges," 132–33. This article was originally delivered as part of Palmer's keynote address for the 2006 Eric Williams Memorial Lecture at Florida International University.

83. Manley, "Fifty Years," 10.

84. For a brief discussion of creole multiracial nationalism and some criticisms of it, see Ledgister, *Only West Indians*, 19–24.

85. D. Thomas, *Modern Blackness*, 12. For a larger discussion of Jamaica's national motto and its relationship to blackness and the Jamaican masses, see her introduction and chap. 1. For discussions and criticisms of this national motto during the 1960s, see Nettleford, "National Identity"; Rodney, *Groundings*, 12–15.

86. For discussions of these two events, see Rodney, *Groundings*; Oxaal, *Black Intellectuals*; Palmer, *Eric Williams*, chap. 8.

87. Chevannes, "Rastafari," 65.

88. Quotes from Allahar, "Popular Culture and Racialisation," 7–8, cited in Deosaran, "Caribbean Man," 81, 114; Rohlehr, "Scuffling of Islands," 100–101.

Bibliography

Manuscript and Special Collections

Caribbean Labour Congress. Monthly Bulletins, Correspondence, Press Cuttings, Information Sheets, Conference Reports and Memoranda 1945–1951. George A. Smathers Libraries, University of Florida, Gainesville.

Casimir, J. R. Papers. Schomburg Center for Research in Black Culture, New York Public Library.

Colonial Office. Records. Public Records Office, National Archives, Kew, Richmond, Surrey, UK.

Communist Party of Great Britain. Archive. Labour History Archive and Study Centre, People's History Museum, Manchester, UK.

Demas, William. Papers. West Indiana and Special Collections Division, University of the West Indies–St. Augustine, Trinidad.

Department of State (RG 84). Foreign Service Posts. National Archives and Records Administration, College Park, MD.

DuBois, W.E.B. Papers. Department of Special Collections and University Archives, University of Massachusetts–Amherst.

Fabian Colonial Bureau. Papers. Bodleian Library of Commonwealth and African Studies at Rhodes House, University of Oxford.

Foreign Office. Records. Public Records Office, National Archives, Kew, Richmond, Surrey, UK.

Hart, Richard. Caribbean Labour Congress Collection. National Library of Jamaica, Kingston.

Jamaica Progressive League. Collection. National Library of Jamaica, Kingston.

James, C.L.R. Collection. West Indiana and Special Collections Division, University of the West Indies–St. Augustine, Trinidad.

James, C.L.R. Papers. Institute of Commonwealth Studies, School of Advanced Study, University of London.

Logan, Rayford. Papers. Moorland-Spingarn Research Center, Howard University, Washington, DC.

Manley, Norman Washington. Papers. Jamaican Archives and Records Department, Spanish Town.

Metropolitan Police. Records. Public Records Office, National Archives, Kew, Richmond, Surrey, UK.

Moore, Richard B. Papers. Schomburg Center for Research in Black Culture, New York Public Library.

National Association for the Advancement of Colored People. Papers. Manuscripts Division, Library of Congress, Washington, DC.

Office of Territories (RG 126). Records. National Archives and Records Administration, College Park, MD.

Prime Minister's Office: General Administration. Records. W.I. Federal Archives Centre, University of the West Indies–Cave Hill, Barbados.

Prime Minister's Office: Information Service. Records. W.I. Federal Archives Centre, University of the West Indies–Cave Hill, Barbados.

Roberts, W. Adolphe. Papers. National Library of Jamaica, Kingston.

Staupers, Mabel. Collection. Moorland-Spingarn Research Center, Howard University, Washington, DC.

West India Committee. Records. Institute of Commonwealth Studies, School of Advanced Study, University of London.

West India Royal Commission. Moyne Papers. Institute of Commonwealth Studies, School of Advanced Study, University of London.

West Indies National Council. Collection. Schomburg Center for Research in Black Culture, New York Public Library.

Williams, Eric. Memorial Collection. West Indiana and Special Collections Division, University of the West Indies–St. Augustine, Trinidad.

Periodicals

Africa and the World
African Sentinel
African Times and Orient Review
Afro-American
Barbados Recorder
Canada-West Indies Magazine
Chicago Defender
Communist
Crisis
Daily Gleaner
Daily Telegraph
Dominica Guardian
Ebony
International African Opinion
Jamaica Times
Journal of the National Medical Association
Keys
League of Coloured Peoples News Letter
Liberator
Messenger

Negro Champion
Negro Worker
New Daily Chronicle
New York Amsterdam News
New York Amsterdam Star News
New York Times
Pittsburgh Courier
Port-of-Spain Gazette
Public Opinion
Times (London)
Trinidad Guardian
Voice of St. Lucia
West Indian (Grenada)
West Indian-American

Printed Sources

Adi, Hakim. *Pan-Africanism and Communism: The Communist International, Africa and the Diaspora, 1919–1939*. Trenton, NJ: Africa World Press, 2013.
———. *West Africans in Britain, 1900–1960: Nationalism, Pan-Africanism and Communism*. London: Lawrence & Wishart, 1998.
Alexander-Gooding, Sharon, Cherri Beckles, and Stanley H. Griffin. *A Photographic Journey Celebrating 50 Years of West Indian Nationhood*. Cave Hill, Barbados: W.I. Federal Archives Centre, 2008.
Allahar, Anton. "Popular Culture and Racialisation of Political Consciousness in Trinidad and Tobago." *Wadabagei: A Journal of the Caribbean and Its Diaspora* 1, no. 2 (1998): 1–41.
Anderson, Carol. *Eyes off the Prize: The United Nations and the African American Struggle for Human Rights, 1944–1955*. New York: Cambridge University Press, 2003.
Andrews, George Reid. *Afro-Latin America, 1800–2000*. New York: Oxford University Press, 2004.
Anglin, Douglas S. "The Political Development of the West Indies." In Lowenthal, *The West Indies Federation*, 35–62.
Ashdown, Peter. "The Growth of Black Consciousness in Belize 1914–1919: The Background to the Ex-Servicemen's Riot of 1919." *Belcast Journal of Belizean Affairs* 2, no. 2 (December 1985): 1–5.
———. "Marcus Garvey, the UNIA and the Black Cause in British Honduras, 1914–1949." *Journal of Caribbean History* 15 (1981): 41–55.
———. "Race Riot, Class Warfare and Coup d'etat: The Ex-Servicemen's Riot of July 1919." *Belcast Journal of Belizean Affairs* 3, nos. 1–2 (July 1986): 8–14.
Ashton, S. R., and David Killingray, eds. *The West Indies*. London: Stationery Office, 1999.
Aspinall, Algernon E. "West Indian Federation: Its Historical Aspect." *United Empire* 10, no. 2 (February 1919): 58–63.
Augier, F. R. "Federations: Then and Now." *Caribbean Quarterly* 35, no. 3 (1989): 16–23.
Augier, F. R., and Shirley C. Gordon, eds. *Sources of West Indian History*. London: Longmans, 1962.

August, Eugene R., ed. *The Nigger Question*, by Thomas Carlyle; *The Negro Question*, by John Stuart Mill. New York: Appleton-Century-Crofts, 1971.

AWIACA (American West Indian Association on Caribbean Affairs). *Caribbean Charter: A Program for the West Indies*. New York: AWIACA, 1942.

Ayearst, Morley. *The British West Indies: The Search for Self-Government*. New York: New York University Press, 1960.

———. "A Note on Some Characteristics of West Indian Political Parties." In *The Aftermath of Sovereignty: West Indian Perspectives*, edited by David Lowenthal and Lambros Comitas, 67–79. Garden City, NY: Anchor, 1973.

Baldwin, Davarian L., and Minkah Makalani, eds. *Escape from New York: The New Negro Renaissance Beyond Harlem*. Minneapolis: University of Minnesota Press, 2013.

Basdeo, Sahadeo. *Labour Organisation and Labour Reform in Trinidad, 1919–1939*. St. Augustine, Trinidad: Institute of Social and Economic Research, UWI, 1983.

Beattie, Peter. *The Tribute of Blood: Army, Honor, Race, and Nation in Brazil, 1864–1945*. Durham, NC: Duke University Press, 2001.

Beckles, Hilary. *Afro-Caribbean Women and Resistance to Slavery in Barbados*. London: Karnak House, 1988.

———. *Natural Rebels: A Social History of Enslaved Black Women in Barbados*. New Brunswick, NJ: Rutgers University Press, 1989.

Benn, Denis M. *The Caribbean: An Intellectual History, 1774–2003*. Kingston, Jamaica: Ian Randle, 2004.

Blackburn, Robin. *The Making of New World Slavery: From the Baroque to the Modern, 1492–1800*. London: Verso, 1997.

———. *The Overthrow of Colonial Slavery, 1776–1848*. London: Verso, 1989.

Blackett, R.J.M. "The Hamic Connection: African-Americans and the Caribbean, 1820–1865." In Moore and Wilmot, *Before and After 1865*, 317–29.

Blanchard, Peter. *Slavery and Abolition in Early Republican Peru*. Wilmington, DE: SR Books, 1992.

Bogues, Anthony. "Nationalism and Jamaican Political Thought." In Monteith and Richards, *Jamaica in Slavery and Freedom*, 363–87.

Bolland, O. Nigel. *On the March: Labour Rebellions in the British Caribbean, 1934–39*. Kingston, Jamaica: Ian Randle, 1995.

———. *The Politics of Labour in the British Caribbean: The Social Origins of Authoritarianism and Democracy in the Labour Movement*. Kingston, Jamaica: Ian Randle, 2001.

Boyce-Davies, Carole. *Left of Karl Marx: The Political Life of Black Communist Claudia Jones*. Durham, NC: Duke University Press, 2007.

Boyle, Kevin. *Arc of Justice: A Saga of Race, Civil Rights, and Murder in the Jazz Age*. New York: Henry Holt, 2004.

Brady, Alexander. *The West Indies: A New Federation*. Toronto: Canadian Institute of International Affairs, 1958.

Braithwaite, Lloyd. *Colonial West Indian Students in Britain*. Mona, Jamaica: University of the West Indies Press, 2001.

———. "'Federal' Associations and Institutions in the British West Indies." In Huggins, *Federation of the West Indies*, 286–328.

Brereton, Bridget. "The Birthday of Our Race: A Social History of Emancipation Day in

Trinidad, 1838–1888." In *Trade, Government, and Society in Caribbean History, 1700–1920: Essays Presented to Douglas Hall*, edited by B. W. Higman, 69–83. Kingston, Jamaica: Heinemann Educational Books Caribbean, 1983.

———. "Contesting the Past: Narratives of Trinidad and Tobago History." *New West Indian Guide* 81, nos. 3–4 (2007): 169–96.

———. *A History of Modern Trinidad, 1783–1962*. London: Heinemann, 1981.

———. "Jubilees: How Trinidad and Tobago Remembered Victoria's Jubilees, the Jubilee of Emancipation, and the Centenary of British Rule." *Journal of Caribbean History* 46, no. 1 (2012): 1–32.

———. *Race Relations in Colonial Trinidad, 1870–1900*. New York: Cambridge University Press, 1979.

British Caribbean Standing Closer Association Committee, Great Britain. *Report of the British Caribbean Standing Closer Association Committee, 1948–1949*. London: HMSO, 1950.

Brown, Judith M., and W. Roger Louis, eds. *The Oxford History of the British Empire*. Vol. 4, *The Twentieth Century*. New York: Oxford University Press, 1999.

Brubaker, Rogers, and Frederick Cooper. "Beyond Identity." *Theory and Society* 29, no. 1 (February 2000): 1–47.

Bryan, Patrick. *The Jamaican People, 1880–1902: Race, Class and Social Control*. Kingston, Jamaica: University of the West Indies Press, 2000.

Bush, Barbara. *Slave Women in Caribbean Society 1650–1838*. Bloomington: Indiana University Press, 1990.

Caribbean Labour Congress. *Federation and Self Government Now or Colonialism and Slavery Forever*. London: CLC, 1948.

Carlyle, Thomas. "The Nigger Question." In August, *Nigger Question*, 1–37.

Carrington, Selwyn. "The State of the Debate on the Role of Capitalism in the Ending of the Slave System." *Journal of Caribbean History* 22, nos. 1–2 (1988): 20–41.

Central Office of Information. *British Caribbean Federation*. London: Central Office of Information, 1955.

———. *Towards a Federation of the West Indies: The Growth of an Idea*. London: Central Office of Information, 1949.

———. *West Indian Federation: A Background Note*. London: Central Office of Information, 1953.

———. *The West Indies: Towards Federation*. London: Central Office of Information, 1957.

Chamberlain, Mary. *Empire and Nation-Building in the Caribbean: Barbados 1937–66*. Manchester: Manchester University Press, 2010.

Chambers, Glenn A. *Race, Nation, and West Indian Immigration to Honduras, 1890–1940*. Baton Rouge: LSU Press, 2010.

Chevannes, Barry. "Rastafari and the Exorcism of the Ideology of Racism and Classism in Jamaica." In *Chanting Down Babylon*, edited by Nathaniel Samuel Murrell, William David Spencer, and Adrian Anthony McFarlane, 55–71. Philadelphia: Temple University Press, 1998.

Cipriani, Arthur A. *His Best Orations*. Compiled by Randolph Mitchell. Port-of-Spain, Trinidad: Surprise Print Shop, n.d. [1950s].

———. *Twenty-Five Years After: The British West Indies Regiment in the Great War, 1914–1918*. Port-of-Spain: Trinidad Publishing, 1940.

Clarke, John Henrik, ed. *Marcus Garvey and the Vision of Africa*. New York: Random House, 1974.

Closer Union Commission, Great Britain. *Report of the Closer Union Commission (Leeward Islands, Windward Islands, Trinidad and Tobago), April 1933*. Cmd. 4383. London: HMSO, 1933.

Clover, David. "Dispersed or Destroyed: Archives, the West Indian Students' Union, and Public Memory." *Society for Caribbean Studies Annual Conference Papers* 6 (2005).

Colonial Office, Great Britain. *Closer Association of the British West Indian Colonies*. Cmd. 7120. London: HMSO, 1947.

———. *Conference on the Closer Association of the British West Indian Colonies—Montego Bay, Jamaica, 11th–19th September 1947*. Part 1, *Report* (Cmd. 7291); part 2, *Proceedings*. London: HMSO, 1948.

———. *The Plan for a British Caribbean Federation agreed by the Conference on West Indian Federation held in London in April 1953*. Cmd. 8895. London: HMSO, 1953.

———. *Report by the Conference on British Caribbean Federation held in London in February, 1956*. London: HMSO, 1956.

———. *Report by the Conference on West Indian Federation held in London in April, 1953*. Cmd. 8837. London: HMSO, 1953.

———. *Report of the British Caribbean Federal Capital Commission*. London: HMSO, 1956.

———. *Report of the Conference on Movement of Persons Within a British Caribbean Federation: Held in Port of Spain, Trinidad from Monday 14th March to Thursday 17th March, 1955*. Col. no. 315. London: HMSO, 1955.

———. *Trinidad and Tobago Disturbances, 1937: Report of Commission*. Cmd. 5641. London: HMSO, 1938.

———. *West India Royal Commission, 1938–1939, Recommendations*. Cmd. 6174. London: HMSO, 1940.

———. *West India Royal Commission Report*. Cmd. 6607. London: HMSO, 1945.

Costa, Emilia Viotti da. *Crowns of Glory, Tears of Blood: The Demerara Slave Rebellion of 1823*. New York: Oxford University Press, 1994.

Cox, Edward L. "'Race Men': The Pan-African Struggles of William Galwey Donovan and Theophilus Albert Marryshow for Political Change in Grenada, 1884–1925." *Journal of Caribbean History* 36, no. 1 (2002): 69–99.

———. "William Galwey Donovan and the Struggle for Political Change in Grenada, 1883–1920." *Small Axe* 22 (February 2007): 17–38.

Craton, Michael. *Empire, Enslavement, and Freedom in the Caribbean*. Princeton, NJ: Markus Wiener, 1997.

———. *Testing the Chains: Resistance to Slavery in the British West Indies*. Ithaca, NY: Cornell University Press, 1982.

Cross, Malcolm. *The East Indians of Guyana and Trinidad*. London: Minority Rights Group, 1980.

Cudjoe, Selwyn R. *Beyond Boundaries: The Intellectual Tradition of Trinidad and Tobago in the Nineteenth Century*. Amherst, MA: Calaloux, 2003.

Cunard, Nancy, and George Padmore. *The White Man's Duty*. Manchester: PanAf Service, 1945.

Dalleo, Raphael. "The Public Sphere and Jamaican Anticolonial Politics: *Public Opinion, Focus*, and the Place of the Literary." *Small Axe* 32 (June 2010): 56–82.

Davis, David Brion. *Inhuman Bondage*. New York: Oxford University Press, 2006.

———. *The Problem of Slavery in Western Culture*. Ithaca, NY: Cornell University Press, 1966.

Davson, Edward. *Report of the West Indian Conference*. Cmd. 2672. London: HMSO, 1926.

DeLisser, H. G. "The Negro as a Factor in the Future of the West Indies." *New Century Review* 7 (January 1900): 1–6.

———. *Twentieth Century Jamaica*. Kingston: Jamaica Times, 1913.

Deosaran, Ramesh. "The 'Caribbean Man': A Study of the Psychology of Perception and the Media." In *India in the Caribbean*, edited by David Dabydeen and Brinsley Samaroo, 81–118. London: Hansib, 1987.

Domingo, W. A. *British West Indian Federation: A Critique*. Kingston, Jamaica: Gleaner Company, 1956.

———. *Federation—Jamaica's Folly*. New York: privately printed, 1958.

———. "Jamaica Seeks Its Freedom." *Opportunity* 16 (1938): 370–72.

———. "The Tropics in New York." *Survey: Social, Charitable, Civic: A Journal of Constructive Philanthropy* 53 (1925): 648–50.

Dubois, Laurent. *Avengers of the New World: The Story of the Haitian Revolution*. Cambridge, MA: Belknap Press of Harvard University Press, 2004.

———. *A Colony of Citizens: Revolution and Slave Emancipation in the French Caribbean, 1787–1804*. Chapel Hill: University of North Carolina Press, 2004.

DuBois, W.E.B. "The Negro Mind Reaches Out." In *The New Negro: Voices of the Harlem Renaissance*, edited by Alain Locke, 385–414. 1925. New York: Simon & Schuster, 1997.

Dudziak, Mary L. *Cold War Civil Rights: Race and the Image of American Democracy*. Princeton, NJ: Princeton University Press, 2000.

Dunn, Richard S. *Sugar and Slaves: The Rise of the Planter Class in the English West Indies, 1624–1713*. New York: W. W. Norton, 1973.

Egerton, Douglas R. *Gabriel's Rebellion: The Virginia Slave Conspiracies of 1800 and 1802*. Chapel Hill: University of North Carolina Press, 1993.

Elkins, W. F. "Black Power in the British West Indies: The Trinidad Longshoremen's Strike of 1919." *Science and Society* 33, no. 1 (Winter 1969): 71–75.

———. "Hercules and the Society of Peoples of African Origin." *Caribbean Studies* 11, no. 4 (1971): 47–59.

———. "Marcus Garvey, the *Negro World*, and the British West Indies: 1919–1920." *Science & Society* 36, no. 1 (Spring 1972): 63–77.

———. "A Source of Black Nationalism in the Caribbean: The Revolt of the British West Indies Regiment at Taranto, Italy." *Science & Society* 34, no. 1 (Spring 1970): 99–103.

Emmanuel, Patrick. *Crown Colony Politics in Grenada, 1917–1951*. Cave Hill, Barbados: Institute of Social and Economic Research, UWI, 1978.

Fanning, Sara. *Caribbean Crossing: African Americans and the Haitian Emigration Movement*. New York: New York University Press, 2014.

Ferrer, Ada. *Insurgent Cuba: Race, Nation, and Revolution, 1868–1898*. Chapel Hill: University of North Carolina Press, 1999.

Fick, Carolyn E. *The Making of Haiti: The Saint Domingue Revolution from Below*. Knoxville: University of Tennessee Press, 1991.

Foner, Nancy. "West Indian Identity in the Diaspora: Comparative and Historical Perspectives." *Latin American Perspectives* 25, no. 3 (May 1998): 173–88.

Franck, Thomas M., ed. *Why Federations Fail: An Inquiry into the Requisites for Successful Federation*. New York: NYU Press, 1968.

Franklyn, H. Mortimer-. *The Unit of Imperial Federation: A Solution of the Problem*. London: Swan Sonnenschein, Lowery, 1887.

Fraser, Cary. *Ambivalent Anticolonialism: The United States and the Genesis of West Indian Independence, 1940–1964*. Westport, CT: Greenwood, 1994.

———. "The Twilight of Colonial Rule in the British West Indies: Nationalist Assertion vs. Imperial Hubris in the 1930s." *Journal of Caribbean History* 30, nos. 1–2 (1996): 1–27.

Frazier, E. Franklin, and Eric Williams, eds. *The Economic Future of the Caribbean*. Washington, DC: Howard University Press, 1944.

Froude, James A. *The English in the West Indies; or, The Bow of Ulysses*. New York: Charles Scribner's Sons, 1888.

Fryer, Peter. *Staying Power: Black People in Britain since 1504*. Atlantic Highlands, NJ: Humanities Press, 1984.

Gaines, Kevin. *American Africans in Ghana: Black Expatriates and the Civil Rights Era*. Chapel Hill: University of North Carolina Press, 2006.

Gallicchio, Marc S. *The African American Encounter with Japan and China: Black Internationalism in Asia, 1895–1945*. Chapel Hill: University of North Carolina Press, 2000.

Garvey, Amy Jacques. *Memorandum Correlative of Africa, West Indies and the Americas*. Kingston, Jamaica: n.p., 1944.

———, ed. *The Philosophy and Opinions of Marcus Garvey, or, Africa for the Africans*. 1923–25. Dover, MA: Majority Press, 1986.

Gaspar, David Barry. *Bondmen and Rebels: A Study of Master-Slave Relations in Antigua*. Baltimore: Johns Hopkins University Press, 1985.

Gaspar, David Barry, and David Patrick Geggus, eds. *A Turbulent Time: The French Revolution and the Greater Caribbean*. Bloomington: Indiana University Press, 1997.

Gaspar, David Barry, and Darlene Clark Hine, eds. *More Than Chattel: Black Women and Slavery in the Americas*. Bloomington: Indiana University Press, 1996.

Gebrekidan, Fikru Negash. *Bond Without Blood: A History of Ethiopian and New World Black Relations, 1896–1991*. Trenton, NJ: African World Press, 2005.

Geiss, Imanuel. *The Pan-African Movement*. Translated by Ann Keep. London: Methuen, 1974.

Gellman, Erik S. *Death Blow to Jim Crow: The National Negro Congress and the Rise of Militant Civil Rights*. Chapel Hill: University of North Carolina Press, 2012.

Genovese, Eugene D. *From Rebellion to Revolution: Afro-American Slave Revolts in the Making of the New World*. Baton Rouge: LSU Press, 1979.

Gomes, Albert. *Through a Maze of Colour*. Port-of-Spain, Trinidad: Key Caribbean Publications, 1974.

Gooding, Earl. *The West Indies at the Crossroads*. Cambridge, MA: Schenkman, 1981.

Goveia, Elsa V. *An Introduction to the Federation Day Exhibition*. Jamaica: UCWI, 1959.

———. *Slave Society in the British Leeward Islands at the End of the Eighteenth Century*. New Haven: Yale University Press, 1965.

Green, James W. "Culture and Colonialism in the West Indies." *Journal of Interamerican Studies and World Affairs* 14, no. 4 (November 1972): 489–95.

Green, Jeffrey. *Black Edwardians: Black People in Britain 1901–1914*. London: Frank Cass, 1998.

Guridy, Frank Andre. "'Enemies of the White Race': The *Machadista* State and the UNIA in Cuba. *Caribbean Studies* 31, no. 1 (January–June 2003): 107–39.

———. "Feeling Diaspora in Harlem and Havana." *Social Text* 27, no. 1 (Spring 2009): 115–40.

———. *Forging Diaspora: Afro-Cubans and African Americans in a World of Empire and Jim Crow*. Chapel Hill: University of North Carolina Press, 2010.

———. "From Solidarity to Cross-Fertilization: Afro-Cuban/African American Interaction During the 1930s and 1940s." *Radical History Review* 87 (Fall 2003): 19–48.

Hall, Catherine. "What Is a West Indian?" In Schwarz, *West Indian Intellectuals in Britain*, 31–50.

———. *White, Male, and Middle Class: Explorations in Feminism and History*. New York: Routledge, 1992.

Hall, Douglas. *A Brief History of the West India Committee*. St. Lawrence, Barbados: Caribbean Universities Press, 1971.

Hall, Kenneth, and Myrtle Chuck-A-Sang, eds. *The Caribbean Integration Process: A People Centred Approach*. Kingston, Jamaica: Ian Randle, 2007.

Harold, Claudrena N. *The Rise and Fall of the Garvey Movement in the Urban South, 1918–1942*. New York: Routledge, 2007.

Harris, Joseph E. *African-American Reactions to War in Ethiopia, 1936–1941*. Baton Rouge: LSU Press, 1994.

Harrison, Hubert. *When Africa Awakes: The "Inside Story" of the Stirrings and Strivings of the New Negro in the Western World*. 1920. Chesapeake, VA: ECA Associates Press, 1991.

Hart, Richard. "Federation: An Ill-Fated Design." *Jamaica Journal* 25, no. 1 (October 1993): 10–16.

Hatch, John. *Dwell Together in Unity*. London: Fabian Society, 1958.

Henry, Paget. *Caliban's Reason: Introducing Afro-Caribbean Philosophy*. New York: Routledge, 2000.

Heuman, Gad. "From Slavery to Freedom: Blacks in the Nineteenth-Century British West Indies." In Morgan and Hawkins, *Black Experience and the Empire*, 141–65.

———. *The Killing Time: The Morant Bay Rebellion in Jamaica*. Knoxville: University of Tennessee Press, 1994.

Hicks, Ursula K. *Federalism: Failure and Success: A Comparative Study*. New York: Oxford University Press, 1978.

Higman, B. W. "The Colonial Congress of 1831." In Moore and Wilmot, *Before and After 1865*, 239–48.

———. "Remembering Slavery: The Rise, Decline, and Revival of Emancipation Day in the English-Speaking Caribbean." *Slavery and Abolition* 19 (April 1998): 90–105.

Hill, Robert A., ed. *The Crusader*. 3 vols. New York: Garland, 1987.

———. "The First England Years and After, 1912–1916." In Clarke, *Marcus Garvey and the Vision of Africa*, 38–70.

———, ed. *The Marcus Garvey and Universal Negro Improvement Association Papers*. Vol. 1, *1826–August 1919*. Berkeley: University of California Press, 1983.

Hinds, Allister. "Federation and Political Representation in the Eastern Caribbean 1920–1934." Paper presented at "Henry Sylvester Williams and Pan-Africanism: A Retrospection and Projection," University of the West Indies–St. Augustine, Trinidad, 7–12 January 2001.

Hinds, Donald. *Journey to an Illusion: The West Indian in Britain*. London: Heinemann, 1966.

Holder, Calvin B. "The Causes and Composition of West Indian Immigration to New York City, 1900–1952." *Afro-Americans in New York Life and History* 11, no. 1 (January 1987): 7–27.

Holt, Thomas C. "The Essence of the Contract: The Articulation of Race, Gender, and Political Economy in British Emancipation Policy, 1838–1866." In *Beyond Slavery: Explorations of Race, Labor, and Citizenship in Postemancipation Societies*, edited by Frederick Cooper, Thomas C. Holt, and Rebecca J. Scott, 33–59. Chapel Hill: University of North Carolina Press, 2000.

———. *The Problem of Freedom: Race, Labor, and Politics in Jamaica and Britain, 1832–1938*. Baltimore: Johns Hopkins University Press, 1992.

Hooker, James R. *Henry Sylvester Williams: Imperial Pan-Africanist*. London: Rex Collings, 1975.

Horne, Gerald. *Cold War in a Hot Zone: The United States Confronts Labor and Independence Struggles in the British West Indies*. Philadelphia: Temple University Press, 2007.

———. *The End of Empires: African Americans and India*. Philadelphia: Temple University Press, 2008.

Howe, Glenford D. *Race, War and Nationalism: A Social History of West Indians in the First World War*. Kingston, Jamaica: Ian Randle, 2002.

Hoyos, F. A. *The Rise of West Indian Democracy: The Life and Times of Sir Grantley Adams*. Barbados: Advocate Press, 1963.

Huggins, H. D., ed. *Federation of the West Indies*. Mona, Jamaica: Institute of Social and Economic Research, UCWI, 1957.

Hughes, Colin A. "Experiments Towards Closer Union in the British West Indies." *Journal of Negro History* 43, no. 2 (April 1958): 85–104.

———. "Semi-Responsible Government in the British West Indies." *Political Science Quarterly* 68, no. 3 (September 1953): 338–53.

Hurwitz, Samuel J. "The Federation of the West Indies: A Study in Nationalisms." *Journal of British Studies* 6, no. 1 (November 1966): 139–68.

Hyam, Ronald. "Bureaucracy and 'Trusteeship' in the Colonial Empire." In Brown and Louis, *Oxford History of the British Empire*, 4: 255–79.

IASB (International African Service Bureau). *The West Indies To-Day*. London: IASB, 1936.

Jagan, Cheddi. *Caribbean Unity and Carifta*. Guyana: Education Committee of People's Progressive Party, 1968.

Jamaica Premier Office. *Federation: How Much Does It Really Cost? Which Is Cheaper? To*

Go it Alone for Independence? Or to Share Everything in Federation. Kingston: Govt. Printer, 1961.

Jamaica Public Relations Office. *Jamaica and Federation.* Kingston: Govt. Printer, 1961.

James, C.L.R. *The Black Jacobins: Toussaint L'Ouverture and the San Domingo Revolution.* 2nd ed. New York: Vintage, 1989.

———. "The Case for West Indian Self-Government." In *The C.L.R. James Reader,* edited by Anna Grimshaw, 49–62. Malden, MA: Blackwell, 1992.

———. *Federation, "We Failed Miserably": How and Why.* Tunapuna, Trinidad: C.L.R. James, 1961.

———. *A History of Pan-African Revolt.* Chicago: Charles H. Kerr, 1995.

———. *Lecture on Federation (West Indies and British Guiana).* Georgetown, British Guiana: Argosy, 1959.

———. *The Life of Captain Cipriani: An Account of British Government in the West Indies.* Nelson, Lancashire: Coulton, 1932.

———. *Party Politics in the West Indies.* San Juan, Trinidad: Vedic Enterprises, 1962.

———. "The West Indian Intellectual." In Thomas, *Froudacity,* 23–48.

———. *West Indians of East Indian Descent.* Port-of-Spain, Trinidad: IBIS, 1965.

James, Winston. "The Black Experience in Twentieth-Century Britain." In Morgan and Hawkins, *Black Experience and the Empire,* 347–86.

———. *Holding Aloft the Banner of Ethiopia: Caribbean Radicalism in Early Twentieth-Century America.* New York: Verso, 1998.

———. "The Wings of Ethiopia: The Caribbean Diaspora and Pan-African Projects from John Brown Russwurm to George Padmore." In *African Diasporas in the New and Old Worlds: Consciousness and Imagination,* edited by Genevieve Fabre and Klaus Benesch, 121–57. New York: Rodopi, 2006.

James, Winston, and Clive Harris. *Inside Babylon: The Caribbean Diaspora in Britain.* London: Verso, 1993.

Johnson, Howard. "The Anglo-American Caribbean Commission and the Extension of American Influence in the British Caribbean, 1942–1945." *Journal of Commonwealth & Comparative Politics* 22, no. 2 (1984): 180–203.

———. "The Black Experience in the British Caribbean in the Twentieth Century." In Morgan and Hawkins, *Black Experience and the Empire,* 317–46.

———. "The British Caribbean from Demobilization to Constitutional Decolonization." In Brown and Louis, *Oxford History of the British Empire,* 4: 597–622.

———. "The United States and the Establishment of the Anglo-American Caribbean Commission." *Journal of Caribbean History* 19, no. 1 (1984): 26–47.

Johnson, Michele A. "The Beginning and the End: The Montego Bay Conference and the Jamaican Referendum on West Indian Federation." *Social and Economic Studies* 48, no. 4 (1999): 117–49.

———. "'To Dwell Together in Unity': Referendum on West Indian Federation, 1961." In Moore and Wilmot, *Before and After 1865,* 261–71.

Joseph, C. L. "The British West Indies Regiment, 1914–1918." *Journal of Caribbean History* 2 (May 1971): 94–124.

Kasinitz, Philip. *Caribbean New York: Black Immigrants and the Politics of Race.* Ithaca, NY: Cornell University Press, 1992.

Kelley, Robin D. G. "'But a Local Phase of a World Problem': Black History's Global Vision, 1833–1950." *Journal of American History* 86, no. 3 (December 1999): 1045–77.

———. *Hammer and Hoe: Alabama Communists During the Great Depression*. Chapel Hill: University of North Carolina Press, 1990.

Kelley, Robin D. G., and Betsy Esch. "Black Like Mao: Red China and Black Revolution." *Souls* 1, no. 4 (Fall 1999): 6–41.

Killingray, David. "'To Do Something for the Race': Harold Moody and the League of Coloured Peoples." In Schwarz, *West Indian Intellectuals in Britain*, 51–70.

———. "The West Indian Federation and Decolonization in the British Caribbean." *Journal of Caribbean History* 34, nos. 1–2 (2000): 71–88.

Kitchen, Martin. *Empire and Commonwealth: A Short History*. New York: Palgrave Macmillan, 1996.

Knight, Franklin W. *The Caribbean: The Genesis of a Fragmented Nationalism*. New York: Oxford University Press, 1990.

———. *Race, Ethnicity, and Class: Forging the Plural Society in Latin America and the Caribbean*. Waco, TX: Baylor University Press, Markham Press Fund, 1996.

Kuczynski, R. R., ed. *Demographic Survey of the British Colonial Empire*. Vol. 3, *West Indian and American Territories*. New York: Oxford University Press, 1953.

La Guerre, John. "The Moyne Commission and the West Indian Intelligentsia, 1938–39." *Journal of Commonwealth Political Studies* 9, no. 2 (July 1971): 134–57.

Lamont, Norman. *Problems of the Antilles: A Collection of Speeches and Writings on West Indian Questions*. Glasgow: John Smith, 1912.

Ledgister, F.S.J. *Only West Indians: Creole Nationalism in the British West Indies*. Trenton, NJ: Africa World Press, 2010.

Levy, Claude. *Emancipation, Sugar, and Federalism: Barbados and the West Indies*. Gainesville: University Presses of Florida, 1980.

Lewis, David Levering, ed. *W.E.B. DuBois: A Reader*. New York: Henry Holt, 1995.

Lewis, Earl. "To Turn as on a Pivot: Writing African Americans into a History of Overlapping Diasporas." *American Historical Review* 100, no. 3 (June 1995): 765–87.

Lewis, Gordon. "The British Caribbean Federation: The West Indian Background." *Political Quarterly* 28, no. 1 (January–March 1957): 49–65.

———. *The Growth of the Modern West Indies*. New York: Monthly Review Press, 1968.

———. *Main Currents in Caribbean Thought: The Historical Evolution of Caribbean Society in Its Ideological Aspects, 1492–1900*. Baltimore: Johns Hopkins University Press, 1983.

Lewis, Rupert. "J. J. Thomas and Political Thought in the Caribbean." *Caribbean Quarterly* 36, nos. 1–2 (June 1990): 46–58.

———. *Marcus Garvey, Anti-Colonial Champion*. Trenton, NJ: Africa World Press, 1988.

Lewis, Rupert, and Patrick Bryan, eds. *Garvey: His Work and Impact*. Trenton, NJ: Africa World Press, 1991.

Lewis, W. Arthur. *The Agony of the Eight*. Barbados: Advocate Commercial Printery, 1965.

———. *Labour in the West Indies: The Birth of a Worker's Movement*. 1939. London: New Beacon, 1977.

Lombardi, John V. *The Decline and Abolition of Negro Slavery in Venezuela, 1820–1854*. Westport, CT: Greenwood, 1971.

Look Lai, Walton. *Indentured Labor, Caribbean Sugar: Chinese and Indian Migrants to the British West Indies, 1838–1918*. Baltimore: Johns Hopkins University Press, 1993.

Lowenthal, David. "The Social Background of the West Indian Federation." In *The West Indies Federation*, 63–96.

——. *West Indian Societies*. New York: Oxford University Press, 1972.

——. "The West Indies Chooses a Capital." *Geographical Review* 48, no. 3 (July 1958): 336–64.

——, ed. *The West Indies Federation: Perspectives of a New Nation*. New York: Columbia University Press, 1961.

Lumsden, Joy. "A Forgotten Generation: Black Politicians in Jamaica, 1884–1914." In Moore and Wilmot, *Before and After 1865*, 112–22. Kingston, Jamaica: Ian Randle, 1998.

——. "Robert Love and Jamaican Politics." Ph.D. diss., University of the West Indies (Mona), 1988.

MacMaster, Neil. *Racism in Europe, 1870–2000*. New York: Palgrave, 2001.

Makalani, Minkah. *In the Cause of Freedom: Radical Black Internationalism from Harlem to London*. Chapel Hill: University of North Carolina Press, 2011.

——. "Introduction: Diaspora and the Localities of Race." *Social Text* 27, no. 1 (Spring 2009): 1–9.

Malliet, A. M. Wendell. *The Destiny of the West Indies*. New York: Russwurm Press, 1928.

——. "Some Prominent West Indians." *Opportunity* 4 (November 1926): 348–51.

Manley, Rachel. "Fifty Years of Jamaican Independence: A Manley Perspective." Keynote address at 14th Annual Eric E. Williams Memorial Lecture, Florida International University, Miami, 26 October 2012.

Mansingh, Surjit. "Background to Failure of the West Indies Federation: An Inquiry into British Rule in the Caribbean, 1920–1947." Ph.D. diss., American University, 1972.

Marryshow, T. Albert. *Cycles of Civilisation*. Grenada: Office of "The West Indian," 1917.

Marshall, Woodville K., ed. *I Speak for the People: The Memoirs of Wynter Crawford*. Kingston, Jamaica: Ian Randle, 2003.

Martin, Tony. "Eric Williams: His Radical Side in the Early 1940s." *Journal of Caribbean Studies* 17, nos. 1–2 (Summer 2002): 107–19.

——. *The Pan-African Connection: From Slavery to Garvey and Beyond*. Dover, MA: Majority Press, 1983.

——. "A Pan-Africanist in Dominica: J. R. Ralph Casimir and the Garvey Movement, 1919–1923." *Journal of Caribbean History* 21, no. 2 (1988): 117–37.

——. *Race First: The Ideological and Organizational Struggles of Marcus Garvey and the Universal Negro Improvement Association*. Dover, MA: Majority Press, 1976.

Matera, Marc. "Black Intellectuals and the Development of Colonial Studies in Britain." *Journal of British Studies* 49 (April 2010): 388–418.

——. "Black Internationalism and African and Caribbean Intellectuals in London, 1919–1950." Ph.D. diss., Rutgers University, 2008.

Mathews, Thomas. "The Project for a Confederation of the Greater Antilles." *Caribbean Historical Review* nos. 3–4 (December 1954): 70–107.

McCartney, John T. *Black Power Ideologies: An Essay in African-American Political Thought*. Philadelphia: Temple University Press, 2010.

McIntyre, W. David. *British Decolonization, 1946–1997*. New York: St. Martin's Press, 1998.

Meikle, Louis S. *Confederation of the British West Indies versus Annexation to the United States of America: A Political Discourse on the West Indies*. 1912. New York: Negro Universities Press, 1969.

Meriwether, James. *Proudly We Can Be Africans: Black Americans and Africa, 1935–1961*. Chapel Hill: University of North Carolina Press, 2002.

Mill, John Stuart. "The Negro Question." In August, *Nigger Question*, 38–50.

Millette, James. *The Genesis of Crown Colony Government: Trinidad, 1783–1810*. Curepe, Trinidad: Moko Enterprises, 1970.

Mintz, Sidney. *Sweetness and Power: The Place of Sugar in Modern History*. New York: Penguin, 1986.

Monteith, Kathleen E. A., and Glen Richards, eds. *Jamaica in Slavery and Freedom: History, Heritage and Culture*. Kingston, Jamaica: University of the West Indies Press, 2002.

Moore, Brian L., and Swithin R. Wilmot, eds. *Before and After 1865: Education, Politics and Regionalism in the Caribbean*. Kingston, Jamaica: Ian Randle, 1998.

Moore, Richard B. "Caribbean Unity and Freedom." *Freedomways* 4, no. 3 (1964): 295–311.

———. "Independent Caribbean Nationhood—Has It Been Achieved or Set Back?" In Turner and Turner, *Richard B. Moore*, 291–301.

Mordecai, John. *Federation of the West Indies*. Evanston, IL: Northwestern University Press, 1968.

Morgan, Philip D., and Sean Hawkins, eds. *Black Experience and the Empire*. New York: Oxford University Press, 2004.

Morris, Mervyn. "Feeling, Affection, Respect." In *Disappointed Guests: Essays by African, Asian, and West Indian Students*, edited by Henri Tajfel and John L. Dawson, 5–26. New York: Oxford University Press, 1965.

Moses, Wilson Jeremiah, ed. *Classical Black Nationalism from the American Revolution to Marcus Garvey*. New York: New York University Press, 1996.

Muhammad, Baiyina W. "What Is Africa to Us? The Baltimore *Afro American*'s Coverage of the African Diaspora, 1915–1941." Ph.D. diss., Morgan State University, 2004.

Munroe, Trevor. *The Politics of Constitutional Decolonization: Jamaica 1944–62*. Mona, Jamaica: Institute of Social and Economic Research, UWI, 1983.

Murray, C. Gideon. *A Scheme for the Federation of Certain of the West Indian Colonies*. London: West India Committee, 1911.

———. *A United West Indies*. London: West Strand, 1912.

Naison, Mark. *Communists in Harlem During the Great Depression*. Urbana: University of Illinois Press, 1983.

Neptune, Harvey R. *Caliban and the Yankees: Trinidad and the United States Occupation*. Chapel Hill: University of North Carolina Press, 2007.

Nettleford, Rex. "National Identity and Attitudes to Race in Jamaica." In *Consequences of Class and Color: West Indian Perspectives*, edited by David Lowenthal and Lambros Comitas, 35–55. Garden City, NY: Anchor, 1973.

———, ed. *Norman Washington Manley and the New Jamaica: Selected Speeches and Writings, 1938–1968*. New York: Africana, 1971.

Olusanya, G. O. *The West African Students' Union and the Politics of Decolonisation, 1925–1958*. Ibadan, Nigeria: Daystar, 1982.

O'Meally, Jaime. *Why We Demand Self-Government*. New York: JPL, 1938.

Orde Browne, Granville St. John. *Labour Conditions in the West Indies*. Cmd. 6070. London: HMSO, 1939.

Oxaal, Ivar. *Black Intellectuals and the Dilemmas of Race and Class in Trinidad*. Rochester, Vermont: Schenkman, 1982.

Padmore, George, ed. *Colonial and Coloured Unity, a Programme of Action: History of the Pan-African Congress*. 2nd ed. London: Hammersmith Bookshop, 1963.

———. *Pan-Africanism or Communism*. New York: Doubleday, 1971.

Padmore, Overand R. "Federation: The Demise of an Idea." *Social and Economic Studies* 48:4 (1999): 21–63.

Palmer, Colin A. *Cheddi Jagan and the Politics of Power: British Guiana's Struggle for Independence*. Chapel Hill: University of North Carolina Press, 2010.

———. "Eric Williams and the Continuing Challenges of a Diverse Caribbean." In Hall and Chuck-A-Sang, *The Caribbean Integration Process*, 129–39.

———. *Eric Williams and the Making of the Modern Caribbean*. Chapel Hill: University of North Carolina Press, 2006.

Parascandola, Louis J., ed. *"Look for Me All Around You": Anglophone Caribbean Immigrants in the Harlem Renaissance*. Detroit: Wayne State University Press, 2005.

Parker, Jason C. *Brother's Keeper: The United States, Race, and Empire in the British Caribbean, 1937–1962*. New York: Oxford University Press, 2008.

———. "'Capital of the Caribbean': The African American–West Indian 'Harlem Nexus' and the Transnational Drive for Black Freedom, 1940–1948." *Journal of African American History* 89, no. 2 (Spring 2004): 98–117.

———. "'Made-in-America Revolutions'? The 'Black University' and the American Role in the Decolonization of the Black Atlantic." *Journal of American History* 96, no. 3 (December 2009): 727–50.

Paul, Kathleen. *Whitewashing Britain: Race and Citizenship in the Postwar Era*. Ithaca, NY: Cornell University Press, 1997.

Payne, Anthony. *The Political History of CARICOM*. Kingston, Jamaica: Ian Randle, 2008.

People's National Party. *The Case of Domingo*. Kingston, Jamaica: PNP, n.d.

———. *Federation Facts. Unity! Freedom!! Progress!!! Independence Now*. Kingston, Jamaica: PNP, 1961.

———. *Great Sayings on Federation: Quotations from Speeches Made at Federation Conferences, in House of Representatives' Debates and at Public Meetings*. Kingston, Jamaica: PNP, n.d. [1950s].

Perry, Jeffrey B., ed. *A Hubert Harrison Reader*. Middletown, CT: Wesleyan University Press, 2001.

———. *Hubert Harrison: The Voice of Harlem Radicalism, 1883–1918*. New York: Columbia University Press, 2009.

———. "An Introduction to Hubert Harrison: The Father of Harlem Radicalism." *Souls* 2, no. 1 (Winter 2000): 38–54.

Perry, Kennetta Hammond. "'Little Rock' in Britain: Jim Crow's Transatlantic Topographies." *Journal of British Studies* 51, no. 1 (January 2012): 155–77.

Plummer, Brenda Gayle. "Firmin and Martí at the Intersection of Pan-Americanism and Pan-Africanism." In *José Martí's 'Our America': From National to Hemispheric Cultural*

Studies, edited by Jeffrey Belnap and Raúl Fernández, 210–27. Durham, NC: Duke University Press, 1998.

———. *In Search of Power: African Americans in the Era of Decolonization, 1956–1974.* Cambridge: Cambridge University Press, 2012.

———. *Rising Wind: Black Americans and U.S. Foreign Affairs, 1935–1960.* Chapel Hill: University of North Carolina Press, 1996.

Polyné, Millery. *From Douglass to Duvalier: U.S. African Americans, Haiti, and Pan Americanism, 1870–1964.* Gainesville: University Press of Florida, 2010.

Post, Ken. *Arise Ye Starvelings: The Jamaican Labour Rebellion of 1938 and Its Aftermath.* The Hague: Martinus Nijhoff, 1978.

Price, Richard. *Maroon Societies: Rebel Slave Communities in the Americas.* Baltimore: Johns Hopkins University Press, 1996.

Proceedings of the West Indian Conference held at Roseau, Dominica, B.W.I., October-November, 1932. Port Castries, St. Lucia: n.p., 1932.

Proctor, Jesse H. "The Development of the Idea of Federation of the British Caribbean Territories." *Caribbean Quarterly* 5, no. 1 (1957): 5–33.

———. "East Indians and the Federation of the British West Indies." *India Quarterly* 17, no. 4 (October–December 1961): 370–95.

Putnam, Lara. "Citizenship from the Margins: Vernacular Theories of Rights and the State from the Interwar Caribbean." *Journal of British Studies* 53, no. 1 (January 2014): 162–91.

———. *Radical Moves: Caribbean Migrants and the Politics of Race in the Jazz Age.* Chapel Hill: University of North Carolina Press, 2013.

Ramphal, Shridath. *Glimpses of a Global Life.* Toronto: Dundurn Press, 2014.

Ramphal, S. S. "Federalism in the West Indies." *Caribbean Quarterly* 6, nos. 2–3 (May 1960): 210–29.

Reid, Ira De A. "The Negro in the British West Indies." *Journal of Negro Education* 10, no. 3 (July 1941): 524–35.

Report of the Commission Appointed to Enquire Into the Disturbances which Took Place in Barbados on the 27th July, 1937, and Subsequent Days. Bridgetown, Barbados: n.p., 1937.

Report of the First West Indies Conference held in Barbados, January–February, 1929. London: Crown Agents for the Colonies, 1929.

Rich, Paul. "The Black Diaspora in Britain: Afro-Caribbean Students and the Struggle for Political Identity." *Immigrants & Minorities* 6, no. 2 (1987): 151–73.

Richards, Glen. "Race, Class, and Labour in Colonial Jamaica, 1900–1934." In Monteith and Richards, *Jamaica in Slavery and Freedom*, 340–62.

———. "Race, Labour, and Politics in Jamaica and St. Kitts, 1909–1940: A Comparative Survey of the Roles of the National Club of Jamaica and the Workers League of St. Kitts." In *Working Slavery, Pricing Freedom: Perspectives from the Caribbean, Africa and the African Diaspora*, edited by Verene A. Shepherd, 502–23. New York: Palgrave, 2002.

Rippon, Joseph. *Unification: United West Indies.* London: Waterlow & Sons Limited, 1912.

Roberts, G. W. "Some Demographic Considerations of West Indian Federation." In Huggins, *Federation of the West Indies*, 262–85.

Roberts, W. Adolphe. *Self-Government for Jamaica.* New York: JPL, 1936.

Robinson, Cedric. *Black Marxism: The Making of the Black Radical Tradition.* Chapel Hill: University of North Carolina Press, 2000.

Rodney, Walter. *The Groundings with My Brothers*. 1969. Chicago: Research Associates School Times Publications, 1990.

Rogers, Thomas D. "Bustamante, the Lonely Fighter: Loyalty, Justice, and Race in the Discourse of a Jamaican Populist." *Contours* 3, no. 1 (Spring 2005): 48–78.

Rohlehr, Gordon. "A Scuffling of Islands: The Dream and Reality of Caribbean Unity in Poetry and Song." In Hall and Chuck-A-Sang, *The Caribbean Integration Process*, 48–121.

Romo, Anadelia. *Brazil's Living Museum: Race, Reform, and Tradition in Bahia*. Chapel Hill: University of North Carolina Press, 2010.

Rout, Leslie B., Jr. *The African Experience in Spanish America, 1502 to the Present Day*. New York: Cambridge University Press, 1976.

Rush, Anne Spry. *Bonds of Empire: West Indianness and Britishness from Victoria to Decolonization*. New York: Oxford University Press, 2011.

———. "Imperial Identity in Colonial Minds: Harold Moody and the League of Coloured Peoples, 1931–50." *Twentieth Century British History* 13, no. 4 (2002): 356–83.

Ryan, Selwyn D. *Race and Nationalism in Trinidad and Tobago: A Study of Decolonization in a Multiracial Society*. Toronto: University of Toronto Press, 1972.

Salmon, C. S. *The Caribbean Confederation: A Plan for the Union of the Fifteen British West Indian Colonies, Preceded by an Account of the Past and Present Condition of the Europeans and the African Races Inhabiting Them, with a True Explanation of the Haytian Mystery*. 1888. London: Frank Cass, 1971.

Samaroo, Brinsley. *East Indian–West Indian: The Public Career of Adrian Cola Rienzi (1905–1972)*. St. Augustine, Trinidad: Faculty of Humanities and Education, UWI, 2006.

———. "Politics and Afro-Indian Relations in Trinidad," In *Calcutta to Caroni: The East Indians of Trinidad*, edited by John La Guerre, 84–97. [Port-of-Spain, Trinidad]: Longman Caribbean, 1974.

Scholes, Theophilus E. S. *The British Empire and Alliances; or, Britain's Duty to Her Colonies and Subject Races*. London: Elliott Stock, 1899.

Schwarz, Bill. "'Claudia Jones and the *West Indian Gazette*': Reflections on the Emergence of Post-colonial Britain." *Twentieth Century British History* 14, no. 3 (September 2003): 264–85.

———, ed. *West Indian Intellectuals in Britain*. Manchester: Manchester University Press, 2003.

Scott, Julius. "The Common Wind: Currents of Afro-American Communication in the Era of the Haitian Revolution." Ph.D. diss., Duke University, 1986.

Scott, Rebecca J. *Slave Emancipation in Cuba: The Transition to Free Labor, 1860–1899*. Princeton, NJ: Princeton University Press, 1985.

Scott, William R. *The Sons of Sheba's Race: African-Americans and the Italo-Ethiopian War, 1935–1941*. Bloomington: Indiana University Press, 1993.

Seigel, Micol. *Uneven Encounters: Making Race and Nation in Brazil and the United States*. Durham, NC: Duke University Press, 2009.

Sheppard, Jill. *Marryshow of Grenada: An Introduction*. Barbados: Letchworth, 1987.

Sheridan, Richard B. *Sugar and Slavery: An Economic History of the British West Indies*. Baltimore: Johns Hopkins University Press, 1973.

Sherwood, Marika. *Claudia Jones: A Life in Exile*. London: Lawrence & Wishart, 1999.

———. "The United Nations: Caribbean and African-American Attempts to Influence the Founding Conference in San Francisco in 1945." *Journal of Caribbean History* 29, no. 1 (1995): 25–58.

Singh, H. P. *The Indian Struggle for Justice and Equality Against Black Racism in Trinidad and Tobago: 1956–1962.* Couva, Trinidad: Indian Review Press, 1993.

Singh, Kelvin. *Race and Class Struggles in a Colonial State, Trinidad 1917–1945.* Kingston, Jamaica: University of the West Indies Press, 1994.

Sives, Amanda. "Dwelling Separately: The Federation of the West Indies and the Challenge of Insularity." In *Defunct Federalisms: Critical Perspectives on Federal Failure,* edited by Emilian Kavalski and Magdalena Zolkos, 17–30. Burlington, VT: Ashgate, 2008.

Slate, Nico. *Colored Cosmopolitanism: The Shared Struggle for Freedom in the United States and India.* Cambridge: Harvard University Press, 2012.

Smith, Faith. *Creole Recitations: John Jacob Thomas and Colonial Formation in the Late Nineteenth-Century Caribbean.* Charlottesville: University of Virginia Press, 2002.

———. "A Man Who Knows His Roots: J. J. Thomas and Current Discourses of Black Nationalism." *Small Axe* 5 (March 1999): 1–13.

Smith, James Patterson. "The Liberals, Race, and Political Reform in the British West Indies, 1866–1874." *Journal of Negro History* 79, no. 2 (Spring 1994): 131–46.

Smith, M. G. *The Plural Society in the British West Indies.* Berkeley: University of California Press, 1965.

Smith, Richard. *Jamaican Volunteers in the First World War: Race, Masculinity and the Development of National Consciousness.* Manchester: Manchester University Press, 2004.

Solomon, Mark. *The Cry Was Unity: Communists and African Americans, 1917–36.* Jackson: University of Mississippi Press, 1998.

Spackman, Ann, comp. *Constitutional Development of the West Indies, 1922–1968: A Selection from the Major Documents.* St. Lawrence, Barbados: Caribbean Universities Press, 1975.

Springer, Hugh W. "The Historical Development, Hopes and Aims of the University College of the West Indies." *Journal of Negro Education* 31, no. 1 (Winter 1962): 8–15.

———. "On Being a West Indian." *Caribbean Quarterly* 3 (1953): 181–83.

———. *Reflections on the Failure of the First West Indian Federation.* Cambridge, MA: Harvard University, Center for International Affairs, 1962.

———. See also under Documentary Film.

Stein, Judith. *The World of Marcus Garvey: Race and Class in Modern Society.* Baton Rouge: LSU Press, 1986.

Stepan, Nancy. *The Idea of Race in Science: Great Britain, 1800–1960.* Hamden, CT: Archon, 1982.

Stephens, Michelle Ann. *Black Empire: The Masculine Global Imaginary of Caribbean Intellectuals in the United States, 1914–1962.* Durham, NC: Duke University Press, 2005.

Taylor, Ula Yvette. *The Veiled Garvey: The Life and Times of Amy Jacques Garvey.* Chapel Hill: University of North Carolina Press, 2001.

Thomas, Deborah. *Modern Blackness: Nationalism, Globalization, and the Politics of Culture in Jamaica.* Durham, NC: Duke University Press, 2004.

———. "Modern Blackness: 'What We Are and What We Hope to Be.'" *Small Axe* 12 (September 2002): 25–48.

Thomas, J. J. *Froudacity: West Indian Fables by James Anthony Froude*. 1889. London: New Beacon, 1969.

Thomas, Roy Darrow. *The Trinidad Labour Riots of 1937: Perspectives 50 Years Later*. St. Augustine, Trinidad: Extra-Mural Studies Unit, 1987.

Thompson, A. O. "Happy-Happy Slaves! Slavery as a Superior State to Freedom." *Journal of Caribbean History* 29 (1995): 93–119.

Timm, Birte. "Caribbean Leaven in the American Loaf: Wilfred A. Domingo, the Jamaica Progressive League, and the Founding of a Decolonization Movement for Jamaica." *GHI Bulletin Supplement* 5 (2008): 81–97.

———. "The Transnational Roots of Anti-Colonial Nationalism in Jamaica: The Jamaica Progressive League in New York and Kingston, 1936–1962." Ph.D. diss., Free University of Berlin, 2011.

Turner, Joyce Moore. *Caribbean Crusaders and the Harlem Renaissance*. Urbana: University of Illinois Press, 2005.

———. "Richard B. Moore and the Caribbean 'Awaymen' Network." *Journal of Caribbean History* 46, no. 1 (2012): 60–94.

Turner, Mary. *Slaves and Missionaries: The Disintegration of Jamaican Slave Society, 1787–1834*. Kingston, Jamaica: University of the West Indies Press, 1998.

Turner, W. Burghardt, and Joyce Moore Turner, eds. *Richard B. Moore, Caribbean Militant in Harlem: Collected Writings, 1920–1972*. Bloomington: Indiana University Press, 1992.

UAPAD (United Aid for Peoples of African Descent). *Memorandum on the Colonization and Development of British Guiana*. New York: n.p., 1939.

Von Eschen, Penny M. *Race Against Empire: Black Americans and Anticolonialism, 1937–1957*. Ithaca, NY: Cornell University Press, 1997.

Wagley, Charles. "Plantation-America: A Culture Sphere." In *Caribbean Studies: A Symposium*, edited by Vera Rubin, 3–13. Seattle: University of Washington Press, 1960.

Wallace, Elisabeth. *The British Caribbean: From the Decline of Colonialism to the End of Federation*. Toronto: University of Toronto Press, 1977.

Watkins-Owens, Irma. *Blood Relations: Caribbean Immigrants and the Harlem Community, 1900–1930*. Bloomington: Indiana University Press, 1996.

Watts, R. L. *New Federations: Experiments in the Commonwealth*. London: Oxford University Press, 1966.

Weisbord, Robert G. "British West Indian Reaction to the Italian-Ethiopian War: An Episode in Pan-Africanism." *Caribbean Studies* 10, no. 1 (1970): 34–41.

Wesley, Charles H., ed. *The Negro in the Americas*. Washington, DC: Howard University, 1940.

Whitham, Charlie. *Bitter Rehearsal: British and American Planning for a Post-War West Indies*. Westport, CT: Praeger, 2002.

Will, H. A. *Constitutional Change in the British West Indies, 1880–1903*. Oxford: Clarendon Press, 1970.

Williams, Eric. *British Historians and the West Indies*. 1966. New York: Africana, 1972.

———. *Capitalism and Slavery*. Chapel Hill: University of North Carolina Press, 1944.

———. *The Case for Party Politics in Trinidad and Tobago*. Port-of-Spain, Trinidad: College Press, 1955.

———. *The Economics of Nationhood*. Port-of-Spain, Trinidad: PNM, 1959.

———. *Federation: Two Public Lectures.* Port-of-Spain, Trinidad: PNM Publishing Company, 1956.

———. "The Historical Background of British West Indian Federation: Select Documents." *Caribbean Historical Review*, nos. 3–4 (December 1954): 13–69.

———. *The Historical Background of Race Relations in the Caribbean.* Port-of-Spain, Trinidad: E. Williams, 1955.

———. *The Negro in the Caribbean.* Brooklyn: A&B Books, 1994.

———. *A New Federation for the Commonwealth Caribbean?* Port-of-Spain, Trinidad: PNM, 1973.

Williams, Zachery R. *In Search of the Talented Tenth: Howard University Public Intellectuals and the Dilemmas of Race, 1926–1970.* Columbia: University of Missouri Press, 2009.

Wolcott, Victoria. *Remaking Respectability: African American Women in Interwar Detroit.* Chapel Hill: University of North Carolina Press, 2001.

Wood, Donald. "Brief Biography." In Thomas, *Froudacity*, 9–22.

Wood, E.F.L. *West Indies: Report by the Honourable E.F.L. Wood on His Visit to the West Indies and British Guiana, December 1921–February 1922.* Cmd. 1679. London: HMSO, 1922.

Worcester, Ken. *C.L.R. James: A Political Biography.* Albany: SUNY Press, 1996.

Wrong, Hume. *Government of the West Indies.* 1923. New York: Negro Universities Press, 1969.

Yelvington, Kevin A. "The War in Ethiopia and Trinidad, 1935–1936." In *The Colonial Caribbean in Transition: Essays on Postemancipation Social and Cultural History*, edited by Bridget Brereton and Kevin A. Yelvington, 189–225. Gainesville: University Press of Florida, 1999.

Zips, Werner. *Black Rebels: African-Caribbean Freedom Fighters in Jamaica.* Princeton, NJ: Markus Wiener, 1999.

Documentary Film

New Nation in the West Indies. Narrated by Hugh Springer. 1958. Montreal: National Film Board of Canada. VHS.

Index

Eric D. Duke is associate professor in the Department of African American Studies, Africana Women's Studies, and History at Clark Atlanta University. He is the coeditor of *Extending the Diaspora: New Histories of Black People*.

Nuer-American Passages: Globalizing Sudanese Migration, by Dianna J. Shandy (2006)

Religion and the Politics of Ethnic Identity in Bahia, Brazil, by Stephen Selka (2007)

Reconstructing Racial Identity and the African Past in the Dominican Republic, by Kimberly Eison Simmons (2009)

Haiti and the Haitian Diaspora in the Wider Caribbean, edited by Philippe Zacaïr (2010)

From Douglass to Duvalier: U.S. African Americans, Haiti, and Pan Americanism, 1870–1964, by Millery Polyné (2010)

New Immigrants, New Land: A Study of Brazilians in Massachusetts, by Ana Cristina Braga Martes (2010)

Yo Soy Negro: Blackness in Peru, by Tanya Maria Golash-Boza (2011; first paperback edition, 2012)

Trance and Modernity in the Southern Caribbean: African and Hindu Popular Religions in Trinidad and Tobago, by Keith E. McNeal (2011; first paperback edition, 2015)

Kosher Feijoada and Other Paradoxes of Jewish Life in São Paulo, by Misha Klein (2012; first paperback edition, 2016)

African-Brazilian Culture and Regional Identity in Bahia, Brazil, by Scott Ickes (2013; first paperback edition, 2015)

Islam and the Americas, edited by Aisha Khan (2015; first paperback edition, 2017)

Building a Nation: Caribbean Federation in the Black Diaspora, by Eric D. Duke (2016; first paperback edition, 2018)